Banking Lite

Bert Harris

ISBN: 1492711853
ISBN-13: 9781492711858
Library of Congress Control Number: 2013916766
CreateSpace Independent Publishing Platform
North Charleston, South Carolina

Contents

Dedication

This book is dedicated to my brother Frank W. Harris, without whose encouragement and constructive critiques this book would have never been completed.

Introduction

Seven years ago my good friend and fellow banker John Clements invited me to attend the *Berkshire-Hathaway* stockholders annual meet in Omaha, featuring Warren Buffett and Charlie Munger. It is an entertaining show as well as being highly educational and informative, not only for the company's shareholders but also for those interested in business and finance.

Arriving late the afternoon on the preceding Friday, John and I started the festivities with a couple of martinis and almost immediately started swapping humorous banking stories from our careers spanning over 40 years in the business. John and I are the same age, so the events from both of our repertoires encompassed the same time frame. Soon the two of us were roaring with laughter until our sides ached. This went on all evening. As it ended John said, "These stories are too rich and too funny not to be preserved!"

On my drive back to my home in Minnesota, yet more tales were recalled and I began collecting stories on three by five index cards. Then I organized the cards coinciding with the various stages of my banking career, starting with how I became interested in a banking career through my final stop as an officer of the Bank of America over 40 years later.

I have used my life's banking journey as a framework so these stories are pretty much in chronological order since that is often relevant to when they occurred. I hasten to add, these stories are not all my own. Some of the tales are from the experiences of John Clements, my wife Jo who worked at

Eastern Heights Bank of St. Paul, and numerous other colleagues in countered throughout my career, which spanned over 40 years.

Many of these stories have been inserted in the narrative as they best fit into banks I have been associated. In each case, the names have been changed to avoid offending persons now living or dead. In addition, I have used fictional names in cases where I enveloped several stories in a single character to avoid confusing the readers with too many characters and in hopes of making the story flow better.

The purpose of this volume is primarily to entertain, as well as to discuss banking philosophy, the profession to which I have devoted my primary working years. With this thought I began writing *Banking Lite* in earnest seven years ago. My hope is the reader will come to understand how personal a banking relationship can be when folks are treated as individuals and banks sit down and workout problems and find solutions. It seems to me the very large institutions treat people as only a number, rather than an individual human being. One of the pieces of my banking career as a CEO I am most proud, was I never foreclosed any families out of their home. "Come to Jesus meetings." Yes! Foreclosure. No! My bank was able to find solutions even for loans we had sold to Fannie Mae or Freddie Mac. For me it was far better to solve a problem than foreclose on a family, whom my kids played baseball and went to school. This book is about the often-amusing people side of community banking.

Acknowledgements

As I began turning out this book chapter by chapter, I shared its contents with various friends and family members: banking colleagues like John Clements, formerly correspondent banker at the Omaha National Bank, Diane Weir, a fellow officer at the Bank of America, Jean Harper, a director at the Security Bank of Glenrock, The late Charlene Collingwood at The First National Bank of Greybull, who was both a participant and shared several stories, Bob Waller, former President of the Midland National Bank of Billings and later the First Interstate Bank of Billings, the late M. J. (Jerry) Swords, noted banking consultant based in Kansas City, and Diane Quinn, formerly President of the Anchor Bank in Woodbury; and my niece Roberta Likes, who both read my material and provided some great stories.

First and foremost I dedicate this book to my brother Frank W. Harris. Frank throughout the long, laborious, endeavor of writing this book has been my number one cheerleader as well as constructive critic. Frank's encouragement and help has been one of the mainstays that have kept me going on this project. Frank is an electrical engineer-medical doctor combined in one body has also published several books over the years.

Another key reader has been my lifelong friend Peter Brakman, who had a career in journalism and like my brother has offered helpful suggestions for amplifying the stories, and improving my writing mechanics, as well as providing encouragement. Other readers include: Pete's brother Hallett and his wife Anne Brakman, a boat dealer and government worker, my daughter Marti Fischbach, Dr. Rod Swift, atomic physicist and boyhood friend, another boyhood friend John and Linda Randolph, paint manufacturer and teacher, Professor Charles R. Larson, Literature Professor at American University in Washington, D.C., a high school-college friend, and Al Lauber, long time friend and the architect who did the architectural design work on two bank remodeling projects.

Colleagues of mine at Data Recognition Corporation in Woodbury including: Cindy Hervig, a biologist, Curtis Jette English and Physical Education Teacher and Michael Fisher, Adjunct English Professor at the University of Wisconsin -River Falls have provided encouragement.

Last and not least my wife Jo who has shared with me some of her stories while working at Eastern Heights Bank, Woodbury office. She has been a loyal life's partner and in many aspects is the star of this book. Thank you Jo, for your help in getting this book to publication.

One

Banking and Table Tennis

Had I seen the famous painting of J. P. Morgan, with his Walrus like mustache, piercing black eyes, bulbous, carbuncled nose, fierce, penetrating look, I can't imagine that I would have chosen banking for my life's career. Certainly, his elegant dress and gentleman's gold watch fob would have discouraged me from this career. At this junction in my life, sneakers, blue jeans and a colorful, button down sport shirt was my preferred attire. As it happens at the point that I decided to give banking a try, I had never even heard of Mr. Morgan, much less seen his picture.

My interest in banking was oddly enough the result of a game of ping-pong with my father, when I was between my second and third year in college. Freshman year I had majored in agriculture, having spent a summer working on Grandfather Harris's Wyoming ranch, enjoying it thoroughly despite the hard physical work and the fact I was allergic to oats, barley and hay, virtually everything in the way of crops we raised.

While in an Animal Husbandry class, livestock judging "lab", we were presented with groups of beef, dairy, sheep and hogs to evaluate for their commercial potential. A good Hereford or Angus steer, would be judged to have "a lot of beef type"; a hog might be described as having "meaty hams". When presented with difficult class of horses, I described a fleshy animal as having "a lot of dog food type" and a scrawny looking horse as having "a lot of glue type". The farm kids burst into great gales of laughter and my interest in being a man of the soil wavered and crashed on the spot.

After my brief venture into agriculture, I took one of those aptitude tests, which suggested I was cut out to be an architect, perhaps even the next Frank Lloyd Wright or Christopher Wren. The University of Colorado taught architecture as an extension of its engineering department, rather than as an art form. The artistic side of building great structures had the most appeal for me. I greatly enjoyed my design and architectural drawing classes, but was frustrated with the applied math courses.

After a year's study of architecture, I visited my Uncle Irv's architecture office in New Jersey. There I saw this 41-year-old graduate architect named Armen, who Uncle Irv employed as a draftsman. Armen was meticulously drawing highly detailed plans for some little joint for putting beams together in the corner of some no doubt grand building. At age 19, I could not envision, waiting 22 years and still not be designing architectural wonders of the world.

Uncle Irv's candor about the struggles he had financially getting to starting his own practice was enough to convince me that I didn't have the patience to struggle to earn a degree in architecture After all 20 years of putzing around drawing boring little pictures, before I could design great buildings. Patience has never been one of my virtues. Since I had always had an interest and flair for business, I decided a career in business was for me. But what business would it be?"

On summer evenings my Dad and I would play furious, fast games of ping pong on the front porch of our family's Boulder, Colorado home. Dad insisted we have a gin and tonic or two while playing to lubricate the conversation. By the time Dad was on his third gin and tonic, he was really hitting his stride: I thought at times there were three balls flying at me on the table at once. As if the gin and tonics were not enough to keep me off balance, Dad was an excellent ping pong player: he played a strategic game and managed to put enough English, or spin on the ball, so that even if I were swinging at the right ball, the ball would not necessarily bounce where I expected. Dad also had a way of looking at you through his grey eyes, while still making eye contact; he never quite looked at you face to face.

My father's conversations were like this too; often they would lead in an entirely unexpected direction. It was during one of these games that Dad would ask me poignant questions like, "What are you going to do for a living?" The implication being, that while he was happy to finance my education, he did expect me to be self-supporting within the next two or three years. By this time the gin had done its work and I was in talkative mood. I unhesitatingly confessed that I saw myself going into business, since I had an enterprising nature, which the family had long ago recognized. I was never very good at sitting on my ass doing nothing, which oddly enough was observed by Mr. Wolcott, our next door neighbor, who was quite content to sit on his patio, hour after hour, doing absolutely nothing. Mr. Wolcott noticed that I was always busy, building a hut in our backyard, repairing bicycles, or mowing and raking neighbor's lawns. I knew I had the initiative to work hard to succeed in business.

However, I had to confess that I had not the slightest idea what particular business that might be. Dad at this point in the conversation suggested I consider banking, in particular commercial lending. Dad's idea was that if I didn't like banking, I would in all likelihood have a customer or two that might be in a more interesting and appealing business. My parents always saw me as an entrepreneur and owning my own business. As it turned out, along with many other pearls of wisdom I learned from Dad, this proved to be excellent advice. I switched my major to finance with a determination to pursue a career in banking.

Dad's first job was with the National City Bank of New York in a branch in Rio De Janeiro, Brazil. I remember a couple of his stories that showed there is a human side to banking.

One story involves the time that a one million dollar check turned up missing at the end of the business day. One million dollars in 1930 was a huge sum of money, so the entire staff of the branch stayed at work though out the entire night looking for the missing check, but it was no use. About 4 A.M., management sent Dad and others home for a few winks of sleep, a shower and a shave. Dad and the others were back at the office by 8 A. M., bleary eyed and still wondering, where the hell that check could possibly be? Shortly after eight, in pops the office boy, and laid the missing check on Dad's desk. Father, always cranky when deprived of sleep, asked the naive young boy, "Where the hell did you find the check?" "We've been up all night trying to find it."

"Oh", the boy replied in an innocent and surprised voice, "I took it home to show my mom. I had never seen such a large amount of money before in my life and neither had she".

Fuming, Dad dragged the boy to the Branch Manager's office. The boss ended the shocked boy's banking career on the spot.

Another story took place also in Rio, where a large international community resided. Father's job at the time was at the foreign currency exchange window, where customers exchanged Brazilian Reis' for U. S. Dollars, British Pounds, or whatever currency desired. Because various currencies fluctuate differently, Dollars up, Reis down and so forth, the foreign exchange window was a haven for speculators. The speculators were hoping they could make a fast profit when two currencies fluctuated in opposite directions and they could make a quick, fat profit overnight. One of Dad's regular clients was a Chinese gentleman, who spoke with a characteristic Chinese accent. While he was enchanted with the possibility of quick and easy profits on a short-term speculation based on currency fluctuations, he frequently took frustrating and painful losses. After one such loss he exclaimed, "Ah so, flucted again!"

I mention these stories, because to appreciate the tales I will be sharing, the reader needs to understand there is a very human side of banking. My earliest recollection of an exposure to a bank was as a child, my mom would take me downtown to the Hackensack Trust Company, in Hackensack, New Jersey where my parents and maternal grandparents did business for many years. The Hackensack Trust Company occupied a fine stone building in the center of Hackensack's commercial district.

One day my mother dragged my little brother Frank and I down to the lower level of the building where the safe deposit vault was located. The vault had an enormous round door that seemed at least ten feet in diameter and perhaps two feet of steel thick, with large round steel pegs to hold the vault door securely shut when locked. Inside were what seemed like hundreds of little stainless steel doors, behind which were the individual safe deposit boxes. Mother would take things in or out of her little box; she was very secretive about such things. While I did not know what mother kept in the box. I knew banks were about money, so I assumed that money was the object of mother's interest.

During the summer of 1946 we spent the entire summer visiting my Dad's parents in Basin, Wyoming. Granddad gave me the chore of washing his green '41 Chevy club coupe every week during the visit, for which I was rewarded with not just a dollar, but a bright shiny silver dollar, which at the time were in common use in Wyoming. Upon returning home to Hackensack at the urging of my parents, I was instructed to open a savings account at the good old Hackensack Trust Company. I took my summer wages consisting of eight wonderful silver dollars to the bank. The teller we saw was Frank Kozlik, a family friend, who mom and dad regularly played tennis with on weekends. I was, therefore, comfortable with handing over my prized silver dollars to Mr. Kozlik.

My vision, of course, was that my eight silver dollars would get their own individual box like mom had in the great vault downstairs, and not be confused with ordinary paper dollars. Even though the spending value was the same, this eight-year-old saw a huge difference in the "total" value of the silver dollars compared with the paper currency. When Christmas time rolled around I decided to withdraw two of my prized dollars for my Christmas shopping. When I went to withdraw my silver dollars, Mr. Kozlik gave me two crummy, ordinary paper dollars. I was shocked and angry. Mr. Kozlik had a very puzzled look on his face as I expressed dismay and my expectation for actual silver dollars; I'm sure he got a good chuckle out of this once I left. He never expected an eight-year-old boy to be a "hard money man". Now that I think about it, I really wanted my silver dollars back!

My parents must have explained about how banks worked as I continued to put money in my account at the Hackensack Trust Company. By the time I reached college age, we had moved to Colorado and I had a checking account at the Bank of Lafayette, where my father kept his business account and took out business loans from time to time. In those days, at least at the Bank of Lafayette, checking accounts weren't numbered. Father had nice blue business checks, printed on fancy banknote paper. I, on the other hand used the free booklets of checks, or counter checks. Ordinarily, Dad used the printed checks, but occasionally he would pick up a counter check to pay for something for the business if he didn't happen to have a printed check on his person. Being a poor college student I ran my account right down to the last dollar or two, but I carefully added and subtracted my transactions so as not to be overdrawn. One day Dad called me over to his desk and with anger in his voice said, "Bert, Charlie at the bank called and tells me you are $48.00 overdrawn: dammit, you can add better than that." Dad gave me $50.00 to get me back in the black.

However, I protested, "Dad, I have added and subtracted over and over and I have two dollars in my account."

"Bert, banks don't make mistakes. Take the $50.00 and go see Charlie. Be sure you apologize too, Charlie is an old and close family friend."

So off I went to Lafayette to straighten my account out. Charlie dragged out the bank's ledger and a pile of the cancelled tan freebie checks and we proceeded to go through them. There it was a $50.00 check, big bucks for my paltry bank account, signed by none other than Dad, written on a tan counter check at the local office supply store. Dad, and I share the same name; it was easy to understand what happened. Charlie, as good a natured man who ever lived, thought the whole incident was quite amusing and laughed heartily at the bank's error. I began signing checks with my initials to avoid future confusion. Dad apologized for his part in the mistake; he had forgotten to write the company name on the counter check. He even let me keep the $50.00. Clearly, I needed to know more about banks and how they operated if this was to be my calling.

With these limited experiences dealing with banks and even less knowledge, I strived to learn more about banking. As the years progressed Dad and I would continue to have our ping pong table discussions, which were different now as Dad shared his knowledge of banking and business over, gin and tonics.

My next two years at Colorado State University went well as I prepared myself for a career in finance. My finance professor, Professor Tueting, was a very knowledgeable and conservative man, and also my faculty advisor. Professor Tueting was tall, with an erect posture, and dressed neatly, but was either color blind or just had plain bad taste in clothing. I can still see him standing in front of the class lecturing wearing this ugly pale green suit, mud brown shirt, set off by a bright orange and red striped tie and purple socks. In spite of his garish attire, I learned a great deal from him and I think he took a liking to me.

In one of his classes we were doing a "case study" of a hypothetical business that wished to borrow $100,000. The company had been unprofitable and had no collateral to offer. One student raised his hand and suggested, that since the company had no collateral, our make-believe bank should lend him the money unsecured. Professor Tueting turn to me and said, "Mr. Harris, what do you think about this loan proposal of Mr. Emerson?"

"Professor", without hesitation I replied, "This is a bad deal. I think the bank should turn down the loan." It was at this point, I think, Professor Tueting decided that I might make it as a banker. As graduation was near, Professor Tueting wrote a letter of introduction to his friend Neil Roberts, President of the Denver U.S. National Bank, one of the largest banks in Colorado.

A couple of weeks later, I drove down to Denver from Fort Collins to meet with Mr. Roberts. Mr. Roberts had, without a doubt, the fanciest office I had ever seen in my young life. We had pleasant chat of short duration and he arranged for me to meet with a Mrs. Gray, who was his personnel officer. Mrs. Gray, a slender, unsmiling lady with dark eyes partially obstructed behind oversized black horn rim glasses, scheduled a lengthy testing process and meeting for the following week. It was scheduled for, as I remember, a Friday, and I drove down to Denver again from Fort Collins, with high hopes and one of the worst colds I had ever had. My nose was running like Niagara Falls; I could barely talk due to a sore throat, and was generally feeling quite miserable.

Mrs. Gray, oblivious to my illness, proceeded to give me and five or six other applicants the timed banking aptitude and clerical skills test. I was busy feeling lousy, blowing my nose, coughing and gasping for breath, but managed to struggle through the test. Mrs. Gray, coldly and analytically, reviewed the results and without further comment told me in so many words that I was too dumb to be a banker. I left feeling dejected and yet determined to prove her wrong. This experience taught me a couple of useful lessons in life. The first was to avoid at all costs trying to do something important when I wasn't feeling somewhere near par. The other lesson was a distrust of putting too much faith in aptitude tests.

Thankfully, the failed aptitude test must not have jinxed my job opportunities. After a dozen interviews, I had two job offers. One with the

Security-First National Bank of Los Angeles, who had interviewed on the Campus of Colorado State University and the other with the Greeley National Bank in Greeley, Colorado. I accepted the job in Greeley because I had a girlfriend at the time, who was to be a senior at the University of Northern Colorado in Greeley the following fall.

Two

Greeley- A Real Banking Experience

Dressed in a new dark blue business suit, white shirt and striped blue and red necktie, I reported for work at The Greeley National Bank, affectionately known as "GNB", promptly at 8:00 A.M. on a bright, sunny Monday morning in June 1960. Mr. Adrian, the gentlemen who I had interviewed with and presumably had at least a part in hiring me, greeted me and introduced me to various people, about 50, I would guess. As he showed me around, he explained the different individual functions at the bank.

I was told that I would start in the bookkeeping department, learn what goes on in the basement, then I would be advanced in a relatively short time to learn to be a teller, then I'd be, perhaps, the Assistant Head Teller and would have the opportunity to learn about the various functions of the bank. The bank, I knew, had no formal officer training program, but I was told that I was a sort of an experiment in developing officer talent in house, as opposed to more formal program a large bank had for potential officers.

In the process of the introductions, I met Dale Hinman, who was the President of Greeley National and had started his banking career in Basin, Wyoming Dad's hometown. Grandfather Harris was a founder and director of the Security State Bank of Basin, where Mr. Hinman's banking career had started, perhaps 25 years earlier. Therefore, Mr. Hinman was not a strange name to me, although I had never actually met him. Mr. Hinman, in the course of our brief conversation, asked me,

"Bert, what job in the bank would you like?

"Mr. Hinman," I replied, "Someday I would like to have your job, sir." Mr. Hinman was probably fifteen years away from retirement at the time, smiled broadly and told me he liked my ambition.

By ten o'clock I was working in the basement, with my suit coat neatly hung up, sorting checks, a very boring job. I was alert to learning how checks were processed and was soon helping customers with their checkbooks. One of my first customer contacts was a lady named Mrs. Krubesheff. Over the phone with the bank's copy of her checking account statement, or ledger in banking parlance, together with her cancelled checks in hand, I dutifully went through the deposits and checks posted on her account to match them up with her on the other end of the line, comparing my items to her check register; it didn't take long to determine that she had written several counter checks and had failed to write them in her checkbook register. She thanked me to which I replied "No problem, Mrs. Kruschev." Nikita Kruschev was then the Soviet Union's top guy and had been banging his shoe on the table at a United Nations summit conference meeting that very week. I was terribly embarrassed at my error. Luckily Mrs. Krubesheff started laughing uproariously and I was off the hook.

After getting a good grounding in the basics of the demand deposit account function and deposit balancing known as proof operations, and the workings of the bank's central accounting system, or general ledger, and the various subsidiary ledgers which record loans, securities and other transactions, I was allowed to advance upstairs to learn to be a teller.

My teller mentor was a lady named Irene Peterson, who had been a teller at Greeley National Bank for many years and was a model of efficiency who treated customers in a courteous and friendly manner. Irene was a smiling woman, 35 years old, of medium height, slender with neat coal black hair. The bank entrusted me with $5000 in my drawer, which was deemed to be sufficient for the customer needs. $5000 was more than my annual salary, the significance of which was not lost on me or Irene. Irene, a devout Christian woman, said, "Bert, in order to avoid the temptation of stealing any of this money, you must think of this money, not as money, but as your *product.* I like to think of my drawer money as *prunes.*"

I couldn't make the conversion from money to prunes, but I did look at it like Monopoly Money, which I couldn't spend. Irene turned out to be a real friend, too.

On the 20th of the month, which was the day that the Weld County Welfare Department handed out public assistance checks to the needy, the bank's lobby was swamped with long lines of welfare recipients coming into GNB to cash their checks. An elderly, short, somewhat stocky lady with pure white hair and sparkling bright blue eyes, probably in her 80s, came to my window to cash her check. Mrs. Holmquist, was her name and she produced her identification and her check for $178.00, mumbled something in Swedish and handed it all to me. I carefully counted the money out of my drawer, and then counted a second time when I handed the proceeds to Mrs. Holmquist. I thanked her. Instead of leaving, she launched into this long conversation, all in Swedish. I had not the foggiest idea what she was saying, so I smiled lamely and listened. The line behind her must have been 10 deep, but Mrs. Holmquist, enjoying the moment, waving her arms expressively and smiling broadly, kept on babbling on and on in Swedish. Several minutes went by and my telephone rang, it was Irene Peterson. "Bert, would you please come over to my window."

I did and Irene explained that poor Mrs. Holmquist lived alone, was lacking someone to talk to, and did this every month, preferably to the most recent addition to the bank's teller line. Mrs. Holmquist then left. A couple months later I was able to assist another teller trapped by Mrs. Holmquist. I now understood why the tellers at Greeley National, in privacy of the employee lounge, referred to the 20th of the month as "Clod's Day".

Our teller supervisor was a competent, white haired lady, who was perhaps in her early 50s. Her name was Maxine Melcher and she frequently conducted teller meetings at which we were admonished to treat customers with the greatest respect and avoid discussing controversial subjects such as religion, politics, sex and anything else that might possibly offend a customer. All of this made good sense to me, a neophyte teller.

That is until I met Barbara Anderson. Barbara was the manager of the Fashion Bar, a women's dress shop located diagonally across Eighth Avenue from the bank. It is a funny thing the way people seek out a particular teller for reasons known only to the seeker. I knew this was very true, because at the First National Bank in Boulder, where I had a savings account, I always went to Betty Napier's window. Betty was a middle aged, cheerful, blond woman, who simply treated me like I was someone special. She treated everyone that way.

Barbara had a cantankerous nature and liked to argue, especially about politics. She almost always preferred me, because she enjoyed coaxing me into a "discussion." This was during the 1960 Presidential Campaign. One day she would argue for Kennedy; the next day for Nixon. I tried not to discuss politics, with Maxine's desk was directly across the lobby from my teller window, but Barbara would pout until she could get me into a polite discussion of the day's politically interesting topic. In my quietest voice, I would indulge her wishes and thus avoid offending my friend while keeping Maxine at bay.

At the end of the business day tellers balance their cash from their transaction tickets in virtually every bank. We were expected to balance to the penny every day, but of course human beings being imperfect, occasionally make mistakes. I was certainly no exception to this. One day I was short $20.00. It was a very slow day and I couldn't imagine where I had erred with so few customers. Irene came over and recounted my cash drawer; however, her count agreed with mine to the penny. I went through my transaction tickets and tried to recall where I might have given out an extra $20.00; nothing registered. Tellers hate to be short, because while some errors are expected, excessive shortages can lead to dismissal. About a week later, one of my regulars, Mrs. Righthouse, the mother of one of my C.S.U. roommates, came in and asked: "Bert, by chance you didn't happen to be short $20.00 last Wednesday?"

"Yes," I exclaimed excitedly. Mrs. Righthouse smiled knowingly and handed me a $20.00 bill:

"Funny, I came in here, cashed a check for $60.00, spent $20.00 downtown and still had the $60.00 when I got home." she said.

"I guess I was too engrossed in catching up. Thank you so much for your honesty," I replied.

Harry Palmer, the Head Teller, and I were the only male tellers in the bank's main lobby, so it was natural that we would become chummy. In addition, Maxine had made explicit instructions to Harry to take me under his wing, as it were, since it was ordained that I was to be Harry's back up. The Head Teller's job was to manage the vault cash, and make up change orders. The bank had a number of large retail customers, who required large change orders. The coins in particular were quite heavy and apparently Maxine thought required a man's muscles to handle. One day Harry asked me to accompany him to the post office and pick up a shipment of money from the Federal Reserve Bank in Denver. As Harry and I walked the two blocks to the Greeley post office, Harry asked casually if I would like to carry the coin order or the one-dollar bills. Not anxious to carry a heavy sack or two of coins the three blocks back I said. "I'll take the ones".

It turned out the order of coins was just a small box of nickels, but the order of ones was a large cube about two and half feet square containing thousands of dollars in one dollar bills. With the great gray cube of ones, marked Federal Reserve Bank conspicuously all over it, we walked in silence back to the bank.

"Miller's Market uses an amazing number of ones," Harry stated slyly as we entered the safety of the bank building.

Every morning Harry and I had the task of emptying the night drop, where the bank's merchant customers would drop their deposits. The bank's tellers would then work the bags, prepare change orders if needed in time for the customers to pick up their bags, when the lobby opened at 9:00 A.M. For internal control purposes bank policy required two people open the night drop save, which required one person with the combination and the other had a key to the collar that fastened around the combination lock dial. Harry had the combination; I was assigned the key to the collar. One Monday morning the vault was quite full, as I pulled the bags out, Harry recorded the merchant's name on special form attached to a clipboard. That morning there were over twenty bags. We distributed the bags among all the lobby tellers. Working quickly, we were barely ready when the store managers came to Harry's window for their bags.

Along came Arvid Hicks, the owner of Hick's Men's Store. Mr. Hicks was a trim, 60ish, dapper gentleman, always dressed in a well-tailored business suit, in hopes of selling customers a suit just like it. Mr. Hicks had been a customer since the 1930s; it was hard imagine that he was trying to make a false claim. Harry checked the list, but Mr. Hick's bag was not in the pile, nor was his bag listed on the register. Mr. Hicks' wrinkled his brow and said. "I know damn well I put the bag in the afterhours drop Saturday night. Where the hell is it?"

Harry looked at him seriously and said. "Well that beats me. We have a procedure that we follow, so nothing goes wrong. I will get to the bottom of this;" he assured Mr. Hicks.

Harry called me over to his window, as Mr. Hick's fumed. "Bert, we have a problem Mr. Hick's bag wasn't on the list or in the actual bags. Let's go down and check this out. We went through the dual control procedure, exactly as we had earlier that morning. Harry opened the safe door. It was bare as Mother Hubbard's Cupboard. Harry and I looked at each other and said in unison. "You couldn't have stolen it."

Harry went and got a flashlight and shined it up the drop shaft and there it was. Mr. Hick's blue bag was hung up on a jagged piece of metal. The construction worker hadn't smoothed over the offending rough spot when the night drop was relocated during a recent remodeling project. By the time, we got up stairs Maxine was attempting to calm Mr. Hicks down. Harry waived the bag in the air, so he could see the lost had been found.

Mr. Hicks smiled, his mood changed completely, as Harry opened the bag and determined everything was in perfect order.

One day I was surprised by a great commotion at the new accounts desk, which was staffed by Margie Overton, an inordinately buxom woman. Margie was bending over her IBM electric typewriter, trying to help an elderly customer select the right checks from the Rocky Mountain Bank Note catalogue. Inadvertently, her watermelon sized breasts simultaneously dropped on the keyboard of the IBM machine, hitting most of the keys at once and jamming the typewriter so it was inoperable. The bank's operations officer tried to tinker with the machine, but finally gave up and called the IBM service man, when the machine started to smoke. The IBM man couldn't figure out how this could have happened. Embarrassed, Margie wasn't about to tell him.

After a few months I gained some proficiency as a teller and would frequently be assigned to work at the bank's annex, which contained the bank's drive-in and walk-up windows. It also contained the bank's mortgage and installment lending departments. At Greeley National the installment loan department was the initial training ground for young loan officers. It was staffed with three lenders and a couple of receptionists, processors, who were young married women. There was a constant turnover in the second desk position, because the women were getting pregnant and leaving to raise their families. Roy Schmidt kept teasing Jeanne Krause, the lady at the front desk that the problem was the chair and he would substitute the number two chair at the number one, Jeanne's station. Jeanne, sensing it wasn't "her chair", would immediately switch the chairs back, reminding Roy. "I already have two kids and can't afford anymore."

My mom had the same problem at Scribbler's Book Company, our family's business, all the young female employees would get pregnant and leave just about the time they were good at their jobs. Mother would say each time, "I just don't trust young husbands."

I enjoyed hanging out with those guys and learning about installment lending, especially the collection side of the business. One day Roy Schmidt, the department head, joined a conversation I was having with Herb Becker and Marv Nix, the other two lenders. Roy, trying to hold back his laughter, said, "You wouldn't believe the conversation I just had with Royal Harrington."

Marv says, "You mean that pompous, ne'er do well mutual fund guy?"

"The same," replies Roy.

"I just turned him down for a refrigerator loan," chimes in Herb.

"That was why he came in," continued Roy. "He's mad at us. I told him, 'damn it, Mr. Harrington, you're two payments behind on the two notes you already have with us.' To which his majesty says, 'Do you mean you expect me to make a payment on each loan *every month?'* Can you believe this guy?" Herb rolled his eyes back. He had a funny way of rolling his eyes so only the whites showed. Then all four of us began laughing.

After the laughter died down a few minutes later, Herb says to me, "Bert, ask Maxine, if she will let you help me repo a car over in Fort Morgan tomorrow afternoon?"

Occasionally, Herb asked me to assist him with a repossession so it was not unexpected that Maxine would approve my absence from my teller duties for the afternoon. However, this trip would prove to be more exciting than most. Herb and I took off in the bank's metallic green Dodge sedan. The drive to Fort Morgan was about an hour's duration. Herb and I got to know each other on our periodic repossession expeditions. It turned out both of us had a fascination for interesting cars, as well as an interest in advancing out respective banking careers. Herb was about five years my senior.

Once we approached Fort Morgan, Herb became all business. "This guy's name is Charles Martinelli and until recently he's been employed at the Fort Morgan plant of the Great Western Sugar Company, but for some unknown reason he was dismissed and hasn't been able to find a new job," stated Herb in matter of fact tone. "I have talked to him numerous times on the phone; he keeps making promises to pay, get caught up, but hasn't done a damned thing. He is almost four months past due. I'm tired of being Mr. Nice Guy," Herb continued.

"I see on his collection card the main collateral is a '57 DeSoto, hardtop coupe, oh, I see there is also a '46 Plymouth too." I observed.

"If the DeSoto is in decent shape, it should cover the loan; that old Plymouth may not even run, probably not worth the time and expense of bringing to Greeley," Herb said, casting a serious frown in my direction. I nodded in agreement.

Charlie's address was easy to find and we parked in front of the house, no cars, and no sign of Mr. Martinelli either. Charlie's next-door neighbor, who was raking up debris from a recent storm, ambled over to us. "Looking for Charlie and Betty?" he inquired.

"Yes," Herb replied. "Can you help us?"

The neighbor said, "Betty said something to my wife about a family reunion of some kind out at her folk's house. I can give you directions. Really easy to get to from here," he said pointing down the street in an easterly direction. "Go down this street, until you can't go no further, hang a right. Then go about two miles down County Road 21. Betty's folks live in a large white house on your right, nice house surrounded by freshly painted red farm buildings, barns, machine sheds etc. No other places like it in the neighborhood." Herb politely thanked him for the information and we took off.

As described, we found Betty's parent's home with no trouble. Charlie's vermillion and white DeSoto hardtop was sitting out front in easy view.

There must have been at least a dozen cars parked in and about the farmyard, so it was evident something was going on. Undaunted Herb and I marched up to the door and knocked.

A gray haired, middle aged, farmwoman of medium height, a little on the plump side answered the door. "Yes," she said as she opened the door.

"We're looking for Charles Martinelli," answered Herb.

"Oh sure, Charlie's here," she said, turning and yelling, "Hey, Charlie, couple of guys in suits to see you."

Charlie appeared momentarily. Recognizing Herb said, "Oh, hi, here about the car, huh?" Charlie said looking quite disheveled, a week's growth of a dark brown beard, grimy t-shirt, but otherwise resigned to his situation.

"Yep," said Herb, pointing to the DeSoto.

"Come to pick it up?" queried Charlie.

"Right, I can't let it get any further past due," replied Herb.

"Yeah, I can see your problem. I ain't got no money or job, so OK, you can have it. Would you mind letting me go back to my house, got a bunch of stuff in the trunk, just personal junk, ya know. I need to unload it at home."

Herb says. "OK, Charlie I guess we can do that for you; Bert and I will follow you." Charlie got in the DeSoto, Herb and I climbed in the Dodge.

"Car looks OK, maybe a little dirty, but no obvious dents," I remarked.

"We might come out whole on this one," speculated Herb. "Old Charlie looks like the picture of that murderer, Charlie Starkweather, they just executed in Nebraska," commented Herb.

"Yeah, I thought that too, but this guy isn't a redhead, the papers said ole Starkweather was a redhead," said I.

"Well," said Herb. "Hopefully, that's the good news. Charlie here seems pretty cooperative and docile." Charlie parked in front of his house; we pulled in behind a car length behind him and got out of the Dodge.

Charlie slowly walked to the rear of the DeSoto and popped the trunk lid open. By this time Herb and I were standing at the front of the Dodge, our minds still thinking about Charlie's similar appearance to the late Charlie Starkweather. Charlie Martinelli reached in the trunk and pulled out a Winchester, lever action, 30-06 hunting rifle. Simultaneously, Herb and looked at each other and said together, "Oh, shit". Our hearts skipped several beats.

Martinelli looked at us with a puzzled look, which turned into a sheepish grin. "Didn't mean to scare you fellers, just my old deer rifle. Here's the keys." said Charlie, tossing the keys to Herb and ambling towards the front door of the house with rifle pointed safely towards the ground and 180 degrees away from us. Charlie came back and unloaded some miscellaneous tools, khaki hunting clothes and camping gear from the DeSoto's trunk and laid them on the curb.

As Charlie took a load of things to his house, Herb said to me, "Why don't you drive the DeSoto and I'll follow in the bank car, seems like repos are prone to car trouble. Why don't you drive over to my house, I'll buy you a beer. I think we earned one today. Who knows, Vivian might even be willing to put on a plate for you tonight." The drive back to Greeley was uneventful and the fin-tailed DeSoto ran smoothly and drove nicely, as well.

Upon arrival at Herb's home, we went in and opened a couple of cans of Coors Beer. "So," Herb said, "how are you getting along with Margie?"

"Margie Overton?" I asked. "Why do you ask?"

Herb took a swig of his beer and said, "Margie drove me nuts when I was on the teller line. She is fixture at GNB. Been there for 20 years, the bank has been her life, no kids you know, very loyal, that's why they gave her the Assistant Cashier title, but unlikely to rise beyond the front desk. Used to drive the tellers crazy with her mindless chatter and always dumping her filing chores on the tellers."

"Oh, I manage to look too busy to be of any assistance to her most of the time. Harry keeps me occupied preparing change orders for the grocery stores; so Margie dumps her chatter and load on Elaine and Charlene. Irene Peterson, my mentor, seems to be off her radar, "I replied.

Herb continued, his face turning red, as his frustration with the thought of Margie intensified. "I didn't mind helping the lady, but her constant mindless gossip and overpowering perfume really bugs me, along with fake looking red hair. I'll bet she puts on her makeup with a putty knife. Damn that woman bugs me." Herb rolled his eyes in that funny way of his so you could only see the whites of his eyes.

Just then Vivian Becker, Herb's tall, smiling blond wife of three years, popped her head in. "Meatloaf tonight guys? Bert, nice to have you visit our humble abode," she said.

After dinner the three of us retired to the Becker's cozy, cheery, living room. I noticed a picture a quaint little white church on the wall. Pointing to it I observed. "Isn't that the Methodist Church over in Windsor?"

"Yeah, Herb's dad has been the pastor there for over 20 years," said Vivian.

"Windsor's is a nice little town, great little bank there too," chimed in Herb.

"Who owns the bank?" I inquired.

"The Hickman brothers, bought it in the 1930s, revived it from its depression troubles. It is a money maker now, so I'm told from my Windsor contacts."

"The old guys must be getting close to retirement," I speculated.

"Yeah", Herb said," they are both past 65 I'd guess, closer to 70, my dad says. They're only two years apart in age. Bert, you and I ought to buy that bank."

"How does one go about buying a bank?" I asked.

"Oh, First National Bank of Denver, or one of the other big banks in Denver or Omaha seem to be anxious to make bank stock loans at cheap rates. Trick is mainly to convince them that you have the ability to do a good job of running the bank," Herb replied. "Greeley National has a reputation for being a good place to learn the nuts and bolts of banking, thanks to Arnie Trautwein, you know, the guy before Hinman. The GNB experience should help us get financing," Herb continued.

"Mr. T seems to be something of a legend. Harry, Irene, well everyone talks enthusiastically about him all the time," I added.

"Bert, we ought to make it our goal to buy the Windsor Bank," Herb restated, grinning from ear to ear.

Vivian looked at him suspiciously. "Herbie, you're dreaming again," Vivian cooed affectionately.

"Well," drawing on my third beer of the evening, "assuming we could catch First of Denver in a weak moment and they lent us the money to buy The First National Bank of Windsor, what would you do with it?"

"First, we'd have to make a lot high yielding installment loans to pay for it," Herb said.

"Seems to me that building looks pretty shabby. I 'll bet it hasn't been spruced up, since it was built in the teens," I added.

"Oh, it hasn't, but do you know what the very first thing I'd do?" Herb said, smiling broadly, with a glint of devilment in his eyes.

"What's that?" I responded.

"Hire Margie!" Herb exclaimed.

"Why the hell would you want to do that?" I asked.

"That way, I could fire her. I've always wanted to fire Margie!" Then we both started to laugh. Vivian frowned at our depravity.

As I worked in the teller line, the more convinced I became that I needed experience in lending. Installment loans would be okay, but following my dad's advice I really wanted to do commercial loans. I was bored as a teller and tantalized by the other more challenging and interesting functions of the bank.

On numerous occasions, I had walked by the loan officers' conference room, but never sat in on any of the decision-making. However, there was a pattern to the meetings I found amusing. First, Mr. Hinman or one of the lenders like Mr. Adrian would place a loan proposal on the table. Then there would be some discussion, especially if it were a livestock or agricultural loan. Greeley National's forte was in cattle feeder lending. As the decision time neared, Herman Pearson, a raw boned, rugged faced man, sort of on the order of actor Charles Bronson, would grunt approvingly. Then Tim Weigand, a fiftyish, gray haired man, with a sturdy build and the look of a weather worn farmer, would let out his "war whoop" as it was referred to around GNB. Then Ralph Mercer, the quiet, red head turning gray, agricultural loan guru would tell them what to do and how to do it. This peculiar little pattern seemed to repeat itself day after day. My participating at this meeting seemed to be years away.

Three

The Bank Examiners Visit

One Monday afternoon during the summer of 1961, GNB was visited by National Bank Examiners. As Assistant National Bank Examiner Harold Blum counted my teller's cash, we began talking. The more I learned about bank examining, the more interested I became, especially when he told me the base salary worked out to be over $100 more a month than I was earning at GNB. Harold Blum was my age and had graduated from college in 1960 like me and like me, had a degree in finance. So I asked Harold how one became a bank examiner and he gave me the address of Paul Ross, the Chief National Bank Examiner in Kansas City.

I wrote Mr. Ross and promptly received an application, by return mail. Upon sending the completed application in, I was granted an interview on the following Monday morning. Kansas City was a good day's drive from Greeley. Early the preceding Sunday morning, I took off for Kansas City in my not so trusty MG-A, an open British sports car. Because the fuel pump had an annoying habit of conking out at inopportune moments, I carried a few tools along, as I had figured out how to repair it quickly in emergencies. The MG performed flawlessly, which I took as a positive omen for my interview the following morning.

I arrived in Kansas City well before dark and found a cheap hotel, whose name I promptly forgot. The hotel was located within walking distance of the Federal Reserve Bank of Kansas City building, where The Office of the

Comptroller of the Currency, a division of the U. S. Treasury, was located on the 4th floor.

Punctually at 9 A.M. I arrived at the office of Chief National Bank Examiner, Paul Ross. Mr. Ross's secretary was a friendly, slender brunette, middle-aged woman, who welcomed me warmly and assured me Mr. Ross was looking forward to the interview. Mr. Ross, it seems, was on the phone with a field examiner. As the phone call lengthened, Mrs. Nelson, the secretary, and I became acquainted. She inquired about my trip, my experience, my family, and my car; she was fascinated by my MG. By the time Mr. Ross had finished his phone call I was quite relaxed, at least as compared with how I was feeling when I arrived 20 minutes earlier.

Mr. Ross appeared at the doorway to his office and motioned me to enter. Mr. Ross was a short, baldheaded bespectacled man with an owl like face, dressed in a gray suit, white shirt and blue tie. He wasn't overtly friendly, but was pleasant in a business like way. Extending his hand, we shook hands. Then he said, "Well, Harris, welcome to Kansas City. Have a seat," pointing to one of two chairs in front of his gray government-issue desk.

Mr. Ross then sat down in his swivel chair, leaned way back and peered over his bifocals at me. He paused for a moment glancing at my application file. "Harris, you seem to have all the qualifications education wise we are looking for. And," he continued, "banking experience too. I'll bet you know how to count cash."

"Yes, sir," I said.

"Surprising how many new examiners, we get that have never counted a bunch of cash," Mr. Ross said. First he explained that the purpose of a bank examination was to determine the integrity of the bank's assets, primarily the loan portfolio, soundness of lending and operating policies and to determine if the bank is in compliance with all Federal banking laws and regulations. Not to be confused with an audit, which is more the verification of the existence of assets and accuracy of the statement of liabilities. Then he asked me a number of banking and accounting questions during the rest of the interview, which I seemed to answer to his satisfaction. After about an hour he said, "OK, Harris, when can you start?"

Stunned at the promptness of his decision to hire me, I replied, "I'd like to give Greeley National two week notice. Would two weeks from today be alright, Sir?"

"Perfect," said Mr. Ross. "I don't know where you'll be assigned. Are you flexible on that point?"

"Oh, yes Mr. Ross. I'm not married, so I can go anywhere." I said.

"Report back to this office at 9 A.M. October 9th and be prepared to go anywhere in the district." Said Mr. Ross. The 10th district consisted of Wyoming, Colorado, Nebraska, Kansas, western Missouri, most of Oklahoma and New Mexico.

By eleven o'clock I was driving across the flat farm country on U.S. 36 in Kansas, the Interstate Highway System was incomplete in 1961, headed to Greeley to tender my resignation. A week or so later, I was surprised when Mr. Hinman, called me into his office for an exit interview. "Bert," he said to me, "Joining the National Bank Examiners is the smartest thing you've done since you joined GNB. You'll learn a lot and reach your goals faster than you ever could around here. We're sorry to lose you, but I believe you have made the right decision. Good luck." We shook hands.

Although a lot of my tasks at GNB were mundane, I realized that I had learned much about the workings of a bank, which would prove to be very useful to me throughout my banking and business career.

Four

Indian Territory

Even though my MG-A was only three years old, it was plain that it was not for a traveling man. My MG-A was a sleek little two-seat sports car. Lots of fun to drive and honestly, the best girl bait I had ever owned. When I stopped for red lights, lovely strange college girls would jump in and ask for a ride. Just a couple of weeks earlier I had taken out a charming gal named Darlene. When I tried to kiss her, while we were sitting in the car she said, "What kind of a girl do you think I am, a contortionist?"

Virtues aside, I needed a car that could carry a couple of decent sized suitcases and the MG could not do that. So, I decided to buy a new car. The weekend before I was to report to Mr. Ross in Kansas City, I tried trading it off in Boulder, the home of the University of Colorado and lots of sports car minded college students, who were potential customers for my MG-A.

My old friend at the Crouch Motor Company, Bill Crouch, the younger brother of the owner, had just the car for me. With winter coming on and the '62 models already on the showroom floor, Bill had several convertibles, and yes he would love to take my MG in trade. As it happened, his remaining inventory of 1961 Plymouths consisted of a gray grocery getter behemoth station wagon and three convertibles, an ugly green one, an even uglier purple one, and a white one, with red interior. The white one didn't have quite as many extras as the other two, and therefore had a lower price tag. It was the perfect car for me. Equipped with my first new car, loaded with virtually all my worldly possessions, I was off to Kansas City to be an Assistant National Bank Examiner.

Again I checked in the "nameless hotel" before sunset the Sunday evening prior to meeting my destiny as a bank examiner. Excitedly, I contemplated my new job. I arrived at Mr. Ross's office fifteen minutes before 9 A.M., as he had requested. Mrs. Nelson was there to greet me like an old friend. She inquired if I was going to take her for a ride in my MG. I had to tell her I had traded it in on a new Plymouth convertible. She looked a little disappointed, then brightened up and said. "Oh, I suppose the new convertible would be OK."

Another man showed up that morning: he was Terry Willoughby, from Denver. Terry was in his mid to late 30s, had a wife and a couple of kids. Terry had worked for the American National Bank of Denver, one of the smaller downtown banks. Like my experience in Greeley, Terry felt his career wasn't moving along fast enough, so he had decided to join the examiners after talking to Harold Blum, my initial contact with the Office of the Comptroller of the Currency, or the (O.C.C.)

The O.C.C. was established in 1863 to finance the civil war by allowing Federally chartered banks to issue currency, or notes of circulation, which were backed by U. S. Treasury Bonds. As a result of the National Banking Act only national banks could issue currency, giving the nation a uniform national currency for the first time.

Mr. Ross greeted us briefly. Terry was to report to Examiner Henninger in Denver. I was to join National Bank Examiner Kenneth C. Olinger's Tulsa "A" crew. We spent the day in Kansas City arranging for payroll details, getting fingerprinted by the F B I for the Federal files and having our pictures taken for our identification cards. We called them "Elliot Ness Cards" in honor of the current popular TV show, the "Untouchables", which had Elliot Ness, portrayed by Robert Stack, always flashing similar ID cards. The analogy was complete, because we also dressed in dark suits, white shirts, tie and frequently a vest.

One of the persons we met that day was a commissioned National Bank Examiner, John Kelly, who was in the office finishing a report. Kelly we soon learned was a World War II veteran and had joined the OCC shortly after the war. John suggested we have lunch and he would give us the lowdown on the new life Terry and I were about to undertake. John came back from the lavatory and exclaimed, "You'll never guess what happened to me. Well, I was washing my hands and looked over at the gentlemen next to me. It was Harry Truman!"

Mrs. Nelson said, "What's so surprising about that? His office is on this floor," Mrs. Nelson said matter-of-factly.

"Oh, I know that," said Kelly. "That wasn't the exciting part. I walked up to him and said, "'Mr. President, you probably don't remember me.' Truman stopped me, looked me over and said. "I certainly do. You were a First Lieutenant in the Army in February, 1945 and were assigned to escort me around Fort Warren in Cheyenne, just after I became Vice President. Your name is John Kelly."

"He remembered me, perfectly. I was amazed," Kelly said excitedly.

"Wow," I said, "No wonder he was such a successful politician, never forgot a person or a name," I observed. The luncheon conversation clued Terry and I in on the life of a National Bank Examiner, at in least John Kelly's view. I drove to Tulsa, Oklahoma, that afternoon and linked up with Mr. Olinger the following day in Oklahoma City.

Mr. Olinger was a few days into an examination of The First National Bank & Trust Company, in Oklahoma City. It was at the time one of the four largest banks in the state. The bank occupied several floors of a 35-floor skyscraper. I found Mr. Olinger in the boardroom, hunkered down over several decks of line sheets. A line sheet is a 5x8 slip of paper and these papers are the nucleus of the bank examiners' examination of the bank's loan portfolio. Mr. Olinger was younger than I expected, about 35 years old, crew cut, trim, sturdy build of medium height dressed in the usual bank examiner garb, dark suit, white shirt, conservative tie. He greeted me cordially and introduced to the other men in the room: Frank Hess, Dick Fitzpatrick, Curtis Smith and Bill Rainey. Frank Hess, was the so-called lead assistant and in charge of the "detail" part of the examination. The detail is everything, except the loan portfolio, which I quickly learned is the province of the Examiner-In-Charge. Mr. Olinger said, "Bert, Frank here will show you the ropes. Mr. Ross told me you would be joining us today."

"We saved the bond account for you. It's quite a job here, this shop has lots of bond issues, both municipal and treasury securities." Frank chimed in.

Without further discussion, we were off to a suite of offices on the fourth floor. Frank introduced me to Henry Davis, who was the bank's investment officer. Mr. Davis was a short, pudgy man, with thinning hair, probably in his late 50s. He had a wide, craggy, unsmiling face and looked at Frank quizzically and disapprovingly to me and said. "Frank, this guy looks a little young to be an examiner." I had the gift, or perhaps handicap, of looking like I was 17.

Frank smiled, with a twinkle in his eye, said, "Mr. Davis, I'm sure you'll get along with Bert just fine."

Mr. Davis pointed to a good-sized table. "Bert, you can work here. Nancy will bring out the ledgers for you; be sure the ledgers are kept in order in the cart." Nancy, a thin gray-blonde middle-aged women, wheeled out two carts of bond ledgers, each about three feet long, containing several hundred cards, one for each issue of bonds the bank owned. The cards provide all the key information about the bond, including rate, yield, maturity, issuer, and type of bond like general obligation or special revenue. In addition, the cards contained record of the income received, cost, and amortization of purchased premium.

Frank explained in great detail how I was to transfer the ledger information, plus price the bonds, determine the Moody's rating of each bond, to special printed up bond line sheets. Then he explained how everything needed to balance and cross balance. Next I was to prepare precise schedules for the examination report. Frank, set me to work and said, "I'll come back at quitting time to collect you. Any questions you can reach me at extension 231. Have fun."

For the next three hours, I prepared line sheets. In fact this process lasted until Thursday of the following week. It turned out to be a huge job, I must have spent over 70 hours gathering information, because Mr. Davis purchased bonds in denominations of as little as $1000 from some rural Oklahoma communities, to blocks of ten to twenty five million in U. S. Treasury securities. I didn't really understand everything I was doing and Mr. Davis, turned out to be quite patient with my ignorance. In spite of his grump appearance, he generously explained detail and after detail of First National's complex bond account. Finally, after 8 days of work, interrupted of course by a weekend in Tulsa. I completed my task, bonds sheets filled out in precise detail and all the schedules completed.

I took my work to Mr. Olinger for review; he looked the securities schedules over with care. Smiling he said, "Well Harris, I can see you have been working." He paused for effect and continued, "You made a mistake." My heart sank. "Bert, this is a really big bond account, probably the most complicated of any bank on our list and it would be unreasonable of Frank and I to expect you would do it perfectly, your first time. This job is all about learning," Mr. O continued.

Frank took me aside and we were able to correct the errors in the schedule easily and I was quite relieved. After we corrected the securities section of the report, Mr. Olinger set me to work spreading financial statements on line sheets, which pleased me as I was starting to get into commercial lending on the second week of my examining career, which I had never touched at Greeley National Bank.

The crew of guys I worked with in Oklahoma was generally a good bunch. Frank Hess, slender build, black hair and an ever-smiling face, was a single man, perhaps 5 years my senior. He had been in the Army at the end of the Korean War, then went to college on the G. I. Bill at Pittsburg State University in Pittsburg, Kansas. Frank had worked for Commercial Credit as a collector in the Kansas City Metropolitan area before joining the O.C.C. The crew generally ate lunch together and took coffee breaks together.

The only other single man on the crew was blond, crew-cut Curtis P. Smith; he had been a F-86 Sabre Jet pilot in the Air Force during the Korean Conflict. No doubt Curtis had some interesting stories tucked away in his mind, but he was silent at meals and we never saw him in the evenings. The story was he came from a wealthy family, and had been raised by his grandmother. Curtis was the mystery man on the crew. He never talked about anything besides work. Evenings, regardless of where we were he would vanish evenings. He drove around in a big black Mafia like Lincoln sedan, which gave some credence to the story of his family's affluence. He was, as I recall an excellent typist, intelligent and a willing worker, but for whatever reason was still an assistant rather than a commissioned examiner, even after 6 or 7 years on the force.

Dick Fitzpatrick was a genial family man, having joined the examining force to enhance his banking career prospects. He seemed to be looking for a bank to light in so he wouldn't have to be away from his family. Fitz, as we called him, frequently joined Frank and me for supper.

Bill Rainey was, who was in his late 50s, a "career assistant" and a 20+year veteran of the examining force. Bill was from Wewoka, Oklahoma and spoke with a slow drawl, a classic Oklahoma accent. Bill seemed to be a good man as far as the credit side of the work, but was not very well educated and apparently never had the confidence to take the comprehensive testing to become a commissioned National Bank Examiner. Bill's wife was a great cook and hostess and the Raineys on more than one occasion hosted our crew's occasional social gatherings.

Mr. Olinger, a devoted father of three, frequently joined us for supper, over the course of my eight months in Oklahoma. He was a rising star among National Bank Examiners. I got to know him quite well and learned a great deal about accounting, banking and life in general.

One evening Frank, Fitz and Ken were having supper at a Furr's Cafeteria in Oklahoma City. Frank and I began to swap collection stories. Frank, while working for Commercial Credit at the time, was instructed to go into a poor, seamy neighborhood in Kansas City, Kansas, to repossess a black 48 Dodge sedan from an old, gray haired black man, named Orville Freedman.

The car was filthy dirty with layers of dust and grime collected at the cement plant, where he labored; in addition, the interior stank, and had great holes in the upholstery. The old heap did run fairly well, as if by some miracle. The old gentleman didn't have the $100 needed to bring the note current or, of course, the $200 to entirely repay the loan. Frank gagged as he prepared to get in the Dodge to drive it away. The old fellow, who had six children in his household, pleaded with Frank to let him keep the decrepit car, explaining he desperately needed the car to get to work. Frank thought fast, decided he didn't want to deal with the odorous of Dodge. "OK, Mr. Freedman, do you have $25.00?" Frank says to the old gent.

"Yas, yas, I can do that, boss," said Mr. Freedman.

Frank, a poor, recent graduated college student, who had just gotten paid earlier in the day, was feeling flush. "Sir, you get paid every Friday, Right?" says Frank.

"Yas, yas," says the old gentleman.

"Tell you what I'll do. I'll catch the loan up for you out of my pocket, if you'll promise to pay me $25 each and every pay day," continued Frank.

"Yas, yas, I'll do it by cracky," says the old gent in his raspy voice. Mr. Freedman was as good as his word and paid Frank religiously every Friday and Frank never had to set foot in the stinking old car.

After I had been in Tulsa about a month, I received a letter from my old high school-college buddy, Norm Bricker. The letter was addressed:

Bert Harris
725 National Bank of Tulsa Building
Tulsa, Indian Territory

Included in the envelope was a used car ad from the Crouch Motor Company in Boulder. Norm had circled the ad, which stated: "1959 MG-A. Black, red leather interior, 35,000 miles. Blackie owned this one drove it only to Mafia Meetings."

Knowing Frank and I both wanted to be far from Tulsa on Thanksgiving Day, Mr. Olinger made us the proposition, that if we would spend Veterans Day in the office at the National Bank of Tulsa Building, straightening out files, destroying obsolete reports, and preparing for the next examination projects, we could both have the Friday after Thanksgiving off. Since I wanted to go home to Colorado and Frank was planning on spending the holiday with his brother Everett in Colby, Kansas, Mr. O's proposal was immediately accepted. We arrived at the office at about 8:00 A.M. and began our work.

We hadn't been at our task very long, when in walks the legendary Mr. Donahue. Mr. Donahue was a lion reincarnated as a bank examiner, or so it seemed. Mr. Donahue was 81 years old, although somewhat stooped over, he was still mentally sharp and had only a year earlier retired as a National Bank Examiner. Apparently he had been with the OCC for 50 years or more. Ken Olinger was his replacement as leader of the "A" crew, which was responsible for the examination of the largest banks in our Oklahoma district. Mr. Donahue still retained his key to the office. I'm sure this was unofficial, but no one had the heart or perhaps the temerity to deny the old examiner this privilege. Donahue loved to hang out at the office, read old reports and reminisce about his glory days. He was feared by some, loved by others, but respected by all in Oklahoma's banking world. Bald, unsmiling, and crusty Mr. Donahue beamed, or as close as he came to that, at the thought that Frank and I would spend our holiday in the office instead of out recreating on this pleasant November day. Of course, he was unaware of our bargain with Mr. Olinger. That day, Mr. Donahue christened me the "Embryo Bank Examiner". Coming from him it was an honor.

I wish I could remember all of the great "Mr. Donahue" stories; my favorite took place during the early 1930s, when the banks in Oklahoma were frequently being held up by the likes of Bonnie & Clyde, Pretty Boy Floyd and John Dillinger. Mr. Donahue was examining one of Oklahoma's many country banks, many of which were in dire straits due to the Great Depression. In those days, field examiners had the authority to put a bank in receivership on the spot, as, many banks had an excess of poor loans. Mr. Donahue, sitting at an oak table, was in deep concentration, studying his line sheets, and contemplating the bank's future in one of the bank's offices. In the lobby, Bonnie and Clyde were robbing the place and proceeded to herd all the bank employees into the vault. Clyde Barrow, spotting Mr. Donahue, walked up behind him, and poked a 38 revolver in his ribs. Mr. Donahue, oblivious to what was going on, says to Barrow, without looking up, "God dammit! Can't you see I'm busy? Leave me alone!"

After Mr. D's outburst Barrow shrugged and continued ushering everyone else into the vault. Sometime after the robbery was over, when his bladder pressure broke his deep concentration, Mr. Donahue became aware of what happened.

Not long after the encounter with Mr. Donahue, we examined the First National Bank in McAlester. The bank's President, George Pemberton, was at gent about 65 years old who had spent his entire career at the bank. He was a friendly, sociable man, who seemed to let his subordinates manage the bank's business, as if on some kind of autopilot. Pemberton seemed to enjoy visiting with me and rest of the crew; not only that, he had all day to do it. Knowing that McAlester was the home of Oklahoma's maximum-security prison and my appetite wet with curiosity for tales of the robberies of the 1930s, I asked if he had any interesting stories.

"Well, there was one rather amusing one." he replied. "It seems Jimmy Drake, a notorious bank robber of the time, although perhaps not as murderous as Dillinger and that bunch, was getting out of prison. People suspected he had killed a robbery victim or two, but he was convicted only of one robbery, where no one got hurt, so he was eligible for parole." Our banker friend continued: "Rumor got out that he was going to stickup the First National Bank," he said with great emphasis. "Well, we contacted the police, so they would be here when he was released. Sure enough, a few minutes after ole Drake's release, he comes strolling in here, dressed in one of those a cheap, ill fitting, brown suits convicts are issued; he walked kinda casual like. I figured part of his act, ya know," he continued. "Half a dozen cops or so planted themselves inconspicuously, dressed in regular clothes and all. Well sir, ole Drake walks up to the first teller, hands him a piece of paper. The cops are ready to pounce. The teller hands him a pen. I'm watching him, careful-like. 'What the hell is going on,' I'm thinking," starting to smile, Pemberton continued. "I'll tell you what was going on. The teller had him endorse his prison paycheck for making damned license plates, which were drawn on our bank. Then ole Drake saunters out with his $123 in cash, just like a regular damned customer, which I suppose he was." Mr. Pemberton started to chuckle. "We were all damned relieved."

As Thanksgiving approached, Mr. Olinger allowed Frank and I to take off after lunch from the Fourth National Bank, where we were working in Tulsa on the Wednesday before Thanksgiving. We drove to Garden City, Kansas, grabbed a few hours of sleep. Then up at 5 A.M. Thanksgiving morning we were off to Colby where Frank was to spend the weekend with his brother's family. I dropped Frank off about 8 AM and drove on to Boulder in time for one of my mom's savory and festive Thanksgiving dinners.

My family endured significant challenges during my first six weeks as a bank examiner. My father had suffered a major health breakdown; he had lost 30 or 40 pounds and spent a couple weeks in the hospital. His face was so drawn and pale; I hardly recognized him. Mom and Dad announced to me that they were starting to liquidate the family business, Scribbler's Book Company, which was a wholesale and retail bookstore in Boulder. It was easily the largest bookstore in Boulder at the time. It was a sad time, since Mom and Dad had worked very hard to make the business a success. They decided to liquidate, rather than sell, in order to get Dad away from the pressures of running the business. Had Dad's health crisis happened while I was working in Greeley, I would have accepted the challenge to carry on the business. But being away for these six weeks, it wasn't possible to join in this discussion; I was simply out of the loop.

Early Sunday morning I took off from Boulder, arriving in Colby about 9 A.M., where I planned to meet Frank for some breakfast and coffee. Frank was waiting at Colby's only downtown hotel when I arrived. However, he was not alone. Accompanying Frank was this lovely, shapely, young, blue eyed, blond woman, perhaps in her early 20s, roughly my age. Instead of only Frank's small single suitcase, there were in addition, three very large suitcases lined up on the hotel's front porch. Smiling broadly Frank gushes, "Bert, I got married over the weekend. This is my wife, Susan. Sue, meet my co-worker, Bert."

Susan smiled brightly and said. "Hi, nice to meet you."

Stunned, I said, "Wow, Frank moves fast. Good to meet you Sue."

Frank said, still smiling from ear to ear, "Susan will be going back to Tulsa with us."

"Good thing this car has a big trunk," I said, eyeing Susan's luggage.

As we ate breakfast, Frank explained that Susan was a niece of Frank's brother Everett's wife and that they had known each other over past several years. But on Thanksgiving Day, "the sparks flew and we got married Saturday morning," Frank explained, still wearing that infectious smile of his. We got in the Plymouth, with all three of us in the convertible's spacious front seat, with Susan in the middle and Frank riding shotgun, his arm around Susan. I was totally amazed at this development and other than congratulating the newlyweds, couldn't think of much to say.

Frank and Susan chatted cheerily as we sped south on U.S. 83, then we turned eastbound on U.S. 50 at Garden City. After about three hours of driving, as we approached Dodge City, Frank said, "Shall we stop in Dodge for lunch?"

"Yeah," I replied. "I need gas, a restroom and a stretch."

After we gassed up, Frank started giving directions. "Left here, right there." I'm thinking he must know a good spot to have lunch, being the Kansas native he is."

He said, "Pull over here." We pulled up in front of large brick institutional looking building. Frank and Susan started laughing uncontrollably.

"What's so damned funny?" I snapped.

Frank smiled, still laughing boisterously. "We're just giving Susan a ride back to school."

"You didn't get married after all?" I gasped. Then I realized that Frank had just pulled the funniest practical joke that had ever been played on me and I joined in laughter. The brick building was the Dodge City Catholic College for Girls. After an uneventful drive, Frank and I arrived in Tulsa sometime after dark ready for work the following day.

As Christmas approached Mr. Olinger, Frank, Curtis and Bill all were planning on taking two holiday weeks off. I didn't have enough vacation for more than 5 days: in fact I had to borrow a day or two to get back to Boulder for the holidays. I was assigned to work for a couple of days for Arlington Smith, "Arlo" as he was known to us. Mr. Smith was a commissioned National Bank Examiner, around 50 years old, who also worked out of the Tulsa office. He was in charge of the "B" crew and did the smaller National banks in eastern Oklahoma. His regular assistants were also taking an extended holiday.

Fitz and I were to assist Arlo in the examination of the First National Bank of Coweta. The Coweta First National was a tiny bank located at the northern edge of cotton farming county in a poor community 25 miles south of Tulsa.

The penurious Mr. Smith always insisted on driving his brown 59 Rambler sedan; he liked the 10 cents per mile the O.C.C. paid at the time, whereas Mr. Olinger let us split up the driving, so we all got some benefit of the mileage. Arlo picked Fitz and me up at our respective homes and we proceeded on to Coweta for an eight o'clock start. Larger banks we started at closing time in the afternoon, since we always tried to have the cash count accomplished by the time the bank lobby opened the following morning, in the case of Coweta 9:00 AM., since there was little cash to count. I was sitting in the back seat and killed the drive time, 45 minutes or so, reading over the old reports. Of special interest, was a confidential section, or yellow pages, the portion of the report the bankers never see, written by none other than the remarkable W. H. Donahue, who was famous for his entertaining confidentials and Churchillian prose. Mr. D wrote: "President Luker, at age 80, is not a competent banker, and it is doubtful that he will ever become one." Nevertheless, in spite of Mr. Donahue's considered opinion, it appeared the bank was solvent, even though it had a few loans of questionable integrity.

We pulled up in a parking space on Coweta's gravel main street, perhaps 50 feet from the bank's front door, and walked around to the side door and knocked. Mr. Luker, who was perhaps 85 by now, greeted us in polite resignation. Mr. Luker was bald, bent over, looked like he might have been Mr. Donahue's elder brother. He, of course, knew Arlo Smith. The bank building was dirty, even more archaic and run down than the dream bank in Windsor, Colorado Herb Becker and I longed to purchase someday.

I was familiar with small country banks; both my grandfather's little bank in Basin, Wyoming, and the Bank of Lafayette, where I had done business, were of less than $2,000,000 in total footings. However, these banks' exteriors and interiors were neat and clean and appropriately maintained. Not so, with Coweta.

Across the street was another tiny bank called Security National Bank of Coweta. Security National had a shabby, small forlorn, brick two story building, with what appeared to be an outhouse in its backyard. The outhouse seemed to echo the outline of Security's building.

Upon entering I wondered, "When was the last time someone took the time to give this place a good cleaning, or even a half assed cleaning?"

The interior was dreary, dust covered and cobwebs everywhere, with three old fashion iron barred teller cages. The varnish on the woodwork was flaking, the oak floor was worn through the finish and the place was filthy. After Arlo introduced us to Mr. Luker, Mr. Luker introduced us to Mr. Fletcher, who was the bank's second officer and Cashier. The title Cashier means the fiscal officer of the bank. Typically it is a desk job that oversees the operations with few if any lending functions.

In the instance of Mr. Fletcher, he was also the bank's head teller. Mr. Fletcher was a portly gent, perhaps 50 years old, about five feet, nine inches tall and looked like he hadn't shaved for a week. His once white shirt was heavily stained with tobacco juice, with a tie so dirty and stained the original colors were hard to detect. Arlo, Fitz and I were a stark contrast in our crisp white shirts, well pressed dark suits and neat, clean ties. I entered his teller cage, which was impregnated with the foul smell of tobacco juice. On the floor was a dirty, brass cuspidor, surrounded by little globs of chewed tobacco. I counted out Mr. Fletcher's cash drawer. I was surprised: It balanced to the penny, as did the bank's vault cash. Fitz counted the other two teller windows and they too balanced precisely. We finished the cash count easily by nine.

Not having any better sense, Fitz and I decided to partake of the bank's coffee, which was fairly potent from infrequently cleaning of the pot. We then ran the checking and savings ledgers. Arlo proved the notes and customer liability ledger (loan ledger). The bank's deposit posting machine was an ancient Burroughs machine, evidently purchased in 1912, when the bank was founded. It was a huge, black monster entirely operated without the use of electricity. The operator placed the ledger sheet in the carriage, carefully lining it up, punched in the previous balance, then added the deposits and subtracted the individual checks, stomped on the foot treadle to record each number and, voila, the ledger was posted. With its' foot treadle and heavy iron construction, it was reminiscent of the old time Singer sewing machines. One of the bank's two female employees handled this function, when she wasn't busy waiting customers at the bank's other teller window.

Arlo insisted we balance the bank's dormant deposit ledger, even though it was still wrapped in adding machine tape and sealed with National Bank Examiner seals from Mr. Smith's previous examination eight months earlier. I was amazed to discover that the dormant ledger was substantially larger than the active demand deposit ledger. It was not hard to figure out why: the bank had never serviced charged out a single account since its founding in 1912. Included were numerous ledgers for 10 cents, even a pennies, were unmolested. Unlike nearly every bank, the Coweta Bank never service charged out even the smallest dormant accounts.

About 11 A.M. I asked where the lavatory was. Mr. Fletcher responded, "Oh, we ain't got one, but they got one next door at the feed store." He pointed towards the rear of the building and said, "Ya go through them double doors of the feed store. On the right there's stacks of feed, fertilizer sacks and such. At the end of the sacks, hang a right. There'll be a door on yer left; that's it."

"Okay. Thanks", I replied, no doubt with surprise and took off towards the side door. Following Mr. Fletcher's directions I found the so-called lavatory; it was nothing more than a drop hole, which smelled like the outhouses I frequented at Boy Scout Camp. Perhaps, one might describe it as an indoor outhouse. Walking back, I glanced across the street and realized the tall slender building across the street behind Security National was indeed an outhouse.

It dawned on me at this moment, that the Town of Coweta didn't have a sewer system and everyone in this poverty stricken little community had an outhouse, while perhaps a few of the more affluent citizens had septic systems.

At lunch that day, Arlo, Fitz and I went across the street to a little Ma & Pa restaurant and each of us had the Blue Plate Special, consisting that day of a generous slice of meat loaf, mashed potatoes, green beans, and a dab of tapioca pudding for dessert, for two bucks apiece. I asked Mr. Smith, how this poor little town of 2500 souls managed to support two banks. Arlo sighed. "Luker and old Johnson at Security National Bank across the street have been so busy being mad at each other, that it never occurred to them to merge the two banks together. Both banks have few loans and both have good liquidity, all treasury securities. Funny, though, they have always managed to make a little money and stay solvent, in spite of their lack of sophistication."

New Year 1962 began for us with another trip to Oklahoma City, this time visiting the Liberty National Bank and Trust Company. Liberty was comparable in size to the First National and also a big lender to the oil and gas industry. The Kerr McGee Oil Company people were among the directors and major stockholders of the bank. Liberty was an aggressive oil patch lender, but what I liked about them was that, it was one of the friendlier banks we worked in. The people were more talkative and cooperative as well. Tuesday of our second week Morrison Tucker, the Executive Vice President of the bank, who had been working closely on the loan portfolio examination with Ken, invited us to join them for dinner the following evening at the Skirvin Hotel, the finest hotel facility in Oklahoma City at the time. Our instructions were to meet Mr. Tucker and his fellow officers in the lobby of the Hotel at 6 P.M.

We arrived a bit early and sat in the lobby, waiting for the Liberty crew, when a very attractive young blonde lady walked in to register at the front desk. Frank, never one to fail to notice an attractive woman, turned to Fitz and me and said. "I've seen that gal before. She must work for one of our banks." Pausing a minute he continued. "Damned if I know which one." He turned to Fitz and me. We both drew a blank and Fitz said, "Can't help you, Frank. I don't place her, nice looking lady though." Fitz wasn't blind to pretty women either.

Frank got up and strolled over to talk to the lovely, familiar looking women and said, "Hi, I'm Frank Hess, the bank examiner. Don't you work in a bank somewhere?"

The young, blonde, woman gave him a puzzled look, frowned a little at first, which changed to a bright smile and replied, "You must have me confused with someone else. I'm Sandra Dee. We're making a movie here in Oklahoma City."

"The movie star, sure, I've seen you in the movies several times. Sorry to bother you." Frank said a bit flustered.

Sandra Dee smiled pleasantly and said, "It happens all the time, have a good evening."

During one of our frequent trips to Oklahoma City, we visited the Central National Bank. The bank's specialty was installment lending and purchasing installment contracts from the local car dealers. The bank was quite clean, an easy bank and we were wrapping up things with time to spare: Ken even had a draft of the confidential section completed.

Curtis was a marvelously fast and accurate typist and always claimed that when typing the words off a draft page, the words somehow went to his eyes and directly to his fingers. He claimed he never actually read, what he was typing. We didn't believe him, especially Ken, who decided to put Curtis' boast to the test. In the middle of the confidential section, management paragraph, usually the most interesting part of the yellow pages, Ken wrote, "Curtis eats shit", immediately after "President Roberts is a competent lender.' After Curtis completed the typing, Ken proofread the report; there it was, "Curtis eats shit," right in the middle of the page. Ken showed it to Curtis, who smiled and said, "See, I told you, Ken." Curtis then proceeded to retype the document without complaint.

Among the more enjoyable banks on our list was The First National Bank & Trust Company in Muskogee, Oklahoma. Mr. Ora Lamb, the President, was our genial host, but the highlight of these examinations was Flossie, a wonderful cook who managed the bank's employee cafeteria. Employee cafeterias were not very common and usually offered less than the finest cuisine. Flossie served up wonderful southern dishes including; fried chicken with her special gravy, the best grits ever, beef stroganoff and cat-fish. Mr. Lamb claimed that by having the cafeteria, the employees got back to work faster and had more enjoyable lunches, too. The lunches were priced right for us, with examiners always trying to save a buck on our $14.00 per day allowance.

While in Muskogee, we stayed at a fairly decent hotel. It had been built during the Oklahoma oil boom of the 1920s and hadn't lost its touches of grandeur, including molded Greek revival columns, spacious rooms, and colorful paisley patterned carpet.

One night Ken, Fitz, Frank, Bill Rainey and I were engaged in one of our occasional penny ante poker games. This particular evening no one made a lot, or for that matter lost a lot. After all it was a friendly game. The game disbanded about 10 P.M. and I was walking back to my room, when out of one of the rooms came a stark naked, 30ish, woman, dark hair, lithe figure, boobs bouncing, running pell-mell and looking behind her, as her "boyfriend," also in the buff, came running after her. As she glanced behind her towards her pursuer, she ran into me and would have knocked me over, except I fell back against the hallway wall. Stunned, but enjoying the view, I watched the bare-ass couple turn the corner down the hallway, heard them laugh and yell at each other. Every time I hear Merle Haggard's song, "I'm proud to be an Okie from Muskogee," I think of that evening.

As we started the first of my second cycle of examinations in Oklahoma, our crew was back in Oklahoma City getting ready for another examination of First National. The bank's lobby was on the second level, mezzanine banking they called it, with escalators going from street level to the tellers and the main lobby. On the first level was a coffee shop, where we met to give out assignments for the crew. We greeted each other and swapped stories, which this time included the story of a couple of F.D.I.C. examiners who got hammered one night and placed their official seals all around the front door of this little country bank in Hollis. I guess the intent was to give folks passing by the bank the impression it was shut down, but of course all it did was get bank management angry. Amusing at the time, but I'm sure their Mr. Ross equivalent would have somehow missed the humor.

The first thing we had to do was count the cash, which was a big job and required organization and coordination: Frank's responsibility. First National must have had 25, perhaps 30 or more tellers. We had the two Oklahoma City crews, plus the examining crew based in Clinton. We had about 20 examiners all receiving instructions for when we entered the bank. The conversation went something like this. Hess would say: "Bert, take tellers two, three, and four. John Duncan, you get tellers five, six, and seven. Fitz, you've been here before, take Tom and Richard and catch the drive-ins. Curtis, Ken's going to have you work with him on the notes, so catch the note teller's cash. Bob, you and I will seal the vault cash and start the count; the rest of the detail guys join us when you are finished with your tellers, to count the vault cash. They usually have several million in cash on hand."

When we entered the bank, 5 minutes or so later, the Oklahoma City Police force was there to greet us. Our waitress must have thought we were out to rob the place and alerted the cops. We all pulled out our "Elliot Ness" cards and showed them to the officers and we were quickly able to get to work.

That wasn't the end to the excitement on that particular trip to Oklahoma City. We were staying at the YMCA up Robinson Avenue three blocks from the bank. The Y was fairly new and had a gym we could use and, best of all it, cost three bucks a night if we doubled up. Fitz and I were sharing a room that faced the street.

Across the street was an ornate dirty stone faced, two-story hotel called the "Carlston Hotel". The place was quite rundown. Its most prominent feature was a wide balcony, 25 feet wide, over the once-grand entryway. Over the years the Carlston Hotel had degenerated into a house of ill repute. At 5 AM, just as it was getting light, Fitz and I were awaken by the sounds of fire engines and police sirens loudly announcing their arrival. We rushed to the window to find that the Carlston Hotel was on fire; we couldn't see flames, but smoke was pouring from second floor windows and from sections of the roof. On the balcony, were the "ladies of the night" dressed in their revealing, flimsy and colorful red, orange, yellow, bright blue, chartreuse nighties, facing the street, waving at the firemen, encouraging them to rescue them. Behind them were the "johns", roughly in equal number, but facing the burning building, hoping when they made their escape down the fire ladder, no one would see.

The following morning the *Oklahoma City Times* reported the hotel fire, noting that fire had done what the police had tried, but were unable to accomplish for years, which was to get rid of this eyesore and public embarrassment.

Following our trip to Oklahoma City we were engaged in the examination of the First National Bank & Trust Company of Tulsa, a large bank. By the middle of the second week, Arlo's crew and the guys from Western Oklahoma were released while our crew was putting together the final pieces of the report, when Paul Ross joined us. President Kennedy appointed James Saxon Comptroller of the Currency, replacing the elderly Ray Gidney several months earlier. Mr. Gidney was a business as usual manager and left the operation of the OCC to the career people. By contrast Mr. Saxon was a lawyer from Chicago who came in to shake up the staid OCC and was now launching forth on momentous changes, including changing the districts. Starting with 1914 the OCC had divided the country into twelve districts, following exactly the boundaries of the Federal Reserve Districts, which often divided states into different regions. For example, Oklahoma and New Mexico had the northern portions in the 10th Federal Reserve District and a southern portion in the Dallas, or 11th Federal Reserve District. Mr. Saxon now divided the nation into fourteen National Bank Regions all along state lines. All of Oklahoma would be joined with Texas in the 11th National Bank Region. New Mexico, Colorado, Wyoming, Arizona and Utah would form the 12th National Bank Region.

Mr. Ross had commandeered an office on the fourth floor and commenced interviews with each of us. Apparently, Mr. Ross never made field visits, except when serious problems existed, which was obviously not the case with First of Tulsa. The bank was viewed by our crew, as one of the top banks in Oklahoma. Ken Olinger, was the first in for a private meeting with Mr. Ross. Ken came out of the meeting looking surprised, but pleased. He was being named an Assistant Chief National Bank Examiner and being assigned to Washington. Frank was reassigned to Kansas City, which for Frank was like going home. Bill Rainey, and Curtis, all Tulsans, would stay put. Fitz had just accepted a good position as V. P. & Cashier of the American National Bank of Sapulpa, a few miles southwest of Tulsa, exactly the kind of job he was looking for.

When Mr. Ross got around to me, I was uncertain what would happen. Mr. Ross leaned back in his swivel chair, peered at me with his owl like face, looking over his bifocals and said, "Harris, I know you're from Colorado and although I can't place you in Colorado, I do have an opening in Cheyenne, working for Mr. Van Dyke. Or, if you like, you can stay here in Tulsa. I don't know who you'll be working for, since Mr. Olinger is going to Washington." I was pleased with the offer and responded, "Mr. Ross, I'd like very much to go to Wyoming, my dad is from Wyoming and my Grandmother still lives there."

"Okay, then it's settled. I'll arrange for the transfer," said Mr. Ross. "Oh, one more thing, Harris. You've been accepted to attend the Inter- Agency School for Bank Examiners in Washington, starts second week in May. Good luck."

Mrs. Rainey hosted one of her crew parties for us at their home. It was a farewell for all of us since our crew of six was being split up in five different directions. The party was a potluck affair with Gwen Olinger, Marilyn Fitzpatrick and Mrs. Rainey providing the food. Frank, Curtis and I bought the liquor. Even Mr. and Mrs. Donahue joined in the festivities. Frank and I had become good friends during the past eight months and we vowed to keep in touch via Christmas cards. As a result of the marriage joke, we even agreed to attend each other's weddings. I knew I would miss this wonderful group of guys who had been my family for the past eight months.

Ken Olinger and I were expected in Washington on the same date. Ken was driving his blue Ford Falcon east, so I rode with him and shared the driving. En route I asked him if he knew Mr. Van Dyke. Ken replied, "Met him a few times at Conference. Can't say I really know him. He enjoys a drink, I'm told. Have a drink with Van now and then and you'll get along fine."

When we arrived in Washington, Ken and I found a decent motel out in Bethesda, Maryland and to save on expenses, we shared a room with two double beds for the four weeks that followed. Every morning we would drive to the Treasury Building, next to the White House. We'd have breakfast in the cafeteria in the basement of the Treasury Building, often with Justin T. Watson, formerly the Chief National Bank Examiner of the Cleveland District. Mr. Watson was now the First Deputy Comptroller of the Currency, the highest career official in the OCC. Mr. Watson was a large robust man in his mid-50s, with thinning hair and an easy, self-confident way about him. Ken was to be his assistant as I understood it. I was surprised Mr. Watson accepted me into his company, as though it were perfectly normal for me the, "embryo assistant examiner," to be having breakfast with the top O.C.C. executive. The conversations between Ken and Mr. Watson were very educational and I felt privileged to attend these sessions; I learned a lot.

I would learn even more at the Inter-Agency School was led by Jerry Swords, a Federal Reserve Examiner from Kansas City, who was exactly nine years older than I. Jerry always had a good story to make even the dullest subject matter interesting. He brought in interesting "speakers" such as a Mr. Anderson, one of the F.D.I.C.'s liquidator, who had recently liquidated the Sheldon National Bank, where Bernice Geiger had literally stole half the bank. The speakers Swords brought in would provide enhancement for various banking issues we were learning about.

Swords and I hit it off immediately. Jerry and I would meet along with other people from the bank examining world, at the Fairfax House for "Happy Hour". Over the years Jerry and I would become good friends.

The month in Washington was great fun. Weekends Ken and I toured the sights. One weekend a boyhood friend of mine, Rod Swift, a doctoral physics candidate at Yale, his roommate George Chamberlain, Ken and I decided to walk to the top of the Washington Monument. After much huffing and puffing on that hot May afternoon, we made it. We decided to take the elevator down, a rather backwards way of visiting the monument it seemed to me. My next stop would be Cheyenne, Wyoming.

Five

Cowboy State Banking

I was to meet Mr. Van Dyke at the Hynds Building in Cheyenne, which was easy to find, since was at the corner of 16th Street and Capitol Avenue, across the street from the Union Pacific Railroad Depot. The office was on the second floor, above the Cheyenne National Bank of which Mr. Trautwein of GNB fame was the President. As I walked in on that warm June day, Mr. Van Dyke was putting the finishing touches on the report for his most recent examination job. Van Dyke's assistant was getting ready for the American National Bank of Cheyenne examination, which we would be starting at 3:00 PM.

Mr. Van Dyke was of medium height, thin gray hair, 59 years old, with a large beer belly. It might have been more accurate to describe his stomach as a whiskey barrel, given his reputed preference for Jim Beam. Mr. Van Dyke greeted me in his quiet cordial way and asked. "Bert, are you up to taking charge of the detail at American National, that's the bank up the street, we'll starting this afternoon."

"Yes. Mr. Van Dyke, I'm sure I can do it." I replied with confidence.

"Oh, Bert, for Christ sake, just call me Van. We're pretty informal here in Wyoming," Van responded with a smile. "This is Jim Cherry, he is the other assistant here," Van continued, nodding towards Jim.

I shook hands with Jim and said, "I'm looking forward to working with you."

Jim said. "Yeah, me too. Bert." Jim was a good sized man, dark brown hair, paunchy, with a somewhat overweight build, not quite as tall as my six feet, and in his mid-thirties. "We lost two guys recently, we're supposed to have a four man crew. Jim Chapin took a job with First National in Casper, a couple of months ago. Kenny Link left a week ago to become Cashier of the American National Bank of Riverton. New bank, just opened for business. I think it opened this morning," Van said.

"Van, that's what Kenny was planning on," Jim Cherry said joining the conversation.

"American, here in Cheyenne, is one of our larger banks. Charlie Hout and a couple of guys from Denver will be up to assist. This will be Charlie's last trip to Wyoming; he's retiring at the end of the month," Van continued wistfully.

Jim and I busied ourselves preparing for the afternoon's business, while Van continued to pound away on his typewriter- he was a two fingered hunt and pecker- finishing the confidential section of the previous week's examination report.

Shortly before lunch Charlie Hout walked in carrying a heavy looking, well worn, bank examiner's briefcase. Charlie was an elderly, slender, short, unsmiling, gentleman, about 75 years old and sporting a full head of pure white hair. Van greeted Charlie warmly; you could tell they had been buddies for years. Charlie said, "Van, the other guys, Ralph Pederson and Al Kris, I think, will be meeting us at the bank at 3 P.M." The four of us walked over to the "Trails End" restaurant, a pretty decent eatery, as I would discovery. Van and Charlie led. Jim Cherry, who seemed to have the lowdown on everyone, and I followed at a distance.

"Charlie and Van are old drinking buddies, been examining banks together here in Wyoming and Colorado since the 1940s," Jim said. "You know, that bag Charlie touts around?" Jim continued. I nodded in the affirmative.

"Sure, looks like a tired version of my bag." I said.

"Well, that's not what is interesting. It's filled with E-Bonds and uncashed paychecks. Ole Charlie is four or five years behind in cashing his paychecks, must be over $100,000 in there. Old bachelor, you know," concluded Jim as we reached the restaurant.

Our three o'clock start at the American National Bank, went off without complications. Ruth Livingston, the bank's Auditor, a friendly, blond lady in her 40s, welcomed us, as if she actually enjoyed having examiners; rarely were bankers glad to see us. She introduced me and the guys on detail to Mr. Rudy Hoffman, the President. Mr. Hoffman was according to the previous exam report was 72 years old. He was a tall man who wore thick glasses and had unruly grey hair, which seemed inconsistent with his otherwise well-dressed appearance. He shook our hands vigorously. Mr. Hoffman many years earlier had been the Wyoming State Examiner whose experience included guiding Wyoming banks through the difficult 1920s; he therefore, understood our mission and was helpful, and his bank was typically always in good order.

A few days later Van, Cherry and I were at coffee break together. Van was wearing his amused smile and said, "Funny thing happened with Rudy a few minutes ago. I was working the Bosler file, you know the rancher from west of Laramie that has the little Town of Bosler named after his family? Couldn't find a financial statement. So, I asked Rudy. 'What happened to Bosler's statement; unusual for you not to have a current statement?' Rudy, hung his head down, looking embarrassed and says to me: 'Van, I did take one, but it looked so awful I tore it up. The guy is land poor, lots of land, little cash and just a couple hundred cows.'" With the help of Ruth and Mr. Kimbro, the Cashier and chief operations officer, the examination of American National went smoothly and Van seemed happy enough with my work.

The following week we were off to the sparsely settled, thinly vegetated, red desert of the southwest corner of the state: Evanston, Kemmerer, Rock Springs and Green River. We were gone for three weekends. Cherry suggested I bring some fishing gear as there were a couple of reservoirs out west and not much else to do. I decided at this time that I could just as easily live in Boulder, which is about 100 miles from Cheyenne and save the rental expense of an apartment. We drove out to Evanston first with me riding with Van.

Jim chose to drive his own car at his own expense. The O.C.C. required three to a car before paying mileage for a second car. It didn't take long for me to figure out that Jim seemed to enjoy being alone, although we did a little fishing together on that trip.

Following Evanston, we went up to Kemmerer, Wyoming, a coal-mining town, dominated by the Kemmerer Coal Company. The bank, located diagonally across the square from J.C. Penney store number one, was an old, but well maintained 1900 style stone and brick building. There were iron bars on all the windows and iron doors in front of the regular oak doors. It could have doubled as a jail, I thought as we approached the bank for an afternoon start. Inside, the tellers were behind the old fashion style iron bars. The bank would have made a great set for a movie set in 1900, or maybe a jail.

The First National Bank of Kemmerer was, in fact, owned by the Kemmerer family. John Kemmerer was the Chairman of the Board, but didn't live in Kemmerer or show up to all the Board Meetings. John A. Reed, the President and C.E.O., was a large balding man of good height. He was also a successor to Rudy Hoffman as Wyoming State Examiner. Like Rudy's bank, Mr. Reed's bank was a very clean shop.

Mr. Reed made what few loans the bank had booked: it had very conservative 20% loan to deposit ratio. Conservative loan to deposit ratios are a clear indication that the bank wasn't making many loans in the community or perhaps there weren't many opportunities to lend. In the case of the Kemmerer bank, I suspect wasn't making all the loans possible, although there may not have been a terrific number of lending opportunities since Kemmerer was a company town with few businesses besides Kemmerer Coal. The bank had an interesting bond account with a lot of corporate securities, unusual in my limited experience, and, of course, the to-be-expected U. S. Treasuries, and a few municipal bonds. The bond account was my project. Cherry, who normally, worked loans, did most of the rest of the detail. Van, of course, examined the few loans the bank had.

The most curious thing about the bank was its Vice President, Nellie Frizzell. Nellie Frizzell was a white haired lady of 60, a little on the plump side and always seemed to dress like she was on her way to an afternoon ladies bridge party. Ms. Frizzell's duties seemed to be to serve as John Reid's secretary, for which she was paid a handsome salary, better than twice the rate for a good secretary. Her board minutes consisted of pages and pages of trivia, about sending out get well cards, flowers to various folks and the responding thank you cards; hardly anything except the bare minimum about loan approvals and other real bank business.

Van wrote in his confidential that in spite of her VP title, she contributed nothing to the bank's actual management. Van, along with every one of the examiners, all of the bank's staff, were inclined to believe John Reed, who was married, was supporting Nellie, his mistress, by this method. Cherry would give out with an evil laugh as he imagined the two in the sack together. First National, Kemmerer was a fair sized bank for a Wyoming town of 2000 population, with over ten million in assets, as I recall. It was an easy job and we were on to Green River ahead of schedule.

The First National Bank of Green River was a little $1,500,000 bank managed and owned by the Chrisman and Toliver families. Outwardly, the bank's building looked to be in good repair and not a relic from the 19th century; however, inside was bizarre looking. Evidently, Mr. Chrisman, the President and chief lending officer, was a hunting enthusiast, for mounted above the old fashioned iron barred teller cages was a whole menagerie of stuffed animals, a couple of mule deer, bobcat, mountain lion and a black bear seemed to doing a balance beam act above the tellers. Mr. Chrisman's golden blond young son, who served as the Cashier and looked after operations. The bank didn't make many loans; they did have a curious bond account. Mostly, U.S. Treasuries, as one would expect, but also a few defaulted railroad bonds, which while actively traded still had some value, had to be written down to market value at each examination. These speculative bonds seemed to lose additional value with each examination.

Van noticed the bank had lost some deposits since the last examination and quizzed Mr. Chrisman as to why. "Mr. Van Dyke" said he in pathetic tones. "Those god-damned big city banks in Rock Spring are taking all of our business away." I don't suppose the dusty, stuffed animals had anything to do with it, I thought. As it happened, the Rock Springs National Bank was next our stop.

Rock Springs in those days had a population of 20,000 and was served by three banks, Rock Springs National, the largest, and a couple of state charter institutions. John Hay, Jr., the President was about 55 years old at the time with a full head of slightly gray hair, a quick wit and a seemingly easygoing manner. Like Kemmerer, Rock Springs was and still is a coal-mining town; many of the old mines honeycomb beneath the town causing buildings and streets to sag and occasionally fall in the now abandoned mining tunnels. The town was then populated with various immigrants from all over the world, but mostly southern and eastern Europe and China.

With great pride, Rock Springs National Bank proclaimed their personnel could speak any language you wished to communicate in. At the time of this visit they claimed they could speak 17 different languages. Talk about having your ear to the community's pulse.

Mr. Hay also was a very savvy gentleman. He set us up in the bank's boardroom, which was adjacent to his office; there was no barrier between the two rooms, so we could hear everything that went on in his office. One telephone conversation, Mr. Hay's side only, went, "It's so hot here today we're farting popcorn balls." Another conversation, with a would-be borrower went. "Harry, you know I'd like to lend you the money you asked for, but after considering your request, I'm going to turn you down." Then John gave him a detailed, thoroughly well-reasoned explanation of the facts that included Harry didn't have enough income to make the payments, especially during the winter, and concluded. "Harry, I would be doing you a hell of a disservice making you this loan."

He got up, as did Harry, shook the man's hand and Harry said, "John, thank you for turning me down. I can see you did the right thing for me." Later when I had to turn down customers for loans I would remember this moment, but I'm afraid I never achieved John Hay's eloquence or graciousness in this situation.

The overwhelming majority of the loans at Rock Springs National were of very good quality. Finally, after going through half the deck of line sheets, Van started hesitating; you could always tell, when a loan had concerns for Van. Mr. Hay knew Van well and recognized the sign. Before Van said a word, John Hay stated. "Mr. Sullivan is a hell of a nice fellow. You'd like him, Van, but he can't pay, better charge it off."

A few weeks later we were off to Lander, Wyoming, over 300 miles from Cheyenne so we took most of the day getting there after spending a few hours in the office. We had made a reservation at the Holiday Lodge, no connection with the Holiday Inns. Holiday Lodge was a Frank Lloyd

Wright inspired, organic architecture structure that seemed to reach out as if to be a part of nature and was one of the nicest facilities we frequented in our travels; the rooms all over looked the scenic, rushing waters of the Popo Agie river. As Van and I drove westward from Casper on U.S. 20-26, there were great herds of over 100 pronghorn antelope roaming this open range country. As the sunset Van, smiles and turns to me and says, "Here we are between Powder River and Hell's Half Acre, Wyoming. Imagine calling into Mr. Thomas and saying were stuck between these two wide spots in the road. Just think we actually get paid to see wonderful sunsets like this." Van had a special appreciation for life as it was dealt him; he never pined for a grander, but seemed to manage to enjoy life as it came his way.

Powder River was a tiny village in 1962 of fewer than 100 people with a couple of gas stations, a bar and a café, which presumable scratched a meager living off the travelers driving by. Hell's Half Acre, another wide spot in the road, is a curiosity of nature. In the middle of this rolling prairie populated by antelope, prairie dogs, rabbits, a few cattle and sheep, and sparse vegetation consisting of grass and sagebrush, lies a miniature "Grand Canyon". Hell's Half Acre, result of thousands of years of erosion, the sometimes filled with water, more often not. The Powder River name as the reader might imagine is owing to there being more sand and silt visible than actual water. Most of the year the Powder River might aptly be described as a river of dust.

During a good summer thunderstorms the Powder River again becomes a conduit for water and carved out Hell's Half Acre. The Powder River cut through epochs of geologic time, thus revealing a variety of colorful red, orange, yellow, shades of blue to gray and assorted colors in between the sandstone and clay walls making up this mini "grand canyon" in the middle of nowhere. We crossed the desolate 100-mile stretch from Casper to Shoshoni, ate supper at the Sage Inn, which proclaimed to be "Shoshoni's finest" and on to Lander ready for an 8 A.M start the following morning.

The First National Bank of Lander, which had recently been purchased by Robert Finkbiner and Robert Bentley, the two Bobs, as Van like to call them. It was at this bank, that I saw firsthand how two guys with not a great deal of money were able to purchase a bank, like Herb Becker and I had dreamed. Mr. Finkbinner had been the chief executive officer for Western

Bancorporation at a couple of Wyoming subsidiaries and must have cashed in his retirement account. Mr. Bentley had sold his small town Pontiac dealership and viola, the two had enough money to satisfy the equity requirement that their Omaha correspondent bank requested.

The bank also had a small insurance agency which helped supplement projected dividends to cash flow their loan payments. The two Bobs had owned the bank for less than two years, but had already made lots of loans. The place was a "workshop" as Jim Cherry described it, meaning it was time consuming to process the loans for examination.

One problem loan involved a restaurant building in Riverton. Apparently, no one had bothered to obtain a survey showing where the building sat on the plot of ground described on the bank's mortgage. It turned out only half of the building was subject to the bank's lien. When the borrower defaulted, the bank discovered to its chagrin, it only had a valid mortgage on half of the building. The borrowers hired a young attorney, just starting to practice law named Jerry Spence, who described the Lander bankers as "greedy, long fingered, dastardly, fellows", as I recall the court transcript in the bank's O.R.E.O. (Other Real Estate Owned) file. The building was razed and the bank's claim was confined to a small parcel of land. Jerry Spence went on to defend Imelda Marcos, wife of the Philippines' notorious President, Ferdinand Marcos and other high profile clients and became famous.

The examination was proceeding along and the bank's Vice President, Harry Hays, invited us out to dinner at Svilar's, an excellent steak house in Hudson, Wyoming. Svilar's was not only known for its fine beef steaks, but also a certain waitress named Millie. Millie was around 50 years old and was Dan Svilar's, the owner, daughter in law. Millie wasn't especially attractive, but what she lacked in looks she more than over came in personality. Millie had a repertoire of funny, sexy stories, told with great flair. She also had a marvelous memory; once introduced she always remember your name, how you liked your steak, even your favorite cut.

Harry Hays, had been with the bank for thirty or more years and he and Van Dyke were great pals. Van and Harry proceeded to get plastered, although Hays was somewhat more restrained. Harry confided in Van that he would be leaving First National at the end of the year. The two Bobs were forcing him into early retirement. Then he told us the story of the night he learned that Bentley and Finkbiner had bought the bank. Harry said, "I went home to Kathryn that night feeling quite dejected and told her the bank had been sold. Kathryn said immediately, 'Harry, why didn't you tell me the bank was for sale? Don't you know I would have bought it for you, Harry honey?'"

Van slurred. "Nice Christmas present!" Cherry and I looked at Harry in wonderment.

Finally Harry broke the silence. "She could afford it you know; her late husband was a big wheel at Honeywell and she has loads of stocks and other investments. I could never ask her to do that, I suppose it's pride." after another pause Harry continued, "I married Kathryn for love, not her money. That's why I work, to support my end of things."

After devouring our choice steaks, we got up to leave. Van Dyke sort of wobbled to his feet, tossed me the keys to his green '61 Pontiac Catalina and exclaimed, "Bert, drive" Thank God! He knew he wasn't in any condition to drive.

Then I watched him stagger, listing to his right side at a 45 degree angle to sidewalk, slowly, deliberately crossing his legs with each step to keep from falling, towards the car a block away. The reader may think I am kidding or exaggerating about the angle. Okay, I wasn't able to measure Van's walk precisely, but as God, Harry and Cherry are my witnesses, Van was walking at a God-dammed 45 degree angle, give or take a degree. He made it all the way to the car, without falling down, honest He really did; I have no idea how he managed to defy Newton's and other laws of physics, but he did.

The next morning I expected Van to be hung over, complaining of a headache. But no, he was fresh as a Morning Glory, for breakfast at 7:00 A.M. He required only a little starting fluid, that is, coffee to get him going.

At the end of that summer of 1962, I took a week vacation and went home to Boulder. My boyhood friend Pete Brakman and his bride, Antoinette, or Andy as we called her, were visiting the folks in Boulder. Aunt Gerda, Uncle Irv, the Frank Lloyd Wright of New Jersey, and cousin Glenn showed up that week too. We rambled around the mountains, talked, played ping-pong and drank gin and tonics too. In an inebriated moment, I mentioned my dream of one day buying my own bank. Uncle Irv burst out laughing. "Bert, people don't buy banks; they aren't proprietorships. Even small banks like the First National Bank of Highland Park are owned by groups of stockholders," said he. Uncle Irv was a director and stockholder in the Highland Park Bank, which was about the size of American National in Cheyenne, one of Wyoming's larger banks.

Back to work in Cheyenne the following week at Stockgrower's National Bank, one of the oldest and largest banks in Wyoming at the time. Finally, the fourth member of the crew joined us in the person of Jerry Magruder. Jerry was 6' 2" or better, roughly 35 years old. As fate would have it, he was most recently employed by Stockgrower's. Jerry was trying to recover from a bitter divorce and was having financial as well as emotional problems. Cherry seemed to want to dive into all the dirt surrounding Jerry's personal life. Jerry apparently took Cherry aside and promised to do him great bodily harm, if he didn't mind his own business. Jerry, on the other hand was a willing learner and was soon ably assisting me on the detail part of the examination.

Soon after Jerry joined us, we were off to Powell, Wyoming, 420 miles away to do the First National Bank. This meant we wouldn't be able to return home for the weekend for the first time since the trip to Evanston, Kemmerer, Green River and Rock Springs. First of Powell was and is an agricultural lender, with a great many loans building up in volume to December, when beet farmers were paid, grain and beans were sold, as well as livestock marketed. First National was a well-run bank, but nevertheless a workshop due to the great volume of loans. The operations were easy and all of us worked on the loan portfolio. The R. A. "Bob" Nelson family owned the bank since its founding in 1910. Bob became President in 1934, when his father died suddenly of a heart attack. Bob's mother, a stay at home mom, according to legend said to Bob. "I don't know anything about running a bank, you'll have to run it." Bob was only 22 years old, but had observed enough and was wise enough to successfully manage the bank.

At supper Friday evening, I suggested we take a drive to Red Lodge, Montana, then up the Cook City Road into Yellowstone National Park. Out of Red Lodge there is a scenic, curvy mountain road, winding ever upward through the pine forests and then above timberline, which leads one top of Bear Tooth Pass. Then several miles driving literally on top of the mountains, over 10,000 in elevation and often actually above the clouds. The visitor some days can get out of the car and walk down into the clouds. One of the most beautiful, breathtaking and stupendous drives in the country.

Magruder was on board immediately. Van Dyke said he needed to finish the Stockgrower's National report, which was due the following week. Once the report was done, Van no doubt would celebrate with his friend Jim Beam. Cherry begged off saying. "I need to polish my shoes." Perhaps just he didn't like our company.

Jerry and I got to know each other, and had a great trip viewing the autumn leaves turning color; we never did get to Yellowstone due to the road being closed because of snow in the high country. On the way back to Powell, we stopped for buffalo burgers and a beer in a rustic little café in Red Lodge. We finished First National Powell midweek and went down to Meeteetse for a Wednesday afternoon start.

The First National Bank of Meeteetse was a tiny $1,000,000 total footings bank located in a small, quaint town of 500 people where the Greybull River emerges from the Absoraka Mountains, east of Yellowstone National Park. In the center of the two block business district is the Meeteetse Mercantile Company, a classic general store, which carried a huge variety inventory, everything from groceries, to clothing, to hunting and fishing gear. The building, although well maintained looked pretty much as it did when it was built about 1900. We arrived about 2:45 P.M. for a 3:00 PM start; 3:00 being the bank's official closing time. The door was locked and the vault door, which was visible from the front door was shut. I was dumfounded, but Van, unfazed, said, "Damned old Angus, must be fishing."

Sure enough, a block away was Angus Linton casting his fly into the Greybull River, which was running serenely, perfect conditions for fishing. Van walked within talking distance and spoke, "Angus, catching anything?"

Angus turned and smiled, he had a kind of shy way of smiling. "Oh, Van, hi. Slow day, great day for fishing, ya know! Bill and I were wondering when you might show up, we're overdue."

We ambled back to the bank, which was an old brick affair that had been painted tan a few years back. The building was the bank's original building built in 1900; the vault door still read "Hogg, Chessman & McDonald, Bankers" in gold leaf. It had been a private bank before obtaining a National

Charter in 1902. I was somewhat reminded of the bank in Coweta, Oklahoma; it still had the classic barred teller cages and Victorian look. Angus phoned Bill, his son, who was the Cashier of the bank and also the main teller. They also had an older lady, about the same age as Angus, about 60. Angus said Ellen always went home after the previous day's business was posted, which today happened to be around 2:00.

Bill arrived in about 10 minutes and opened the vault, which apparently didn't have a time lock or dual control; either Bill or Angus could open it. Cherry and Magruder proved the deposit ledger records. Van balanced the notes. I tried to balance the cash drawer; it was short about $3.17 or some such odd figure. I asked Bill how come it was off.

He looked at me quizzically and said. "We're always off a little, ya know?"

"Well, no I didn't know. Why, is that, Bill?" Said I. Cherry started chuckling to himself and then out loud. He'd been here for a couple of previous examinations.

"We don't mess with pennies. Fella comes in with a check for $5.99 we give him six bucks. A check for $6.02, he just gets the six bucks." The vault cash, ledgers, and notes all balanced to the last cent though. The bank only had about $90.000 in loans, significantly less the bank's $120,000 in capital. A typical bank would loan out 6 or 7 times its capital. Virtually all the bank's assets were tied up in U.S. Treasury securities in laddered maturities. The building, well actually, just the lot was carried at $500, apparently the original cost of the land. The building had been depreciated out to zero years ago. The bank's equipment was all electrically operated, and was a type of Burroughs widely used in numerous banks around the country; hell, they even had indoor plumbing.

Van was done with loans by noon, discussion and all, the next day; he went to his motel room to finish the Powell report after penciling in the changes he wanted on the Meeteetse confidential. As Van put it, "Pretty hard to spend any time worrying about old Angus." Cherry typed it up. By noon, we had the Meeteetse report in the mail to the Chief National Bank Examiner and were on our way home.

When we got back to Cheyenne it was late, about 10:00 P.M., and I decided I'd get a motel room before driving on to Boulder the next morning. I stopped at the Stage Coach Motel, pulled right up in front of the office and proceeded to register. I wrote my name, my folk's Boulder address on the registration card, but put down Wyoming license plate 2-34V, a Cheyenne number. The clerk looked at me suspiciously, looked at the car to verify the license tag and said, "There must be two of you? Something's funny going on here."

"No just me," I replied wearily.

"I ain't renting you no room so you can entertain your girlfriend and make a big mess" said the clerk. I was too tired to argue with him and managed to find a more hospitable innkeeper the next try. I also decided to rent an inexpensive apartment in Cheyenne.

Early in December, we found ourselves at the First National Bank of Rawlins, owned by Robert Bible and his family. Mr. Bible was a crusty old banker, around 65 years old, steel grey hair, stocky build. He told Van he was getting ready to sell and retire to Arizona. "Tired of these damned Wyoming winters," said he.

Wyoming winters can be cold and windy, with snow coming at you horizontally, especially on the high plains around Rawlins. Probably, tired of Rawlins too. Rawlins is home to Wyoming's maximum-security prison for men. According to Mr. Bible, as the Union Pacific Railroad was being built, Rawlins, a division point, had its choice of the prison or the University of Wyoming. In the wild west of the latter part of the 19th century, the Penitentiary seemed like the better economic play. 100 years later Rawlins is a rather dreary town, populated with inmate wives and others hanging around until some inmate was released or perhaps, so they might often visit their wayward relative. These folks are often at the bottom of the economic and social ladder.

Rawlins was also the county seat and served as a trading center for ranches for miles around. The countryside around Rawlins was dry open range, especially well-suited for sheep production. As Harold Johnson, a local lawyer and director of Mr. Bible's competitor put it: "If it don't smell like sheep shit, it can't be a very good loan."

For a good time in Rawlins there were a number of sleazy bars along Front Street, which was also the town's red light district. The bars and dance halls all faced the railroad depot and other railroad buildings. Van's favorite bar was "The Green Mill" owned by Joe Huner, who Van came to know during the three or four visits he made to Rawlins annually; there were two National Banks in Rawlins in those years. The four of us made our way to The Green Mill after work, where to our delight Joe had a "Happy Hour Special" whisky and water for only 25 cents. Van stated, "At these prices I can't afford to be sober."

Cherry was working the installment loan department this trip and came up a collection card for a loan on a Lincoln Continental sedan to one of Rawlins's fallen doves; attached was a letter from Sadie, it read. "Sorry, to be behind; I've been sick. As soon as I get back on my back again I'll get my payments caught up."

A few weeks later, we paid a visit to Sheridan's First National Bank. It was winter by now and Sheridan had at least a foot of snow on the ground. The president of the bank was Clarence Meyers, well into his 80s and quite senile. Mr. Meyers was quite forgetful, except for things that happened long ago. I was amazed when he noted my name and said, "You must be Dr. Bert Harris' grandson, I remember him well." Grandfather Harris had left Sheridan for the then developing town of Basin across the Big Horn Mountains to the west in 1908.

The Sheridan bank was populated with all male tellers. One gentleman had been a teller for 25 years and thought he was an expert on banking given all his "experience". He proceeded to make light of my youth and, from his view, lack of experience. Of course he didn't know beans about loans, operations or investments; only tellering. The bank used a hand written, archaic Boston Ledger to record cashier checks and other official checks. Ken Walker, one of the more enlightened staff members was in charge of official check records. Magruder, and I, convinced him to use the more modern method of keeping copies of outstanding cashier,s checks as the record. He protested at first, then grinning said. "I think we can slip this by Mr. Meyers."

Over the years, with Ken Walker and some of the other senior officers we were able to help First National up date, without Mr. Meyers even being aware of improvements in record keeping and improved internal controls.

Sheridan was another workshop, with lots of loans, confusing or missing documentation. We were running behind and anxious to get an early start home Friday, due to the snowy roads. Van asked management if we could work late Thursday afternoon after the staff had all gone home. We were working with just us and the janitor in attendance when the phone rang. The janitor picked up the phone: "Yes, this is First National Bank of Sheridan." Pause. "You say you're the Flamingo Casino in Las Vegas and Marvin O' Reilly wants to write a check for $2000." "Oh, yes sir, he is a really good customer, give him anything he wants!" Pause. "I'm Carl Barnes, good night."

Bank management confirmed Carl Barnes assessment of Marvin O' Reilly's credit worthiness the following morning. I am not sure Carl Barnes might not have been a better judge of people than some of the 20-year veterans of the teller line, who might soon become lenders.

When reviewing officers' positions it was apparent, that the positions though out the back were entirely by age, except for the janitor, who was part time. The bank had some competent people, but advancement seemed to be in chronological order, rather than on the basis of ability. In the confidential section Van, wrote: "The management succession program is the oldest guy gets to be President."

While in Sheridan by chance, I happened to meet Barbara Boatman, a pretty, tall, slender school teacher, who taught elementary grades and also music. It turned out she was the stepdaughter of Carl Ralston, a VP and one of the senior men at the First National Bank of Sheridan. At her mother's suggestion I took her out to Story, a quaint little town that lies up against the Big Horn Mountains. We had a pleasant dinner and somehow the conversation turned to music. I said to Barbara, "I'm not very musical, but I love a variety of kinds of music."

Barbara replied, "Everyone has some musical gift. I'll show you."

We took in a movie and I hoped the she would forget about educating me musically. The movie turned out to be totally forgettable; I have no idea what it might have been about. Afterwards I took Barbara, who still lived under her parents' roof. The home was a white one-story rambler and Barbara invited me in for a nightcap. By now it was 10:30 or later. No sooner had we gotten in the door and sitting on the couch, then Barbara dashes into her room and comes back carrying a guitar. She says, "I'm going to teach you how to play the guitar."

Not knowing what else to say I said, "Okay."

She began strumming the instrument, singing, and demonstrating several basic chords. I said, "Barbara, aren't you worried about waking your folks?"

She smiled coyly and said, "Don't worry about it." And started to sing and play briskly and even more audibly.

Then she handed the guitar to me and I attempted to play and even sing since I was pretty relaxed. Pretty soon we were both singing and taking turns strumming on the guitar. She was playing the instrument and I was fumbling with it. I fully expected her folks to come charging out of their nearby bedroom, but they stayed put.

Years later after I married someone else, I happened to see the Ralstons at a Wyoming Bankers Association Convention and talked to Dolly Ralston. She told me much to my surprise that she liked me, never mentioning the guitar incident and said, "I was hoping somehow you and Barbara would get together, but as it happens she married a fellow teacher."

The winter of 1962-1963 was a very cold one and filled with new changes, thanks to Mr. Saxon, President Kennedy's Comptroller of the Currency, who was charged with moving the banking system forward with vigor. Mr. Saxon believed in aggressively chartering new National banks. In Wyoming it started slowly with the American National Bank of Riverton in 1962, but by January 1963, we were charged with doing frequent new bank charter investigations.

Van preferred to work with me, as opposed to Cherry, who he described, after a few drinks one night, as a "horse's ass."

When sober, Van kept silent about his opinions about controversial topics, as well as subjects that might be offensive to crewmembers. However, when Van was participating in his "sport"- he regarded his binge drinking as his "Olympic Sport"- you never knew what pronouncements or observations he might share with anyone in earshot.

The first new bank investigation I participated in was in Pinedale, Wyoming, the county seat of Sublette County. Pinedale, population 1000, was the only county seat town in the state with no bank. Located on the western side of the "Wind River Range" of mountains, Pinedale was rather scenic, with Bridger National Wilderness Area and year round snowcapped peaks, towering to over 10,000 feet in elevation, as Pinedale's backdrop.

It was so darn cold that week, 30 below zero, its beauty escaped me as I trudged around on foot interviewing various people about the character of the organizers, their opinion as to the need for the bank, and the key question: would they use the bank? Even Bob Seivers, a lawyer and the apparent leader among the organizers seemed to be well regarded.

Again and again it was pointed out to us the nearest bank was 35 miles away in Big Piney, famous for even colder weather, like 45 below that week. The population of Pinedale was quite keen on having a bank in their town; hell yes, they'd use the proposed bank. One morning it was so cold in Big Piney they didn't know how cold it was since the thermometer mercury collapsed into a little ball, totally off the scale. It was a comparatively balmy 30 below in Pinedale. In spite of the fact Van's Pontiac had to be jumpstarted each morning, Van and I felt the folks in Pinedale needed, and would support the proposed new First National Bank of Pinedale. Mr. Thomas, our new Chief National Bank Examiner in Denver agreed and the charter was granted. The examinations of the Pinedale bank were assigned to the Salt Lake district office, so I never saw personally how well they did, but from all reports it succeeded and in a few years passed the State Bank of Big Piney in total asset size.

Van Dyke and I were off to Gillette to do another charter investigation. In this instance there was a well-established local bank, The Stockman's Bank, managed by Howard Esmay and Kenneth Naramore. Gillette in 1963 was an ugly, dusty little town of perhaps 3500 souls, primarily a ranching trading center in the middle of Thunder Basin National Grasslands. Recent discoveries of oil, gas and coal suggested the town was about to boom. Van met with the organizers and I walked around town talking to various merchants and towns people. The Stockman's Bank seemed well regarded, but at the same time there were a good number of people thought another bank in town was needed. Gillette's tap water smelled like rotten eggs; Gillette was only place where a person smelled worst after stepping out of the shower, than he did when he entered.

Even though the water was putrid, the charter was granted for the First National Bank of Gillette. It didn't hurt that Teno Roncalio, a prominent Democratic Congressman, with close ties to the Kennedy political camp, was to be a major shareholder.

As the Wyoming prairie was turning green in May of 1963 Van, Magruder, Cherry and I were examining the First National Bank at Thermopolis, which is about 325 miles from Cheyenne our headquarter city and too far to justify returning home for the weekend. The Thermopolis bank was fully loaned with a mix of farm, ranch, main-street, plus a number of business making a living off tourism. Thermopolis has several mineral hot springs, which are touted to have curative powers. There are several mineral baths there and in addition the town is located on a main route into Yellowstone National Park..

In downtown Thermopolis at the intersection of U.S.20 and Thermop's main street, which turns westward into State Highway 120 stood until the mid-1960s the old Wind River Hotel, which must have been built about 1905 when the railroad arrived in town. The hotel was built of purplish red sandstone and had a forsaken appearance; they had stopped renting hotel rooms at the Fire Marshall's insistence, but the bar and dining room still operated. The food was decent, and as Van put it. "The bar couldn't figure out a way to screw up Jim Beam and water." The best thing about the restaurant was Nancy, a sweet, friendly, cute, petite lass with light brown curly hair and deep brown eyes to match. Nancy was missing her two front teeth, so at breakfast, while holding a miniature box of Wheaties, she would ask "Would you like Weanies or Cheerios for breakfast?"

The President of the bank, Charles M. Smith, owned a sizeable highway construction company was 72 years old and left the active management of the bank to Vern Eastman, Executive Vice President, who was in his mid-fifties. Thermopolis was a week and half project, so Van had planned to go up and pay Angus Linton at Meeteetse a visit, 50 miles northwest, an easy two-day job. Poor old Angus received more examinations than needed, because the bank took so little time to examine.

Friday night, after a week at Thermopolis, Magruder and I were planning to drive up to Shell, Wyoming to visit my Dad's ranch. About 6 P.M. I talked to Dad just before we left for supper and he had a few questions about crops and water for Art Collingwood, Dad's tenant. The Shell Valley is one of Wyoming's more picturesque spots and Shell Creek is one of the better fishing streams around if the water isn't running too rapidly. Cherry as usual decided to "Polish his shoes and write a letter to Betty." Our favorite waitress, Nancy was on duty at the restaurant, with her usual good cheer. The girl, perhaps in her early twenties had two small children to support, since her apparently abusive husband had taken off for parts unknown. She was in sharp contrast to Cherry, who was never happy, unless he was unhappy.

Nancy waited on us, with her typical efficiency and friendliness. This evening she offered us peanuts to munch on with our drinks, "Penises, guys" she said.

About half way through happy hour, I became very ill with severe stomach pains. After rushing to the men's room and losing my drink and the remains of lunch, I had Magruder take me back to the Colonial Motel. I gave Magruder the keys to my car, since he needed to be able to go back to the restaurant to enjoy his supper and the upcoming weekend.

By the time I got back to my room I was in terrific pain and asked the motel manager to get me a doctor. Within 20 minutes Dr. Kunkle showed up at my room, ushered in by the motel manager. I told him I thought I was having an appendicitis attack. Dr. Kunkle, with cold hands, poked around at my gut, hit the hot spot, and I yelped in pain. "Excellent diagnosis for an amateur. We'll take it out tonight," said the doctor.

I called my parents, who I had just talked to less than a hour earlier, and advised them what was going on. They were to say the least, surprised. Dad said he would call Adriana "Van" Harris, his aunt who lived at the Pioneer Home, a retirement facility in Thermopolis, so as to have a family member present while I was under the knife. About 7:15 P.M., Dr. Kunkle gave me a shot of something, that put my lights out for the operation and I was asleep until the next morning.

When I awoke that Saturday morning at about eight, there was my octogenarian Great Aunt Van at my bedside. Aunt Van was smiling broadly. Her bright blue eyes twinkled, her pure white hair was tied in a neat bun, and she was hunched over from osteoporosis. She still seemed to quite spry, even if she did wield a cane to walk. She was dressed in blue on white print cotton dress, which was pretty much the way I remembered her three years earlier. Aunt Van had spent her entire career as a surgical nurse, assisting Uncle Chester, her surgeon husband, pretty much from the time he graduated from medical school in the early years of the twentieth century, practicing medicine in the pioneer days of rural Wyoming until he retired in 1936, due to a stoke and died in 1944. She began. "Bert, dear, I was worried as hell about you. You were on the damned operating table for over two hours, and I'm sitting in the waiting room all this time. Finally, your young whippersnapper of a doctor, Dr. Kunkle comes out."

"Why, Mrs. Harris, I didn't know you were related to this young man," said Dr. Kunkle, having deduced there was some connection given the common last name. Van recited the previous evening's conversation with the doctor.

"Grandnephew, I told him," said Aunt Van. "Dr. Kunkle, how the devil did it take you over two hours to take Bert's appendix out?" Aunt Van continued, without Dr. Kunkle having a chance to respond. "Could have taken it out in half an hour myself, you know!" Aunt Van emphasized.

"Then, Kunkle tells me you appendix was hotter than a July 4th firecracker. And to make matters worse, it was perpendicular to the intestines, instead of parallel, the way they are normally. Very ticklish operation to get it out whole without bursting and spreading all that nasty, poison pus and infecting your innards. Course I forgave him for his slowness. You've got a really big incision there, needed more room to get that hot thing out, but he did it okay. He put it in a jar so you can see it. He'll show you when he makes rounds." Aunt Van said. She would visit me daily for the next week.

During the week I was flooded with visitors. Charlie Smith the Thermopolis bank's President, was in the hospital at the same time, so he'd come by in a wheel chair and talk banking with me in the afternoon. Van Dyke and Magruder would come in evenings after work, along with many of the employees from the First National Bank at Thermopolis. The best part of the hospital visit was, it turned out Charlie Smith, age 72, and I, age 25, were the two youngest patients in the hospital that week. Conversely, the nurses and their aides were all less than 30, so I would get almost constant attention in the form of back rubs and massages from all the young nurses. I was quite spoiled.

By Friday I was ready to be released, although still felt pretty weak, like I'd been hit by a Mack truck. Van Dyke had arranged for me to have the following week off to recuperate in Boulder. Magruder drove my car to Cheyenne with me sleeping off and on for the whole trip. I was sufficiently rested enough to make it home to Boulder by eight in the evening.

Finally, towards the end of my "vacation" week, I got around to washing and vacuuming out my Plymouth convertible, which had been though several rainstorms and needed attention. In cleaning out the car, I discovered a pink cigarette lighter and a tube of lipstick, along with other feminine paraphernalia. I was curious to find out what Magruder was up to, while I was in the hospital.

The following Monday the four of us, Van, Magruder, Cherry and I, gathered in the Hynds Building to prepare for an afternoon start of the Cheyenne National Bank. When Magruder and I went to coffee break I handed him a lunch sack containing the lipstick, hairbrush, and cosmetics. "So Jerry, did you find a lady friend in Thermop?" Said I.

Jerry looked a little stunned, then a little embarrassed. "Yeah," he replied.

"That's okay Jerry, I met a good looking nurse, you know," I said.

He still looked a little funny. Then I guessed. "Nancy, right?"

"Yeah, why not, she's a nice girl, cute too. Hot to trot as well," said Magruder.

"So what do you do on date with old Nancy? Take her out for a bowl of Weanies?"

"Wise guy!" he growled.

Cheyenne National was a fairly new bank having been opened early in 1960. After three years it was growing rapidly and had some loan problems; in particular the bank had bought a bunch of Mack Truck paper from the O'Dell Motor Company. It had a dozen or more repossessed heavy duty Mack trucks, plus even more slow paying trucker loans. Since the bank was still fairly small, $10 million in assets, we didn't require help from a Denver crew for this examination.

At five minutes in front of 3:00 P.M. we walked in. Van as usual grabbed the notes, while Magruder and I started balancing teller cash. Uncharacteristically, Jim Cherry started chatting with Betty Corbett, the front desk receptionist and installment department girl Friday. The number one teller was a stunning redhead named Carol Holt, who for some unknown reason took a shine to me. As I was counting Carol Holt's cash, Magruder, nudged me and said, "Cherry's in love. That's the "Betty" he was going to write that weekend in Thermop."

"Ain't love grand, Jim's actually smiling too," said I.

Betty Corbett, a divorcee, was an attractive brunette, with a full figure, pleasant disposition and roughly the same age as Cherry, that is mid to late 30s. Van had Jim work with him on the commercial loans and assigned me to work the installment loans, with all the O'Dell truck loans. Normally, Van would have assigned Cherry to this task, but Van was engineering a way to keep Jim away from Betty, so lovesick Jim could get some work done, at least during working hours.

The following morning, I got over to the installment loan department and there was Harry Palmer, my old friend from Greeley National days. Harry was smiling broadly and said he was glad to see me. "Harry, how the hell are you anyway." I said.

"I'm good learning from the school of hard knocks! Trying to collect these damned Mack truck loans." Said Harry.

Bob Gravatt, also a Greeley National alumni was the manager of the department, although he left Greeley National Bank when Mr. Trautwein left; so I hadn't met him before. Between Gravatt and Harry Palmer, they seemed to have the truck loans under control, but not without a lot of long hours and hard work.

Mr. Trautwein set us up to work in the boardroom, which was adjacent to his office. So like the set up in Rock Springs, we could hear everything that was going on at Mr. T's desk. One day an irate customer, Paul Pierson, came into Arnie Trautwein's office. He was totally in orbit over the fact that he had been turned down for a loan and proceeded to unleash his vast vocabulary of foul and colorful language on Arnie. Arnie Trautwein, a tall, trim, bald man, whose bald head lit up like a red light bulb, when he was angered, was quietly studying a credit file when Mr. Pierson entered, arms waving and spouting obscenities. Arnie's temper was legendary, I had recalled from GNB days, so I was expecting Mr. T. would respond in kind.

But no, Arnie was calm, cool and collected and said, "Paul, that's it, just let me have it, bankers are mean S. O. B.s and we deserve whatever insults you can heap on us."

Pierson stammered and continued the tirade, "You God damned old skinflint of a no good son a whore."

Staying calm, Arnie egged him on saying, "Come on keep the insults coming. You can do better than that, Paul."

Pierson by now was out of breath and uttered almost inaudibly. "Ah, shit, I guess you ain't gonna change your mind."

Coolly Arnie said. "That's right, but don't you feel better getting, this off your chest, Paul?"

Pierson, nodded affirmatively, turned on his heel and left. Arnie, went back to reading his file as though nothing had happened. It was a great lesson in letting angry customers defuse themselves.

As we were preparing to leave, I went to redheaded Carol Holt's window to cash a check for the weekend. The lady in front of me was familiar looking and when she turned around, I realized it was Barbara Anderson, the Fashion Bar manager from Greeley. "Hi," I said.

"Bert, what shall we argue about today?" said Barbara. We had a brief discussion of the Kennedy administration's initiatives after I cashed my check. For the most part we agreed with many of the progressive things the administration had done. I told her about some of the changes in banking instituted by Mr. Saxon our illustrious leader. Barbara was at least ten years my senior, so there was no romantic interest going in either direction, but she was interesting to visit with.

By mid-summer 1963, someone in Washington had looked at a map and realized the Casper was closer to the center of the state than Cheyenne, which is in the extreme southeast corner. Our sub-district headquarter city was designated to be Casper, so we moved our office as well as our individual households to Casper. Not only did I get an apartment in Casper, but I also decided it would be useful to have my own telephone for the first time. I went to the office of Mountain States Telephone and Telegraph Company in Casper. A stern faced man with dark horn rimmed glass informed me that I would need to put down a $50 deposit. I looked at him a moment contemplating parting with the fifty bucks.

Picking up on my concern he added. "We pay six percent interest and then if you pay your bill promptly you'll get the deposit back."

After thinking for a moment, remembering my savings account was only earning three percent, the maximum allowable by law I responded.

"In that case I'll give you a check for $1000, might as well make it worth my while, don't you think?

Mr. Horned Rim Glasses, started to smile, "I don't think we need a deposit from you." And I now had telephone service in Casper. My bluff had worked.

Once we all settled in Casper, we were surprised to learn that 37 year old, confirmed bachelor, Jim Cherry had proposed marriage to Betty Corbett. Even more surprising, she accepted. Jim decided to accept a position as Auditor of the Wyoming National Bank of Casper, so he could stay a home nights with his bride and her eleven year old daughter. Just as we lost one of our crew, the demands for new bank investigations picked up. Van and I continued to do new charter investigations in Cheyenne, Newcastle, Glenrock, Dubois, Powell and Casper as 1963 evolved.

One of the more enjoyable banks on our list was the First National Bank of Lovell. Jack Pearson was the president and in his forties. His father, Wallace Pearson, then in his late seventies, was the chairman. The Pearsons ran a solid little bank, which had for many years operated in the same building since its founding in 1906. By 1963 they were in the middle of constructing a modern, spacious new facility. Wallace Pearson had assumed the role of elder statesman and was content to allow his able son Jack to manage the bank's affairs. Wallace was a great help in explaining the details as to how they did things. I noticed that they had two ledgers of charged-off loans and asked why. "Well," said Wallace,. "We divide them up into two categories. This one we call the 'hospital'. They're loans we are working and hope to be able to collect ultimately. The other ledger tub we call the "Cemetery"; those would be charged-off loans to bankrupts, deceased folks, or people who have skipped town and we haven't been able to trace."

Wallace continued. "We work the charge-offs aggressively. By that I mean we phone, write, institute legal action if we think there is the possibility it will result in our getting paid. You can see our recoveries are quite good, better than 50% of our charge-offs."

Wallace told me he used to play tennis with Grandfather Harris, Lovell being about 40 miles from Basin, where Granddad lived, and they were good friends. I asked Wallace if he still played. "Oh, yes, I still play with my grandchildren. Course I don't run after the ball like I did when I played with your Granddad."

Wallace had been widowed for a number of years and lived with his daughter, Frances, and her husband, a local dentist. On some of my official visits, Wallace would invite me over to his home for dinner. After dinner and some red wine he would share some of his stories about banking in the early days.

"Did you know that the banks in Wyoming had a much more difficult time in the 1920s, than the 1930s? In the 1920s there were seven banks serving the area we now serve and we were all broke. In those days the field examiners could call in the receiver to liquidate your bank on the spot; we always worried each visit that they would close us down. Paul Henninger, he was just a young man then, used to say to me. Keep on trying, I'll let you go this time. We were the only broke bank that didn't get caught," he said.

Jack Pearson had a great sense of humor. When we entered a bank, we sent requests to the bank's correspondent banks in cities like Denver, Omaha, New York, etc. for correspondent bank statements so they could be reconciled to the bank's general ledger. On one visit to Lovell we were delayed in receiving our cut off statements that is statements in the middle of the usual statement period, from the Denver Federal Reserve Bank and the bank's account at The First National Bank of Denver. I asked Jack if he knew what the problem might be. "We get our mail off the train, you know the C.B. & Q. We call it the Cheyenne to Billings & Back Maybe Railroad. The problem is yesterday's train didn't get here until today. So your statements won't arrive until tomorrow, because they will be on today train," said Pearson.

Jack told a story on himself: one cold January night he woke up in the middle of the night, sat up and said to Laurie, his wife, "My God, I think I left the vault door open. So I got dressed drove down to the bank; it was colder than all Billy Hell, at least 20 below zero. Opened the side door and there was the vault door shut tight, time lock set for the usual 8:00 AM.. Why the hell would I think I left the damned vault open?"

After Cherry left, we took on a new man. Ted Ernst, joined our crew. The first bank Ted did with Van and I was the Stockman's National Bank of Lusk. Stockman's was managed by Max Bird and his tall, redheaded wife Madeline. Max was a gray haired gent in his mid- fifties, slender, with a rather harried look about him. Max and Madeline were both workaholics and attempted, without 100% success, to all the important-decision making jobs themselves, spreading themselves rather thin. So if one of us examiners needed to ask a question, one needed to ask Mr. or Mrs. Bird. As I remember this particular examination, it was just Van Ted and I. Ted was good help from the start, as he had worked several years at First National Bank of Laramie and was thoroughly familiar with the operations side of banking.

The examination got off to a rocky start, as several tellers operated out of the same cash drawer, which is a poor practice we continually bugged the Birds about. The cash was off a few bucks, which is always hard to trace when you have several people working out of the same cash supply. In addition, the notes didn't balance because Max, always in a hurry to take care of the next customer, forgot to post a couple of payments during a busy Monday. It was 7:30 P.M. before we got the cash and notes in balance and under control. Van said he'd like to buy us a drink in commemoration of our hard work and to welcome Ted to the crew.

Being the Olympic drinker he was, Van was not thinking of a single drink what he really meant was he wanted to get tanked and polish off an entire fifth of Jim Beam, his instrument of choice. We all went up to Van's room in the Lusk Hotel diagonally across the street from Stockman's Bank. The hotel was a five-story brick edifice, built in the early1920s when Wyoming was enjoying an oil exploration boom. Van's room had several chairs so we settled down and started to visit, as Van poured us each a generous slug of whiskey in paper cups, provided by the Lusk Hotel. We each down our first drink rapidly and Ted started to talk about his enjoyment of hunting and fishing. Van asked Ted. "Ted did you do any hunting this fall? Ted responded, "Oh yeah, my brother Ed and I went into the Snowy Range west of Laramie and we both were able to bring down a big 5 point elk."

In Wyoming hunters only count the antler tips on one side in case you're thinking five points isn't a respectable sized elk. It is. Then Ted proceeded to fill Van and I in on all the details of his memorable hunt, kind of rifle used, the difficulty and challenge of dragging the two large elk out by sliding them on the snowy trails down the mountains, where Ed's pickup was parked.

By this time Van decided we needed another drink and proceeded to pour another round of generous drinks. I took mine into the bathroom to dilute it, as I could see where this evening was headed. Ted then said to Van, "Van did you get anything this fall?"

Much to my surprise, as I didn't know he was a hunter, Van replied, "Boy did I ever. It was up near Chugwater. I got this six point mule deer buck, biggest one I'd ever seen, must have dressed out at 350 pounds."

Ted said, "Wow! What did you get him with?"

Van paused a moment for effect, then with a serious, sincere look said, "A green Pontiac."

Feeling no pain, we all laughed uproariously at Van's little prank and proceeded to kill the bottle, although I made several more trips to the bathroom to pour out whiskey and add water. By the time we were out of whiskey it was 10:30. Van was fully anesthetized and slurring every word and Ted was likewise feeling no pain and wobbled on his way to his room.

The next morning Ted, Van and I met at 7:15 in the hotel's restaurant for breakfast. Van was fresh, as a daisy as he always was after the evening festivities. Ted was obviously under the weather, suffering from a hangover and had a throbbing headache. Ted ordered aspirin, orange juice, and coffee. Van and I ordered our usual hearty bacon and eggs for breakfast. Since this was Ted's week on the job with us, I spent most of the day working with him on teaching the detail part of the examination. During our coffee break that morning, while Van was working with Max and Madeline, Ted said to me, "Jesus, Bert, I have never seen anyone hold his liquor like you!"

"Ted," I confided, "I've worked with Van for a year and a half and one of the things I've learned is to pour out some of the whiskey with each drink. Hell, I don't want to get schnockered like Van. There's no way I can keep up with him drinking."

By now the coffee and aspirin were working and Ted started to grin; he had a pleasant wide smile and said, "Well, that's a good trick to know."

In November 1963, just before Thanksgiving, Magruder, Ernst, and I were sent down to assist National Bank Examiner Robert Jennett, one of the senior Denver examiners, at the First National Bank of Pueblo, Colorado. Van was taking some vacation time to visit his daughter for the Thanksgiving Holiday in Bozeman, Montana, which Van enjoyed. I was working the installment loan department, which was good size, but clean and well run. At coffee break with Magruder and Ernst said Chuck Mitchell, one of the guys on Jennett's crew was having trouble with a number of detail problems. "Chuck is pretty sharp, why would he be having problems." I observed.

Chuck joined us and said to me. "Bert, you were here eight months ago and we worked the detail together, well they have a new guy in charge of it, Bob Armstrong. He has totally screwed up the I & D report, internal controls have gone downhill. We'll it's just chaotic."

"Chuck, Armstrong was a lender eight months ago when we were here," said I.

"One of the head guys must be mad him because he is in charge of operations now. This outfit doesn't put much emphasis on operations, I think they change every year or so," said Chuck. "Operations is treated as an ill legitimate stepchild; whichever officer is crossways with the top guys gets to be Cashier and is therefore operations officer." Chuck smiled knowingly and continued. "The reason the place has such crummy earnings is they ignore the money they could be making if operations were a smooth running machine."

"Like First of Casper, which is about the same size, but makes twice as much money," I added.

"Exactly, First of Casper and old Curtis Brekjern, who has masterminded their operations for last 15 years or more," observed Chuck.

On Wednesday, November 22nd, we were winding down the examination. Mitchell, Ralph Pederson and I decided to have lunch at a great little Italian place, Rizzoto's, which was about a 15-minute drive from the bank. We stopped at a stoplight when over the car radio came the announcement that President Kennedy had been shot during a visit to Dallas. As all Americans, we were stunned by the terrible news. The irony for Chuck and I was eight months earlier we had seen President Kennedy riding by us in the same open Lincoln limousine, while we waited at the same stop light in Pueblo. The President had been in town to dedicate the Arkansas Valley Dam Project nearby.

It gave all of us an ironic feeling to have President Kennedy murdered and to receive the news under almost identical circumstances where we had actually seen the President eight months earlier.

Six

Ignorance Is Not Bliss

January of 1964 brought a number of changes to our lives as National Bank Examiners. All the new National charters were creating more competition in the banking industry as well as more problem banks. This was especially true for the newly chartered banks. Mr. Saxon, our illustrious leader in Washington, decided a part of the problem might be that the examiners were too cozy with the bankers and people like Mr. Van Dyke, Mr. Jennett and Mr. Henninger shouldn't be examining the same institution year after year with no other examiner taking a look at the bank. A new rule came out that the same examiner could only examine the same bank two times consecutively, then someone else would be assigned to be the Examiner in Charge. After two exams the previous examiner could return.

In Van Dyke's case, some banks he had done ten or fifteen times consecutively, perhaps more, since he had been the Examiner-in-Charge of the Wyoming field office for many years. This change also meant there would need to be two commissioned examiners in the Casper Field Office, instead of only one. The idea being that eventually, there would be at least one examiner in the district eligible to examine any given bank at any time. Vern Bliss, out of the Salt Lake City, or "Shit Lake Salty" as he liked to call it, received his commission as a National Bank Examiner and was transferred to Casper to be the second commissioned Examiner under Mr. Van Dyke. Vern was about 37 years old and had received his commission after being an assistant for six years. He had previously worked in a branch of First Security Bank of Idaho, so he had good practical banking knowledge, along with his experience as an examiner.

Vern was a tall, slender man on a wide frame, dark brown hair, piercing, closely set, brown eyes and a peculiar sort of a nose. His wife was a tall, attractive woman, with medium-length light brown hair and the same nose as Vern, both of which appeared to have been plucked from a ski jump. There must be something in the water in their mutual hometown of Gooding, Idaho. They had two sons, ages 10 and 12 at the time, who were also equipped with the characteristic Bliss nose. Nearly all of Mr. Bliss's banking and examiner experience had been in branch banking situations. At the time, Utah had two large National Banks with branch systems: First Security Bank of Utah, National Association, and Zion's First National Bank. Plus fewer than a dozen small unit, or single office National banks, were scattered about the state.

Our Wyoming crew knew Mr. Bliss from a couple of trips we had made to Salt Lake City. It was apparent that these system bankers did things much differently than we did in Wyoming. For one thing, the branch managers were on some sort of autopilot. They were not capable, or perhaps not authorized, to do their own thinking. Branch managers, particularly in large branch systems, are guided by bank policy as dictated to them in a manual which attempts to cover all eventualities. The problem is individual situations don't always fit the book; human nature is more unpredictable than any manual writer can possibly imagine.

Ted came back from one encounter with a branch manager scratching his head. Ted had requested the manager to write off a bunch of old overdrafts, standard OCC policy. After accounts were overdrawn with no deposits of over 30 day nearly all banks we had encountered would write them off. The branch manager told Ted he didn't want to charge-off the stale overdrafts because he didn't want to lose the accounts. Ted politely said to the manager, "Look at it this way, since they don't have any money on deposit and these customers are no longer depositing with you regularly, you don't really have an account do you?"

The man looked at Ted in utter surprise and said. "You know, I never thought of it that way." He complied with Ted's request.

At another branch, I was reviewing a large, ever increasing, million dollar unsecured line of credit to a fair-sized auto dealer. The dealership had lost $100,000 plus in each of the last three years; so, in effect, the bank was financing losses. The branch manager's defense of the loan was the sizable compensating checking balances carried. These deposits were not discretionary balances, they were monies collected from car sales waiting for checks to clear in payment to G.M.A.C., the General Motors finance arm that was financing the dealer's new car inventory. In other words these funds in this account was already committed and offered no collateral support for the bank loan. I classified the loan as substandard. At which Mr. Pollard, the little cherub faced branch manager, became very angry with me; his face turned lobster red. Although his language was not abusive, it was obvious he was seething inside and he wanted to erupt.

I took a page from Cheyenne National's Arnie Trautwein's management text and just let him vent on me. Once he stopped talking and calmed down, I suggested that he attempt to collateralize the loan if possible and put it on an orderly repayment program. I wrote in my management comments that Pollard was an expert on compensating balances, but was sadly deficient in credit judgment and administration for failing to do anything to secure the bank's position concerning the customer's declining fortunes.

Mariner Eccles had put the First Security System together in the 1930s from an assortment of troubled banks. With the booming U.S. and Utah economy after World War II, the bank had grown and prospered. The management was now in the hands of his son, perhaps Grandson, Spencer Eccles. Because of Mariner's revered position in the banking world, Spencer thought he could do no wrong. In my opinion, he was an arrogant jackass. I was always happy to leave Salt Lake City on our periodic visits.

Bliss arrived in Casper with his picturesque family, along with his pride and joy, a well-kept, yellow 1955 Cadillac Coupe deVille, He then followed Van in the Wyoming banks, now that Van was a lame duck examiner, as he described it. One of the first banks I accompanied Vern Bliss on was the examination of the First National Bank in Worland. The Bower family owned the largest block of First National's stock. Ray Bower, Senior, and his identical twin brother Earl dominated the board and bank policy. They were about 75 years old and were intensely interested in the bank's affairs, but had turned the day-to-day management over to Vernon Bower, Earl's son, who was then 48 years old.

The twins were always looking over Vernon's shoulder. Ray Bower, Junior, was the Cashier and responsible for operations, which while not really troublesome, were certainly not outstanding. Ray, Jr. had little sense of humor and a bland personality; he seemed more interested in flying his Cessna 172 airplane than learning anything new to improve his bank's operations.

Examiner Bliss was a much more technical examiner than Van Dyke, who relied heavily on his knowledge of the particular banker's ability and history. Bliss seemed to enjoy writing up long lists of technical exceptions, unsigned financial statements, various collateral document exceptions, and on and on.

One day Ray, Sr., walked into the boardroom where we were working, and introduced himself as a director, and grilled Vern on the progress of the examination. Vern spent a good hour with him going over in precise detail his findings to date. The following morning twin brother Earl came in and asked identical questions. Again Vern dutifully went through his findings, virtually repeating exactly what he told Ray Sr. on the previous afternoon. When Earl left, Vern, clearly annoyed, turned to me and said. "Jesus Christ, that old fart is senile. I just answered all of those same damned questions for him yesterday afternoon, less than 24 hours ago."

I couldn't help but smile. "Vern" said I, "You talked to the *identical twin brothers*, Earl this morning and Ray, Sr. yesterday."

"Boy, those two old boys are identical. I was puzzled how a guy so seemingly senile, could ask such valid and salient questions." Vern said.

When Vern Bliss sat down with Vernon Bower, I fully expected the sparks to fly, as Bliss had substantially increased the volume of criticisms. Vernon Bower politely, but vigorous countered and defended Bliss' criticisms for several hours. After all the vigorous discussion, a bewildered Vernon Bower asked Bliss point blank, "Do you think we are really all that bad?"

"Mr. Bower," Vern Bliss stated. "No, I think you are a capable lender and, all and all, this is a pretty decent bank." Vernon smiled for the first time since our arrival, and they shook hands. We were on our way home to Casper. Ray Bower Junior to my knowledge has yet to smile.

If Vern Bliss thought the documentation was lacking in Worland, I was consumed with curiosity and trepidation as to how he would get along with the volcanic Royce Tibbett at the Citizens National Bank of Torrington. The old gentleman had taken over the management of the bank in 1923. Banks in Wyoming were failing constantly in the 1920s. As Lovell banker, Wallace Pearson put it when comparing the 20s with the 30s, when the Congress passed legislation to establish the Federal Deposit Insurance Corporation, or F.D.I.C as it is commonly known. "Where the hell were you (the government) when Wyoming banks really needed help."

I remembered my first encounter with Mr., Tibbett. Mr. Saxon had changed the title and format Earnings and Dividend report. (E. & D. Report). Previously it was called the Income and Dividends report (I. & D. Report); the report, along with the quarterly call report (the bank's Balance Sheet) was required to be filed with the OCC. The new I & D Report, filed semi-annually, changed the components and arrangement of some of the key data: however, Mr. Tibbett, hadn't bothered to read the new instructions. After all he had been filling out these reports for many, many years; before I was even born, in fact.

Consequently, the I. & D. Report, as well as the Call Report, were hopelessly incorrect and would have to be revised and a corrected version would need to be filed with the O.C.C. Mr. Tibbett exploded when I pointed out the errors and that the reports would need to be corrected and revisions sent to Washington. He let go a torrent of defamatory language and summarized his rage with the crowning insult, "You no good, god dammed Nazi Hitler Youth."

"Mr. Tibbett," I replied, shaken and trying to calm myself. "Mr. Tibbett, I am only the messenger here and have no authority to influence, create, change, or ignore this problem. But I will make the necessary changes for you and all you need do is to sign them and we can send them off to Washington and they will be happy." He kept all his work papers in his private office, so he led me into his inner sanctum where I was able revise the report for him. On the shelves of his office I noticed a couple dozen of green bound Scott Specialty Stamp Albums and I was able to turn the topic of conversation to our common hobby. We talked philately for 20-30 minutes. We became friends after a fashion, and I was no long treated as a "Hitler Youth".

Mr. Tibbett was a collateral lender and didn't bother with balance sheets for his farm and ranch customers. This is not to say he didn't know what was going on with his loan portfolio; he did, but in his own unique and very effective way. Every morning starting at five Mr. Tibbett would visit a farm, check machinery, count cattle, inspect crops and talk to his customer. He knew his customers, the value of the collateral, their farming abilities, and how their crops were progressing.

Bliss, being a very technical examiner, wrote up as financial statement exception, every agricultural loan in the bank. Mr. Tibbett was enraged, turned beet red and showered Bliss, with his litany of profanity, although he did save Bliss the "Hitler Youth" insult. In the past Van Dyke and Charlie Hout had ignored these exceptions, since it was obvious that Mr. T. managed a very clean, well performing loan portfolio. In addition, it was obvious that with the well documented collateral files, that he had have sufficient information to make intelligent judgments on his farm customer's loans. A year or so later when I followed Mr. Bliss as the examiner in charge, Mr. Tibbett, had obtained the missing financial statements, so I never had any problems with my friend Mr. Tibbett.

After Vern Bliss arrived on the scene, Van allowed me to conduct an examinations under his watchful mentorship. Van could still examine the American National Bank of Riverton, because it was a new bank. The bank president, Del Crouse, had spent years managing the Stockgrowers State Bank of Worland for his father- in-law, George Muirhead. When Mr. Muirhead died, his prodigal son George Muirhead, Jr. returned from a bank in Colorado Springs to claim his birthright and Del was out of job.

Mr. Crouse organized, with a group of Riverton businessmen and ranchers, to form the American National Bank. Del was a tall angular man, with greying curly hair and winning smile and was more experienced than most folks who start new banks. On his desk was a huge clothespin-like clip device embossed with the moniker, "BIG DEALS".

Del had recruited Harry Hays from the First National Bank of Lander, who knew Fremont County banking and was well known in the community. Kenny Link, the cashier, had been Van's assistant for several years and was helpful to us, although he conceded he was, "Up to his ass in alligators with a volume of annoying minor problems, which wouldn't be so bad there weren't so damned many of them." Pretty typical for a new bank.

One of the problems was the teller Mary Beth, a somewhat chubby, cheerful, middle aged, grey- maybe blue is more accurate- haired lady, who never seemed to be able balance to her till. As I was going through the examination findings with Del Crouse, I showed him the transcript of Mary Beth's over and short record. Del looked at them over his bifocals and said, "Let's see, dollar here, nickel, a dime there, maybe $7.00 dollars for the month. God, how I wish all my advertising dollars were this little."

"What are you saying, Mr. Crouse?" said I.

"Bert, go over to teller line and watch this wonderful lady in action: she has a helpful, friendly way with customers. Hell, it's obvious she isn't stealing; the amounts aren't significant and are just as likely to be long as short. Right?" Del said, looking me straight in the eye, then motioning to Mary Beth, who was greeting her customer. "The customers just love her and I do too! Advertising money well spent I'd say." I had to agree.

In 1964, Van and I continued to do new charter investigations, two in Casper, one each in Dubois, Powell, Lovell, Laramie and Douglas, while Bliss and the rest of the crew conducted the examinations. One of the more interesting persons we met was a lawyer and organizer of First National Bank of Glenrock, Western National Bank of Casper and First National Bank of Douglas, Mayne Miller.

Mayne Miller was a Tennessee transplant who had worked as an aide to Senator Estes Kefauver, served in the U. S. Occupation forces in Japan after World War II and had somehow manage to court and marry the daughter of the Japanese Ambassador. Mr. Miller confessed to me that he moved to Wyoming in hopes of launching a political career, which, appeared more hopeful due to Wyoming's small population as compared with, say, his native Tennessee. Of course, the then incumbent Democratic Senator Gale McGee must have been something of an inspiration since he was a very liberal Senator whose interests and political ideas more closely fit New York or Massachusetts, than the right leaning Wyoming voter. McGee, nevertheless, was able to get elected at least twice with his eloquent speeches.

Mr. Miller, perceived that a banking connection would give some credence with conservative Wyoming voters. In the meantime, Mr. Miller had a little law practice in Casper and, as I worked with him I enjoyed his company. His office was in the old Wyoming National Bank Building at Center and East Second Street in downtown Casper, a couple of floors above our National Bank Examiners Office. I got to know him fairly well and thoroughly enjoyed his wit and sense of humor.

The Wyoming National Bank of Casper had just moved into a great futuristic looking round building, which we examiners dubbed "The Great Pumpkin." Mr. Miller and I were discussing the ongoing charter investigation for the Western National Bank of Casper, when the topic turned to Wyoming National's new building. Mayne commented. "How does one turn down a customer's outlandish loan proposal in such a fanciful building as that?" Even forty years later it remains the most non-traditional bank building in the state.

In 1965 I had purchased a gorgeous tan 3-year-old Buick Electra 225 Convertible. Even though it had but 25,000 miles on the odometer, it was a great luxury to me. My Casper home was a little apartment, which I shared with fellow assistant Ted Ernst, and I had to park on the street. One morning, I came out to discover a dent in the driver's side door; the good news was that there was a note from the driver, Mrs. Davis, who had been babysitting her grandchildren in the neighborhood. She explained that she dropped something on the floor of her car and bumped into my car when she reached to retrieve it. I called Mrs. Davis and she said she had contacted her State Farm Insurance agent, Hugh McCarthy, no doubt a relative of comedian-ventriloquist Edgar Bergen's dummy, Charlie McCarthy.

When I contacted Mr. McCarthy, he informed me that State Farm wanted me to take my beautiful luxurious, Buick-leather seats and all-convertible to Bergstrom's Body Shop, which was generally regarded as the shoddiest and cheapest repair shop in town. So I called Mayne Miller, the only lawyer in Casper I knew, and asked him if State Farm could legally shove these unworkmanlike fender pounders down my throat?

Mayne said, "I'll write State Farm a letter for you. You go out and get three bids from shops acceptable to you." I asked him what the letter would cost me. He said, "Free. I'd sue those State Farm bastards just for the fun of it."

I told Mrs. Davis of my difficulties with State Farm and Mr. McCarthy and my desire to be sure I'd get a nice job. Mrs. Davis told me her brother had just opened a new body shop and she promised her brother would not only give me a good bid, but would do a perfect job. So I got three bids. Mrs. Davis's brother, was the low bidder and the repair job was flawless.

By the time summer rolled around Magruder a transfer to Denver so he could marry his girlfriend Frankie. We were once again short a man.

That's when I met Verne Sorheim, Magruder's replacement, was, perhaps four and half feet tall. These people like to be called "Little People," rather than dwarfs or midgets. Verne explained his height with an interesting story. According to Verne, he had been playing basketball as a young boy when he was knocked down scrambling for the ball. Another player coming down from a jump shot landed on him and broke his pelvis and leg bones. This stunted his overall growth, especially his legs. By the time I met him, he had been through countless surgeries to fix the damage and relieve his pain. Verne somehow managed to retain his good sense of humor through his pain. Verne was an accountant who decided to become a bank examiner.

Like Ted Ernst, Verne's first on the job experience was to be at Stockman's National Bank of Lusk. We were gathered in the coffee shop of the Lusk Hotel before what we knew would be a long afternoon. Ted, Van, Vern Bliss and I all ordered our usual coffee and pie. Verne, ordered a glass of milk. A tall, happy drunk cowboy had observed Verne's small size and happened to be standing nearby when Verne ordered his glass of milk. "Sonny," he said, with a bit of a slur in speech, "You should have started drinking milk years ago and you wouldn't have this problem," holding his hand up to approximate Verne's short height.

Verne turned to me and without hesitation said, "Hold me up, so I can hit him." The cowboy started laughing; then he tottered away towards the bar.

As Ted and Verne worked the detail at Stockman's; I was working with Bliss and Van on the loan portfolio when I came across a mortgage note for a conventional home loan signed by Barbara Johnson and James Outhouse. This would have been in 1964 before unmarried couples might typically buy a home jointly. I asked the bank's managing officer the relationship between the two mortgagors. He started to chuckle and replied, "Oh, they're married alright. She isn't about to be known as Mrs. Outhouse and Jimmy is too damned stubborn and proud to change his family name to something more bride friendly."

If you really wanted to press Vern Bliss's buttons, it was to drag out the expression "Ignorance is Bliss." Bliss, after all was an intelligent and capable guy. But of course the very name, "Bliss" invited snide remarks from every wise guy he encountered.

During the summer of 1964 Bliss got a job offer he couldn't refuse, as senior internal credit review officer at Zions First National Bank of Salt Lake City. Wyoming Examiners referred to it as the "Bank of Mormon" since it was owned by the Church of Christ and Latter Day Saints, commonly known as "Mormons" or "LDS".

The bank was the result of consolidating three church owned banks: The First National Bank of Salt Lake City, Zions Savings Bank, and Utah Savings Bank. First National was a pretty decent bank, as was Zion Savings, which specialized in home loans to the Mormon faithful. Utah Savings Bank, on the other hand, was a cesspool of poor defaulted loans made to borrowers on the basis of their fidelity to the church rather than any kind of normal credit criteria. I remember going through ledger card after ledger card of defaulted loans, where the so called "collection notation" was not about bringing the loan current or otherwise solving the delinquent status, but rather about what a good "Brother" or "Sister" the borrower was and how he or she always tithed 10%. The condition had gotten so deplorable church officials decided to get out of the banking business and negotiated a sale to Roy Simmons, who was a faithful Mormon and a competent banker.

The church had one uninsured savings bank in Arizona fail causing many depositors to lose their savings. They certainly didn't want a repeat of this sad event, especially since the bank's main office, was directly across the street from both the Mormon Temple and Tabernacle. Joseph Smith's hand reached ironically towards the bank.

Shortly after Vern Bliss's departure "Wyoming Visiting Fireman," as Wyoming examiners were dubbed, were in the Zion's First National employee lounge" taking coffee break. True Mormons of course don't drink coffee and other caffeinated beverages, with the exception of Pepsi Cola, which at the time the church owned a sizable block of stock in. I admire the way the Elders of the Church managed to grant exceptions as it fit their commercial interests, but I digress. We were enjoying our morning coffee, when Sorheim starts talking about a terrible new drug LSD, except he didn't have the letters in the correct order and referred to it as LDS. The Mormon ladies at the next table, who were drinking their Pepsis, were horrified, since they thought we were speaking ill of the LDS or the Latter Day Saints. Fortunately, Bliss got wind of the lady's dismay and was able to quiet them down and explain the error.

When Bliss left Wyoming, the need for examiners becoming more acute. Van saw the problem and recommended to Mr. Thomas, our Chief National Bank Examiner for the 12th National Bank Region, that I should be considered for the promotion to commissioned National Bank Examiner. Of course, I would have to pass a rigorous test on banking laws, credit analysis, and general banking knowledge. I had not been an Assistant National Bank Examiner for even three years. Normally it took at least five years to obtain the vaunted commission; in some parts of the country 20 years was not unusual. Obtaining a commission was a very big deal, for it meant that I had the authority to conduct examinations and sign reports in my own name. Even better than that my salary would double.

Mr. Thomas, invited me to spend a week in Denver, where he would prepare me for the deciding test. I arrived at the Denver Office in the Farmers Exchange Building on a Monday early in August 1964 and began studying the laws and National Bank Examiners Handbook. Mr. Thomas was a tough World War II, Battle of the Bulge, tank commander veteran. He had a muscular build, thinning crew cut, brown hair mixed with flecks of gray, and was always chomping on a cigar.

After lunchtime he called me into his office along with Harold Blum, my first contact with the examiner's world, who was also going to be taking "the test." "Boys," Mr. Thomas said, "we have a crisis out at the Brighton National Bank. The president, Hugh Best, is a god- damned crook. The bank is insolvent and should be closed. But his highness, Mr. Saxon, refuses to believe that any of his new crop of banks could possibly be broke. To make matters worse, Best and his cronies have purchased a little bank in Clayton, Missouri, which is flush with cash and treasury securities, which they obviously plan to loot." Mr. Thomas was on a roll, as Harold and I sat there in amazed silence.

"What I need you boys to do is to go out there and sit with Mr. Best and crew and try to stop things from getting any worse, while I try to cajole

Mr. Saxon and the guys in Washington to shut this bank down, before the F.D.I.C. fund is more impaired," continued Mr. Thomas. "You need to check on their cash position and check to see if they have stock certificates for the First National Bank of Clayton. You don't need to do anything with the loans; all they have is a bunch of horseshit for loans, anyway." Harold and I looked a little stunned.

"You should have some time to study for the test out there. I'll find someone to relieve you so we can keep your commissioning on course." said Mr. Thomas, now more relaxed.

Harold and I drove out to the suburb of Brighton and the Brighton National Bank, which was lodged in an old, white clapboard, circa 1910 two-story house, with a sign in the front yard, "Brighton National Bank". It was on a commercial street, so the sign didn't look as out of place, as it might if the bank had been in a residential area. We entered the bank and flashed our "Elliot Ness" cards at the bewildered employee at the front desk. A concrete vault had been poured into what once had been the dining room. The old living room was the lobby with a couple of teller stands on one wall. Mr. Best was not happy to see us. He didn't say anything, just glared at us, as we explained our mission.

We counted cash and checked the bank deposits with the Federal Reserve Bank and correspondents. All of the cash came to less than $40,000. It was obvious that a good-sized cash letter, a bundle of checks drawn on the bank, could put them out of business. We did figure out that the bank had drained its liquid resources to loan Mr. Best and his buddies the $400,000 to pay for the Clayton bank stock. They did have the stock certificates on hand and we learned Mr. Ross in Kansas City had stationed some guys in Clayton to prevent any hanky-panky at that end. We sat there until Wednesday afternoon and were assured that some other guys would replace us at Brighton Thursday morning.

Harold and I took our written tests on Thursday and both managed to pass; now we just had to get past the oral test with Mr. Thomas Friday morning. As I remember, Harold went first into Mr. Thomas' office at 8 AM. At 10 Mr. Thomas was ready for me. He spent the better part of two hours quizzing me on everything from laws to credit analysis. The test was also quite instructive as Mr. Thomas gave me various philosophical insights.

The main pearl of wisdom, not to be afraid to be firm, as he was just a phone call away if I needed back up. Just before noon he said, "Bert, you passed. Congratulations! Let's you, Harold, and I go over to the Profile Room for lunch, my treat."

Over at the Profile Room, which turned out to be swankier than anything the State of Wyoming had to offer, Mr. Thomas ordered us each a large gin martini in a frosted glass. He didn't ask if we wanted a drink, he just ordered it. I guess he figured as stressful as the week had been for the three of us, we needed to relax. It turned out Mr. Thomas had gone to Rutherford High School, a football rival of Hackensack High, where I had gone to my sophomore year before my family moved to Colorado. We talked about everything, except banking and examinations.

The Brighton National Bank was closed a week or two later along with the San Francisco National Bank, another notorious bank failure. In San Francisco, the bank's sumptuous quarters was replaced by a bar, called the San Francisco National Bar, which required a minimum change in the sign. The word Bank was changed to bar. Their motto was "put your mouth where your money was."

Van was nearly out of banks he could examine and with Vern Bliss gone the Wyoming district needed my services as a commissioned National Bank Examiner. I was now officially a National Bank Examiner, ready to go to work. My salary had doubled. Of course my responsibility more than doubled, so it was a win-win trade for the OCC and yours truly. However the benefits of the promotion did not negate the fact that I still had a lot to learn. Luckily, Van accompanied me on many of my initial examinations, so I was able to draw from his experience and knowledge for counsel.

One of the first examinations assigned to me was Rawlins National Bank, in Rawlins, Wyoming. The president, John France, was quite gray, although only in his forties, but very much young at heart. On the second floor of the bank one room was a museum devoted to the town of Rawlins association with outlaws, who had passed through town and were inmates at the State Maximum Security Prison, which was located a half-mile from the bank building. Most notable was a pair of shoes made from the hide of "Big Nose George Parrott", a 19th century bad man who was hung in Rawlins many years ago

Seven

A Promotion

Rawlins National was one of the few banks that still employed predominately male tellers, several were former railroaders. Karen Clark, the female exception, was a tall attractive blond gal. She took a lot of ribbing from "the boys, but never let the attention get to her. In defense of "the boys," they were not particularly offensive, just noisy. They were a boisterous lot and every day after the lobby doors closed, they would let loose, with whooping and hollering, and an endless stream of practical jokes and jests upon each other.

Mr. France, by contrast, was generally a quiet man and above all the commotion generated by the tellers. He did, however, have a keen sense of humor. Although he kept his dignity and rose above the tellers' fun, nevertheless he seemed to enjoy his staff's hijinks! Overall Rawlins National was a well-run bank and enjoyable to examine, since Mr. France was a good credit man and always candid with examiners. Mr. France and I sat down to discuss the bank's loan portfolio. I came to a line sheet that Van and Bliss had both marked with a big "W" for watch. This exam, however, the loan showed a zero balance. From the data it was hard to see how the borrower could possibly have paid it off. So I asked, "John how did Mr. Jenkins manage to retire this loan?" Did he incorporate and the loan is now a part of some corporation I have missed, when selecting loans for review?"

John looked at me seriously and said, "Bert, in the course of growing up, didn't you mother ever teach you not to ask people embarrassing questions?"

"What are you talking about, John?" I replied.

John grinned sheepishly and said in a low voice. "You guys were right, I charged it off, when Jenkins skipped town."

Not long after the visit to Rawlins National Bank we were back in town at the First National Bank of Rawlins. This time Mr. Bible was gone. Mr. James Ivins from Nebraska was in his place. Under Mr. Bible's leadership First National was a staid quiet somber, almost gloomy institution; rather the opposite of the Rawlins National. Mr. Ivins set about to change that and tried to invigorate his employees. He wasn't afraid to take on issues like personal cleanliness, dressing to look professional, and plain good manners.

The interior of the bank was redecorated to reflect his enlightened attitude. One chubby little teller I remember from past visits, dressed carelessly, used no makeup and seemed to limit her bathing to every third week of the month, judging from the odor surrounding her. Her personality seemed dour as well. This visit she was, as Mr. Ivins described her, "a cute little fat girl," She was wearing a stylish dress, hair done attractively, with makeup tastefully applied, no noticeable odor, and when I talked to her she reflected a pleasant, if not exciting personality. The place seemed to glow from Mr. Ivins' revitalizing.

Mr. Ivins enjoyed story telling. Once he told a story about his father, who owned two very small banks in western Nebraska:. One was at Crawford, and the other, The Sioux National Bank at Harrison. During the early years of the twentieth century many banks had their capital and surplus accounts written in gold leaf on the street facing windows; one window might read something like "Capital $100,000.00, Surplus $50,000. During the 20s and 30s these numbers overstated the facts and, should the bank fail, the bank owners could be liable for misrepresenting their true condition to the public, who had entrusted their savings with the bank. While it was not illegal to make a bad loan and have the bank fail, misrepresenting the bank's condition could prove to be a serious liability, perhaps even criminal.

The Sioux National Bank had such a sign and the elder Mr. Ivins pondered the best course of action. If he removed the gold leaf Capital and Surplus pronouncement, the public would be wise to the bank's deteriorating condition, perhaps precipitating in a run, which is a banker's worst nightmare. If the bank failed, Mr. Ivins realized that he could be personally and perhaps even criminally liable. Months went by as Mr. Ivins mulled over a course of action, but was unable to find any kind of solution to the dilemma. One night at 2:00 A.M., he received a phone call from the local police. A drunk driver had driven through a window down at the bank and he needed to come down to the police station to press charges. Mr. Ivins deliberately drove past the bank in route to the police station and noted that a Model T Ford had indeed crashed through the bank window, the one with the gold leaf Capital and Surplus advertised.

Upon arrival at the police station the desk officer said, "Mr. Ivins, I have the drunk driver responsible for the damage in a jail cell." pointing over to the disheveled drunken man in the Harrison's two-cell jail. "No doubt, you'll wish to press charges"

"Hell no!" Replied Mr. Ivins. "I'd like to pay for his bail."

The stunned desk officer, didn't know what to say. Mr. Ivins paid the $200 for the man's bail and left before the policeman could ask why he would do such a peculiar thing.

If I thought Jim Ivins' entertaining stories were the prelude to an easy loan discussion, I was certainly wrong. Mr. Ivins wanted to defend every loan in the portfolio, regardless of obvious problems. We had a heated discussion over a number of loans, but the one I recall clearly was a loan made to a young tenant rancher, who was renting a place over 100 miles away in the high country near South Pass City. The tenant's financial statement showed heavy debts and would have shown a deficit net worth had it not been for the highly inflated value of the livestock. Mr. Ivins argued, until his face turned beet red, that the values were justified because of the superior quality of the livestock. The problem I had with the loan was there weren't enough cattle to liquidate the loan and not enough cows to generate calves over time to amortize the loan in an orderly manner. I held my ground.

By the end of the examination, I was glad Joe Huner's Green Mill Bar on Front Street was still featuring 25-cent drinks during happy hour.

Shortly after the Rawlins visits, I was off to examine the First National Bank of Gillette, . Gillette in those days was a dusty little town of perhaps 3500 people, miles from a larger city. My assistants, Ted and Verne accompanied me on that trip. On the way north over the prairie on a narrow two-lane State Highway we drove by the B-Bar-B Ranch, which raised buffalo commercially. Ted started to chuckle a little and said, "Can you imagine the guy that owns this ranch sitting next to the fellow down in Laramie that's in the Jackrabbit fur business, sitting next to each other on a plane?"

"Just picture B-Bar-B guy saying to Mr. Jackrabbit, "What business are you in?"

The Jackrabbit guy says. "I'm in the Jackrabbit business."

Mr. B-Bar-B says, "Yeah right. I'm in the buffalo business"

"Sure you are." Replies Mr. Jackrabbit.

Telling this little story shortened the long ride just a little. After we checked into the Best Western Motel, we went down to First National Bank. The bank was housed in a tired old retail store building with a 25-foot front and reaching back perhaps 100 feet. It wasn't a very impressive appearing bank, especially when compared to Stockman's Bank's modern brick building a block down the street, which had been planned as a bank. Mr. Mathews, the president, and Mr. O' Halloran, the Cashier, seemed on edge; not that we expected them to be glad to see us. Verne and Ted quickly counted the cash, ran a few ledgers, which seemed to balance okay. I proved the notes and immediately noticed a high volume of past due loans. Since the bank's total assets were only about a $1,000,000; this new bank appeared to be off to a slow start.

By the end of day two, I realized this bank had far more serious problems than anything I had encountered on my own. Late in the day I called my boss, Jack Thomas, and reviewed my findings with him: 20% of the loans were past due, half of those were seriously delinquent. I had a long list of loans to be criticized and Ted had uncovered a defalcation while reconciling the bank's correspondent bank account with its' primary correspondent, First National bank of Lincoln, Nebraska. It seems Mr. O'Halloran had made himself a $20,000 loan several months earlier, which he reflected on the bank's books as though he had borrowed the money from the First National Bank of Lincoln. The problem was the Lincoln bank never granted the loan. In addition, several laws were violated, the bank had poor serious internal controls, and many important documents were missing. In short it was one hell of a mess. Mr. Thomas, said. "Bert, you need to call a board meeting and I'll come up and join you for it." He paused a minute and said. "I can fly into Gillette?"

"Well, Mr. Thomas, the nearest airport with scheduled service is in Casper. You could fly there and rent a car, but it's another 160 miles to Gillette from Casper," I said.

"In other words, I can't get there from here." Mr. Thomas sounded frustrated and then thought a minute. "Tell you what. You go ahead and call the board meeting and I will have Mrs. Tassi (his executive secretary) keep my phone line open for you, no matter what I'm doing. You're going to have to do this by yourself, but remember I'm as near as your phone and if needed I'll talk to anyone there that wants to give you a bad time."

So I informed Mr. Mathews that I wanted to call a board meeting with all members present. He reluctantly agreed and we set the time for 1 PM. Because of the bank's small size, it didn't take long for Ted and Verne to put together the body of the report. I was too nervous to eat lunch. I had sat in on a number of board meetings with Van Dyke, but they were a courtesy that Van extended to the bank, rather than for the purpose of addressing serious issues.

I started the meeting promptly at 1PM, with all the local board members present. They were all men in their 50's and 60's, roughly the age of my parents, with the exception of Director Ray Saunders. Mr. Saunders was a lumberman and had a solid slim figure, was in his late 30s with red hair showing a few gray strands mixed in. I was 26 at the time. The board members came from a variety of backgrounds: a couple of ranchers, an oil and gas operator, and the local lumberman. O' Halloran never came back from lunch. The women tellers were handling the bank's few customers as we gathered in a back room, which was more of a storage room than a boardroom.

With trembling fingers, I cautiously, went through my findings on the report pages and on my line sheets. Except for a cough and the rustling of papers, the board members sat in total silence. Finally, after an hour I finished my comments. My invitation for questions was met with silence.

Finally, Ray Saunders, the lumberman, said turning to Mr. Mathews. "God dammit, things are really fucked up here. I don't pretend to be no banker, but I do know that folks are supposed to pay their notes on time. We've got a bunch of shitty loans here! Where the hell is that crooked son of a bitch O'Halloran?" Ray Saunders was taking charge now. "Mathews, call the god-dammed F.B. I. O'HALLORAN needs to have his ass fired and prosecuted. God dammed thief!"

Suddenly, the board awoke and agreed with Ray Saunders. They would do their duty and straighten out the bank's problems. Saunders immediately called another board meeting for the rest of the afternoon without us being present. Ted and Verne had the report in good shape and all I had to do was write the confidential section of the report. We left around 3 PM for the trek back to our homes in Casper. As we traveled down the narrow road, Ted asked, "Well, how did it go with Mr. Misfit and Old Hooligan?" referring to names we had dubbed them with at dinner the previous night. I told my assistants that it went quite well given the circumstances and that it appeared Ray Saunders was already providing the leadership needed to turn things around.

That afternoon, Ray Saunders took immediate charge of things in Gillette and both Mathews and O'Halloran were fired. The board members elected Ray Saunders, President of the bank.

The following week I was assisting Bob Jennett at the First National Bank of Pueblo, Colorado; my third trip in that institution. I had written my confidential section over the weekend, but hadn't mailed it. Since Van wasn't available, I asked Jennett to read the yellow pages before I sent it on to Mr. Thomas. "Jesus, what a mess. Tell me, Bert, wasn't there anything you liked?" Bob laughed, adding a little levity to this otherwise serious situation. "Seems to me you covered everything. Mr. Thomas might want to make a few revisions, but you'll learn from it."

The day the Gillette report landed on Jack Thomas' desk he called me. "Bert, you know that Congressman Roncalio is the major shareholder in the Gillette Bank. He is tight with the Kennedy wing of the Democratic Party and he could get you fired. Reports like yours can be very political."

"Mr. Thomas" I replied. "Mr. Roncalio's bank is going down the tubes, like Brighton National, if they don't get on the ball and start fixing their problems quickly. As for me, I can find another job, if it comes to that."

"Bert, I think you have drawn the correct conclusions, given the facts provided. I will add my name, approving and agreeing with your report, but I wanted you to know you might be somewhat at risk." Said Mr. Thomas and so the report went in as I had written it without any revisions.

In those days problem banks received a visitation every 60 days to monitor progress made or not made towards resolving the bank's problems. The Denver office sent Doug Krogh, a Denver based examiner, up to do the first 60-day visitation. Doug and Ray hit it off immediately and before the visitation was over Mr. Saunders had hired Doug, as Executive Vice President, to work under Saunders' direct supervision. The bank's problems were rather quickly put on the mend as subsequent visits to Gillette would prove.

Not long after the Gillette examination, we were assigned the pleasant task of visiting the First National Bank of Buffalo. Buffalo is a pretty picturesque, town of 3200 people nestled against the eastern slope of the Big Horn Mountain Range. Historically, the town boasts being host to the Johnson County Cattle War in 1892, one of the last fights over open range country between cattle ranchers and sheep ranchers. Executive responsibilities were shared by Robert Holt and Robert McBride, both in their late forties, the two Bobs seemed to be on top of the bank's relatively few problems, a welcome change after Gillette. The interesting thing about Buffalo was not the bank, but the town itself.

A crooked main street winds through the center of the business district consisting mostly of circa 1890-1900 brick buildings, many with a kind of Victorian decor flavor. At the low spot on Main Street, Clear Creek comes rushing out of the mountains. Cantilevered over the creek was the "Busy Bee Café", a tiny little restaurant with perhaps 15 stools. The grill was presided over by a man named Hollis and his wife Peggy. Hollis was a large rotund, jovial man, who was the cook and proprietor. Peggy, a petite lady with a winning smile, was the waitress and cashier. Between Hollis and his wife, they knew pretty much everything, the patron might want to know about the local sports teams. Watching Hollis prepare the meals reminded me of the patter and showmanship one sees in a Japanese restaurant; I always ordered eggs over easy if for no other reason, but to watch Hollis flip the eggs high over the grill, then watch them land perfectly, squarely on his spatula. Next to the Busy Bee was the Occidental Hotel.

Off the lobby of the Occidental was a bar with several pool tables. One night Ted, Van, Verne and I were having a few drinks and playing pool. Uncharacteristically, I was hot, playing pool, handily beating all comers. Van, who knew I really wasn't much of a pool player, had just seen Jackie

Gleason's movie "The Hustler," about Minnesota Fats, the renowned pool master. Van slurred, "tonight, Bert I think you could beat Jackie Gleason!"

I was assigned to make a trip up into Wyoming's Big Horn Basin, a desert region that receives less than 9 inches of annual rain. The region is completely surrounded by high craggy snow-capped mountains which according to local legend stall the storm clouds, dumping the snow and rain in the high country, leaving the valley below comparatively dry. On this particular trip we drove westward from Casper in the Morning as we crossed on U.S. 20-26. We had slowed down as we passed through the village of Powder River. Just as we began to accelerate, suddenly, as if appearing from nowhere, a handsome buck antelope ran past us doing about 60 miles per hour, then crossed in front of us, as though we were just traveling too slow.

The Shoshone First National Bank was managed by Sam Allen, who by this time must have been in his late 40s. His father, R. W. Allen, had been the bank President for many years was now about 80 and enjoyed visiting the bank. R. W. believed in running a good clean bank, and instructed me to, "Give 'em hell, Bert."

The senior Mr. Allen had been the Cashier of the bank during the 1920s and early 30s. In those days banks issued their own currency called National Bank Notes, which were backed by the bank's investment in U.S. Treasury Bonds in an amount equal to the bank's outstanding "notes of circulation". This currency looked like paper money issued by the Federal Reserve Banks or the U.S. Treasury and was in fact printed by the treasury on the same linen paper used for other currency. The difference was it read "Shoshone National Bank of Cody" or other issuing bank. This was prior to the 1958 merger with The First National Bank of Cody. Each individual note was personally signed by the bank's President and Cashier. The notes were not negotiable without both signatures. Mr. Allen smiled broadly and added. "I used to take bills signed only by Sammy Parks, then put my signature on them as I needed to spend the money. I used them as traveler checks, before American Express and other traveler checks were in wide use, whenever I went on vacation. Quite handy!"

Mr. Allen had many banking stories. One of the stories involves Sammy Parks, who was the bank's President for more than 20 years. Mr. Parks was an extremely conservative person and a banker and took nothing at face value. One day when inspecting and counting a rancher-borrower's sheep, the rancher noted as the sheep trotted by Mr. Parks that the sheep had all recently been sheared.

Mr. Parks replied. "I can see the left side of these sheep have been sheared."

The Shoshone First National Bank was owned by a group of local investors, who were represented on the Board of Directors. One of the directors, Oliver Steadman, had a son Don, who joined our crew about this time. Don and Ted knew each other from their time at the University of Wyoming.

At the time Ted and I were sharing an apartment in Casper. Shortly after Don joined us, Ted and I were enjoying whiskey and water, or "Bourbon and ditch" as the Wyoming expression goes. The phone rang and it was Don, "I need help; can I come over?"

"Sure" I said. "Ted and I are just enjoying a little libation. Come on over and we'll fix you a drink and you can tell us your problem." I turned to Ted and said. "Don's on his way over. Says he has big troubles."

"I wonder why? You would think he would want to be home with his wife and daughter after being gone all week." Said Ted.

Ten minutes later Don arrives at our apartment and out of breath from running up the steps to our second floor apartment and says. "I'm moving out. I can't live with that woman any longer. She just spent my whole month's check on shoes! Can I crash here until I can get things worked out?"

"Don, we don't have what you would call deluxe accommodations here, but you're welcome to sleep on the floor; Ted when he's here sleeps on the couch." I said. "I've got a sleeping bag you can use."

Ted said. "I'm going drive to Cheyenne in the morning to see Alice in the morning. So you can have the couch Saturday night."

As the reader might expect, Don and his wife divorced. Since Don's job didn't allow him to assume the role of "Mr. Mom," his mother-in-law took on the actual raising of the little girl, with Don providing support and visits as he could schedule them. Don had a surprisingly close and friendly relationship with his mother-in-law, who also recognized her daughter's irresponsible nature.

The Denver office assigned Ted, Van, and I to examine the Dubois National Bank, a new bank. Dubois is a small town of fewer than 1000 people and located in the Wind River Valley about half way between Riverton and Jackson, Wyoming. The town elevation is about 8000 feet above sea level. The town's economy revolves around tourism and a saw mill. Prior to the chartering of the Dubois National Bank, the town's residents had to travel 85 miles to either Riverton or Lander, or alternatively across Togawatee Pass, over the Rocky Mountains to Jackson, Wyoming. Directors of the American National Bank of Riverton, along with several local merchants and ranchers, founded the Dubois National Bank.

Harry Hayes, who was an active Vice President of American National, became the President. The day-to-day management was placed in the hands of George Blevins. Mr. Blevins was enthusiastic about the town and the challenges of getting the new bank off to a good start.

Mr. Blevins had a long career as a Bank Examiner for the State of Wyoming, but had never actually held a management position in a bank.

The quarters for the new bank were in the original red sandstone building built in 1913 for Amoretti, Welty, Helmer & Company, a private bank, meaning it was organized as a partnership and not chartered by state or federal authorities. It closed in 1927. It was a small building that was constructed of red sandstone. It did, however, have a fireproof vault complete with a steel door. Since the building was under consideration as a possible physical location for the proposed bank, Van and I were invited to go inside during charter investigation. It was inhabited by a tough looking old lady with brilliant red hair. She kept her ample liquor supply in the vault along with her wardrobe. She reluctantly showed us around, although it was evident she wasn't anxious to leave what had been her home for at least 15 years.

Mr. Blevins was very cautious when making loans and provided good documentation when he made one. He had a good handle on operations, so the examination went very smoothly and we were finished with everything, except Van writing the confidential section, by 5 PM of the second day. We were scheduled to meet the rest of the crew for a 3 o'clock start at the First National Bank of Riverton, eighty miles away. Harry Hays had driven up from Riverton to discuss loans and the five of us: Ted, Van, Harry Hays, George Blevins and I when out to dinner.

At dinner Van started to tell George he needed to try a little harder to make loans and not to be paranoid of taking a small loss now and then. Van told us the story of the first loan he made in his long banking career: Van had grown up in Mendota, Missouri, a small farming community on the Missouri-Iowa line, near present day Unionville, and had worked for the local bank. One Saturday in 1924, the bank's staff was clerking a farm auction sale and a farmer, who Van had known all his life, asked for a $15 loan to purchase an old cow at the sale. Van made his first loan. Van said looking at George, "I knew that old farmer all my life. It never dawned on me he wouldn't pay for that old cow, but he didn't."

George looked at Van in silence, then looked over to Harry Hays. Harry said, "George, you are going to make a few bad loans, some mistakes, but you need to learn from them."

Van looked at his friend Harry and smiled. "George, Harry here has been making loans to these folks in Fremont County for years. Sure he has had a few small loans go sour, but these are good people, here in Wyoming. The great majority will pay."

I repeated a comment Del Crouse made to me on a recent examination: "Most people are entitled to some credit, the question is how much?"

After our steak dinners we talked about non-banking topics. Harry told us that the Wyoming Fish and Game Department had sequestered a large herd of big horn sheep just outside of town. Harry said, "I can see you are pretty much finished with the examination; if you have time I'll take you up there first thing in the morning to see them in my Jeep Wagoneer." A Jeep Wagoneer is a civilized version of the universal Jeep, but has the all-important four- wheel-drive, which made them very popular in mountainous Wyoming. Ted and I immediately decided to go.

Van, who was by this hour pretty well anesthetized, said, "You boys go with Harry and I'll finish the confidential."

"Good," said Harry, "I'm also staying at the Sage Motel. I'll knock on your door at seven sharp."

Van wobbled out to the car at his usual 45-degree angle to the boardwalk in front of the *Elkhorn Restaurant* again without falling down. It was a cold January night. By seven o'clock the following morning, it was at least ten degrees below zero. As promised there was a sharp knock at the door. I opened the door and there was Harry Hays standing there in nothing but blue boxer shorts, a white T-shirt, and brown leather bedroom slippers. "Ready to go? Said Harry, seemingly totally unaffected by the cold.

Ted had also come to the door to watch Harry amble the two doors down to his room, as though it was July. "He must have been drinking anti-freeze last night," mused Ted.

After a hearty breakfast at the *Elkhorn Restaurant* we were off to see the big horn sheep. As Harry had promised there was a herd of about 50 male and female big horn sheep enclosed in a tall makeshift corral, lured inside by fresh hay bales. The Fish & Game Department people were tagging the sheep, so they could be tracked in the future. Never before or since had any of us ever seen so many big horn sheep at once; it was quite a magnificent sight.

By the time the spring of 1965 rolled around, Steadman was romancing a young lady, who worked at the First National Bank of Powell. While we were in the middle of the examination of her bank, Dorothy, a cute, slender, flat chested, brunette, with bright brown eyes, was stricken with an appendicitis and put in the local hospital. Steadman, decided to try to gain favor with her, by presenting her with roses to cheer her up. He talked Verne Sorheim, who by now had become our crew humorist, into accompanying him for moral support for the visit to her bedside.

At coffee break the following morning Verne recalled the visit for the rest of us. "We walked into her room and she was wearing this thin, tan nightie that came up to her neck. Quickly, she pulls the covers over her bosom. Why the hell would she bother to do that? All she has is a couple a pancakes with raisins in the middle."

Following the examination of the Powell bank I examined Angus Linton's First National Bank of Meeteetse. It was spring and the Greybull River was running wildly, the fishing wasn't any good, Angus and Bill were still at the bank when we arrived a few minutes before three that afternoon. The cash, as usual, was off a couple of dollars, the notes balanced and we were wrapping up things for the afternoon start. Angus reached for a string on the wall, pulled it a couple of times, and said, "I like a beer after a long work day."

Staying until after five constituted a long day for Angus. A couple of minutes later there was a knock on the door. Angus let the guy in, who was carrying a tray with two cold beers in frosty glasses. The man said, "Angus, you rang?"

"Yes, we'll need three more," said Angus, pointing to his son Bill, Verne and Steadman. And the man was off to draw the additional beers. Angus pointed to the string on the wall. "We have a bell on the other side that rings when Bill and I get thirsty for a beer, then Art comes over with a couple of beers; he runs a tab for us," he said, with his sly little smile that I had come to enjoy.

Friday morning, Angus and I discussed the loan portfolio, which had grown, perhaps to $100,000, still less than the bank's capital, so there wasn't much to discuss. However, there was one loan that was nearly a year past due. The loan was secured by a first mortgage on a small store building located a few doors down the street and occupied by a cabinet maker and short order carpenter. "Angus, what is going on here? Mr. McDougal hasn't paid you since last June? It seems like you should think about foreclosing or negotiating a deed in lieu of foreclosure if you can," I said.

Angus looked at me very seriously and said. "It is a problem, but the building and lot are easily worth the amount of the loan, so I'm not worried about actually taking a loss. The real problem is, if I were to foreclose on Mr. McDougal, then his wife would be mad at my wife. Even worse Emily McDougal wouldn't invite my wife to her Tuesday bridge parties. Then my wife would be mad at me and I don't like having her mad at me. I guess I could charge it off. Then you wouldn't be mad at me."

Flabbergasted, I said, "Angus, go ahead and charge it off, then everyone will be happy."

Angus gave me his sly smile and said, "I'll do it. When McDougal sells the property someday he'll have to settle with the bank to give good title."

Shortly, after the trip to Meeteetse examination I received a call from Mr. Thomas. "Bert, I'd like to transfer you to Albuquerque, you're about to become a lame duck examiner in Wyoming, Van is eligible to examine most of the Wyoming banks. Clair Gamble down in New Mexico is limited on the banks he can do, so I need you in New Mexico."

"I can go; when do you want me there?" I said.

Mr. Thomas said, "May first, you worked down there last year for several weeks, so you know all the guys. Clair will be looking for you; just meet him that morning at the office, which is still in the Sunshine Building. He's planning an afternoon start close by. Good luck!"

Eight

Land of Enchantment

On May 1st, 1965, I arrived to commence my duties as Supervising National Bank Examiner of the New Mexico field office. Prior to being transferred to New Mexico, I became somewhat familiar with the territory, having worked with Clair Gamble and his crew for several weeks approximately a year earlier. At the time Gamble's crew were all relatively new to the examining business. I remembered that particular month having started in Roswell, New Mexico, at the First National Bank and ending the month at the First National Bank of Sheridan, Wyoming, from one of the most southern cities in the 12th National Bank Region to the northernmost bank in the region, a distance of 900 miles, yet I never left the "First National Bank". In those days some people were under the impression that all the First National Banks were either branches of one giant bank or otherwise related.

The name First National Bank originated with the National Banking Act of 1863. Banks in various towns were required to be named: "First National Bank of Philadelphia." Then the next charter in the city would be Second National Bank and so on. However, the law wasn't popular. Several old banks, such as City Bank in New York, wanted to become National Banks, but didn't want to give up their well-established names. Moreover, when the numerical banks in New York City got up to around seventeen, the ridiculousness of the system became apparent and banks were allowed to name themselves. By that time there were many First National Banks around the country and the name became popular, as a kind of marketing device, which is true to this day.

Clair Gamble had the reputation of being an easy going examiner, both as to his handling of the banks and the guys on his crew, so I wasn't sure how well I was going to fit in down in New Mexico. The banks and Gamble's crew were accustomed to his *laissez-faire* attitude. Although I believe I was a fair examiner, I had observed that I held banks under my supervision, as well as my crew, to a higher standard. Since I now had a commission and was nearly 500 miles from Boulder, going home on weekends wasn't going to be convenient or easy and I realized I needed to make a life for myself on weekends. I moved into a fairly new apartment complex at 1200 Madeira, SE in Albuquerque, which had about 50 units, populated mostly with young people. The place had a good-sized swimming pool and a recreation-game room too. Best of all, there were a number of lovely single young ladies in residence.

The first examination I participated in was assisting Denver- based Paul T. Henniger, who had been a National Bank Examiner since the 1920s, at yet another First National Bank, the First National Bank in Albuquerque. First National was easily the second largest bank in New Mexico, quite complex and therefore assigned to a senior examiner.

P. T. Henniger was about Van Dyke's age, 62, and had spent his whole career with the OCC since leaving his hometown of Hay Springs, Nebraska. Mr. Henniger was a large, heavyset man with an ever-present cigar in his mouth. P.T., as his crew called him, was highly respected: he was a man I could learn a lot from.

P.T.'s mantra was, "The secret to being an effective examiner was to examine the banker first, then exam the bank." I was happy for the opportunity to work with P.T; I had worked for him on a number of assignments and already knew and admired the man.

Mr. Henniger had assigned me the responsibility of examining the East Central Avenue Branch of First National, which had a sizable loan portfolio. It was the first time I had been chosen for a lead position participating in one of P. T.'s jobs; I was anxious to do first class work.

The Branch Manager was Neil Monihan, who I enjoyed working with at East Central. We were scheduled to discuss loans with P.T., Clyde Hill, the bank's President and C.E.O., at 9:00 AM on Friday morning. However, the morning got off to an inauspicious beginning. With the exception of Central Avenue, Albuquerque's main east-west thoroughfare, downtown Albuquerque is a network of one-way streets. Turning right off Central Avenue on to a one-way street four lanes wide, I made it to the third lane to make my left turn as I headed to the bank's parking ramp. In New Mexico a driver was expected to turn left from the fourth lane, or far left lane. As luck would have it, a cop was right behind me and I received a ticket for the unlawful turn. P. T. was behind me and recognized my Buick convertible as I was being given a ticket. As a result, I was a few minutes late. P. T. cigar clenched in his mouth, looked up from his line sheets and said, with a completely deadpan expression. "Bert, were you planning to discuss the East Central Branch loans with Mr. Hill from jail?" He began to chuckle and his great belly shook heartily.

Picking up the tail end of the conversation, Neil Monihan walked in and said, "What's this about discussing loans in jail? Bert, you look like you could use a cup of coffee, I'll buy."

We walked next door to a busy little coffee shop, where it seemed all of downtown Albuquerque gathered for a morning eye opener. As we waited for our coffee, I explained with embarrassment my illegal turn and the resulting ticket. As I was concluding my story, a tall 50ish gentlemen greeted Neil. Neil turned to me and said, "Bert, this Mike Kelly, Chief of Police. He is an old high school buddy of mine. Chief, this is Bert Harris, my bank examiner, who just moved to Albuquerque this month. Bert, tell him your story."

I shook hands with Chief Kelly, and with even more embarrassment repeated my story for the third time in less than 20 minutes. Kelly sat down with us and he motioned the waitress to bring him a cup of coffee. Kelly grinned first at Neil, then me. "Bert, let me have that ticket. This is no way to welcome a newcomer to Albuquerque."

This was the first and only time anyone fixed traffic ticket for me. We chatted for 15 or 20 minutes and then it was time to meet with Mr. Hill and

P. T. for the loan discussion. Fortunately, I was saved the indignity of telling my traffic ticket story a fourth time. Mr. Hill was a distinguished, white haired gentleman, who looked like a stereotypical bank president. Luckily, we got right down to business. The East Central Branch had a decent loan portfolio, with the exception of one loan, which had been put together by the Chairman's eager young son, who had a special knack for making complicated deals. The line of credit consisted of a Small Business Administration, or SBA loan, which by themselves involve a large volume of paperwork. The SBA advance was accompanied by an account receivable line of credit, plus some equipment financing. All of these were documentation nightmares. Neil made a comment about the mountainous file: "Quite a few trees died to create this guy's file."

P. T. chimed in. "Any loan this complicated couldn't possibly be any good."

Mr. Hill looked at me thoughtfully.

"I believe it is substandard; the borrower is struggling to make the payments. Basically, he is making payments out of his declining inventory. Balance sheet is not impressive and cash flow is marginal," I said. P. T. waived his cigar in agreement. Mr. Hill nodded his ascent to the verdict. I was off to the next bank.

One of the first banks I visited was the Hot Springs National Bank of Truth or Consequences, or "T or C", as the town is locally known. T or C got its' name from a television show call "Truth or Consequences". The City of Hot Springs was offered funding for some otherwise unaffordable improvement project if it would change its' moniker to Truth or Consequences. The name change was no doubt hotly debated within the community. The bank sided, naturally, with the conservative populace in the community and retained its' original name, Hot Springs National Bank.

Even though the town changed its name, Hot Springs was still a good name for the bank. The bank's building sat dead center on one of the town's famous thermal springs. The bank's president and chief planner of the new building project built a rather elaborate mineral spring bath within the bank building which is accessible only through the president's private office. As I remember, the president at the time of my visit was on vacation. Our host banker was Robert Grady, executive vice president and a former New Mexico State Trooper. He had lived in T or C long enough to be well versed in the community lore and the bank's loan portfolio. As a result, the visit went smoothly. He suggested we all go out to eat at a quaint little Mexican restaurant at Chucillo, a tiny village northwest of Tor C.

Chucillo's entire population spoke Spanish. Few of the residents spoke or even understood English. In other words their English was as bad, if not worse, than my Spanish, which is pretty damned awful.

La Buenos Gardenia, was a charming little adobe place set in the middle of a well-tended garden, where presumably the proprietor grew much of the produce served. Mr. Grady encouraged, perhaps cautioned is a better word, us to order the Mexican fare off the menu, and we wouldn't be disappointed. With the exception of Dennis Hogerheide and me, all of the guys on my crew were from either Texas or New Mexico natives and were connoisseurs of Mexican cuisine.

The proprietor, Jose, a genial, middle aged, somewhat portly gent, always a good sign in an unknown eatery, greeted us. "Ah, Señor Bob! Buenos noches, Señors."

You could tell Bob Grady was a regular. Motioning, with his hands Jose guided us to a table for six. We sat down on benches at a crude picnic style wooden table decorated with an inviting vase of flowers, paper place mats and a large earthen pitcher of water. Jose handed out six menus, written entirely in Spanish. I selected a combination plate, the others chose various Mexican dishes, with the exception of Dennis.

Dennis, who hails from Michigan, ordered a broiled steak, medium rare, with a salad. Jose diligently wrote down the orders and looked in disbelief at Dennis and said, "Boiled steak?"

Dennis had sufficient beer that he missed the meaning of Jose's question and answered, "Yes."

As we sat enjoying our Corona beers, when Jose brought the meals, five plates with generous servings of various Mexican dishes, beautiful to look at and which proved to be as delicious as they looked. A bewildered Jose served Dennis this pitiful steak, boiled white along with a gorgeous garden fresh salad. Jose shook his head and said to Dennis in disbelief, "Senor, You ordered a *boiled* steak."

Dennis shook his head, admiring the wonderful meals served the rest of us, said to Jose, "I guess this must be what I ordered?"

I don't think I could have been as good a sport as Dennis. On the other hand, it reinforced my belief in following the local's leads as to menu choices. Sammy loved spicy food and poured Tabasco Sauce over his already spicy burritos and devouring the meal with great enthusiasm, sweat pouring off his brow he exclaimed, "Wow, this is really, really good!"

That pretty well summed up our meals that evening, except for the "boiled" steak.

The following day was Friday and we put most of the finishing touches on our report and went home to Albuquerque. My crew were all married and with the exception of Dennis had young children. My crew had other things to do on weekends. Fortunately for me, one of my brother's college roommates, Steve Negler, was an Air Force Officer stationed at Kirtland Air Force Base. Occasionally on my weekends in Boulder, Steve, my brother Frank and I would go hiking or flying together. Steve held a private pilot license for several years. Steve's bachelor officer quarters turned out to be a few minutes from my apartment, and like me, he had time to burn on weekends. Weekends we hung out together; frequently we would go flying.

On one of those weekends we were flying up the Grand Canyon of the Rio Grande in a single engine, two seat, Cessna 152. The scenery, with its' craggy rock ledges and occasional evergreens clinging to the stone canyon walls, was quite beautiful. We were flying about level with the canyon rim and Steve says to me. "Bert, drive; I want to take some pictures."

Flying was totally new to me. Steve gave me brief instructions: "Pull back on the yoke to go up, push to go down. Turn the yoke left will tip the plane to the left; turn right to tip right. This operates the plane's ailerons. Easy on the controls, I'm right here."

Wow, I thought, this is great fun. I was bitten with the flying bug. After the flying it was back to work Monday morning.

Our crew's next assignment was the First National Bank of Artesia in southern New Mexico. I rode with Rod Smith and read over my predecessor Gamble's previous reports. The bank's loan portfolio didn't look too bad, but there were very few internal controls. Internal controls are designed to protect the bank from both internal and external theft. These can be very difficult to achieve in a very small bank, like my friend Angus Linton's bank in Wyoming. But in a bank the size of Artesia, twenty times the size of the

Meeteetse bank, there was no reason why most of the standard precautions couldn't be implemented. Even Angus' internal controls were better, despite his tiny staff of four. Gamble had made a special point of the internal control issue in his confidential section, which in itself was unusual.

Rod Smith was the detail man on this examination. Rod was a bit older than I and the rest of the crew and had spent a number of years as an auditor at the Albuquerque National Bank. I was glad to have Rod with me for what promised to be a challenging situation. We arrived at the bank and Charlie Evans, the President, greeted us, "Well, you fellows are overdue. We've been looking for you."

I shook hands with Mr. Evans, and he showed me to the bank's boardroom where we were to start to work. Rod reported the teller's and vault cash balanced to the penny. I proved the loan ledgers and notes and they too were in perfect balance. By Thursday Rod came in the boardroom to talk internal controls.

"Chief," says Rod. "You're not going to believe this, but the internal control problems, all three pages of them, have been fixed, except for a couple of minor items."

"Really, that seems unlikely, but if true, that's terrific. Let's talk to Mr. Evans. Gamble's report says he was quite belligerent about fixing problems," I said.

Rod went out and collared Charlie Evans. Charlie Evans was about 60 year old, with a decided paunch and a round, red face. Evans said with a smile, "What can I do for you boys?"

"What's the story on the remarkable improvement you folks have made with your internal controls?" I replied.

Charlie sat down in one of the boardroom chairs and said in his southwestern drawl, "Well, it's kind of a long story." Turning to Rod, who had been in Artesia for the previous exam, "Rod, do you remember Grace Thomas, the little spinster lady. Gray hair, kinda skinny?

Rod said, "Sure, handled the insufficient fund checks, as I recall."

"Right. You know what that sweet little old lady was doing?" Mr. Evans said.

Rod and I shook our heads in the negative. Mr. Evans continued his tale. "Well gents, she had a system. We charge $2.00 for a "NSF" check.

She'd give the bank a dollar and pocket a dollar for herself. Been doing if for years. You'll never guess what she did with the money."

I said, "I don't have a clue, Charlie."

"Well, Mr. Harris, get this: she had a God dammed savings accounts at Peoples Bank, across the street. There was over $60,000 in it. Of course she might have stolen more, we just don't know. When I told the board about it, the shit hit the fan. They were furious. Got out the last examination report. Told me to get my ass in gear and fix all the exceptions and I have done the best I know how," Charlie said and bowed his head in embarrassment.

Rod and I looked at each other in amazement. "Well, Mr. Evans, Rod tells me you have done a fine job of clearing up this problem," I said.

"Funny, I always thought all of our people were honest, especially Gracie," Evans answered. She worked here for over 25 years. Shame to ruin a career like that. We learned a hell of lesson and those dammed internal controls weren't that hard to install, either. Should have done it years ago."

If I thought Mr. Evan's bellicose streak was a thing of the past, I was wrong. The loan discussion was slow and tedious as Mr. Evans chose to argue about nearly every substandard or poorly performing loan. The one I especially remember was a $50,000 unsecured loan to one Richard R. Arnold, President of Pacific International Oil, Limited, a large Big Board listed company. The loan hadn't had a principal payment applied since it was originated five years earlier, although interest payments had been made punctually. To make matters worse, there never had been even a personal balance sheet in the file.

Charlie's explanation was that the loan was a goodwill gesture by Mr. Arnold, to this community bank, since Arnold owned a good sized ranch in the county. I shook my head in disbelief and said, "Mr. Evans, there is not the tiniest evidence in your file that this isn't a forged note; that someone just wrote Mr. Arnold's name on the note. Moreover, there is no indication Arnold has the capacity to pay this loan. Sure he makes the big bucks, but if he is dumping his surplus funds into that ranch, he might be losing money hand over fist. The ranching business can be a great way to lose money. I am going to classify this loan substandard and suggest proper documentation, especially financial statements and an amortization program."

Charlie Evans face got even redder than usual. "Well, damn it, I suppose you have a point. I am embarrassed to ask Mr. Arnold for a financial statement."

"Mr. Evans, why? Mr. Arnold wasn't too embarrassed to ask you for the fifty grand!"

Happily, the next examination Denver scheduled for us was a bank run by the elder brother of one of the assistants on our crew, Jeff Carlisle. Jeff came from a distinguished west Texas banking family. His father, Marvin Carlisle, owned and managed the First National Bank of Tulia, Texas. Winford, Jeff's brother, owned and managed the Lovington National Bank in the southeastern corner of New Mexico. Jeff didn't accompany us to his brother's bank in compliance with OCC regulations, but assured me Winford would give us a cordial reception.

Winford Carlisle was around 40 years old and spoke with a distinctive Texas accent. What I remember most about this visit was the way Winford talked about some of his rancher customers, whose oil wells made ranching in this dry country profitable. "We find in our country, cattle do best when they can graze in the shade of an oil derrick," Winford would drawl.

He made that pronouncement several times during the course of our otherwise uneventful loan discussion.

Another interesting bank in southern New Mexico was the First National Bank of Dona Ana County in Las Cruces. Much of the countryside around Las Cruces is devoted to raising the highly prized long staple Pima Cotton, which commands a premium price over short staple varieties. Frank Pappan, the Chairman and a major stockholder, had the dubious distinction of being a nephew of Franz Von Pappan, one of Hitler's henchmen. Frank Pappan was a large, bald, friendly man with a keen sense of humor. When discussing the loan he made to an elder retired army officer and his wife he could hardly control his laughter.

"What is so funny?" I asked.

Mr. Pappan, restraining his amusement said, "Gerry and Evelyn are building this house with the biggest shower I ever saw, dual nozzles, exquisitely designed, like a damned Roman bath. I asked Gerry 'Why?' He says, 'Evey and I like to shower together.'"

Mr. Pappan then exploded into a loud boisterous laughter. "Can't you just picture these two eighty year olds in the shower, lathering each other up, getting it on? God, I hope they don't fall and hurt themselves."

That evening after work entire crew, retired to a quaint open air Mexican restaurant, which had an adobe look about it. We sat under a vine-covered pergola on this hot summer evening. Jeff Carlisle ordered a Margarita. I had seen him drink those before and I thought, "what the hell, I'll have one too. Jeff leaned back and told an amusing story about his wife, Janice. Jeff and Jan did their personal banking at the Yoakum County Bank in Denver City, Texas. Jan, a very pretty blond gal, went to cash a check in Albuquerque. The clerk looked at Jan, then the name of the bank, and said. "Daisy Mae, I can't cash this check for you, even if Lil' Abner signs it too. Out of state check you know, this ain't Dog Patch."

By this time Sammy Spikes had consumed several beers and was feeling no pain. Truth be told we were all feeling quite jovial. It was at this time Spikes told us how he was going to make his fortune. "I'm gonna buy me a piece of desert land out there by Lubbock, get an inflated appraisal, borrow a bunch on it, then do it again and again till I got a million bucks, sorta like that ole boy Ponzi in the 1920s, ya'll know. Then I'll buy my own bank."

We all laughed heartily, especially the humorous and playful, Sammy. We did not know how prophetic this story would be. Even Stan Braun, a crusty, cocky, crew cut guy from San Antonio, who didn't typically share Sammy's off the wall sense of humor, laughed. Stan was more at ease talking about the glories and wonders of Texas! He could be the stereotypical Texas blowhard, although at heart I discovered he was a pretty decent fellow.

"Stan, while were down here lets you, Rod and I drive up to Hatch and catch that bank, while Sammy, Jeff, and Dennis finish the Las Cruces report," I said.

The First National Bank of Hatch was tiny, the smallest National Bank in the state with only a couple of million in deposits. The bank was a neat sand colored brick building. There wasn't much work, since the bank had few loans, a small installment department for cars, trucks and farm machinery, and a remarkable portfolio of operating loans to Pima Cotton farmers. These operating loans were booked in March, then advances were made during the farming season until harvest, then they all were paid in full in the fall. I mean every damned loan zeroed out! If an examiner had been in there in January, the bank would have no loans. Our visit was in July, so the loans were within three-fourths of their peak. They were superbly documented. As Stan put it, "We were in and out of there like a thief in the night."

A few weeks earlier, Mr. Thomas asked for a volunteer to teach at the O.C.C.'s school for newly appointed Assistant National Bank Examiners. This annual happening was to be held in Dallas, Texas at facilitates offered to us by The First National Bank in Dallas. This year the instructors from the three Regions were: Harold Hackstock, the office administrator, from The Tenth Region out of Kansas City; Jerry Dunn, a Field Examiner like me, from Eleventh Region headquartered in Dallas, and myself representing Region Twelve. Our students were from the same three regions, which gave us a suitable class size of 25 students. Our job was to teach these new hires the basic things they need to know in the field. By this time, per Mr. Saxon's mandate, only college graduates would do. Actually, working in a real live bank wasn't much of a qualification in the New World of National Banking. Mr. Saxon was a fancy Chicago lawyer, who had neither appreciation nor proper respect for people, who have learned by practical experience; rather he was impressed by university degrees.

It is amazing how little a college education teaches a student of practical use. One guy I especially remember was Igor Chevonovich, who informed us at least once a day that he had a Master's Degree in Economics and counting cash, reconciling correspondent bank accounts, preparing investment schedules, reviewing Income and Dividend, Call reports, verifying bank balance sheets, were far beneath his dignity. Unfortunately, these were the tasks he was required to do on the job. But his majesty, Crown Prince Chevonovich, refused to take even a remote interest in the class and sat sullenly through the whole two weeks staring at us, after all he was the one with the Master's Degree.

Another curious member of the class was a fellow named Ed Cook from Arizona.

Ed fell asleep in class, which, I admit, could be a little dry. I think the real problem for Ed was that he was having a great time enjoying the nightlife in Dallas. One day I threw a piece of chalk at him and hit him squarely on the noggin. He jumped up and yelled, "What, what the hell is going on?"

"Why Ed, I knew you wouldn't want to miss this exciting talk about call reports," I replied, mustering all my efforts to resist joining the rest of the class in laughter.

In all fairness to Ed, he did turn out to be a decent assistant examiner. Unlike his highness Mr. Chevonovich, who was fired after he proved he wasn't even capable of the simplest duties of an Assistant National Bank Examiner.

Of the other two instructors, Harold Hackstock was a different kind of guy. Harold was a kind of "fuddy-duddy" 50-year-old bachelor. Harold had held the National Bank Examiner mantle long before I became an assistant back in 1961. I had met him when I worked out of Mr. Ross's Kansas City Office. Harold's job was reviewing reports as they came in, making sure all the numbers added up, making the t's crossed and i's dotted. The astonishing thing about Harold was he had never actually gone into a bank as the Examiner-In-Charge. His perspective was entirely from the viewpoint of turning in the perfect report to send on to Washington. Nevertheless, he did bring useful insight to the table, if not for the class, than Jerry and I. The Dallas instructor, Jerry Dunn, had previously worked in Salt Lake, so I knew him slightly from visits to First Security and Zions, "The Bank of Mormon", if you prefer.

Jerry and I had earned our commissions about the same time and spent several lunches and evenings swapping stories. One day on our way out to lunch, we passed through First National's modern, high ceiling lobby with its great white marble columns. Standing in the middle were two gentlemen. Jerry recognized Robert Stewart, the chairman and C.E.O. of the First National Bank in Dallas.

Jerry says to me, "Let me introduce you to Bob Stewart."

Mr. Stewart immediately recognized Jerry and shook hands with both of us, as Jerry introduced me. Turning to the elegantly dressed gentleman standing next to him, he says, "You all know Dave."

The gent was David Rockefeller, then the globetrotting chairman of Chase Manhattan Bank of New York City. Yeah right, like a couple of bumpkins from Wyoming and Texas would likely know David Rockefeller. I was so stunned I didn't know what to say and neither did the gregarious Jerry Dunn. Mr. Rockefeller was cordial enough, but seemed intent on his business with Bob Stewart and we left for lunch. It was fun meeting "Dave".

After my tenure as an instructor, I returned to New Mexico. George Lowry from Clinton, Oklahoma had joined our crew. George had recently graduated from the University of Oklahoma, with a Business Finance major. He was soft spoken and had a distinctive western Oklahoma accent. H-e t-a-l-k-e-d s-o s-l-o-w-l-y. His accent is forever etched in my mind as how an Oklahoman should talk. Sammy Spikes had earned his commission as a national bank examiner so the crew could now be divided to perform two examinations at once. One of the split crew jobs I drew was the American National Bank of Silver City.

Silver City was nestled in the mountains and, as the name suggests, was a mining community. The American National bank was managed by Rhodes Scholar Frank Wright. Mr. Wright, was of average height with a great mane of gray. He dressed in tweed with leather patches on his arms. He was a very bright gentleman who looked more like a college professor than a banker. The first thing I noticed was the bank's commercial note form, printed on yellow-gold paper; the notes called for payment in U.S. gold coin. Mr. Wright was obviously a frugal and conservative fellow to be using these note forms, after all the common use of gold coins was abolished by the Roosevelt administration.

The bank was quite clean, most of its assets were in U. S. Treasury securities with orderly maturities out to 5 years. Mr. Wright explained to me that he always bought deep discounted bonds to insure a gain in his securities account, which made up 85% of the bank's assets. The small loan portfolio was a mixture of installment loans, local real estate mortgages, and a few choice commercial loans. Choice with the exception of a $10,000 note to "Los Pinos Altos Mining Company", which was a real stinker. The company, had claimed mining properties worth $2,000,000. By the time we arrived, the mining claims had proved to be bogus according Mr. Wright. The file was devoid of any useful information, except for the balance sheet boasting of the grossly overvalued mineral rights. Mr. Wright was waiting for our arrival to charge off the loan for fear the Internal Revenue Service would question a total voluntary write off. Rod, George and I quickly put the report together and had some time to explore Tyrone.

We drove out to the copper mine, which had been closed for many years due to uneconomical copper prices. It was in effect a ghost town with the most beautiful deserted art deco, circa 1920's shopping mall. It had apparently been the company store, in this case stores, for Phelps-Dodge employees, whose row after row of empty, identical, company houses sat beyond the mall overlooking the great open pit mine. The mall itself was done in exquisite, pictorial tiles in a full range of pastel colors. It was quite a site as we imagined what this must of looked during the roaring 20s when copper prices were high. We were able to make it back to Albuquerque early Friday afternoon for the weekend, where I was in for a pleasant surprise.

This Saturday in late August was sunny and hot. I decided to amble down to the swimming pool, for a cooling dip, and perhaps a conversation with one of the lovely ladies in residence at 1200 Madeira Ave. SE. As it happened, there was just one shapely, blue eyed, blond gal, in a blue bathing suit. I had noticed her, a time or two before. She had always been accompanied by a bleached blond chatterbox. But now she was alone; I started a conversation and introduced myself.

She was a first grade teacher and proved to be easy and interesting to talk with. We quickly discovered we had a lot in common. We liked a lot of the same things: books, activities, including skiing, my favorite winter sport, and dogs. We discovered our parents even owned Sealyham Terriers, a rather scarce Scottish breed. After talking for three hours, we were both sunburned and I asked Mary Cramer out for dinner that evening. She said. "Give me an hour to shower, change and make a couple of phone calls."

We went out to eat at a charming, adobe Mexican restaurant in Old Town, called La Placita. The ambiance and food and atmosphere were great; I'd recommend it to you. Mary's company proved to be even better. From this date forward, Mary and I spent the better part of each weekend together, although once in while Steve and I would go flying, when Mary had personal things to do.

During the winter we went skiing virtually every weekend. By the middle of January we were skiing Santa Fe Basin. On the last run of the day, as it was getting dark, Mary lost her balance on the steep slope, trying to make a sharp turn and broke her leg. We were planning on having dinner with her parents, Dr. and Mrs. Cramer. I had met Mary's family once, on Thanksgiving, when they graciously invited me to have dinner with them. Since it was dark by the time the ski patrol had brought Mary down from the mountain and put a splint on her leg, we were quite late when we arrived at the Cramer's home. Mary stayed in the car, as I knew she needed to go to the hospital to get the leg x-rayed, and getting out would be added pain for her. I rang the doorbell and Mrs. Cramer answered. She said cheerfully, "We wondered when the ambulance would arrive."

Embarrassed I explained briefly the afternoon's accident. By this time Dr. Cramer was at the door and said, "I'll meet you at the emergency room at Bataan and we'll get Mary's leg fixed up."

Bataan Memorial Hospital is connected to the Lovelace Clinic, where Dr. Cramer was one of the senior physicians. Mary insisted on enduring the pain while the nurse removed her ski pants instead of cutting them off, since they were brand new. A testament to her strength of character, I thought. The break proved to be a hairline fracture and healed quickly. By 9:30 we were back at the Cramer's home, which oddly enough reminded me of my parent's home. I was quite nervous and feeling guilty, as I had urged Mary to make the last run of the day, which is often when ski accidents happen. Dr. Cramer looked at me and said. "Bert, you look like you could use a martini!"

Of course the good doctor was right; in fact we both had a couple. Mary's mom broiled some steaks and we had pleasant evening, or what was left of it. I became comfortable with Mary's family and I believe they with me. Mary's mom had a behemoth sized Plymouth station wagon, which had an automatic transmission. She lent it to Mary, since operating the clutch with her left foot in cast would be a problem driving Mary's V.W. Beetle. Typical, Mary, though she didn't like driving mama's bus, quickly figured out how to operate the clutch by hand using a cane.

My career as an examiner continued with my personal life, I was off to examine the First National Bank of Roswell, which was a good-sized bank in 1966. The President of the bank was J. C. Powell, an amiable Texan, in spite of his Texas bravado. He greeted us with a smile. Since the previous OCC visit the bank had purchased over two million dollars-worth of second mortgage paper from Blue Sky Developers, a Dallas real estate developer, who were buddies of Mr. Powell. The Bank took about two weeks to complete. As I neared the time to review the loans with Mr. Powell, I received a call from my boss, Mr. Thomas.

Mr. Thomas told me that Washington had some information concerning the principals of the Texas developer, indicating that they were rather unsavory characters. The loans themselves were all paying according to the terms of the note, which were extra generous, since there was virtually no equity and the source of the cash flow wasn't documented. Mr. Powell and I agreed on a mild "Special Mention" classification. I considered a more severe Substandard Classification, but remembered Van and P.T.'s adage. "If the loan is really bad, it will be there next examination." Mr. Powell didn't seem particularly concerned and was able to talk intelligently about the bank's various problems. I wrapped up the report and sent it to Mr. Thomas.

My next assignment was to do a charter investigation for a new National Bank in Socorro. Socorro is quaint little town with the central business district in the form of a town square, with adobe like buildings and a partially covered sidewalk, reminiscent of the scenes from western movies depicting gunfights. As was customary, I interviewed the president of the Socorro State Bank, a small bank that seemed to be making a reasonable effort to service the community's needs. The gentleman was not enthusiastic about another bank coming to town; certainly not an unusual reaction. What did surprise me was he didn't know the organizers.

The organizers spokesman and agent was Mr. Harvey Sullivan, a large blustery man with a pox marked face from Clovis, New Mexico. As a means of breaking the conversational ice with Mr. Sullivan, I mentioned that I had recently bought a new Ford Mustang from the Ford dealer in Clovis while examining the Clovis National Bank, managed by Joe Sisler, who I liked and thought to be a an able banker. Mr. Sisler was also the Democratic Party Chairman for Curry County. Mr. Sullivan, also an avid Democrat, launched into an emotional lambasting of Mr. Keller. "God damn Joe Sisler is a no good, dirty rotten, son-of- a-bitch!"

Unable to image what Mr. Sisler had done to deserve such a vile outburst, I meekly asked, "What is your grievance with Joe Sisler?"

Sullivan burst forth with, "Why, the rat is so dammed honest, he won't even stuff a ballot box to deliver Curry County to the party."

Funny, Mr. Sisler's honesty was one the virtues I liked most about him. The investigation went downhill from there and I recommend a turn down for the new bank charter application, Mr. Sullivan's application was also turned down in Democratic Washington as well. As I was writing my Socorro report, I received another phone call from Mr. Thomas. "Bert, I have some bad news. Van has some kind of cancer and has requested a transfer to Denver to be near his doctors and his son, Jerry, who lives in the Denver area. I need to transfer you back to Wyoming."

"Whoa, just as I was getting used to the guys and the banks. I even have a wonderful girlfriend here," I said and paused a minute, then continued, "Well, I guess I'm a company man and I do love Wyoming. How soon?"

"First of May," Mr. Thomas said.

Mr. Thomas wasn't done yet. "Also, I need to have you reopen the First National Bank of Roswell examination. Coey Eggertson in Washington has some more information on the "Blue Sky Development Company." I want you to re-exam those second mortgage loans, based on Coey's new information. I'm thinking they should be classified doubtful."

"Doubtful? That amounts to a technical charge-off of over a third of their capital," I said.

"Right, I've already sent the report to your office, so you take one assistant with you and reopen the examination. I'll make arrangements to fly down there Thursday and we'll have a full board meeting. I especially want Mr. Fielding there. He is the bank's biggest stockholder and has the most to lose. There is airline service into Roswell, isn't there?" Mr. Thomas said.

"OK, I'll set it up. Mr. Thomas, I believe Roswell is served by two regional airlines, Solar and T.T.A., that's Trans Texas," I said.

Mr. Thomas said, "I recall Gamble called it Tinker Toy Airlines."

"Everyone down here calls T.T.A. Tinker Toy Airlines, they fly a lot of DC 3s and other prop driven planes for shorter runs." I chuckled a little, glad Mr. Thomas hadn't lost his sense of humor.

As I drove back to Albuquerque, I thought mainly about Mary, much more pleasant than the Roswell situation. I decided to pop the question as soon as I got home. Mary and I went out to supper that evening. The first thing I did was propose. Even though her foot was still in a cast, she accepted. She said laughing, "My mother said you would marry me after you broke my leg."

We both laughed. Saturday we went to Fogg's Jewelry, Mary's favorite store at the Winrock Mall. We were waited on by Donald Fogg, who was one of the owners and a neighbor of Mary's folks. We selected rings. That evening we went to see the latest Matt Helm movie starring Dean Martin at the Sunshine Theater in Albuquerque. I was particularly interested in seeing the movie because it was filmed in Santa Fe while the boys and I were examining the Santa Fe National Bank the previous summer. We stayed at the Inn of the Governors, a Downtowner Motel, where many of the crew making the movie were staying and we had a few drinks with the gripper, cameramen and others. The stars, of course, had more elegant quarters.

The movie was entertaining and seemed be enjoyed by the audience, but what really brought down the house was when Matt Helm, played by Dean Martin, relaxing in his traditional Spanish styled Santa Fe home, is asked why he is planning a trip to Mexico. Matt Helm's answer: "Because I like Mexicans"

You do not need to leave Santa Fe to see Mexicans. The movie viewers roared with laughter. I couldn't help but wonder if the line even got a titter in other venues like New York and the rest of the east coast. Rested and relaxed, I was ready to tackle Roswell.

Much to my surprise, Mr. Powell was just as gracious, pleasant and cooperative as the previous visit, even with the disagreeable task we had before us. He immediately contacted his board and got Mr. Fielding, the bank's principal stockholder, to come in. Mr. Fielding was a very tall gaunt man in his 60s, with a craggy, unsmiling face, black hair with just a few flecks of white. He looked scary to me, but was polite, gracious, and candid. I revised the report and disturbing findings based on the added information. I became increasingly nervous about the board showdown and Mr. Thomas' impending visit. I felt like I had a real bomb on my hands, since the report results would seriously impair the bank's capital and the meeting had the potential for verbal fireworks. At noon Rod and I went over to a cafeteria a couple of blocks from the bank for lunch. My stomach was cramped, hurting and rumbling; I needed to sit down and do some serious business to relieve my discomfort.

The men's room didn't have privacy stalls; however, I wasn't in a position to be picky. As I my bowels were erupting, when this 70-year-old codger, with a raspy voice walks in and wants to visit. "Son, what are you doing in Roswell? What do you do for a living?"

I suppose my necktie, clued the old boy into the fact I wasn't a local. I replied, "I'm a National Bank Examiner."

He says, "You must be an assistant examiner. You look like you just graduated from high school."

I let go with a great blast and turned to this unwelcome intruder. "As it happens I am the Examiner-in-Charge."

The old fart says, "You can't be, you don't look old enough."

I turned to him and said in triumph. "It ain't how old you are, it's how smart you are."

Finally, he shook his head and left. Although I had several other things on my mind, it struck me that, the senile old busybody hadn't taken care of his own business. I hoped he peed in his pants!

That afternoon Mr. Thomas arrived at the Roswell Municipal Airport on a TTA DC-3, and got off the plane, smiling from ear to ear. What the hell is he so God damned happy about? I wondered. He greeted Rod and I warmly and we all piled into my red GT Mustang Fastback. Lucky, Rod was limber enough to fit in the back seat, with Mr. Thomas' overnight bag.

"Why are you smiling?" I asked.

Mr. Thomas said, "I just love those old "goony birds." Flew in them during the war. Thought I would never get to fly in one again."

Since we were dealing with wheeler-dealer Texans, I told Mr. Thomas my Dad's story about the plane with 50 Texans flying into LaGuardia Airport in New York. The pilot calls the tower for landing clearance. The tower comes back and says, "I need you to circle, were backed up."

The pilot comes back and says, "Look I have 50 Texans aboard, were coming in from Dallas and I'm low on fuel."

The tower comes back, "That can't be; DC-3s only carry, max, 25 passengers. You're way over loaded."

Pilot says, "No I'm not over loaded, but I am running low on fuel."

Tower comes back, "OK, you are cleared to land on runway 33. I'll have the emergency equipment to greet you and I'll come down in person. I gotta see this."

The pilot makes a perfect, smooth landing and taxis over to the gate. The tower controller watches as 50 midgets walk off the plane, with the pilot right behind them.

The Tower operator says to the pilot, "Where the hell did you find 50 midgets in Dallas?"

To which the pilot replies, "These guys are just regular sized Texans with all the hot air squeezed out of them."

The story set a relaxed mood for the meal that followed. At dinner we discussed the plan for tomorrow's board meeting. "Bert, I want you to go through your findings, just like you did in Gillette. What I want these jokers to do is to find a way to get the 'Blue Sky Development' loans out of the bank. Hopefully, Fielding and Powell are in Republic's good graces. They have the bank stock loan on First of Roswell's shares."

The meeting went off as scheduled and Mr. Thomas allowed me to make my presentation, without interruption. He sat and nodded agreement. Finally, after I finished, he re- emphasized the highlights of my report. Mr. Powell and Mr. Fielding, gracious and calm as ever, promised to get matters straightened out. They would be dealing with Mr. Thomas directly until the next examination. I drove Mr. Thomas to the airport. On the way I asked Mr. Thomas about getting married on June 11th.

Mr. Thomas smiled and replied. "Bert, you don't need to ask my permission to get married." There was a pause, then he continued, smiling. "Sure, you may have the time off."

I had been in New Mexico exactly one year.

Nine

Changes and Opportunities

While Mary and her mom planned the wedding in Albuquerque, I found myself driving Mary's pale pea green Volkswagen Beetle on the 800-mile trek from New Mexico to Casper to make my arrival time of May 1, 1966. The VW's lack of power was especially noticeable as I drove north out of Medicine Bow, location of the Virginian Hotel, center of the action in Owen Wister's book "The Virginian". The barren country, which only sheep, antelope, and rabbits could survive on, rises, as I arrived at the top of Shirley Rim. I found myself down shifting and unable to maintain even 50 miles per hour. No doubt I was missing the fun and great performance of my V-8 power- packed Mustang. In spite of the VW's slowness, I have always enjoyed the solitude and naked, untouched beauty of this open range part of Wyoming.

During the year I had been in New Mexico, Ted Ernst had received his commission and had married Alice Larson, an elementary school teacher. In addition, with the exception of Verne Sorheim, all the crewmembers were new. Ted and Alice had us over to their apartment for dinner, the weekend Mary flew up to look over the housing situation. Since Alice and Mary were both elementary school teachers, they hit it off immediately. Mary and I had decided to purchase a home, since we were expecting to live in Casper for several years.

On the way north, I had spent a night with my folks. To my surprise, Dad reached into his desk drawer and gave me two $1000 U.S. Treasury bearer bonds. They had been there for a few years, judging from Dad's scramble to find them. I was struck by the oddity that my father and mother, who were conservative and secretive about financial matters, would have totally negotiable U. S. Treasury Bonds lying in an unlocked desk drawer. Dad insisted we use the proceeds for the down payment on a house.

Mary liked the idea of buying, so we spent Saturday looking at various houses in our price bracket. We stopped at one well-kept house, which was for sale by owner. The owner was wheezing badly, as he puffed on his cigarette. He explained to us he was moving to Arizona to relieve his asthma and emphysema. I was tempted to open my big mouth and suggest quitting smoking. This particular house smelled like someone or something had died in it, which turned us off. We did find a home on a one-acre lot in an area adjacent to the City of Casper, called Allendale. It was about eight blocks from my cousin Bill Harris, who also lived on the same street, but within the city limits. We were quite excited about our first home. The trip gave Mary some comfort about moving to the wilds of Wyoming.

By the time of Mary's Casper visit, the invitations had gone out and I received a response from my old Oklahoma bank examiner buddy, Frank Hess. We had pledged we would attend each other's wedding. But this wasn't to be, as Frank and his bride were scheduled to marry on the same day as Mary and I. By this time Frank had taken a job as President of the Bank of Excelsior Springs, Missouri, a Kansas City suburb.

The wedding took place at St. Mark's Episcopal Church, block or so from the Cramer's home. Both of my grandmothers were there. My grandfather Kempe, age 86, was in failing health and decided against the trip. Mary's grandparents Loren and Clara Cramer from Ponca City, Oklahoma also came. My brother Frank served as my best man. Mary's twin brother John, described by Mary as her womb mate, was joined by his wife Martha, who was one of the bridesmaids. Mary's younger brother, Dick, had just graduated from New Mexico Military Academy. I learned Dick had been chauffeuring Mary around in my Mustang. I couldn't be mad at him, after all the Mustang was an absolute hoot to drive and Dick no doubt enjoyed it as much as I did. Dick, John, and Steve Negler, my flying buddy, were the groom's men and ushers.

The wedding was a joyous occasion. My relatives mixed well with Mary's family. The funniest picture was of Mary feeding me a piece of the wedding cake. I had managed to lose my lunch from nervousness and by the time we got around to cutting and eating the wedding cake, all I had consumed since breakfast was champagne. Well, I was feeling little pain but was quite happy. I had parked my shining red Mustang in a downtown parking ramp and rented an Oldsmobile sedan for the wedding. This way, the guests had a car to decorate, paint up and tie tin cans to. Mr. Hertz had the task of cleaning up the mess.

Our honeymoon consisted of a tour of several National Parks. First stop was the Grand Canyon, where we got up late and couldn't get any breakfast. All we could get was apple pie a la mode and thus the first tradition in our marriage: apple pie a la mode on our anniversaries. Then we traveled up through Brice and Zion National Parks in Utah. From Zions we headed north to Wyoming and Grand Teton and Yellowstone National Parks and home to Casper.

On one of the first weekends after we settled into our home, while we were having a romantic interlude in the afternoon, the doorbell rang. Mary and I called it our "Mormon Cocktail", since we presumed the non-drinking Mormons would have a little romance in lieu of a cocktails. At the door were our friends, Ted and Alice Ernst, with a wedding gift for us. We got up, dressed quickly, haphazardly and answered the door, since we were at this point just enjoying each other's company. The gift was a fire extinguisher, which seemed appropriate at the time.

Luckily, Mary was able to travel with me that first summer and I was able to show Mary my favorite state of Wyoming and get paid for it too. One of the new guys on our crew was Bart Neville. He and his wife Pat had also recently married: Pat also traveled with Bart. Mary and Pat were able to spend the days sightseeing, while Bart and I worked. We were fortunate in our assignments that summer as well. One of our first assignments was a charter investigation for a new national bank in Jackson, Wyoming, surely one of the most beautiful places in America.

It was not my first charter investigation in Jackson. Eighteen months earlier, I had investigated a proposed new bank in the middle of winter. I remember vividly, driving in a snowstorm over Togowatee Pass, a few miles behind the snowplow, with my head out the window for better visibility. The proposed organizers apparently had some mob connections, according to the Washington Office. They also lacked local participation. In the end the charter was denied. The skiing was great so the winter trip wasn't a total waste.

The organizers took Bart and I on a helicopter tour of the Jackson Hole, which was quite spectacular. After that we couldn't deny Mary and Pat a similar ride. The Grand Tetons rise to 13,500 feet above sea level, 7500 feet from the valley floor, with Jackson Lake and Grand Teton Lodge in the foreground. Wildlife including moose and the National Elk Refugee, with some 600 elk grazing in the lush green pasturelands live in the Jackson Hole valley.

One of the most interesting things about the trip was one of the organizers I got to know fairly well, Abi Garaman. Mr. Garaman was a first cousin of the Shah of Iran. He looked quite a bit like him too. Garaman had attended U.C.L.A. and met his wife there. Mrs. Garaman was a Jackson native, whose family owned a Western Clothing store on the "square" in Jackson. Abi joined in the family business and went on to establish several enterprises of his own.

Mr. Garaman's family, the Royal Family of Iran, was mystified by Abi's decision to become a U.S. citizen and live in Jackson, Wyoming, which had a population of perhaps 3000. The grandeur of Jackson Hole is evident in pictures, but it is not the same as actually being there. Abi's family lived in something of a goldfish bowl and took delight in "being someone important". They chided Abi about being a nobody in the U.S. Abi assured them he enjoyed his station in the U.S. and to demonstrate that he was known in the America he prepared a post card addressed only: "Abi", Jackson Hole, U.S.A." and mailed it from Tehran. When he arrived home in Jackson, the card was waiting for him. He mailed it back to his family in Iran. The family decided that he was somebody in the U.S. and supported his decision.

Another fun place we visited that summer was Dubois, Wyoming, just 80 miles east Jackson. George Blevin's Dubois National Bank was an easy shop. The Denver office always allowed more time than we needed, so we had time to enjoy ourselves. Dubois had a good summer stock theater and we happened to catch Peter Fonda in a western spoof one night. We were there for three nights and each night we visited the Rustic Bar, which had a good price for happy hour drinks and free post cards to boot. Each day we mailed Mary's brother Dick a picture card of the bar. Every day, our handwriting became more uncontrolled, as though were spending our entire time in Dubois getting sloshed at the bar. I don't know if Dick thought it was as funny as we did, but we had a good time.

After Dubois we made a trip to Gillette and the First National Bank; Ray Saunders and Doug Krogh had done an excellent job of turning the bank into a success. Mary and Pat made a day trip to Devil's Tower another one of Wyoming's scenic wonders. Otherwise, I don't suppose Gillette was that much fun for the girls. As fall approached, Mary was notified that she had been accepted for a second grade teaching position at the Wherry School in Casper. Just before school started Mary and I decided to have a party for the crew.

Two new men had joined the crew over the summer; Patrick Sharpe, a dislocated Texan, and Don James, a Casper native. The weather was beautiful for the event and we had a little barbeque on our patio. Although we knew Sorheim, the Ernsts and the Nevilles and, of course, the team members, the spouses and girlfriends of the new guys were new to us. So the first order of etiquette was introductions. Pat Sharpe and his wife were quite gregarious and immediately Mrs. Sharpe introduces herself: "Hi, I'm Sharon Sharpe."

Don James' girlfriend, smiling and extending her hand, says, "Hi, and I'm Sharon Sharper."

We were flabbergasted and at first thought it was a joke. After all, what are the odds? Once we realized that Sharon Sharper was really her name, we all had a spirited laugh. It got the evening off to a festive start. It was good to know I had such a compatible crew to look forward to working with them.

Mary started her teaching duties the last week in August and I was once more on the road. We were both dog lovers and thought a dog would be good company and offer Mary some measure of protection, too. One weekend in October, we visited my family in Boulder and we decided to look for a dog, preferably a large dog, in Denver. On Saturday evening we got a copy of the Denver Post, Sunday Edition, and searched the classified ads for possible dogs. There were several St. Bernards and one Newfoundland. We made some calls and prepared a circular route around Denver to look at the canines.

As it happened the first stop was the Newfoundland. The dog's name was Brutus and he was about a year old and housebroken. Brutus was a magnificent specimen, everything and more dog books say a Newfy should be. We both fell for this black, large, docile giant and bought him on the spot. Brutus seemed to take to us immediately, and willingly piled into the back of the Mustang, filling both rear seats. On the way back to Boulder, we stopped to see the Van Dykes, who were living in Arvada.

The Van Dykes hadn't met Mary and, although I had talked to Van on the phone a few times I hadn't actually seen him since my return from New Mexico. They sent us a very nice silver tray for a wedding present and Mary was curious to meet them. Van and Leta were glad to see us. Van had lost quite a bit of weight since I had last seen him 16 months earlier, but considering, how ill he was, seemed to be in good spirits. While Leta and Mary got acquainted, Van and I talked as Van petted Brutus. Van suggested that I come down for dinner if I was working in Cheyenne or Denver, should the opportunity present itself.

We continued our journey and had dinner with my folks in Boulder, who, both being dog fanciers, were interested in meeting Brutus. Then we took off for Casper, again with Brutus filling both back seats. We arrived in Casper by 11:30 and prepared a sleeping spot for Brutus and then went to bed ourselves. As we lay in bed I asked Mary, "Have you noticed something odd about Brutus?"

Concerned Mary replied, "What do mean?"

I said. "He hasn't let out a peep since we acquired him this morning."

Before Mary had a chance to respond, Brutus let out a loud "woof". Just one woof, to let us know he was in good working order. Brutus, with his heavy, black, hairy coat, was an outdoor dog and once we got to know him, we realized he preferred to sleep outside, preferably on a pile of snow, if one was available. Yet he quickly realized his job was to be Mary's protector. On his own, he decided to sleep next to Mary's bed while I was on the road.

When I was home on weekends or working in town, he would sleep in the yard. He was a very smart animal and was easy to teach, although he often figured out his proper place by himself, without prompting from us.

The first time Mary and I sat down for a before dinner martini, Brutus tried to climb up in Mary's lap. Mary weighed about 125 pounds and Brutus' weight 165. Mary placed her hand to a spot beside her, next to the couch and Brutus was never on the furniture again. He would allow the neighborhood children to on our driveway during the day with nothing more than a wagging tail. After dark no one passed and of course, he was big enough to be respected. The kids never challenged his authority.

As winter approached Mary and I started skiing at Hogadon Ski Area on Casper Mountain, just 15 minutes from the house. It occurred to me that we might enjoy a weekend skiing at the Antelope Butte Ski Area, 35 miles east of Greybull. I had heard it was an excellent ski hill, with nice dry snow and a much greater vertical drop than Hogadon. One Friday afternoon in mid-December, on the way back to Casper from Powell, I decided to stop in to visit with Gerry Williams at The First National Bank of Greybull, who, I had discovered was not only the bank's president but also an avid skier. Mr. Williams was at his desk and fortunately wasn't tied up with a customer. I said, "Gerry, you told me that you skied Antelope Butte frequently. I thought you might be able to tell me what the ski conditions might be like."

Mr. Williams replied, "Not real good yet, we need a really good snow for the best skiing. Say, do you have a few minutes?"

"Sure," I said, "I'm not in a big hurry."

Gerry said, "Good, let's go downstairs to visit."

We walked downstairs. The lounge was empty. He poured us each a cup of coffee, finishing off the pot. We sat down and started to talk.

He looked at me and said, "You've made half a dozen examinations here and I am impressed. You seem to know your banking. I have a heart condition and my doctor has suggested that I don't need the stress of running the bank."

I looked at him. He certainly, looked more like a much younger man. I knew he was physically active, enjoyed skiing, hunting and golf. Moreover, he looked fit, probably close to the ideal weight for his 5' 8" frame with more pepper, than salt, in his hair. I was surprised by the revelation.

Mr. Williams continued, "You have a connection to this community with your Granddad coming to Basin, about the time my dad came to Greybull. Anyway, what I'm getting to is I'd like to sell you this bank."

I was stunned. "Well, I can't exactly, write you a check for it."

Gerry laughed. "Oh, I know that. What I had in mind was to sell it to you over a period of time. Here's the deal, If you raise $100,000, we'll enter into a deal where your financing institution would lend you money against the stock you buy. I'll give you the right to buy the rest of my shares, so as to keep control together. That right would be assignable to your lender. I own 60%. I'll fix the price at year-end 1967. I'm not in a big hurry, give you time to round up some money."

"Wow, I wasn't expecting this. Funny, I just came into find out about ski conditions. I need to talk to Mary, and get a handle on financing. I'm definitely interested, "I said.

"Tell you what, talk to your wife, a correspondent bank or two. Then sometime in January you and Mary come on up, we'll go skiing, have dinner and see what we can put together." Gerry said.

We shook hands and I took off for Casper to discuss the deal with Mary. Mary was weary of me being on the road so much and was already thinking family. The idea of settling into a community and as a bank president was very appealing. I managed to talk to Bob Bryans and Jack King at First National Bank of Casper, which had some trust business with our family and knew both my dad and my late grandfather. They gave me a dose of encouragement and indicated a desire to work with me. We were planning to go to Albuquerque for Christmas, spending an evening in Boulder with my parents en route, so I'd have a chance to talk to them as well about financing.

Mom had fixed one of her simple, but delicious roast beef dinners. We had a couple of drinks before dinner. Afterward, we retired to Dad's favorite room, the den. He had a fire going and offered another round of drinks. Mom and I declined, but he fixed himself a strong looking bourbon and water. I outlined Mr. William's proposition. Both Mom and Dad seemed to be listening attentively. However, Dad was uncharacteristically silent. Mom asked a number of astute questions including, "How much money do you kids have to put into this venture?"

I responded, "Mary and I have something over $15,000."

Mother was astounded. "I thought you were examining banks, not robbing them."

I smiled and said, "Well, since Wyoming and New Mexico are both districts where an examiner is on the road 80-90 percent of the time, I was able to save my salary and live on my per diem. I invested and had some good fortune in the stocks I bought. With the mileage allowance we get and the high usage, I received enough reimbursement to keep myself in new cars too. I paid cash for the Mustang."

My frugal mother was truly impressed: in those days you could buy a nice house almost anywhere for $15,000. In fact that was the amount we paid for our house in Casper, although we did have a 5.25% mortgage against it. The following morning at breakfast, it was clear that Dad hadn't remembered the previous evening's conversation at all. Absolutely zilch! As we prepared to leave for Albuquerque, Mom walked us to the car and said, "If you kids have saved $15,000 to put in this bank deal, your father and I will back you. I will handle your father. Count on it!"

Relieved that my folks were going to back us, we drove on to New Mexico. Shortly after our arrival at Mary's folk's home we got into one of those "what's new" conversations. We explained in general terms the deal with Gerry Williams and The First National Bank of Greybull. I had no intention of asking for in-law participation. However, after we explained the proposal, Dr. and Mrs. Cramer looked at each other and said, "We'd like to help."

We had a nice Christmas holiday, with the exception of one minor blemish. It turned out that beneath the bed we were sharing, was the Cramer's Sealyham, Top's favorite hideout. I had managed to accidentally drop a pair of rolled socks under the bed. As I reached under the bed to retrieve my socks Top bit my hand without any warning. It hurt like crazy. I guess he wasn't as friendly as I thought.

As we drove north we stopped in Boulder. Mom had handled the situation with Dad. Dad promised we could borrow $10,000 from Grandfather Harris's Trust; plus Dad said he and Mom would buy some additional shares. Armed with this news I revisited Bob Bryans and Jack King and explained our situation. Of the $100,000 Gerry required down, we would only need to borrow $55,000. In those days prime was about 5%; not too painful, so we were ready to get back to Greybull to see Gerry Williams.

On a cold, clear weekend in January we went up to Greybull, spent a couple of days skiing and had an excellent steak dinner at Bluejacket's, a picturesque log structure overlooking Shell Creek at the mouth of Shell Canyon. I explained to Mr. and Mrs. Williams the financing we had been able to arrange and the Casper bank's willingness to work with us. The First National Bank of Greybull was already doing business with the Casper bank and Gerry knew Bob Bryans and Jack King quite well. As the deal progressed, Mr. Williams agreed to throw in the small insurance agency he owned, which Mrs. Williams managed on a part time basis. It was a great weekend and we were excited that things were coming together. Monday morning, it was back to work and off to Cheyenne.

We were examining The First National Bank & Trust Company in Cheyenne. It was a shop that typically took two weeks; it was an old guard, fuddy-duddy bank that in some respects was a throwback to earlier times. The bank's president was Robert Dubois, referred to behind his back as "Mr. Dubious". In most respects he was very conservative; he was also a pleasant enough man and treated us cordially. The bank had more loan problems than one might have expected given the low loan to deposit ratio, strong capitalization, and reserved attitude towards lending. Rather than make many consumer loans for cars, appliances and home improvements, the bank preferred to make loans to finance companies.

Finance company loans are not categorically bad, but they do require good supervision and documentation, which was lacking. In short this was hard for the bank to evaluate its collateral and measure the performance of the loans, since they tend to be what bankers call "evergreen credits"; they don't pay down. To analyze these lines of credit the examiner must determine the quality of the finance company's loans. I noticed that Van, in the previous examination had his trademark "WW" on the line sheets for these loans. Indicating he had extra concern about the borrower. During the second week I decided to give Van a call and he, with Leta's blessing, invited me to dinner. I quit work a little earlier than usual and managed to make it to Arvada by 6:30. Van and I had one cocktail before Mrs. Van Dyke had dinner on the table. This was her way of keep Van sober for the dinner hour. Van had lost some more weight, so it was evident that the cancer was taking its' toll. Van was cheerful and didn't talk about his illness and wanted to talk about banking.

We talked a little about the First National Bank in Cheyenne, which I had in process. Van reached into his remarkable memory and credit knowledge and proceeded to tell me exactly the loans I would be classifying. I sat there in amazement, as he named every problem loan in the place. Next, I told him about the about my opportunity to go to Greybull as president. Van then made a pitch for staying with the examining force.

Van repeated his story about being the first Cashier of The Englewood State Bank in the south Denver suburb and how the bank was sold and he was then out of a job. The Comptroller's Office had been very good to him. In fact he stated that he had been on sick leave for the past eight months and had six more months to go before it was used up. Van had never, in over 20 years, taken a day of sick leave.

"Bert" he said. "You really want to think it over carefully, before quitting. Being a National Bank Examiner is a really wonderful career. Look you already have your commission. It takes some guys over 20 years to get where you are today."

I responded. "Van, Gerry is letting me buy control over a period time, so I'll end up owning the bank in a few years."

"Well, that's a totally different deal. Why the hell, didn't you say that first?" Van chuckled.

That would be the last time I would see Van. On a Monday morning three months later, I received a call from Max Paulson, Mr. Thomas's administrator, giving me the sad news that Van had died. "Bert, Mrs. Van Dyke would like you and Ted to come down and be pallbearers. I've arranged for you guys to assist Bob Jennett at the First National Bank of Denver; he has in progress, lots of work there you know."

"When is the funeral?" I asked.

Max said. "It will be Friday morning at Olinger's. Oh, kind of an aside you might want to know. Well, you know Leta is understandably quite upset and a bit of ditz. I've been helping her notify people, especially old examiners and some bankers too. Anyway, I was going through the list of who should be notified and I asked her, 'What about pallbearers?' And she says, 'We don't know anyone named Paul Bearers!'"

The funeral was well attended by examiners, a few bankers and, of course, Van's family, including his first wife, Virginia, who was employed at the First National Bank of Denver.

After lunch with Mr. Thomas, Ted and I drove back home to Casper. Ted said. "We're all going to miss Van. What you think his epitaph should read?"

I thought a minute and replied. "Charles Clifford Van Dyke, National Bank Examiner. He was very proud of his position and strove to give it everything he had."

"I don't suppose putting that inscription on his grave marker at a 45 degree angle would be appropriate." Ted responded.

By June Mary and I had all of our ducks in a row. We were ready to move to Greybull. We made a trip to Greybull to find a house. Gerald Williams had lined us up with a local realtor; it didn't take long, since there weren't a lot of choices. One house we looked at was for sale by owner. There was a slight, perhaps 5 miles per hour breeze blowing. Since we lived in Casper, where the wind blows frequently and often at gale force, we didn't think anything of it. The sellers commented that is was windy. Mary and I looked at each other and said simultaneously. "It is?"

Getting away from the Casper wind would be a benefit we would enjoy in Greybull. We bought an older, four-bedroom house, only four blocks from the bank, so I could walk to work. I was looking forward to starting work at The First National Bank of Greybull on August 1, 1967.

Ten

New Challenges

On the glorious bright and sunny morning of August 1, 1967, I began my first of many walks to The First National Bank of Greybull. Feeling quite chipper, virtually walking on air, I walked downtown to the bank. I immediately encountered a slender, erect, elderly gentlemen, who walked with a brisk step; he wore a brown Fedora hat. Of course, I had no idea who this spirited gent was. I greeted him, "Good morning, how are you sir."

The old man smiled and doffed his hat, "FIRST RATE!"

The aged gent proceeded north as I proceeded south. When I arrived at the bank, Mr. Williams showed me to a steel grey desk, next to his steel grey desk and to the right of my desk was a conference room. I said, "Gerald, before we get into introductions, I am curious, if you can tell me who I just encountered walking north on Yellowstone? An old gentleman, with a vigorous walk. I asked how he was and he answered, 'First Rate!'"

Gerry Williams smiled and said, "Oh that would be old Doc Myers, a retired dentist. He goes for his morning constitutional walk every day, pretty much every morning; he must be around 90 now. Been here for as long as I can remember."

"Sorry for the diversion, his lively manner struck me,"

"Old Doc is a regular customer, you'll see him frequently."

We walked to the desk in front of his. Jack Linderman was a slender man of 50, medium height, and a pleasant smile; he put down his pipe as he stood up. He extended his hand and we shook hands. "Welcome to Greybull," Jack said.

We visited briefly, and Jerry Holm joined the conversation. Jerry was a short blond man, about 40, with a crew cut, who exuded enthusiasm with both his mannerisms and speech.

Gerry, "Jack is on the board and is mostly a lender. Jerry is our Cashier and works with the newspaper on our ads. Come on over and meet Gracie."

I already knew all of the officers and most of the staff from prior visits as an examiner. We walked over to Grace Larson's teller station, on the bank side. Grace was a tall, strong looking farmer's wife, white haired lady of at least 65. Her cash drawer was open, as she counted out a change order a customer called in. I shook hands with her and discovered that she had a strong firm grip. "We knew you were coming today, welcome!" Grace said.

I peered into her cash drawer and there was an Army 45 Automatic pistol. Pointing to the gun, I asked, "Is it loaded?"

Grace looked at me as though that was a stupid question, "Of course it's loaded. Guns ain't no use without bullets, you know!"

I refrained from asking if she ever used it and decided to change the conversation to something different. "Grace, how long have you worked here?"

She paused for a minute to ponder the question. "Well, let me think. I remember when the bank across the street closed in 1930, so I suppose it in must have been 1928 or 1929 when I came. Yes, it was 1928."

The next teller was Jeannie Copp. "Jeannie's husband, Frank, is our Mayor. He works over at Core Chevrolet, used to work at the Greybull Elevator Company," Gerry said.

Jeanne was a portly, yet in an odd way athletic looking, 50ish lady with glasses, greying hair and engaging smile. I asked her how long she had been at the bank. "18 years in June."

The next lady was Charlene Collingwood, an attractive, full figured, sturdy, brunette with a pleasing smile and an especially infectious voice. I knew her better than the others since her father-in-law, Art Collingwood, and her husband, Don, leased a farm my Dad owned. It also struck me that she, at 34, was one of the youngest persons in bank.

The last teller in the row was Ronald Wright, age 20, who I hadn't met. Ronald was definitely the youngest member of the staff. Gerald gently, but firmly, grabbed Ronald by the arm and said, "Ron, you, Bert and I need have a little chat."

Mr. Williams sat us down in the two customer chairs facing his desk. "Bert, this is Ronald Wright, my grandson"

Ron and I exchanged glances and shook hands. Gerald continued, turning to Ron. "Ronald, from now on you will be working for Bert, your job is to please him; he will be running this bank, not me. After the annual meeting in January, I'll be playing golf in Arizona."

Mr. Williams looked at Ronald seriously, but not in an unpleasant way, and said, "I want everyone here to understand me clearly on that point."

Ronald and I nodded our assent. Ron got up and went back to his teller station. Gerald smiled at me and said, "I want Ron, and everyone, to understand that you will be the boss. Frankly, I just want to play golf, ski and hunt. I don't want to worry about the bank. You remember the conversation about titles we had on one of your visits while we were putting this deal together? You asked if I wanted to keep the president's title until you satisfied the contract terms."

I nodded my recollection of the conversation. Gerry continued, "I told you then, that I wanted you to have the President's title because you'll need it. My dad kept the title until he died six years ago, even though I have been managing this bank since old George Hinman died. Bert, take my word for it. Having the title will come in handy."

I said, "Thank you! I've thought about that conversation quite a bit. In order to show the public continuity, I was thinking you and Herman Mayland could be Co-Chairmen of the Board."

Modestly Gerald replied, "I am not much on titles, but I think your idea is a good one. I guess it would look a little funny if I demoted myself to vice president."

I was glad he liked my idea, since I didn't want to alienate Herman Mayland, a well-respected farmer, rancher and politician. Gerry continued, "I do want you to know you can call me anytime to talk things over. Come over to my house for cocktails and we can visit about anything on your mind."

Gerald got up from his desk and ushered me over to meet Marie Ward, his secretary. Marie was a slightly greying middle-aged woman, with a pleasant smile and manner. She was busy typing a letter on a manual, new appearing Royal typewriter. Gerald said, "Marie is our secretary and kind of a girl Friday assistant. She will be leaving us soon, but in the meantime feel free to have her take your dictation. I've hired her daughter, Dorothy Derryberry, to take her place. She is well trained as a secretary. I'm sure you'll find just as efficient as Marie. Dorothy is out for a few days tending to her daughter."

At about that time a weathered, tall, elderly man, wearing overalls and a straw hat. Obviously he was a man of the soil. He sat down at Gerry's desk and looked me over carefully. Apparently, he knew I was joining the bank, too. He said, "Bert Harris III, I remember you."

I had no clue who this old farmer could be.

The old gent smiled, "Your granddad was my family doctor for years. Oh, I don't suppose you remember me, I'm Frank Pierce."

The old boy grinned; even more widely and continued, "Do you remember the Old Timer's Picnic in Hyattville; must have been summer of 1946? You and your brother about drove your old granddaddy crazy chasing you two around."

He started laughing. I had to laugh too. After all, I was only eight years old at the time, I remembered the picnic, having a good time, and catching a little Rainbow trout out of Paintrock Creek. Mr. Pierce turned to Gerald to discuss his business and I decided to checkout my desk.

The desk contained the expected promissory note forms, collateral documents and a five-page type written list entitled "Shit List". I had seen in my travels as an examiner, many country banks kept such a list in order to avoid making the same mistake twice. On the left side of the page would be a name: Alfred Dunn, then to the right a comment such as: No Good, or Slow, In Prison, Took Bankruptcy, Charged Off and one I especially recall: Garrisons - All of them- no damned good!

As I sat there diving further into the contents of my desk, a balding man, who looked to be a few years my senior came in, carrying a Speed Graphic camera, and introduced himself. "Hi, I'm Bruce Kennedy from the Greybull Standard. Gerry told us you were coming today and I'd like to do a story, including a picture."

Bruce took my picture and we talked at length; he had grown up in Basin and of course knew my family very well. He was, like everyone else I met that morning, a total news flash to me. I have to admit I liked Bruce immediately, especially when I discovered he was as enthusiastic about skiing as I was. We talked for half an hour and I gave the requested information; he took a picture of me that turned out so nicely I sent a glossy copy to my folks.

I couldn't help wondering who would be coming through the door next. A little while later a forties-something gentleman in bib overalls, horn rim glasses, sat down at my desk and started talking to me. He was quite friendly. I kept wondering who this guy could possibly be. I had not the faintest recollection. We talked for fifteen minutes. He told me granddad had been the attending physician when he was born. Of course Granddad had delivered half the babies in the south end of Big Horn County for over 30 years, so that information was of no help. Finally he says to me, "I'd like to borrow $10,000."

$10,000 in 1967 was a good-sized loan for our small bank and as I looked at him I realized that I had never made a loan to anyone in my life. A pronounced flutter went through my entire body, centering in the pit of my stomach. I said, "Sir, I'm sorry, but I haven't the foggiest idea who you are?

"Oh, I suppose you wouldn't know me, we all know the Harris's. Tis I who should apologize to you. I'm Art Smith- Art's Electric."

"Art, good to meet you," I said as I got up to find a credit file. Fortunately, The First National Bank of Greybull consistently maintained good credit files. I grabbed the file and the documents were all in good order. Except for a small remaining balance on his service truck installment loan, Mr. Smith had nothing on the books. Best of all, I referred to the copy of the bank's "Shit List", which Gerald had conspicuously placed in the top drawer of my desk. Mr. Smith's name was entirely absent.

Art explained that he needed to buy materials for a large wiring job and that he would pay the loan, as he did in the past, when his customer paid him. Pretty much a generic accounts receivable loan. Gerald had already filed a financing statement, so all I needed to do was fill out a collateral form note and Mr. Smith would be all set. After meeting with my Mr. Smith, it was lunchtime and I went home for 45 minutes to catch Mary up on the events of this busy morning.

When I got back to work I ventured into the back room, where the bookkeepers and proof operator were housed. Nearly all were older than my mother, who was 55. Although it wasn't obvious to me at the time, I was about to have a creditability problem with these ladies, especially, since I looked like I was a teenager. I still had to show and ID to purchase a drink on a routine basis.

The head bookkeeper was Mrs. Orpha McGee, a red headed, thanks to Breck or some other hair color maker. She was tall, pleasant enough and had been with the bank longer than anyone else in the back room. Then there was Setzka Breakey, a petite, slender, pretty little lady, with a wrinkly face, whom I would guess was quite stunning as a young woman. Alma Warne was next in line in the age and seniority. She had black hair with some gray, struck me as intelligent and well groomed. The only youngish lady was Thelma Kost, who was about 36. She was the proof operator and an excellent detail person. As I would discover Thelma would turn out to be one of the most loyal, able, yet complex persons on the staff.

After getting acquainted in the back room I rummaged, through my desk to see what other treasures I might uncover. As I sat there Herman Mayland, the Chairman came up to my desk. He was a wiry man of less than average height, friendly smile, a surprisingly deep voice, wearing a crisp Stetson Hat. I had met Herman during the course of past examinations. He had an outgoing personality and it was hard for me not to like him. Herman sat down and we spent some time getting acquainted. He seemed glad that I had come and was looking forward to working with me. I asked him if he would be willing to join me on some farm and ranch visits. He liked the idea and invited me out to his place on the Emblem Bench.

Just as Herman got up to visit with Gerald, Carroll Durkee walked in. Mr. Durkee, had sold his "Big Horn Drug Store" and retired a few years earlier and was now retired. His wife was an invalid and he was quite devoted to her welfare. Carroll was a chubby gentleman, who spoke with a slight stutter. As Mr. Durkee and I talked we were joined by Drew Prugh. Drew was in his seventies and had been Gerald's second man for many years. He was quite tall and slender. He spoke quietly, but with deliberation. I had met him on my first couple of trips to the bank as an examiner, while he was still active in bank management.

By 3:00 P.M. I had gotten acquainted with all the directors and most of the staff. After the lobby closed Gerald and I visited further. As he had told me at our earlier meetings, he felt it was important for me to get involved in the community. He and Jack were members of the Lions Club. He suggested I join Rotary, along with Jerry Holm, which met Tuesday at noon. He also thought I might enjoy the Midway Golf Club, perhaps play on Men's night and during the fall join one of the bowling leagues. I asked how the bowling alley did here, since in my examining experience many of them were lending disasters.

Gerald replied. "Oh, this one seems to do well. I think perhaps because it is small, only 10 lanes, and no competition. Operates out of an old auto dealership building. The leagues are always plumb full and it seems like everyone in town enjoys it. Hell, even old Doc Myers was a bowler until recently."

Gerald Williams had arranged a series of dinner parties to acquaint Mary and me with key customers and people in the community. The parties started the following week. The first party included Lee and Caroline Kunkle, owners of Lee's Grocery story, which was located on Yellowstone at 4th Avenue North, near our house. Lee was telling Mary a story. "The other night, I had just closed up the store and was getting ready to go home, when I saw a bear."

Mary smiled knowingly. "Perhaps, a black bear?"

Kunkle went on. "Exactly, I went home to Caroline and I said. 'Honest, I haven't been drinking, but there was a black bear walking up the street towards the river, just ambling along.'"

Mary started to giggle. "Mr. Kunkle that was Brutus, our dog. He is a black Newfoundland. Quite harmless and friendly, I assure you."

Kunkle started to smile. "Well, I'll be damned, just a big black dog. Aye."

By this time everyone at our end of the table was laughing, especially Caroline Kunkle, who teased, "Lee, you're sure you weren't drinking?" It seemed that even Brutus was doing his part to acquaint us in our new community. The first board meeting I was a part of went off smoothly. I mentioned a couple of things I thought we needed to do. The O.C. C. was requiring bank's report earnings for the purposes of Federal bank reporting on the accrual accounting method. I recommended that we also report to the Internal Revenue on the accrual method to avoid extra record keeping.

Several board members weren't familiar with accrual accounting. I explained the main difference would be that we would accrue, that is take into income, interest income on commercial loans and securities, on an as earned basis, rather than as the interest income was actually received. We were already on a partial accrual for our installment loan portfolio, so it wouldn't be very difficult to convert it to the new system. Likewise we would expense interest of deposits, as it occurred, rather than at the time we paid it. The process would involve some extra work to set up, but once in place wouldn't be appreciably different or more difficult than the cash method. I asked. "Any idea, where we might find a temporary person, familiar with accounting to take on this task."

Drew, who had been totally silent the entire meeting, suggested. "My wife, Myrtle, could come in and do that for you. I will ask her."

"That sounds great. I'm looking forward to meeting her." I said.

Drew, who was well over six feet tall, elected to ride with me to the "Five Sisters" restaurant, where we had our traditional dinner after the board meeting. Drew had never ridden in a Mustang before and seemed to have a little difficulty squeezing into the passenger seat. The seat was pulled forward to accommodate Mary's shorter frame and to ease Brutus' access to the backseat. His lanky legs were nearly up to his chin, until I told him how to get some more legroom using the seat adjustment lever. With this modification, he was able to sit in reasonable comfort. I was rather surprised he wanted to ride in the Mustang, as conservative as he was. He was more of a full sized Pontiac man.

We arrived at "Five Sisters" and Earl Clifton was one of the owners poured drinks from memory, until he got to me. This had been such a ritual with the board that he knew that Herman and Drew drank Cutty Sark Scotch, Gerald, brandy Manhattans, Jack and Carroll, Bourbon and ditch. Since it was summer I ordered a Gin and Tonic. Earl didn't even ask for an ID. I was making progress, indeed!

An elderly lady, who was already three sheets to the wind, slid up on the stool next to me. "You're Doc Harris's Grandson ain't you? My name is Alice."

She slurred her last name, but I didn't catch it; didn't want to either, to be truthful.

"Yes." I replied, as I looked over this ancient lady, with her war paint piled on in thick layers, trying to figure out, if this was someone I should know.

The old woman continued. "I knew Granddaddy *quite* well, if you know what I mean. He was one handsome man! As, a matter of fact, he had a number of extracurricular girlfriends. Did ya know that sonny?"

I shook my head in the negative, although it wasn't the first time I had heard this. Granddad had confessed to my brother and me a few months before he died, that he had had several marital transgressions and deeply regretted them. He urged me to not follow in his footsteps. My Aunt had also told me on one occasion, that Granddad had been a "philanderer" as she put it. It was hard to believe, that this old biddy had ever been sexually provocative.

"Alice, I need to visit with these gents." I said, anxiously, wanting to terminate the conversation. I rejoined a buzz session with Gerald and Herman, who were talking about ranching, banking and business in general. Thus leaving Alice Who-z-watsit to enjoy her drink. Luckily, I never encountered her again.

We all had perfectly done T-bone steaks and the conversation drifted away from business as the evening progressed. Herman grabbed me by the arm and said. "I'll give you a call."

A few days later at 6:00 A.M. the phone rang insistently. Herman, the farmer, was an early riser, who assumed everyone got up early too. I awoke out of a sound sleep and picked up the phone, wondering, who the hell would be calling at this ungodly hour. As if the phone ringing wasn't enough, I picked up the phone to hear Herman's very deep voice. "THIS IS HERMAN!"

I damn near jumped out of my skin. Mary, also, quite sleepy, looked at me as though some great tragedy had befallen the family.

"Yes." I replied tentatively.

Herman continued. "I just finished breakfast and was thinking I'd like for you to come out this afternoon after the bank closes. I'd like to show you my place. Bring Mary along too. LaRoice would like to get acquainted with Mary. They can talk girl talk and you and I can go irrigating."

I was starting to become awake. "OK, I'm sure Mary would enjoy that and I would love to see your place. I need some directions."

"Nothing to it. Go past the white Lutheran Church and Emblem Post Office on your right on the Cody road. Our place will be on the left about a mile, orange brick house, only one like it, you can't miss it." Herman said.

"We should be able to get out there by four, depending on how quickly I can finish with customers." I replied.

"Four it is, then. See you this afternoon." Herman said and hung up.

Gerald had been ushering the more important customers over to my desk, pretty much from my first day on the job. As it happened, I was able to clear my desk by 3:15, walk home, ditch my tie and put on clean jeans. I didn't want to go irrigating in my banker suit garb. Mary and I arrived at Mayland's a few minutes after four. LaRoice took Mary into her homey, country kitchen and launched into to whatever it is ladies talk about. Herman and I walked out to his pickup.

Herman's pickup was a little four-wheel drive International Scout, outfitted with a small cab over the two bucket seats and a pickup bed behind. The green truck was mud spattered. The bed contained a couple of spades-irrigating shovels and Herman's knee-high boots and a couple dozen aluminum irrigating tubes. The little four-cylinder engine started immediately. Herman pointed to a tiny little cottage behind his house surrounded on two sides with groves of evergreen trees. He stated. "That's the house where I was born in 1903, Brother Martin was born there too, but in 1901."

We drove back on the highway, east bound a couple of miles and pulled off by a neat, weed less field of malting barley. Herman and I got out. Along the upper end of the field was a concrete lined ditch with irrigation tubes; like I'd seen in the back of in the back of his truck. First, Herman set the dam ahead, perhaps 50 yards, of the water. Then he pulled the upper dam out, releasing the water to flow in order to irrigate the next several rows. As the water began to flow towards the new dam setting, Herman and I carried the tubes forward. Once Herman saw that I was helping to carry the tubes, he began to artfully dunk the tubes in the water, setting up a siphon in a single motion. He never missed, the water flowed out of the tubes down the rows into the field. Herman smiled and said. "Pretty slick, aye!"

"Absolutely! I don't know if you knew, I worked for Dick Fagenstrom down at Manderson and did some irrigating, but it was all with shovels and ditches. This is much quicker and easier. I am impressed," I replied.

Herman said. "Whenever, Brother Martin and I have a good year, a little extra cash you know, we invest in leveling, concrete ditches, and other improvements. Saves a lot of time and irrigates more uniformly, increasing yields. This barley will be ready to harvest next week. I give it a shot of water now to increase the plumpness of the grain - just the way Coors likes to receive them."

We were done in less than an hour. Arriving at the brick house just in time for "Happy Hour". Herman poured all the four of us generous drinks of "Cutty Sark", obviously his favorite and we talked. Herman began, "I'm really glad you're here. Gerald is a good man, but I think he has kinda lost interest. I believe the bank could be much more and I'm hoping you can give it a shot of life. Always been an honest and sound bank. To be fair Gerald cares about the community, that's why he wanted to bring you in. Wanted someone with a connection to Greybull and Basin, not some dude from Denver or God only knows where."

I savored my Cutty Sark scotch and said. "I have a number of ideas. It seems to me that the building is out of date. I think we really ought to have a drive-in - nearly every bank does. Customers really like the convenience."

Herman replied. "Gerald and I have thought we should be up dating. The bank's in the original 1907 building. Put a brick facade, over the original sandstone in 1950 and expanded into the building next door. We had paid off our Reconstruction Finance Corporation capital infusion during the war. Drive-Ins weren't in vogue in 1950. Gerald decided to let you, or who ever bought the bank, do a building project. He'd rather play golf, ski - Well, you get the picture."

I left Herman's feeling good that the key board member would be supportive of change, but I still thought there was more basic work I need to do.

One of the early tasks I tackled was collections. Although the loan portfolio was generally pretty clean, there were some installment loans that needed more work. I remembered Bob Bryans, at First National Bank of Casper, saying once that they wanted to make loans, but they also expected borrowers to pay them promptly and they had a vigorous collection system, which minimized delinquencies. "We want people to pay us first."

With that in mind I proceeded to contact delinquent borrowers, before they became seriously behind. First we'd send notices if they were 10, then 20 days late, about the time the second payment came up we would phone them if possible, otherwise we would write the errant customer a letter: First a mild letter, then a more insistent message, then one threatening letter, after which we would repossess the car, furniture, or other collateral.

I sent out a series of letters to a schoolteacher who had left Greybull and taken as position in Roundup, Montana. I received no response after four letters and sure as hell didn't want to go up to Montana to pick up a few crummy pieces of furniture. I wrote a fourth letter promising repossession and a lawsuit for any deficiency. I received the following letter back:

"Dear Mr. Harris:

I don't like your nasty letters. Moreover, they won't get you your money. Enclosed please find $100 (Two Payments).

Sincerely, Keith Adams

Not only did Mr. Adams catch his loan payments up to date, we never had any difficulty with him again. It was this kind of action gave us a reputation in the community for being aggressive collectors that cut down delinquencies and reduced losses.

By November I was getting pretty well in the groove at the bank. Gerald Williams invited me to join him for an afternoon Chukar hunting expedition. Chukars are formally known as Hungarian Partridge. They are fun to hunt and challenging to shoot, because they fly in an irregular, unpredictable pattern. I had bought a 12 gauge Winchester, lever action shotgun for this kind of hunting, which I hadn't brought home yet. It was a beautiful Indian Summer Day as I walked out with the gun over my shoulder. There was a regular customer at Jack's desk, negotiating a loan. Knowing damn well what I was up to Jack said. "Where are you going with that shot gun?"

Being in a happy, jovial mood, I replied. "I thought I'd go out and collect a few loans."

The gentlemen at Jack's desk got up and said. "I guess I don't need that loan, after all."

One of the first loan requests Gerald passed my way was a loan to a company called Big Horn Canning located at Cowley, in the north end of Big Horn County. The corporation canned locally grown peas and corn. The principal stockholder was a pompous, fat, old lawyer from Cody, Ernest Goppert, Sr. He was requesting a $500,000 loan and we were asked to participate to the tune of $25,000. I had seen the loan at many of the banks around the Big Horn Basin where we were located, although never in the Greybull bank. I looked over the application documents provided and noticed that, although the loan was intended to pay off entirely from sale of the "pack." It never did. The carryover increased annually as a result of the company's mounting losses.

Gerald and I talked about the deal over high balls one night, at his house. I confessed to him I had seen the loan in a number of area banks and that it had been examiner criticized. The argument the lead bank made was, "Mr. Goppert was a wealthy man and would bail the banks out." Gerald and I both felt if we were to participate in the line of credit, we would require the great Mr. Goppert's financial statement and personal guaranty. Being a lawyer, Goppert knew he had no legal obligation to bail the banks out, should a loss occur; my Dad had an encounter with Mr. Goppert that proved to me he was a slippery, sly character.

Dad's Basin Land & Livestock Company had at one time tried to engage Mr. Goppert to do some work concerning a lack of reporting from his co-stockholder in the company; Mr. Goppert's mishandling of this case instilled a distrust in me for the man. We turned down the deal, but the other area banks went along with Mr. G.

Another challenge was Earl Madsen, which I was able to solve amicably. Gerald had been lending to Mr. Madsen to finance money installment contracts on appliances and furniture, sold by the local Gambles Store. The contracts were assigned to us, but had no documentation to determine the integrity of the collateral. The names on the contracts were all local people who we knew, but some of the names were on Gerald's infamous "Shit List". So it was hard to evade the question: "how good was the collateral?" Mr. Madsen, was a recently retired Wyoming National Guard Colonel, in addition to being the former owner of the Gambles Store. I invited Mr. Madsen in to discuss the matter.

Being the old Army man that he was, Mr. Madsen could be quite resolute and inclined not to change, particularly for a young whippersnapper like me. I explained our situation and that I wanted a better handle on the payment history on the contracts. Mr. Madsen stated that he kept a payment record of each borrower on a 4" by 8" card and that he posted every payment as they came in. I said. "Good, why don't you bring those cards in every quarter and I'll check out the delinquencies and dollars outstanding."

Mr. Madsen said. "Seems like a lot of trouble, but if you insist I'll do it."

"Good, I'll even provide a cup of coffee or pop, if you prefer to enjoy, while you wait." I said.

Once Mr. Madsen became accustomed to the procedure, we had some interesting conversations, while I poured through his records. It turn out that Mr. Madsen was a pretty good collector and even most of those on our "Shit List" seemed to pay him reasonably well. December arrived and our farmer and rancher customers came into pay their crop loans. Finally a few people, I actually knew came in. Art Collingwood, a short rugged appearing man, was the tenant on Dad's Shell farm, came in with his bean check and retired his entire line of credit. We visited for a minute and he didn't mention, thankfully, the day I had visited him in September with my dog Brutus. While we talked about farming, livestock and different types of beans, Brutus had come up to us with a chicken, very recently deceased, in his mouth. I had taken Brutus bird hunting a couple of times and apparently he thought birds in general were fair game. I apologized profusely and offered to pay for the chicken. Art said. "Oh, shucks, that chicken was old, too tough to eat. I was gonna have to kill him anyway. I don't want your money. Your dog did me a favor."

As he left he invited me out to his place for another visit and I told him I would, when we set up his operating line for the New Year. After Art left, Gerald came over to my desk and said. "Art is fine man. I've been here since

1938 and old Art has never failed to pay off his operating loan. I can't think of another farmer I can say that about."

Another farmer I knew was Jay L. North, known all over the county as "Northie". Northie farmed the place our family called the "River Ranch," getting its' necessary water out of the Greybull River through the Cockins Ditch. Northie raised sugar beets, an excellent cash crop. Northie was a tall erect man, always wore a hat. I'll bet I knew him at least fifteen years, before discovering he was bald. One of the stories I always liked about Northie was his famous bow tie, one of those leather pre-tied affairs that hitched in back. He wore the tie all the time. Gerald told me he would do farm visits to Northie's place: he would be irrigating on a hot day wearing his bow tie, suspenders, denim shirt and jeans and, of course, the ever present hat.

My Granddad had sent me out to the River Ranch to get acquainted with farming, when I was 16. Northie had two foster sons, Doug and Winston Miller. Legend has it that Northie's son, Jack, had married their mother and when Jack and the mother decided to leave town, the boys decided they preferred living with Northie and hid out for days in the surrounding hills, until Jack and Mom were gone. Doug, who was about my age and I got acquainted and managed to get a tractor stuck in an irrigation ditch that summer. It was refreshing for me to see Northie, who I really did know.

Northie and I took care of his banking business and we started to visit. Northie told an amusing tale about his watermelon patch. Northie had a unique accent and speech mannerisms, that I was never able to put a label on, but it did make most everything he said, sound quite profound. One hot August day, when the watermelons were ripe to perfection, he caught a couple of townies stealing and smashing watermelons. Northie, shot gun in hand, caught up to the boys and says. "Now dammit, I don't mind you swiping a few of my watermelons to eat; I have plenty and I don't mind sharing. But I take exception to smashing the melons, waste makes me terrible mad. I'd hate to be putting buckshot in your fannies." The town boys returned, but never smashed another melon.

With December upon us we need to set up the accrual accounting system. I hired Myrtle Prugh to do the work. Myrtle was a frail looking, but surprisingly energetic, white haired lady in her mid-sixties. She had a quick mind, excellent with figures and a sparkling sense of humor. She was exactly what I needed. I explained to Myrtle what I needed and in short order, she did all the preliminary work needed. On January 1, 1968 we would be on a complete accrual accounting system, including all new subsidiary ledgers.

Gerald, meanwhile was very supportive of my efforts. In fact he seemed to be enjoying the whole process of change I was putting the bank through. At the end of the first week in December Jerry Holm, the Cashier and the chief fiscal officer of the bank, (or as I liked to call him the "Chancellor of the Exchequer") came around to all the staff members with an envelope containing a deposit ticket for a whole month's salary. Since I had only been at the bank for four months, I was delighted to, received a whole month's salary.

Gerald's wife let it be known she wanted to play bridge with her friends and no longer wanted to manage the insurance agency. After looking the staff over and talking to Gerald, I decided to name Charlene Collingwood as my insurance department manager. Gerald gave her high praise saying she was an excellent worker, dependable and honest. The problem was neither Charlene nor I had the required Wyoming Insurance Department Licenses. We each obtained a manual, studied ferociously, passed the test and were granted our licenses for all categories. We were ready for January first. A few days later I was in for another surprise.

Jerry, our "Chancellor of the Exchequer" came around with another round of envelopes. Yet another month's salary for each employee. I was quite amazed to get two bonuses in one month. I asked Gerald what was going on. Gerald smiled, as he said. "We don't have an accrual accounting system so I can't predict the bank's yearly earnings until nearly Christmas. As the earnings picture becomes clearer I give out bonuses. I don't like to pay the I.R.S. taxes. Besides, I really like my employees much more than the taxman."

The bank had its annual Christmas Party at the Five Sisters Restaurant. Helen and Earl provided great food and drinks. Somehow Myrtle was in charge of the so-called entertainment and we played a silly game of bingo, which the older people enjoyed, but I could see the younger set was rather bored with it. The last week of the old year was a busy time preparing ready for the New Year.

Eleven

Boy Bank President

On the second Tuesday of January 1968, I was elected President and Chief Executive Officer of The First National Bank of Greybull. I was 29 years old. As I recall, only a few of the bank's stockholders were in attendance, although we had close to 100% represented by proxies. Gerald wished me good luck and took off for his winter retreat in Arizona the following morning. I was on my own. As winter set in my thoughts turned to skiing. My new friend, Bruce Kennedy, suggested Mary and I join he and his wife, Betty, for a day of skiing at Red Lodge, Montana.

We all piled into Bruce's maroon Buick convertible with all our skis mounted on the lid rack. During the two-hour drive to Red Lodge, we had a great opportunity to get acquainted. We started talking about Greybull and its history. I asked, "How did the town get its' name?"

Bruce grinned and said, "There are actually two stories; you can take your pick. The Greybull part is from a legendary, dirty, albino, buffalo bull, hence the Greybull. The Greybull River was named after the albino buffalo; that's pretty solid. Washington Irving wrote about it in the 19th century and the town took its name from the river which, of course, flows into the larger Big Horn River at the south edge of town. To me that's the most plausible story."

"What is the other story?" I inquired.

"Well, that would be the more romantic story. You know the bluffs east of town?" said Bruce.

"Sure, can't miss them," I replied.

"Ah, legend has it, a pretty murky one at that, the Indians stampeded a small herd of buffalo off the bluff. It was easier and safer than trying to shoot them with a bow and arrow. Accidentally, the Greybull was killed in the stampede. The Indians believed the albino buffalo had mystical powers and felt they had offended their great spirit by killing him. They, therefore, named the site Greybull in the buffalo's honor."

Mary said, "I like the second story better!"

The skiing was great and we learned a lot about Greybull that day. However, I was back to work Monday morning. I had several ideas for improvement on my mind. One was the building and I began to assemble ideas for a remodeling project. Another issue that troubled me was our board of directors seemed to be isolated from the community. Jack, Gerald and I were insiders. Herman obviously brought many things to the table, being active in the agricultural community, politics, and many other goings on. As much as I liked Mr. Durkee and Drew Prugh as individuals, they were no longer connected or active in the business community. I had seen as an examiner a number of situations in which a bank board had become something of a retirement club. I saw this was happening in Greybull.

At one of our earliest Board Meetings, I presented new director criteria. In order to not offend Carroll and Drew, I grandfathered in all the present board members. I have never liked the idea of arbitrary age limits for board members which some institutions impose. Rather for a bank board, I think the key to an effective board is that members be active in the business community, regardless of age. Our new policy was for directors to retire, when they become disconnected from the business community; no age criteria were included in the policy statement. The first order of business was to begin to get some new vigor on the board.

Towards this end, I first wanted to get an active main street merchant on the board. We elected Larry Probst, the owner of Probst Western Store. Larry was 51 at the time, was well-liked, and ran a highly successful business which was located directly across the street. Larry had shrewd business acumen. He was able to control his temper and tried successfully to be pleasant to everyone, even people he disliked. His way of "getting even" with someone was to sell them something at Probst Western Store. That way he "got some of their money". Of course he didn't mind selling to people, he liked. Larry started his business doing shoe repairs and selling leather goods such as saddles and tack for horses. Over the years the shop had evolved into western style clothing store, along with the horse gear.

In the 21 years since Larry and his wife Ora came to Greybull, he had built Probst Western Store into a destination business for people wanting western wear and merchandise for horseman and women. He was well acquainted with all the farmers, ranchers and everyone in town, too. In the pre-credit card days, merchants extended credit to customers they trusted. Larry was an excellent judge of credit worthiness and character in general. Larry provided a wonderful perspective and immediately contributed much wisdom and knowledge to the Board of Directors, as well as the loan committee.

Another peculiarity of The First National Bank was that tellers were considered royalty, at least within the bank. The tradition was that an employee would serve as a bookkeeper, then to proof (the balancing of each transaction), and advance, after many years, to the teller line. There was a maximum salary one could earn, which was based on length of service. While I did not cut any one's wages, I let it be known that people could increase their earnings based on the different jobs they knew. My idea was to have back-up people in all the operating positions in the bank. It also meant that people in bookkeeping could get salary increases by learning to be proof operators, tellers, and, later, general ledger bookkeepers, the most complex of the non-officer positions.

It was the new policy that those who liked bookkeeping could stay there, even if he or she had learned the tellers' job. We might even hire someone directly from the outside to be a teller, assuming they had the personality and other abilities to be one. I was quite proud of myself, for I thought I had devised a set up designed to work for the bank and its employees, a win-win for all parties. That was what I thought until the "Night of the Revolution".

On a chilly Friday night in February, about a week after announcing the policy, all hell broke loose. We closed the lobby in those days at 6:00 P.M. and I had managed to clear my desk and went home. Mary, Brutus, and I were settled down for "happy hour". I mixed a shaker of martinis and Mary had a fistful of large dog biscuits for Brutus. The phone rang. I picked up the receiver and it was Jerry Holm, our operations officer. "Bert, you'd better get down here. The ladies in the back room are on the warpath."

Dumbfounded, I asked, "Why!"

Jerry replied, "They are really unhappy about the new personnel policy regarding bookkeeping, tellers and so forth."

I replied, "Oh, Jesus. I'll be right down."

As I hung up the phone, I explained the situation to Mary and asked her to put dinner on hold. I rushed down to the bank in my new turquoise Chevy bank car to try to make sense of the situation. When I got there, I quickly discovered that Myrtle was the ringleader. Sweet bright witty Myrtle had turned into a union organizer, with the ferocity of John L. Lewis, without bushy eyebrows. She was madder than a nest of hornets and unloaded on me: "How could you be so unfair, unkind to poor Orpha and her girls?"

Shocked, I said, "I don't get it. I am trying to establish a system of cross training and employee education and you think I'm being unkind?"

Myrtle came back, fire lighting up her blue eyes. "What about seniority?"

"Seniority? My program appreciates the loyalty of everyone here. This idea is about everyone having the opportunity to learn new tasks. Earn a better salary, too! I could understand your anger if I was cutting wages, but I'm not," I fired back.

Myrtle shook her head, "You mean you're not cutting wages?"

"Damn it, Myrtle! Of course not. In fact everyone will get at least a cost of living increase and the opportunity to learn something new and earn a bit more. I'll put it in writing, which obviously I should have done before I went public with this decision. I am really sorry for the confusion," I said calmly and firmly.

The ladies had finished their work, having posted both ledgers and proven everything was in balance. Myrtle left still fuming. Orpha and the others seemed placated at least for the moment. After all, how could this young kid possibly have any worthwhile ideas?

Our demand deposit system used old outdated posting machines. We posted the customer's statement and the bank's ledger copy in a separate operation. In addition, the operators had to manually pick up the previous balance. Many banks were using NCR Postronic machines, or a similar Burroughs product. The Postronic technology utilized a magnetic strip to record balances and eliminate pick up errors. I decided that we needed to update. Some of the banks were converting to computers, but it seemed plain to me that this crew wasn't ready to leap into the computer age just yet. As a result was there were some good used Postronic machines available from small banks converting to computers.

My friend Jim Chapin at the Hilltop National Bank of Casper had a couple NCR Postronics he offered to sell me at a good price, so I sent Ed Rech, pronounced "wreck", owner of the local Greyhound Moving and Storage franchise, to Casper to pick up the machines. Ed was a very strong, husky man, with biceps greater than most men's legs; he could pickup damn near anything, it seemed to me. Yet he was a kindly gentle giant, mild mannered gentleman.

When Ed arrived in Casper, Jim Chapin, called me and said, "There's a guy named Wreck here to pick up the posting machines. Are you sure you want to entrust this sensitive equipment to a guy named Wreck?

Jim, first let me tell you he moved all of my personal stuff up here and not a scratch. If it helps your piece of mind any, Ed's name is spelled R-E-C-H. Fine old German name, I believe," I said.

"Well, OK, I was just checking. Oh, and thanks for the check," he replied.

The new machines improved our efficiency and we cut our demand deposit accounting staff in half. We also, later on bought a Burroughs Sensitronic for posting on general ledger, savings, investment and the loan ledgers. With the change to the accrual system, the general ledger bookkeeping job, became a full time position and no longer a part time job for the cashier. Having a cashier, who also had authority to write official checks and originate other accounting entries was a poor internal control practice. I put Ronald Wright on this task, since he was recently married. He needed the opportunity to earn a better wage and I saw him as a bright young man I could mold into a competent banker. Just as I was feeling my oats as a bank president, a young lady demonstrated the value of my new title.

On a dreary winter's day, a petite, pretty, young, redheaded lady walked up to my desk wanting to borrow $10,000 to purchase a mobile home. I took her application, studied it, but decided that this wasn't a loan I wanted to make. Her income was from welfare and wasn't sufficient to make the payments. To make matters worse, she wanted 100% financing. Since it wasn't our policy to make mobile home loans without a good down payment, and it was evident her income wasn't enough to make the payments, I politely declined the loan.

"I demand to see the president!" She shrieked, as her face lit up to match her flaming red hair.

Calmly, I said, "I am, the president."

She glared at me, swished that lovely head of red hair in my direction and without another word she walked out, never to return. How right Gerald Williams had been about the usefulness of the president title; this day I really appreciated it. While I was enjoying my new life as bank president, Mary was adapting slowly to small town life. One thing that bothered her was that it was evident people in the community were constantly talking about us and interested in everything we did. Or in her mind, it seemed that Greybull's people were too nosy. She wasn't able to land a teaching job, as there were none to be had, but she did get a job as a teacher's aide and was able to make a few friends at school. I pointed out my dad's wisdom about small town living: "People talking about you is not malicious: they are just interested and most only care about their neighbors."

"Mary," I said, "Look at it this way. If people are talking about us, they are leaving other folks alone. Speaking of meeting new people, Wally and Martin Mayland, Jr. and wives have invited us up to the Bear Creek Ranch Saturday for supper Saturday. While I am there I need to do a livestock inspection. They are Herman's nephews and are about our age. It should be fun."

On the last Sunday in February, we drove up to the Bear Creek Ranch, about a 45-minute drive from town, mostly on gravel roads. The ranch buildings lie at the foot of the western slope of the Big Horn Mountains. Bear Creek runs by it. I believe there is a Bear Creek in every county in the State of Wyoming. This would be Big Horn County's edition of Bear Creek. As the countryside rose, we past a number of cattle ranches, mostly populated with either Hereford, a red brown and white critter, or Black Angus, both beef animals.

We did see a small herd of Holstein, angular looking black and white dairy cattle. Mary said, "Look police cows!"

We both chuckled at her little joke. As we approached the Bear Creek Ranch, the grazing land became more sparsely vegetated, indicating rangeland more suitable for raising sheep than cattle. We looked to our left and there was a tall stately rock outcropping 50 or perhaps 60 feet high. Sitting on top was a bald eagle, a wonderful Bald Eagle, symbol of America. Bald Eagles as this time were considered close to being an endangered species. Neither of us had ever seen a bald eagle before, so we stopped to get a good look. The great bird remained totally motionless for the ten minutes or so, while we were enjoying the view, before we continued our journey.

When we arrived at the house occupied by Wally and his wife Carolyn, Mary and I told them, our eagle viewing. Wally and Carolyn started laughing.

"What's so damned funny, Wally?" I asked.

Containing his hilarity, Wally managed to say, "The eagle was up on a big sandstone out cropping, 60 feet tall or so?

"Yes, how did you know?" I said, but now suspicious of something fishy.

Wally and Carolyn smiled broadly; Wally said, "It's not a real eagle, it's one of those Case farm machinery dealer eagles, John Bayne put up there years ago. If you take the time to climb up there, you'll see it's nothin' but a steel statute. God only knows how many guys have tried to shoot it, thinking it was the real thing."

"I suppose that's better than having them shoot at a real live eagle," I said.

Wally said. "We do occasionally see the real McCoy here. Mostly, we see only the golden eagles. They are a bit of a menace to sheep; they'll attack a young lamb, you know. Let's go down to the lambing sheds. Martin and the boys are down there; we're in the middle of lambing. A good time for you to get a look at our operation and get a look the sheep, instead of trying to run them down in the hills."

We walked down to the lambing shed. Shed seemed hardly the word for it, since it was a good sized, well-constructed wood barn, perhaps 100' by 20'. The interior was divided into a series of small pens, each containing a ewe and one or two lambs. Wally explained, "We mate a Suffolk, a black faced sheep, with an all white Columbia. We breed for a high ratio of twins, which boosts our productivity of lambs per ewe. Occasionally, we get triplets. The mothers can't nurse those so well, so we match those up with a ewe that has lost one of her lambs. We do this by taking the pelt off the dead lamb and putting it on the surviving triplet. That way it smells right to the momma ewe and she accepts it. This also works with lambs that are orphaned when the mother dies giving birth."

Wally's brother, Martin, was assisting a ewe in the birth process as we entered; I didn't get to talk to him until later during the visit. While Wally, Martin, Martin's young sons and the sheepherders, managed what was a maternity ward for sheep, I managed to get a fairly accurate count of the livestock on the place. As nearly, as I could tell, all 2700 ewes, plus the assorted rams were present and accounted for. Wally and Carolyn treated us to an excellent lamb chop dinner. When I got back to office the following Monday, I called Bob Bryans at First National Bank of Casper, the bank we sold a participation to in this loan. This was for us a large line of credit.

Bob Bryans was surprised that I had gone out to do an inspection so early in the season, since the sheep operators around Casper and Rawlins generally lamb later, in late March and April to take advantage of the warmer spring weather. I said. "Bob, I asked Wally and Martin about why they timed their lambing in February. They said that after years of observation, they had discovered that the last two weeks of February were consistently mild enough for lambing. If they did get a cold snap, it wasn't as dangerous to the lambs as a wet spring snows that freeze on the sheep's backs. You don't get wet snows in February. The other advantage is they get an extra six to eight weeks growth on the lambs, come marketing time in the fall."

Bob said. "I noticed their lamb production figures per ewe from last year is much better, than we see around here, or John France sees down at Rawlins."

"As I understand it is the combination of early lambing, high twin ratios, and extra care given during birthing. They use indoor lambing sheds instead of trying to do their lambing out on the range. They have a regular obstetrics ward for sheep," I said.

After talking to Bryans, I received a call from Doug Krogh, my former examiner pal, who had become the managing officer at First National Bank of Gillette. Doug said. "You'll never guess what happen. The bank is in the hole!"

"What the hell happened? I thought you guys were doing well." I replied.

"Oh we are, very well. We were excavating for the foundation for a new building on the lot next door. The contractors got too close to the old building and it collapsed into the hole." Doug said laughing at his mischievous and misleading presentation of the story.

"Was anyone hurt?" I asked.

"No, fortunately, it happened after banking hours, as we were getting ready to go home. Happened in a kind of in slow motion, so were able to get out safely. The equipment was on the side of the building that didn't go in the hole, so we were up and running in a couple days. Say could I borrow $2500 from you? Joyce's old Chevy has become a motorized repair bill." Doug said.

"Well, I don't know if I should lend any money to a guy, whose bank is in the hole," I teased.

I paused a minute and said. "I'll drop a note and blank financial statement in the mail to you today."

Many bank executive officers feel it is a good ethics procedure to justify their credit to another banker rather than borrow from their own bank, which at the time was restricted under Federal Reserve Regulations. Meanwhile, I was progressing with our plans to remodel our bank building.

We determined that we needed some additional property for a drive-in facility. The Pruitts, who owned the shoe store next door, had been wanting to sell for some time, as they were up there in years and desired to retire. I went next door to talk to Melvin Pruitt. The building was for sale all right, but there was a catch. Melvin also wanted to sell the shoe business, too. Not what I expected. I called Larry Probst and asked for his advice.

I explained that I really wanted to buy the building, but wasn't very interested in the shoe store. Larry suggested that we buy the whole ball of wax as it were: "We can liquidate the shoes, have a going out of business sale. When the inventory gets picked down, so there are limited sizes and selection, we can sell the remains to a distressed merchandise outfit. I know a couple of honest Jewish gents from Denver that do that."

We consummated the deal with Mr. & Mrs. Pruitt and we had the land for our new drive-in window, plus a whole building full of shoes. It was generally known in town, that we were the purchasers of Pruitt's Shoe store. Jim Mockler, a local real estate agent and owner of some farmlands, came in as we were liquidating of the shoe inventory and said, "How are things at the First National Bank and Shoe Company."

"Luckily, we won't be in the shoe business very long," I said.

With the land tied up, we began deciding how to proceed. At the time we had no local contractor customers capable of doing the job. We elected to go with Bank Building Corporation, which is a company that specializes in building banks. Their representative was a gentleman named Donald McDonald, no relation to Ronald or the hamburger factory, insofar as we were able to determine. The plans looked very spiffy and certainly gave the fresh look we were looking for. The main thing that bothered me was the space allocated to bookkeeping and operations seemed too small. Another issue was the drive-in couldn't be seen from the bank building and was isolated; the teller would need to carry cash as well as the checks and deposits about 50 feet to the nearest door to the lobby. This seemed like a potential security issue.

Being naive, inexperienced, and having never planned a bank building, I figured they knew more about building banks than I. The board didn't have any experience in that arena either, so we went along into the building project pretty much as Mr. McDonald had proposed. During the first year, as I had discovered the night of "The Revolution", proved I didn't know much about personnel and a number of other issues.

One of the problems that came up was when I was visited by the wage and hour regulatory people concerned Fred Marcus, our janitor. Fred was, a white haired, retired employee of the Greybull Elevator Company. The elevator stored and acted as a harvesting agent for farmers selling grain and beans. We paid Fred a wage he felt was reasonable; Fred's wife Elsie came along to keep him company. She was not at all well; very heavy, and perhaps disabled by a stroke, a diabetic condition, or both. Elsie moved with zombie-like slowness. While she kept Fred company, she did move a dust rag about now and then.

The wage and hour people discovered Elsie accompanied Fred on his nightly two-hour visits to the bank and insisted we pay her the minimum wage. To be truthful, until the wage and hour people arrived, I never gave the matter a thought. I called Gerry and he suggested I talk to our bank attorney, Stan Davis.

Stan had a practical manner of dealing squarely with issues. He suggested that we make a contract with Fred as if he were a contractor. Stan Davis was a colorful character in his own right and, in addition to having excellent, sensible and fair solutions to legal problems we encountered. Stan was a rather effective trial lawyer too. My favorite story about him goes like this:

A few days before hunting season began Stan was asked to be the public defender for a 19-year-old accused of stealing a $50.00 radio from his employer Hawkins and Powers Aviation. The young man had returned the radio. However, Big Horn County's erstwhile County Attorney Bob Gish insisted on prosecuting the case, since it was considered a felony at the time under Wyoming law. He even insisted on a jury trial.

One of the potential jurors, all decked out in a red shirt and red hunting hat, asked to be excused so he could go hunting. Stan Davis got up and told the judge, "Elk hunting season only comes once a year; I'm a hunter and understand. I think he should be excused."

The judge launched into a long "civic duty" speech about the responsibilities of a citizen to serve on a jury and to no one's surprise refused to excuse the gentleman in the red hat. Of course he was selected and the trial commenced. Mr. Gish spent a day and one half providing evidence about the crime. Then it was time for Mr. Davis's defense.

Stan got up and called no witnesses and made his closing argument: "The defense has never disputed that the defendant stole the radio. We admit; he did it. The real question is should this boy be incarcerated for swiping a $50.00 radio that has already been returned to its rightful owner. We think not."

Stan sat down and the jury was out and back in less than 10 minutes. The guy in the red hat was, as it happened, the foreman of the jury and said, "We the jury find the defendant not guilty."

Speaking of practical solutions to problems, one of our important bank and insurance agency customers was Hawkins and Powers Aviation. Their banking business was a simple seasonal operating line of credit that paid out in full every fall. The bonding part of the insurance business was another matter. H & P was a slurry bomber, forest fire fighting contractor and. since they worked for the Forest Service, Bureau of Land Management and some state government agencies were required to provide performance bonds. They were preparing for three slurry bomber contracts. Every year Gerald told me that it required a selling job to convince George to write the performance bonds, because H& P "s financial statement, didn't resemble a construction customer, the usual customer for performance bonds.

Gerald instructed me that the best way to get this done was to go down to talk to George Mayes at the United States Fidelity & Guaranty Company's bond underwriting office in Denver. "Take Charlene along so she can talk to the fire, commercial and personal lines underwriters," Gerry advised.

Charlene was the newly appointed manager of the insurance department and Gerald had found that a personal acquaintance with the insurance underwriters was useful, especially when insuring large risky lines like grain elevators, lumberyards and other commercial insurance risks.

Of course I didn't know any more about bonding than was in the brief coverage in the State of Wyoming Insurance Manual, about two pages. Then Gerald surprised me: "George is a skier. Let him know you're a skier too! George is really a decent guy, but he will want to get to know you. Once he knows you are a skier you should get along with him real well."

With that advice, Charlene and I went to meet the people at U.S.F.& G. in Denver as well as some of the other fire insurance people we represented. First George and I talked about skiing. I had skied most of the Colorado ski areas he frequented, so I didn't sound dumb, as I knew I would when it came to bonding. Finally, we got around to bonding. George looked at the paperwork and shook his head, "It doesn't look like a construction company."

Without thinking, I said, "Of course not, it is an aviation company."

George said, "They don't show much of a net worth."

"George, they buy those airplanes at salvage auctions, many of the planes were bought after World War II, at surplus sales. They have long since depreciated them to zero. They expense the upkeep and upgrades, which is plenty. The planes are in first class flying condition. Dan Hawkins and Gene Powers tell me they are flying PB-4Y-2s, the Navy version of the B-24 bomber and they are easily worth over $100,000 each. They have five in good flying condition, plus several helicopters and other equipment. There is a great deal of value here!" I said.

George said at this point, "OK, I think I understand."

"George, I don't pretend to know much about bonding. But as I understand performance bonds, it is all about making sure the job gets done. H & P has the pilots and airplanes to do the job," I said.

George said, "Bert, you're a banker, right?"

"Right, sir," I replied.

Then George startled me, "Bert, if you understand banking, you should understand bonding. We bondsman are looking for good current ratios, net worth, same as you bankers. Keep that in mind and you can sell lots of bonds." With that wonderful lesson, which I have never forgotten, the world of bonding opened up to me.

My next bonding customer was Eyre Preator, a sturdily built man of medium height, an excavation contractor who mainly did work for farmers like the Mayland brothers, but also occasionally did work for public entities. Eyre was a man Gerald Williams held in high esteem ever since a new Caterpillar tractor he was hauling on a trailer over Tensleep Pass got loose on him and tumbled, several thousand feet to the bottom of the Canyon. It is still there as far as I know. Eyre tightened his belt and made his payments punctually, without a hitch. With the loss of this expensive, uninsured piece of equipment, Gerald was amazed that he was able make his payments as though nothing had happened.

This day Eyre was looking for a bond to do some excavation work for the State of Wyoming. We talked as I filled out the forms and I asked him, "Do you have the experience to do this job?"

"Oh, yes, I know how to do the job. I'm not doing it for the experience. Frankly, it is the money I'm interested in," he answered. We were able to get Mr. Preator bonded with my new friend George, without difficulty. Now I understood bonding. Bondsman are looking for liquidity, good earnings and a good balance sheet, exactly the way bankers evaluate loan applications. With spring Mary and I were pleased to learn she was expecting in November. Life in Greybull was going very well.

That spring I started playing golf on Wednesday evenings in the Men's League at the Midway Golf Club. We played "best ball" in that league;

whichever player has the best score for each hole counts his score. My partner was Del Atwood, who was a good twenty years my senior. However, we had similar handicaps and it turned out we were pretty compatible. Del owned the Atwood Family Funeral Home. The business was established by his parents in 1930 and was the only funeral parlor in the Basin- Greybull community.

That summer we had an application for the establishment of a second funeral home. A guy named Carlson from Casper was the applicant. He had been employed by one of the undertaking establishments in Casper, so he had the experience. He also had the equity to put into the venture, an excellent credit report and, on the surface, looked like a decent loan applicant. I knew very little about the funeral business, so I asked Del Atwood to teach me some basics. Del said they had about 100 cases per year in the community. Surprisingly, some years 102, others 98, but year after year they provided about 100 services each year. Their breakeven point was around 70 cases. Armed with a few funeral home facts, I talked to Gerald and got his opinion.

As was becoming our custom, I went over to the Williams house for "happy hour" and we discussed the loan proposal. The problem with the funeral business is the number of cases the operator gets to handle is finite, unlike a Vincent Price, Boris Karloff movie, where the "entrepreneurs in death" went about murdering people to drum up business. Another major part of the problem was that the Atwoods were well regarded in the community and it would be difficult to take enough business away for the proposed funeral home to be successful. Moreover, Gerald pointed out, the Atwoods were significant depositors and he thought we shouldn't rock the boat. We turned down the loan. Our competitors at the Security State Bank in Basin made the loan. Our judgment was vindicated when Mr. Carlson called it quits six months after opening.

Mary was a couple of days overdue, so I took her for a ride one evening in our International Scout on a bumpy jeep road not too far from the hospital just in case events unfolded unexpectedly quickly. The following day our son Oliver Burton Harris was born on November 12 and we were quite excited. It was the first grandchild for both of our parents. Mary's folks were on the next plane. My parents managed to contain their excitement until

Christmas, when they paid us a visit. The year for the farmers and ranchers in our service area was a good one with good yields on crops coupled with good prices. As a result the bank had a 25% growth in assets and deposits.

According to many of the younger employees, the biggest improvement was in the bank Christmas party. Same place, same great food, but instead of bingo, we had dancing. Even the older people danced and didn't seem to miss the bingo.

Twelve

The Building Project

By the time the new year of 1969 rolled around our lives in Greybull had settled into something of a routine. About a month into the New Year we were visited by our National Bank Examiners. Verne had now earned his commission and was the "Examiner-In-Charge"; I had always enjoyed working with Verne when he was my assistant and was looking forward to visit. This would have been the third examination since I joined the bank and I felt pretty good and had been able to address issues I thought examiners might have questions about. Moreover, our agricultural customers had had a good year thanks to favorable crop yields, coupled with decent cattle prices. Our loan portfolio was in good shape and we had a 25% growth in assets.

Verne and I sat down to discuss the loans and other issues. It turned out we only had a single loan subject to criticism. The loan was a weakly performing loan to a car dealer, who was not able to curtail his used car inventory. In this case due to the relatively small line of credit, and I had no quarrel with Verne's evaluation or the loan being in the report. Finally, he dragged out the year end, call report, compared it the previous year. The report showed total footings of $4,999,509.

Verne looked at me over his thick glasses and said. "Mr. Harris, all you had to do was empty your pockets and you would have made it over the $5 Million mark."

We both broke into smiles and then we talked in about the bank's remodeling plans. With growth like this, we needed better facilities. We talked about Gerald's mentoring, in particular our recent success with SBA loans, and our recent ad campaign. One of the many things Gerald Williams had been right about was Jerry Holm's talent in putting together quality ads. Jerry and Bruce Kennedy got together the idea of featuring children of our customers in bank ads.

For example Art Sylvester, our highly skilled local carpenter's young son was posed with a hammer and saw, with a caption about how daddy used us for construction money while a project was in the works. One of the pictures was of my son Oliver, sitting on top of my desk with a caption about our savings accounts. The ads were a huge success. Several women said they turned to our ad first when they received their Greybull Standard and Tribune each Thursday morning. We ran the campaign for about six months.

At the bank, about mid-morning one spring morning, shortly after Gerald had returned from his Arizona winter retreat, all of us were alarmed by a loud, blood-curdling shriek emanating from the bookkeeping department. Those of us who were not busy with a customer rushed to the back room. There was Setzka, fashion and style conscious Setzka, starring in disbelief at her feet, hidden from our view by her chocolate brown NCR Postronic machine.

Jack, looking concerned, said, "Are you OK, Setzka?"

"Setzka, what's wrong?" Asked Charlene.

Setzka looked up at us and started to smile slightly, "Oh, I guess, I'm OK, but I just discovered I have a red shoe on my right foot and a brown one on the other foot."

Being last in the room I arrived just in time to hear Setzka's explanation. I just shook my head in disbelief and said, "My God Setzka, we thought you were being murdered."

Embarrassed, she said, "I guess it took me by surprise. I'm usually quite particular about such things. Sorry to trouble you all. Thanks for your concern."

At this point all of us, especially Setzka, started to laugh.

A few days later, at mid-morning, I noticed a pleasant middle-aged lady at Gerald's desk. Gerald motioned me over and said, "I'd like you to meet

Louise Stadfeldt. Louise worked for us for a number of years and was an excellent employee. She quit to be a stay at home Mom. Now, Lonna, her daughter, is in High School and Weezie wants to come back to work."

I shook hands with her and said, "Louise, we don't have any openings right now. But that all can change pretty fast and with Gerald's high recommendation I'll definitely keep you in mind."

Later that very day, when I got back to work after lunch Setzka, was sitting primly at my desk.

"What can I do for you?" I asked politely, resisting the temptation to remind her of the shoe episode.

She smiled knowingly and said, "I've decided it's time to retire."

"I hope this doesn't have anything to do with the shoe incident? I said.

"Well it made me put my life in focus. I am well past 65 and my sister wants me to come live with her in Arizona. I think I'd like to accept her invitation." She replied.

"We'll miss you around here. When do you want to leave? I asked.

"I was thinking, perhaps the end of next week. I'd like to get down to Arizona and catch some warmer weather." She said.

"That sounds good and it will give me a few days to line up a replacement. Thank you for your reliable and loyal service." I said.

Immediately, I called Louise Stadfelt, "Louise, you'll never guess what happened this afternoon. Setzka decided to retire and we now have an opening in bookkeeping, if you are interested."

Louise replied. "I'm amazed. I never thought this morning that an opportunity, would come so quickly. When do you want me to start?

"Neither did I, I was thinking next Monday. That way there will be a week or so overlapped with Setzka and it will give you a chance to break in gracefully. We have new posting machines and procedures have changed some since you left, 14 years ago?" I said.

"I'm looking forward to coming back. Do we still start at eight?" She said.

"Sounds perfect, see you Monday." I said.

With the New Year launched we were ready to start construction on the remodeling of our 1907 building. It was to be a radical change in appearance from the old building. It would include a drive-in window, modernized lobby, three private offices for the senior officers, private conference room, and improved safe deposit vaults and, most importantly, a bright fresh modern look. In order to complete the construction quickly, which involved removal of a bearing wall and supporting the second floor with a column in the center of the lobby, we needed to move our banking operations to temporary quarters, to allow our contractor to work unobstructed.

We rented a small masonry store building about 25 x 100 a couple of blocks east on Greybull Avenue. The building didn't have a vault so we added a reinforced steel concrete vault to the back of the building. The building wasn't up to our usual security standards, so we decided to hire a night watchman to look after the place during non- banking hours. Louise Stadfeldt volunteered her husband, Lon for the night watchman job. By spring we were moving into the temporary quarters. Ed Rech, our gentle giant moving man, moved us. It was amazing the pieces of heavy equipment Ed picked up, with no effort, including nests of safe deposit boxes and safes I never dreamed one man could possibly pickup by himself.

Our quarters were cramped, but it was well organized. The new arrangement, arranged along functional lines, worked out quite well. Several members of the old guard left us including Orpha McGee during these months. We hired Darlene Hanson to fill the proof operator slot. Darlene was a pretty, 40ish, red head, with a perky, outgoing personality. It turned out that being a proof operator was not Darlene's forte.

For the first time I was faced with the unpleasant task of firing someone. In this case someone, I genuinely liked and could envision her as a teller or receptionist kind of position. However, at that moment we had nothing that fit Darlene's talents and personality. I sat Darlene down and explained to her that things weren't working out for her as proof operator. Moreover, I pointed out our overtime costs looking for her errors were costing approximately her salary every month. I gave her a month's salary to ease her financial burden, while she found a new vocation..

The next day "Honey" Hanson, her irate husband, came storming into the bank. Honey, whose given name was Darrell, was a large, well-built man, a good deal bigger than me. For many years Darrell had been a beekeeper, hence the nickname, "Honey." I had no desire to tangle with him. Honey, hardly seemed to be the right moniker for him this day; he wasn't in a very sweet mood. Additionally, the Hanson family, various members were very good customers and I a major public relations situation on my hands as well. I sat "Honey" down at my desk. I didn't have a private office and the lobby was busy and humming with customers. I needed to keep this as low key as humanly possible.

"Darrell" I said. "I'm really sorry about terminating Darlene's employment; however, for the proof position she was a terrible fit. Square peg, round hole, if you understand what I mean."

I went on the explaining the issues in polite, firm, but as quietly, as I could. I saw Darrell was reluctantly nodding his understanding of my position. Finally, he said. "I'm concerned that she won't be able to collect unemployment compensation, since she was fired for cause."

"Darrell" I said. "We pay into the fund for this kind of situation and I will interpose no objections whatever to Darlene collecting unemployment insurance. By all means, she should file. Be assured that I will help in any way I can. I am not angry with Darlene in a personal way and feel terrible that this was necessary."

"Well that sounds better, Bert." Darrell said as he got up to leave.

"Good luck to both of you." I said hoping, he wasn't too mad at me.

About a month later a smiling Darrell and Darlene came in and I couldn't help wonder what was going on. I stood up and shook hands with the couple and asked how I might help them. Darrell started the conversation, "The Decker's want to sell the Montgomery Ward Catalogue Store and we're thinking this might be a good business for Darlene to run."

"Fine, let's see if we can't put together a financing package." I said, as I imaged Darlene's pleasant personality and helpful attitude in this role.

The Hanson's had a good credit history with us and the Wards Store financial information supported the loan request. It was good application. Once the loan package was complete it was one I easily granted. In January when Darrell and Darlene brought in their tax return it was obvious that Darlene had found her niche; she had earned three times the salary we were paying her. This proves that sometimes firing someone can be the best thing you could possibly do for them.

From this experience I learned testing people for jobs might have some merit. My experience with the abrasive Ms. Gray at the Denver U.S. National

Bank made me cautious of using a test as a sole determining factor in hiring a potential employee. But my experience with Darlene told a different story. I found a clerical aptitude test for bankers and decided perhaps I should try it. I decided to order some tests and experiment with the test. I selected all of our clerical people, whose abilities I was well acquainted with.

The test we chose confirmed the abilities and aptitudes of our star employees like Thelma, Charlene and Louise. With this knowledge, I started to use the test on applicants. One lady, who was well known to us in the community and without knowledge of how she would work in a banking job was given the test. I wouldn't have hesitated to hire her based on her personal reputation in the community. Mrs. Burgess took the test and bombed it. While really good, well suited, people scored around 150 points, poor Mrs. Burgess, scored a miserable 90. We went with the relatively unknown person who had something like 140 points. After that decision, we learned that Mrs. Burgess was hired by our competitor. But within three months was fired. The test seemed to have some merit. By this time the building project was moving along at a decent clip.

Our building superintendent was a man named Tony Berith, a transplanted German, with a jovial, but-never-the less, professional workman attitude. Tony was middle aged with a wiry build and curly gray hair. Every week, we would go on a tour of the building as it was being torn apart then reassembled. Our new space started to take shape. As if the building project didn't create enough turmoil in our lives, we were visited by Mr. Douglas Sotham of the Internal Revenue Service for an audit.

I was quite confident that we had nothing to worry about, since our C. P. A. firm was Peat Marwick, Mitchell and Company, which was a big eight firm and did more bank tax returns than any other accounting firm in the nation. Our bank was one of the larger taxpayers in his district and consequently we were audited nearly every year. We were also the first bank in our corner of Wyoming to switch from a cash to an accrual accounting system for tax purposes. It was on this issue Mr. Sotham landed on me with both feet, figuratively speaking. Of course, he wasn't a violent man.

Mr. Sotham said, "You re accruing interest on certificates of deposit, savings certificates. Those are savings accounts and the "Code" prohibits accruing savings interest expense."

"No, sir, that law pertains only to savings accounts. We pay our savings depositor's interest on December 31st on their accounts, so there is no accrued interest reported. Certificates of Deposits are in essence a promissory note, like a note a customer might give us for a loan. Peat Marwick says it is OK to accrue interest on certificates." I replied.

We went round and round on this for at least fifteen minutes. Charlene, whose desk was next to mine looked at me doubtfully and said. "I hope you know what the hell you are doing!" I decided to be cautious and called Ken Eide, my tax man at Peat Marwick, just to verify the point and boost confidence in my argument. He verified my information.

"Mr. Sotham, I just talked to my tax guy at Peat Marwick and he assures me accruing interest is permissible under the code. And they see many more bank tax returns than you." I said with renewed defiance and confidence.

Sotham glared at me and refused to change his mind.

Frustrated, I said. "Call your Grand Imperial Leader, or whatever you call your source. I know damned well, I am correct in this matter."

Douglas retreated into the area surrounding the conference table and sat down at the telephone and began to dial.

Charlene looked at me dolefully and said, "Are you absolutely sure you know what the hell you are doing?"

I looked at her confidently and said, "I wouldn't put up a fight like this if Peat Marwick weren't backing me up on this. Thanks for caring."

A few minutes later Douglas Sotham came back to my desk, tail between his legs like a whipped dog, and said, "My boss said, you are correct. I'm sorry. I misunderstood the law."

I didn't want to have him angry with me, so I said, "Doug, I can see why you were confused. Not being able to accrue interest expense on the CDs would have been a big tax bit for us and after all we don't want to over pay our taxes."

Doug nodded agreement and silently went back to the conference table where he was working. He was silent for the rest of the week until Friday when he finished his audit. "Mr. Harris, can I have a few words with you, before I leave?"

"Sure." I said, wondering what mischief he had dug up during the past two days of silence.

"Mr. Harris, we found an arithmetic error on your depreciation schedule and the I.R.S. owes you $641." Douglas said with a smile.

"Well, thank you Doug. I hope you'll come back every year; we can always use and extra $600!" I said and we shook hands.

Although Doug audited every year for as long as I was in Greybull I never saw him in person at our bank again. He always scheduled his audit when I was on vacation or on a business trip. When I returned there would be a note from him on my desk which read, "I performed your tax audit and everything is OK. Your friend, Doug."

About midway through our construction project I received an invitation to an open house at the First National Bank of Gillette, my friend Doug Krogh's bank that fell in the hole. Mary and I went over to join in their celebration on a warm summer day. We looked over the new tan brick building and visited with Doug Krogh and Ray Saunders, the President, who had engineered the bank's remarkable recovery from near disaster. Mary and I were standing in the buffet line with Ray and his wife Cynthia, when Ray said to me. "If it weren't for you blowing the whistle on us that day five years ago, this day never would have happened. We would have gone straight down the tubes."

I thanked Ray for his kind words and we helped ourselves to a fine assortment of excellent meats, salads and desserts.

By this time we were getting acquainted in our community as well as various Wyoming bankers. Mary was becoming accustomed to small town living and developed a number of friendships. One of those people was Diane Frank, the wife of Peter Frank, a doctor in the next town of Basin. One day, when our son Oliver was about 6 months old, Diane called at about 4:30. "Why don't you and Bert join us for dinner tonight? We're going out to Blue's. We'll pick you up at six."

Mary was concerned about finding a babysitter on such short notice, but decided on Lee Ann Greiner, who lived across the street with her grandparents. Mary played cards with Mrs. Greiner weekly, so she offered Lee Ann the opportunity to baby sit. Lee Ann arrived at about quarter to six and confessed, "I'm only eleven and have never baby sat before."

Mary thought quickly, "Your grandmother's home right?"

Lee Ann nodded in the affirmative.

Mary went on, "Do you know how to change a diaper?"

Lee Ann said, "Yes, I help my aunt with that occasionally."

"You know what? That's all I need to know, we'll be at Bluejackets. Your Grandma is across the street. I think you'll do just fine." Mary said.,

And she did. Another of Mary's adventures with Diane was grocery shopping at Wheeler's Market in Basin. Dalton Wheeler, the proprietor and my Dad's closest boyhood friend saw her in the store with Diane.

"Mary." he said, "I see you in here with Diane periodically, but you never buy anything. Why is that?"

Mary answered, "Mr. Wheeler, you don't bank with First National and Bert wants me to do my business with bank customers to the greatest extent possible."

Mr. Wheeler shook his head, "I guess, I can understand that."

That afternoon Dalton, or "Bandy" as my Dad affectionately called him, came into the bank to open a very large checking account and buy a Certificate of Deposit. Mary had turned out to be a good salesperson.

Mary and I were also becoming a part of the community and developed an active social life. One Friday evening we were invited to Dave and Rose Lindsey's for drinks and dinner. Other guests were Tony and Betty Rogers, our philosophical and humorous local doctor; Jim and Eileen Horn. Jim was a fastidious, neat-nick, very particular about many things, but especially his vehicles. Dave was a "mud engineer", that is he developed various concoctions used in oilfield drilling fluids. All three couples were more our parent's age, than ours. In fact Dr. Rogers and Mary's Dad had been classmates at the University of Colorado, Medical School in the 1930s. When we arrived, Dave was working late and had yet to arrive, but Rosie was prepared for us and poured the drinks. Dr. Rogers started telling a story about a young unmarried lady, who had come in the office that afternoon for an examination, because she was feeling nauseous.

"I carefully examined her and determined she was about three months pregnant."

"The girl said, 'Oh. Dr. Rogers that's not possible, I haven't been having sex with my boyfriend.'"

"So I moved over to the window and began looking skyward. Didn't say anything."

"The young lady then said, 'Doctor, why are you looking out the window?' 'Because,' I said, the last time this happened a star rose in the east.'"

About the time Dr. Rogers finished his story Dave came bursting through the front door and greeted us. "Sorry to be late, but old man Markley needed to talk to me about some drilling problems and it took longer than expected."

Rosie stared at Dave, the message was clear: he needed to get cleaned up. Without a word Dave retreated into the bedroom, showered and change clothes. While Dave was changing Jim Horn stepped outside to smoke one of his long odoriferous cigars. By the time Dave was finished changing, Jim was back and pounced on him. Jim had recently sold Dave a blue six-month-old Jeep pickup truck in showroom, like new condition. This day, truck had been in the oilfield southeast of town and was like Dave, covered with black mud.

Jim said, "Dave I am really disappointed that you aren't taking better care of that truck I sold you last month; it is a filthy mess."

Dave said, "God dammit Jim, when I buy a truck, it is a work truck and I take it into the oilfield which is where I go to work! Oil field roads are often muddy this time of the year."

He continued breaking into a broad smile, "Jim, God damn it, I don't have time to breast feed your damned truck."

Jim shook his head and took a hefty gulp of his Bourbon and ditch.

We did develop other friendships of people closer to our age too. Don and Charlene Collingwood, a couple closer to our age, invited us out to dinner one Sunday.

Charlene had prepared a lovely pork roast, complete with applesauce and all the fixings. Donnie, their teenage son, who was active in Four-H as many farm kids are asked, "Mom, is this Vera?"

Charlene replied casually, "Why, yes it is."

Mary and I looked at each other curiously. Then Donnie piped up, "Vera, is my Four-H project. Good isn't she?"

We had to agree "Vera" had turned into quite an excellent roast.

After about a year we were ready to move back into our newly remodeled building. We spent the weekend moving machines, safes, and safe deposit boxes. Ed Rech moved us back into our building. It was beautiful, with a bronze buffalo sculpture behind the teller stations, three private offices, a board-conference room, plus a small conference room where the original cash and safe deposit vault had been. We weren't able to reuse it as a vault facility as it was too narrow for safe deposits on either side and we needed a better facility for the cash vault. Mr. Berith and his designers poured concrete with steel reinforced walls within the old oversized records vault, so the exterior wall was over two feet thick. Tony Berith said it was "burning bar" proof; the latest device in bank burglary technology.

So on sunny Monday spring morning we were ready to begin operations in our new quarters. The exterior had a cedar facade on the up level, which broke up the lines of the old austere ivory colored brick walls. With great excitement, we all arrived to work early in anticipation of the big day. Jack and Ron Wright, who had the dual control lock combinations for the safe deposit and cash vault, proceeded to open the vault for business. It wouldn't open.

Jack and I huddled to determine what went wrong. Jack drew on his pipe. "I can only think of two possibilities. One is we simply set the clock wrong and it will open later. The other is something is wrong with the locks. They've just been serviced by the Mosler people, so it should be OK. Meanwhile, we need to get some cash."

I said, "I'll call Ray Faurve (pronounced four) down at Basin and get some cash. We'll send Ron and Jerry down after it."

I called Ray down at the Security State Bank of Basin and explained the situation to him. Of course he burst in to great gales of laughter. Finally, when he goes over laughing he said, "Sure I'll help you out, $40,000 be enough to get you open?"

"Thanks very much for your help. I'll send Ron and Jerry Holm down with a Cashier's Check immediately." I said.

The boys didn't quite get back by 9:00, our opening time. Within a few minutes they arrived and we were able to offer cash services to our customers. Jack and Ron tried the vault again at 10:00 AM and it open as if nothing was ever wrong; the timer was erroneously set an hour later than it should have been.

As might be expected, the media got a hold of the story and it was on the surrounding local radio and TV stations in Casper and Billings the nearest TV stations to us in our somewhat remote part of Wyoming. Well, what the hell, at least everyone in Wyoming and Montana knew we had a new building.

The new building added excitement to the community and, as Donald McDonald had predicted, we had a sharp increase deposits and other activities as a result. There was one important lesson for me; however, that was to trust my own instincts. Despite the grandeur of the new remodeled facilities, the workspace for the bookkeeping department was cramped, as I had feared it would be.

Thirteen

A People Business

No matter how many new inventions come along - computers, automatic teller machines, on line banking, and countless other devices to streamline banking - operations one thing that never changes is that banking is a people business. The mega banks that have evolved in recent years have reduced their customers to a mere number, but they have not altered the fact that an individual's finances are very personal. Banking remains a people business and the personal relationship many of us have with the people at our particular bank.

So it was at the First National Bank of Greybull, we wanted customers to feel a kinship with our personnel, especially tellers who are often the customers' sole contact with the bank. We had a lovely young lady working for us, I'll call her Victoria Gilbert. Vickie was blonde, with bright blue eyes, and was tall with a drop-dead gorgeous voluptuous figure. She seemed to attract a curious lot of novel customers. Vickie had a bright and cheery personality with a winning smile; small wonder the customers were attracted to her.

We hadn't been in the new building very long when she rented Mr. Wilbur Browning a large safe deposit box. A few months later Vickie, processed the entry of Mr. Browning into his new box. Vickie ushered Mr. Browning into the small conference room; he shut the door, and he rummaged through the contents of the box.

After half an hour or so Mr. Browning emerged red-faced and angry." Someone from the bank has been in my safe deposit box!"

Vickie responded calmly to Mr. Browning's accusations, "Mr. Browning, that's not possible. After we issue you the box keys, there are only two and they are yours. If you lose them we have to get a locksmith to drill the lock. The guard key held by the bank doesn't get us in the box; it only permits your key to work, once we have checked to see the person holding the key is on the entry signature card."

Mr. Browning was not satisfied, "You must get in from behind!"

"What? You think we can get in from backside of the box?" Victoria asked.

Thinking he had scored a major point here, Wilbur said, "Exactly!"

Victoria smiled patiently at Mr. Browning and locked her money drawers. "Let's you and I take a little walk."

Fortunately, it was a quiet day and a momentary absence from her teller slot would cause no snag in customer service. As it happens the back of the wall of the safe deposit box vault is a two-foot-thick, steel reinforced masonry wall. The back side is in the driveway for the drive-in window. Vickie guided Mr. Browning to view the brick wall, which ran the entire length of the west wall of the building, clear up to the roof.

They stood silently and viewed the wall and Vickie sweetly said, "Mr. Browning, this wall, two feet worth, is behind your safe deposit box. Can you see there is no way anyone from the bank can possibly get into your safe deposit box from the rear?"

Mr. Browning stared wordlessly, at the wall for a moment as he digested Vickie's words. Finally, he said, "Yeah, I see what you mean. Guess I misplaced that certificate somewhere at home, I'll look."

Mr. Browning showed up the next day and apologized to Vickie, waving the missing documents in his hand and asked to be readmitted to his box, just long enough to tuck the wayward certificates in his box.

Another day, a gentleman decked out in dark gray pin striped business suit complete with a red and white striped power tie, who was more than a little out of place in Greybull, came to Victoria's teller window. He asked to cash his paycheck from Dresser Industries. Dresser had a good size bentonite mining and processing plant just north of Greybull, which employed over 100 people. The man himself was apparently from Houston, Dresser's headquarters, and properly identified himself with both a Texas driver's license and a Dresser identification badge.

Vickie asked, "How would you like your cash?"

The Texan replied, "In twenty-five-dollar bills."

Vickie thought she had misunderstood him, "You mean twenty dollar bills?"

"No, I want twenty-five-dollar bills," he insisted.

Vickie started to grin a little, but managed to contain her amusement, "I'm sorry but U.S. currency doesn't come in twenty-five dollar denominations."

Jack Linderman had been standing in the adjacent teller cage delivering some money to Jeanne Copp, who needed some vault cash to fill a large change order from the local Safeway Store. Jack started to laugh and dashed off to his office and shut the door so he would not embarrass either Vickie or the customer.

"Well then, how about thirty-five dollar bills?"

"U.S. currency doesn't come in thirty-five bills either." Vickie was about 20 years old and still retained most of her girlhood silliness, was making a huge effort to contain her laughter.

Vickie continued to talk to the Texan, "Let me tell you what we have. We have: ones, fives, tens, twenties, fifties, one-hundreds. I guess I could get some twos from the vault if you really wanted them, but they're not used much, except at racetracks. What would you like, sir?"

The Texan, acting as though all of this was totally new to him said, "How about $500 in fifties, the rest in twenties, and of course the small bills you need to get to the $835.52, the amount of the check."

Vickie smiled brightly, still refraining from laughing said, "That I can do!"

She quickly counted the money out of her teller drawer and handed it back to him and said, "Have a lollipop and a great day."

As soon as the Texan was gone, Vickie and Jeanne, joined by Jack, were finally able to release their pent up laughter.

One hot July day, I noticed a long line of six or seven men at Vickie's teller station. A single woman was in line at each of the other teller stations.

Since we tried earnestly to keep teller lines to no more than three, I got up to determine why Vickie's line was so long. Vickie had chosen to wear a very revealing peasant blouse, giving her male audience a wondrous view of her ample bosom and deep cleavage. I did call her and suggested she cover up. Miraculously, our teller waiting lines became approximately even once Vickie adjusted her attire.

People stories are not limited to the teller line. About the time my son Oliver turned three years old, I bought a bright red, little Austin Healey Sprite roadster. The reader needs to understand these cars are quite small and just barely have enough room for two people. The car was fun to drive in sunny weather, but miserable due to a loosely fitting top in rain, and a habit of skidding in snow, or other winter weather. When I brought the car home, Oliver asked me, "Daddy, is it a toy car?"

Of course he was exactly right. It was a toy car; a true "garage princess" driven only in fair weather. We even had Wyoming vanity plates on it which read "TOY." I had owned it for a couple of years when Bud Duggan came into the bank and wanted to buy the car. Bud was one of those customers who always wanted to negotiate interest rates for his short term-business borrowings. Having picked up on this habit of Bud's, I always quoted a rate half a percent higher than I needed, so I could say to him, "OK, Bud, since you are such a good customer and a good fellow, I'll knock off half a percent, just for you." Bud would leave thinking he had conned me.

This day proved to be different. Bud said, "I'd like to buy that little Austin Healy Sprite from you."

I said, "Bud, I really enjoy this little car and don't want to sell it."

Bud replied, "Well, Bert, why don't you put a price on it?"

"OK, wise guy," I thought as I dragged out my National Auto Dealer Association's Blue Book. I looked up the N.A.D.A. value, which was $1,250, in prime condition, somewhat more than I had paid for the car. I pointed to the value of the car and said. "Bud, like I said, I don't want to sell the car, but if you want it that bad, you can have it for $2,500."

Mr. "Nick Me for Half a Percent" without flinching, wrote me a check for the car, on the spot for the $2,500. Being a man of my word, I accepted the check and delivered the car. I thought I could find another like it or at least similar, but in Wyoming they are scarce and not very popular either. I never did find another Sprite.

There is no part of the banking business that is more human than the lending side. Banks are here to serve the public; however, it is not always easy and I remember a couple of banker's stories to that effect. Del Crouse, who I knew when he was President of the American National Bank of Riverton, once said, "Most everyone is entitled to some credit. The question is how much."

Marlin Jackson, an Arkansas banker, had a glass eye, for which he had paid a handsome price. One day a gentleman came into his bank and presented one of the agonizing borderline loan applications. This particular deal seemed to have equal arguments for either making the loan or declining it. Finally, Jackson said to the would-be borrower, "Your request is one I'm having a difficult time deciding whether to grant or not. I'll tell you what I will do. I have a glass eye; if you can correctly identify the glass eye, I'll grant you the loan."

Without a moment hesitation the customer said, "Mr. Jackson, your left eye is the glass eye."

Jackson was surprised how quickly he made the correct guess and said, "You are correct. I'm curious how you could tell?"

The man replied, "I thought I saw a little sympathy in the left eye, sir."

Of course there are some loans that are impossible to make. One day Larry Mulligan came into the bank and wanted to see me. Larry was definitely not first in line when God passed out brains; he was often referred to as our town's village idiot. He subsisted on odd manual labor jobs and welfare payments, a very meager existence at best. Despite his deficiencies, Larry was a pleasant person to talk to and since nothing special was going on at that moment, I agreed to talk to him, "What's going on Larry?"

"Oh boy, Collingwood Motors has the most beautiful car down there. It is a new red Pontiac convertible; I want to buy it!" he replied.

I was familiar with the car, Faye Collingwood, the wife and partner of Cub Collingwood, the dealer, had been cruising around in it for the past month or so.

"Nice car, but it is pretty expensive, must be about $5,000 or so."

Larry said, "I get a welfare check each month and could pay $20 per month for sure."

"Larry, $20 won't pay the interest on that car. I'm sorry I can't help you," said I.

Larry got up to leave and looked at me and said without rancor. "I guess I knew you wouldn't lend me the money."

Then Thelma Kost, who eventually became one of our consumer lenders, had Glenn Evenson come in. Glenn, who like many poor people in our community, struggled to make a living and support his family. He came in to borrow enough money to purchase a used pickup truck for $2,000. Thelma looked him up in our internal credit rating records. The record showed he was slow, but somehow he always managed to get us paid. Thelma shook her head doubtfully as she reviewed his credit record card. Before she could say anything, Glenn said, "I know my credit isn't very good here, but it's the only credit I have."

With this remark Thelma couldn't help but smile. She got Glenn's active loan cards; there were three, most a month or so behind. Finally, Thelma said, "How badly do you need this truck?"

"Well, the engine went out on my old Chevy and I need the truck for my work. You know I work for my Dad in the oil patch, when he needs me. Otherwise I do odd jobs that require I have a pickup. The old Chevy is nearly paid, two payments to go I think," said Glenn.

Thelma sat him down, took his application and helped him figure out a budget. Finally, she said, "Glenn, let's wrap all these loans into one and make a payment that fits your income."

One of the things about community banking that I came to love was the honesty and integrity of nearly all of our customers. Occasionally, however, I encountered people who were not honest. One summer day, Elmer Mann, a rugged, weatherworn old rancher from up at Hyattville, came in with a problem. He discovered that his bookkeeper, Angela Baker, had forged checks with his signature on the ranch account, payable to herself. Angela had been his bookkeeper for several years and recently quit and taken off for Montana. Mr. Mann explained that after she left he reconciled his last few bank statements and discovered she had embezzled about $3,500.

Elmer was hopping mad, but wasn't inclined to prosecute, provided we reimbursed the amount of the theft since we obviously hadn't recognized the checks as forgeries. We immediately admitted our responsibility and agreed to make good. Jack told Mr. Mann that we would turn the matter over to our bonding company, U.S. F. & G. Moreover, Jack and I both assured him that we would make up anything the bonding company didn't cover. I called my friend George at U.S. F. & G. for some guidance. Charlene and I prepared the claim form and within a couple of weeks we were able to reimburse Mr. Mann in full. George suggested that we should jointly prosecute Angela. We handed the money over to Mr. Mann and told him that the bonding company was inclined to go after Angela criminally and for damages.

Within a week I received a phone call from Bill Baker, Angela's ex-husband, with a proposition. "Look, Mr. Harris, Angela is the mother of my children and I don't want her to go to jail. After all, the kids really need her. I'm working down here in Flagstaff as bulldozer operator. I don't make a whole lot of money, but I can and will send $200 per month, until it's paid."

"Bill," I replied, "Our bonding company has paid Mr. Mann off, but I'll talk to my friend George down there and see if he'll call off the dogs and accept payments from you."

I told Bill I'd let him know as soon as I had a decision from George. I called George that afternoon and without hesitation, he said he would be willing to forgo a criminal action if Bill would make good on his promise. "Hell" George said, "If Bill comes through for us I wouldn't even ask for interest." I called Mr. Baker back and told him that George was willing to work with him on his proposal. Bill said he'd get a check off to me that day and within a week we had the first $200 payment which, of course we forwarded to U.S.F. & G. Bill made all the payments promised each month until the debt was paid.

The Bill Baker story doesn't quite end there. A year or so after the stolen money was returned to the bonding company, I received another call from Bill, who was still located in Arizona. Bill's old pickup was about to breathe its last. He explained that he wasn't established with a bank in Arizona and needed $2,000 to buy a newer vehicle. Although we ordinarily don't make "out of territory loans", I readily agreed to do so and sent him the paperwork. The loan performed flawlessly. But because Bill was living in Arizona, our eagle-eyed bank examiner proceeded to verbally criticize me for making loans to borrowers located so far away. I explained the history of the Bill Baker loan and he seemed to accept my explanation; at least it didn't appear in our examination report.

What did appear was rather bizarre, The Equal Opportunity Housing Act states that banks must not discriminate on the basis of race, religion or ethnic background, when granting home loans. In order to provide public awareness and to enforce the law, banks are required to post a notice that informs the public of the act. In the entry way to The First National Bank of Greybull we had a large bulletin board, where we obediently posted the notice. The board also was used by the general public to let folks know about meetings, sporting events and various other goings on in the community. At times, the bulletin board would get crowded. Apparently, on the morning before our National Bank Examiners arrived, one of our local church ladies posted a large notice advertising a bake sale at the Presbyterian Church, which completely covered the Equal Housing notice.

Of course "old eagle eyes" caught the absence of the sign and we were cited for a violation of this regulation. We tried to explain that a customer had covered the notice with the bake sale notice just recently, and repaired the damage by reshuffling the notices on the board as soon as the problem was discovered, but he still insisted that it needed to go into the report. At this point I decided to do him one better by posting multiple notices, mounted in picture frames in several places throughout the bank.

In spite of bank examiners and the serious nature of the business of banking encountered almost daily, bankers can be a fun loving lot of people. Well, perhaps not all bankers; but at least at The First National Bank of Greybull we did manage to have fun. Even Myrtle, union leader and inciter of "the revolution," had a wonderful sense of humor. At our bank for many years we tried to make something of an event of April Fools' Day.

On one particular April 1st, Myrtle baked a large sheet cake with chocolate icing, or so it appeared, complete with the inscription "Happy April Fools' Day". By this time she was pretty much a part time employee, but on this day she took it upon herself to act as hostess. She began serving little squares of the Chocolate frosted white cake to customers, employees and anyone else, who was interested, along with a cup of coffee. After a while she encouraged others to do the cake cutting while she visited with folks. It turned out only half of the cake was actual cake, the rest was chocolate frosting covered Styrofoam. Myrtle howled with laughter as people tried to cut into the highly resistant Styrofoam "cake." I wasn't angry with her. After all, in a small community which lacks the entertainment choices found in a large or even medium sized city, one must make his own fun.

One of Greybull's most amusing summer diversions was "Crazy Days." Merchants offered special deals on discounted merchandise from tables set outside on the sidewalk. Many people dressed in absurd costumes. On this day everyone on Greybull Avenue, the town's main street, participated in "craziness." We encouraged the bank staff to come to work in the bizarre outfits of their choice. One year Charlene showed up in a buckskin looking outfit, complete with headband and a nice tall pheasant feather. Jerry Holm and Jeanne Copp, dressed as Haight-Asbury, San Francisco hippies. Donna Dalin, came as a freckle-faced farmer complete with Beverly Hill Billies, kind of tattered straw hat. The topper that year was Ron Wright, who arrived, attired as a baby with nothing but a diaper made of an old white sheet. Ron has quite a bit of black body hair, which made the whole outfit, or lack thereof, even more amusing.

Another year I came as a drunken derelict, complete with simulated egg on my maroon necktie and carried around an old whiskey bottle about half filled with bourbon colored tea. Charlene showed up, with an excess of makeup, in a bright red dress and a blond wig. She further adorned herself with all the jewelry she could muster from her jewelry box, as well trinkets and necklaces from the collections of her mom and daughter. She was the perfect caricature of the Madame of a whorehouse. With the business of banking and insurance, Charlene's department, ground down to a virtual halt, the two of us decided to take a walk down Greybull Avenue to see what others on the street had come up with for the community's amusement.

Our receptionist and secretary at the time was Ann Martin, tall, elegant looking and every bit the lady. Ann was dressed in a simple yet stylish blue dress, in complete contrast to the spirit of Crazy Days. Ann was assisting a middle-age man and his wife, both of whom were quite obviously tourists and certainly not tuned into the local Crazy Days celebration. I was pretending to be drunk, staggering and slurring my words. I had played drunks in college plays and was considered good at it. As Charlene and I passed by Ann's desk, the lady stared at us aghast and remarked to Ann. "I'll bet the bank is glad to see that couple leave!"

After we made our tour, Ann told us she explained to the travelers the Crazy Days tradition, but added she didn't have the heart to tell them that we actually worked here. Making your own fun is a part of small town life.

Since we only had one movie theater in Greybull, we didn't get all of the good movies Hollywood puts out. One of the movies we did get was "Bonnie and Clyde." It was over coffee one morning that Ron Wright and I decided that we would make a spoof of the Bonnie and Clyde movie. After all, we had a bank we could use as a setting.

I wrote a simple plot and by Sunday we were ready to start filming. Ron and his wife Stella were to star as Bonnie and Clyde; my wife Mary was to be a teller. We enlisted Jerry Kurtz, since he had recently taken in trade a couple of Wyoming Highway Patrol cars. So we had a genuine police car for the chase scene. Jerry, wearing a big white hat and with a cigar, impersonated George Warfel, our Big Horn County Sheriff, was our lawman. Wayne Wright, Ron's brother, served as the deputy. Before trading in the patrol car the state had removed the sirens and lights and makings, although not the spot light and distinctive paint job. We painted the lens on the spot light red and painted stars on the white doors and deck lid. We used my top down Austin Healey convertible roadster for the getaway car. I planned to film the chase scene, from the back of Ron's International Scout pickup. We were ready to film 'Bonnie and Clod.'

Ron was the perfect Clyde, or "Clod", as we dubbed him in our rendition. He was every bit the ham, carefully combing his hair as he passed in front of the security cameras, stopping for Greybull's solitary traffic light and even used hand signals when turning. After the stickup part, our procession headed east on U.S. 14 towards the Big Horn Mountains, with Ron and Stella in the roadster, tossing water balloons at our mock police car. Jerry turned the red spot light on and to our surprise and embarrassment a couple of cars actually pulled over. We decided to have the shootout scene at Post Creek, a little picnic-camping area just above a series of hairpin turns, which made for great pursuit scene filming.

As we began to organize the finale of our little epic, who should come along but six Wyoming National Guard trucks, including one towing a small artillery piece. We filmed the entire procession and didn't even need to splice it in, since it fit perfectly into our filming sequence. With the help of a bottle of Del Monte catsup, we were able to imitate the bloody, last act of 'Bonnie and Clod.'

The film was a local hit and I showed it at Rotary club meetings in Greybull and Basin. After these two showings, I received a phone call from Bill Breining, who was the senior warden at St. Andrew's Episcopal Church, where I was a member of the vestry. Bill said, "We at St. Andrews have a sense of humor; therefore, I am ordering you to bring your 'Bonnie and Clod' movie to the vestry meeting on Wednesday evening."

The movie did add a little levity to our meeting, which was usually embroiled in a serious discussion of the church's precarious finances.

It was during these good times that Martha Frances, our daughter, arrived on July 23, 1971. Oma the sole surviving grandparent on either side of the family, flew out from New Jersey to Denver and joined my parents for the drive north. She explained that my generation of grandchildren had not produced a single granddaughter, only the five boys. She was delighted to note that Martha was first female born to our family since my mom's younger sister in 1915.

The year 1971 had been a good year for our farm and merchant customers, even though there was a rise in interest rates. Our little family and the bank were doing well and as Christmas approached we were in a festive mood. I was reminded that not everyone was enjoying the general prosperity and sense of wellbeing that our family felt. At Christmas time it had been the custom at our bank to have available for our customers a nice piece of remembrance advertising. Each year it would be a piggy bank, lighter, perhaps a pocketknife, and always a choice of calendars. We also brought our leftovers from the previous years, so the customers had a choice. All of this merchandise was free. This particular year I happened to observe Larry Mulligan's mother scooping up about a dozen items. This seemed a little odd to me but, realizing these folks were very poor, I said nothing. After Mrs. Mulligan left I mentioned it to Charlene. Charlene said, "Oh, didn't you know, Mrs. Mulligan does her Christmas shopping with us every year."

Fourteen

Prosperity and Difficulties

The winter of 1972 brought us good skiing snow in the mountains. One Friday morning in February I was surprised that Mary wasn't dressing in her red ski outfit: it was Ladies' Day at Antelope Butte Ski Area, our local ski hill. Mary always went with her friends on Fridays.

"Mary," I said, "How come you're not going skiing with Ginny and the girls?"

"I just feel very tired today and decided not to go," she replied.

"Maybe you should take some Gerital, perhaps you're a little anemic," I said.

She smiled weakly and said, "I think I'll just take it easy and look after the kids today."

Without thinking much about this uncharacteristic decision on Mary's part, I trudged off to work.

It was about this time we were breaking in a new Burroughs Sensitronic machine for our General ledger and lending records. The new machine, like the one we used for our checking account accounting, had a magnetic automatic pickup for balances of these ledgers, hence saving manually transferring balances for each day's activity. This cut the posting operation time in half. It was during this streamlining of operations that I observed that we were actually posting the loan ledgers three times for each transaction. While the input into each posting was somewhat different, the new equipment allowed us to post these records only once, which would save a lot of time in the long run.

Myrtle wanted to continue posting the loans the old way and produce three separate, but very similar records; I suppose out of tradition or habit. I explained to her that the new machine provided a printout of the loans, which we could use at our loan committee meetings, along with the records needed for the loan accruals and general ledger record. The new machine had eliminated the need for the second posting and third creation of the loan records.

"Myrtle, there's no reason to post the notes three times; it's very time consuming when one run will do the job, I said.

Myrtle's ire was up and she sputtered, "We've always done it this way."

"Dammit Myrtle, we don't make loans around here to give you something to balance! Hereafter, we'll do this in a single operation," I replied.

I still was having credibility problems with Myrtle and some of the older people, but I did finally get Alma Warne on my side. Alma was now the full time general ledger bookkeeper and auxiliary records bookkeeper. One day I passed Alma's station at the posting machine. She had a puzzled look on her face.

"What's the matter, Alma?" I asked.

"I can't get the general ledger to balance and I'm off by $500,000." she said as she shook her head and handed me the out-of-balance daily statement.

I looked it over quickly and identified the problem; "Here it is; the commercial loans are overstated."

As I handed the statement back to her, she said, "How in the world did you figure that out so quickly?"

"Easy," I said, "there is no way we could have made $500,000 worth of loans yesterday without me knowing about it."

Finally, the old guard was in my corner, except for Myrtle, who retired shortly thereafter.

One the day Fred, our former janitor, came in to see me about setting up an escrow for the sale of a Marcus family farm property to another member of the family. He was accompanied not by Elsie, his wife, but by Evelyn Reinke. Mrs. Reinke was the wife of farmer from Emblem Bench, located west of Greybull. The Reinkes had been customers for years and I was also acquainted with her. What struck me was that Fred and Evelyn were brother and sister. They looked so much a like it would have been hard to miss; yet I never realized the two as related until they were seated next to one another. It was poignant reminder of my dad's words: "In a small town you want to keep your ears open and your mouth shut. You never know whose relative you are talking to."

Luckily, I hadn't said anything offensive to either of them. I had taken Dad's advice and was very careful about remarks I made. My competitor, fortunately, wasn't always careful about such things. I came back from lunch shortly after 1 PM to find the lobby packed with merchants from our neighboring town of Basin. I was pleasantly surprised, but I had no idea why all of these businessmen were here.

The first in line to see me was Ray Cummings, who owned and operated Thompson Lumber and Hardware, one of Basin's oldest businesses.

I greeted Ray, who I knew fairly well from St. Andrews Episcopal Church, where we were both vestrymen: "Ray, what can I do for you?"

Ray said, without a moment's hesitation, "I want to move all my business to First National Bank, operating loan, business and personal checking, savings, the works!"

"Ray," I replied, "I've tried to wean you over here for years without any luck, why the sudden change of heart?"

"You'll never guess what Del Crouse said at the Chamber of Commerce luncheon today."

"I can't imagine, Ray."

"He said, 'Security State Bank was ONLY interested in making loans to farmers.' That's in front of nearly all the Main Street merchants; it made everyone in the room mad as hell. That's why everyone is here to see you today!" Ray replied.

"Well that explains the Basin delegation being here." I said.

That afternoon, a number of Basin's merchants became First National customers. On that day it became clear to me why some of the farmers and ranchers closest to our bank insisted on driving the extra seven miles to Basin to do their banking. I remembered a conversation I had with Jim Whaley, a Shell Valley farmer-rancher whose place was located just across the road from our family place on the Shell Road. I tried to persuade him on more than one occasion to bring some of his business to our bank, with not a glimmer of interest from him.

He said, "That damned old George Hinman, Senior, wouldn't lend us any money in the 1930s, when we really needed help. We moved over to Basin in 1935 and been there ever since. They've been real good to us."

"For Christ sakes, old George died in 1938, which is incidentally the year I was born; how come you wouldn't give me a try?"

Mr. Whaley replied, "Bert it is called loyalty!"

It was apparent that he wasn't about to move any Whaley family business our way, so I didn't press the issue. I wanted to retain what friendship I had with him. It was ironic to me that in 1935 my grandfather, Dr. Bert Harris, was titular president of the Security State Bank and one of its founders.

With all our farm loans set up for the season and other recent activity at the bank it was about time to take a vacation. Although Mary's chronic fatigue loomed over her, she always enjoyed traveling and we thought a vacation to California, might somehow energize her. It was May and we were driving our family car, the orange Jeep Wagoneer. We were delighted with the Jeep; it was a great highway as well as mountain vehicle, useful for livestock inspections on mountain range pastures, and good for skiing trips.

We took off on our vacation driving though Yellowstone National Park. The roads had just been cleared a week earlier and the snowdrifts were twice as high as the Jeep. Yet the elk, bears, buffalo and other wildlife were out to greet us along the roadside as we drove through the park. Then we went on to Teton National Park, visually inhaling in the magnificent scenery. During the spring the Grand Tetons were capped with their winter's coat of heavy snow and Jackson Lake was still frozen, although the ice was starting to break up.

From the Tetons we motored on into Idaho. Once in Idaho, we decided to check out the ghost towns in the mountains above Boise. On our way up to Silver City, we came upon a huge snowdrift lying across the road. It was taller than the Jeep and there was no way around it. I thought about trying to go through it, but I remembered that I have never owned a four-wheel-drive vehicle that I hadn't gotten royally stuck. I already proved that on my first livestock inspection tour last fall shortly after taking delivery on this particular Jeep. While looking at a herd of Hereford cattle I became bogged down in some mud and my rancher customer had to pull me out with his tractor. We decided to save that adventure for another day and drove on to Nevada. We did manage to find some ghost towns in Nevada and didn't even come close to getting stuck.

We arrived in Sacramento at our friends Rich and Jo Weeks' home and called Mary's dad to check on Mary's mom, Rhoda, who was to have surgery earlier that day. To our shock and sorrow, we learned that Mary's mom had died on the operating table. We flew to Albuquerque to be with Mary's family. After the services we returned to Sacramento to continue our journey.

While in California, we took the children to Disneyland, where Oliver enjoyed meeting the Disney characters he'd seen in person. Martha was only a ten-month-old toddler, so I can't tell you if she enjoyed it or not, although she did get a severe case of the giggles as Oliver plowed through a large bowl of spaghetti, getting most of it on his face. On the way home we checked out some more ghost towns in as we drove across Nevada.

Upon our arrival back home we asked Oliver, "What part of the trip did you enjoy the most?"

To our amazement, he replied after careful consideration, "I liked the animals in Yellowstone Park the best!"

The three-week trip proved to be very tiring for Mary, and I finally persuaded her to see Dr. Frank, who was our family doctor and friend. He ran some tests; the results were inconclusive, even though she had lost weight. The weight loss was attributed to losing the pounds she had gained leading up to Martha's arrival ten months earlier.

1972 was a year of rising interest rates, and customers were more sensitive about the return they received on their savings dollars. Commercial banks such as ours were regulated by the Federal Reserve Regulations as to the rates we could pay on both ordinary savings accounts and certificates of deposits. Saving and Loan institutions, and more specifically Big Horn Federal Savings and Loan Association, half a block up the street, operated under similar regulations issued by the Federal Home Loan Bank Board. However, they were always authorized to pay one half a percent more than us. On the street customers began to move their savings to Big Horn Federal and I was routinely accused of being "too cheap" to pay the same rate or, as they saw it, "the going rate." The accusation annoyed my competitive spirit.

I began to search for some way of leveling our competitive playing field. Our New York correspondent bank, First National City Bank, came up with a partial solution to this problem, which they offered to share with us gratis. The program allowed us to pay certificate of deposit rates, which brought out savings account in line with our savings and loan competitor. Jerry Holm, our marketing guy, dubbed it Gold Savings, while he named a regular passbook accounts Blue Chip Savings. One of the first people to open a Gold Savings account was my dad, who promptly referred to it as his 'Gold Sock' account, where he kept his joy or hobby money.

A year or so later dad, who had become an avid stamp collector in his sunset years, called me from Buenos Aires, Argentina, requesting I transfer $800 from his 'Gold Sock' account to his farm checking account. He had written a check to a stamp shop in Buenos Aires for a whole bunch of prized stamps, which he decided was a good value, especially some 19th century United States stamps. In Argentina they were just some foreign stamps of no special interest or value to local collectors.

Early in July, Mary confessed to me she had fallen asleep while driving the seven miles between Basin and Greybull in the middle of the morning. With her were both children and our Newfoundland dogs, Brutus and Cleo. Under normal circumstances, there was no way this noisy lot of passengers would allow her to fall asleep. Her tiredness was getting worse and it was time for a complete physical examination, including x-rays. Dr. Frank suspected something serious was going on and arranged for her to have a complete physical in Billings at the regional hospital there.

We drove north to Billings and left the children with Viola Reilly, our neighbor who frequently babysat the neighborhood children during the day, with the explicit understanding that all children picked by their parents by six. The Reillys' had a tiny house, at least three children living at home at the time, and no way of accommodating overnight visitors. We had expected to be home easily by five P.M.

Starting at ten o'clock Dr. Swenson began to run a series of tests including chest x-rays. He discovered a large, grapefruit-sized tumor in her right lung. Dr. Swenson was a thoracic surgeon and decided that it was imperative to operate in order to determine if it was malignant or benign. He wanted to operate the following morning at seven. I called the bank and talked to Charlene and ask if she could find someone to look after Oliver and Martha. She said her 15-year-old daughter Diana was available. Diana had a lot of babysitting experience and in fact had babysat our kids on several recent occasions. The kids liked her; Charlene and Diana would get them set up in our home. I called Mary's dad to let him know what was going on. Being a doctor, he must have suspected what might be going on and said he would fly up to Billings from Albuquerque on the next possible flight.

Mary got out of surgery at about 10:30 the following morning. Mary's dad had arrived by this time so he was on hand for the post operation conference. Dr. Swenson had a somber expression on his face and began talking, "The good news is Mary came through the surgery in very good shape. She has pretty pink lungs, obviously she has never been a smoker. I am wary of the tumor because of its size, but we won't know if it's cancerous for sure until the lab results are back in a couple of hours. She should be coming around in the next half hour and you can visit her."

Mary's dad listened stoically, as I tried to understand what was going on. We went into visit Mary as she came out from under the anesthesia. As expected she was groggy at first, but once the drugs wore off seemed to be reasonably comfortable and in good spirits. Neither Mary nor I could imagine this giant, ugly tumor could be anything but benign. When Dr. Swenson came back with the lab results, we were shocked and terrified to learn the tumor was malignant. Dr. Swenson did further tests and we learned that the cancer also had showed up in her lymph nodes, indicating it was spreading throughout her body.

Mary's dad and I stayed at the Cherry Tree Inn in Billings so we could be close to the hospital. I was curious as to why the motel was called the Cherry Tree Inn, since there were no live cherry trees in evidence. I asked my Billings banker friend, Bob Waller, who was the President of the Midland National Bank, a bank we corresponded with about the name. Bob chuckled a little and said it's really quite simple and said, "Why, Bert don't you know it's owned by George Washington?"

"You're kidding!" I responded.

"No. This George Washington is an executive for the Northern Pacific Railroad, invested in this motel. Must have wanted at least one motel in the country where he and his wife could spend a night without being suspected of some kind of philandering mischief," Bob replied.

Mary recovered quickly from the surgery and we went back to our lives in Greybull; Dr. Cramer went back home to Albuquerque. We were all wondering what the future had in store for us. After a week of tending to Mary in Billings, I brought her home and I was back to work, where something was always happening.

The first day back, an irate Art Brooks was at my desk and proceeded to dress me down for a comment my teller Victoria had made to him about his new pickup truck. He said, "That damned Victoria has been spying on my accounts and blabbing my business."

"Art, I am shocked to hear that about Vicky. She is an experienced teller, and worked for us for four or five years and knows our secrecy policy, which is very strict," I replied.

"Just how strict is your policy, Bert?" Art came back at me.

I took a couple of seconds to contemplate my response and said, "Let me put it this way. We operate this bank as though it were a Swiss bank, at least to the extent that U.S. banking laws will allow us. This means we terminate employees who go around discussing bank matters, by that I mean customer business, with anyone outside of the bank. Every employee signs a secrecy agreement on day one; it's a policy Gerry Williams started that I vigorously continue to enforce."

Art said, "You mean you're going to fire her?"

"Perhaps, but first, I'll get her side of the story. I'll get back to you as soon as I decide on the appropriate action," I replied.

Art had calmed down by now and said, "Then I'll hear from you in a day or two."

"Absolutely, perhaps as soon as this afternoon, just as soon as I can have a sit down visit with Vicky," I answered.

After Art left, as soon as there was a break in the steady teller traffic, I called Vicky over to my office for a little chat. I repeated Mr. Brooks' narrative to Vicky and asked for her side of the story.

"Mr. Harris," she began in earnest, "I have been a teller here for four years and I know and agree with the bank's secrecy policy. I believe I have always complied with it. What happened was this: Art Brooks is my next-door neighbor and he bought a beautiful new blue and silver Chevy Silverado pickup from Core Chevrolet. When he was in this morning, I was intending to compliment and tease him about his new truck. What I said was, 'If I had your money, I'd buy a nifty new truck just like it, but maybe red instead.' He must have thought I was looking at his balances."

"Vicky, as it happens, Art and Rachael have a large five-figure savings account with us, which he perceives that you had been peeking at," I said.

"Oh my God, I didn't even know he had a savings account with us. Honest, I was just trying to compliment him and rib him a little about his new truck." Vicky pleaded.

"Vicky, I'll call Art and explain this to him. I know him to be a reasonable man; I'm sure he'll understand. Be assured I will not fire you. You have been a top-notch teller for us and I appreciate it."

Vicky went back to her teller station, and I called Art Brooks and repeated Vicky's version of the event. Art chuckled over the phone. "I'll be dammed, she didn't even know I had a savings account with you. I get it now; she was just jealous of my new truck. It is a beauty!"

"Well Art, I'm glad you understand; there was no inappropriate intent on Vicky's part. We think she is an excellent teller and don't want to lose her," I responded.

"Come to think of it, Rachael and I have found Vicky and Gary to be damn fine neighbors too!" Art said.

Our parade of unique and interesting customers continued. One of them was Ken Jones, a retired gentleman, who, with his wife, lived on a little hobby farm east of town. He always carried nice balances and when in the bank was friendly and usually had something amusing to say.

On this day particular day, he came in wanting to borrow $5,000 for 90 days. Since I had been at the bank, he never requested a loan. Ken asked specifically to see me. I told him we would need a personal financial statement or balance sheet.

"You need a what?" He asked.

"Ken, you know, a balance sheet, a list of what you own and what you owe, tell us how rich you are," I said and handed him the form.

Ken said, "OK."

And he began filling in a few figures on the asset side, value of ranch, a number for his total investments. He looked at the liability side and said, "I don't owe any money, except for monthly bills, phone, electricity, that sort of thing. Do you really need that?"

I replied, "No, we don't need information on the regular household stuff, since you zero them out monthly; you can just write none, if your place and vehicles are unencumbered. Then please sign it."

I watched as he wrote something and applied his signature. He handed the finished document to me. It read, "I am a Rich Son of a Bitch, Kenneth C. Jones."

I had to laugh as I prepared a disclosure note for the requested loan.

Mary called and asked if I could come home early, as she was feeling severe pains in her lower abdomen. Fortunately, it was a relatively slow September day and I was able to break away quickly. When I got home her face was white and it was obvious she was in tremendous pain. I called Pete Frank, who said to meet him at the hospital. He did a quick examination and discovered that the pain seemed to be coming from a tumor that was lodged in her ovaries; he decided to operate immediately. It turned out to be a baseball-size growth, which seemed to have been absent when Dr. Swenson had examined her and removed the lung tumor in July. The tumor appeared despite the chemotherapy treatments with Dr. Clarissia at the University of Utah Medical Center in Salt Lake City the previous month.

The reality of the rapid progression of the cancer and its' grim outcome settled upon us. We made monthly trips to Salt Lake for the treatments with Dr. Clarissa and made it a point to have some fun in the process. A gourmet dinner and show of some kind became part of the ritual.

By 1972 time I had gradually put together an excellent board of directors, comprised mostly of men who were active in the business community. Carroll Durkee had retired due to failing health and move to Billings; he died a couple of years later. Herman and Gerald Williams were still interested and active board members. Larry Probst was brought on board the year I became president. Soon to follow was John Anderson, a hardworking, successful rancher, whose picturesque ranch lay east of town against the magnificent Big Horn Mountains. He also had a beautiful herd of quality

Hereford cattle. When cattle prices were low, he would complain, "To think I spent a year shoveling shit only to lose money!"

We also brought on Jerry Henderson, who was a lifelong resident of Basin and a Harris family friend and neighbor. He was president of the Wyoming Gas Company, our local natural gas utility. Jerry known as an enthusiastic citizen's band radio user, whose CB handle was "gas passer".

My board of directors were acutely aware of Mary's deteriorating condition. At the October board meeting, Larry and Jerry confronted me on my need and responsibilities to both run the bank and take proper care of Mary. They pointed out the bank was having a banner year, with excellent sugar beet prices, good cattle prices and strong loan and deposit growth. Larry said, "We think you need a strong credit person as your second man, so your time is more flexible to take care of Mary's needs. We all know Jack is a competent operations man, but is weak, too kind hearted, when it comes to credit administration."

All the board members supported Larry's motion to seek an experienced senior credit officer. This was one of those events that reinforced the idea of having a good board comprised of members, who are more than "Yes men" to the C.E.O. I made a few calls to Ted Ernst and Bart Neville, a couple of my old examiner buddies I thought might fill the bill, but they were both employed in promising situations in their hometown banks. As I contemplated how I might find someone to fill this need, Ann Martin said there was a gentleman named Robert King who wished to see me. I didn't have a clue as to who Bob King was although I heard the King family had moved into the community. Bob was dressed in a conservative gray suit, white shirt and blue tie. This was not typical dress in Greybull, Wyoming, except for bankers and lawyers. He had the face of a middle-aged man, and his hair was prematurely white. I said, "Bob, nice to meet you. What can I do for you?"

"Mr. Harris," he said as he handed me his résumé, "I am looking for a job. I have been in banking for over 20 years."

I quickly scanned the document and saw that he had good lending training and experience at Wells Fargo Bank in San Francisco, and a couple of V. P. positions at two Dallas, Texas banks. One of the banks, Texas Bank

& Trust Company, a fair sized institution, I'd heard of. The other appeared to be a smaller suburban bank. He had also spent three years as a V.P. sales manager of an agricultural products company, also in Texas. I replied, "You seem to have excellent banking credentials and as it happens we are looking for a senior credit officer, but I'm fearful that we might not be able to pay the salary you are looking for. I am curious how you wound up coming to Greybull?"

"Mr. Harris, let me respond to your questions in reverse order. We moved here because my wife, Mary Ann, felt the need to be close to her kid sister, Amy. Amy Ogle, married to Ed Ogle, he works at the Dresser plant. As to my salary needs, I am pretty flexible. We came here knowing that duplicating my Dallas bank salaries wasn't likely to happen. Besides, we live inexpensively, and the cost of living here is much cheaper than Dallas," he answered. We talked at length and after a few calls to board members I hired Bob as executive vice president.

Since Bob now worked for me as VP, I had more flexibility and could help Mary through her illness. Bob also provided some expertise that my examiner experience could not. Mr. King was also a Mormon, which proved to be useful in obtaining a number of accounts from individual Mormons. Some of those accounts were good and others not too good. He was even able to wrestle the South Big Horn County Stake account away from our competitor in Basin. This big account was the main account for all the Mormon activities in our community. The move allowed me the ability to concentrate my efforts on key issues both at the bank and in my personal life.

As Christmas approached, it was apparent that this could be Mary's last, so we decided to make it special. We invited both families, including our brothers, my parents and of course Mary's dad, who had become a widower in May. We were determined to have a memorable, fun holiday season. The way this year had gone, more obstacles were to be expected.

Shortly after Thanksgiving we had a small fire in the kitchen, which we were able to put out ourselves and no serious damage was done. Luckily we had a fire extinguisher, received as a wedding gift that had been idle all these years; it worked just fine. However, the kitchen looked like something from

Dante's Inferno and needed to be repainted pronto. I called Art Baugh, our local painting contractor.

Art was a small solo operator, but took great pride in his workmanship. Art was also a chief petty officer in the Navy reserves and his service predated Pearl Harbor and in fact he was there on the "day that will live in infamy." Art promised he would get the job done in time for our Christmas festivities. The other issue was getting Mary's chemotherapy done so she was over the nausea incurred by the time our guests arrived.

We were able to charter a Piper Aztec airplane for a day, in this way Mary's urgent care in Salt Lake City would be taken care of expediently and I would only miss a day of work during this very busy month of the year. The chemotherapy finished a week earlier than usual to allow for the time it took to recover from the massive dose of drugs. By this time Mary's hair was falling out in massive chunks. As a result, Mary purchased three wigs, which she cherished. As she explained it, "I've never had a hair color choice every morning before: redhead, blonde or brunette. It is kind of fun." Mary was remarkable at remaining cheerful, even under these trying and difficult circumstances.

Art Baugh finished the kitchen redecoration in a cheery bright green, blue and white. With the house in shape, the next question became: how do you entertain all seven of these people for a week?

We decided to make a movie. At the time a number of airplane hijackings were taking place around the world and airport security was being tightened, especially in the U.S. We owned a Super Eight movie camera with a zoom lens. I wrote a simple script and called the film "Skijacked". We began filming as our guests began to arrive, before they even were aware of our plans. Our family, at least our generation, were all ski enthusiasts.

We cast Mary's brother Dick as the hijacker and filmed a Frontier Airlines Convair 580 as it landed at the nearest commercial airport at Worland, Wyoming, and caught Dick as he deplaned. Mary's twin brother John and his wife Marti flew in from Ada, Oklahoma, where he had set up an oral surgery practice. My brother Frank now in medical school at the University of Colorado in Denver, joined with my parents driving up from Colorado. Mary's dad flew up from Albuquerque. On the first evening we had everyone together, we went over the plot for "Skijacked". We were determined to include every interested person in our motion picture enterprise.

The storyline started with Dick boarding the airplane and demanding to be taken to "Ski Valley." We filmed the hijacking scene in the cockpit of a Hawkins & Powers C119, which is a cargo plane with a very roomy "flight deck"; which made for easy filming. Frank played the part of our blind pilot, and four-year-old Oliver was the co-pilot. We synthesized pilot uniforms by fastening gold ribbons on their blue jackets. Marti and Mary were the good time gal flight attendants, dolled up in flannel leopard like sleepwear. Dick, wearing a red ski cap, extracts a small ransom and bails out over "Ski Valley." We faked this by having him jump out of the parked C119 wearing skis and using an umbrella for a parachute. Bear in mind this was a very low budget film.

Dick, being a very accomplished skier, landed parachute in hand, making a stunning, perfect skis-together touchdown on the steepest part of the mountain. Meanwhile, the plane crew radioed the local sheriff who just happens to be skiing that day. I played the part of the sheriff, doing an impersonation of our colorful cigar-chewing local Sheriff George Warfel. The sheriff chased Dick down the mountain. Dick was wearing a red ski cap, but Dick being the superior skier gives the sheriff the slip and seizes the opportunity to give John the red hat, who neglected to wear a hat that day and was feeling the effects of the cold weather on his bald head.

Seeing John ambling along with the red hat, the sheriff mistakenly thinks he has caught up to Dick and stabbed him with a ski pole. At the hospital - our freshly painted green, blue and white kitchen- a "skipolectomy" is performed by Dr. Cramer, with brother Frank serving as the anesthetist, assisted by party girl nurses Marti and Mary. The operation is performed on our kitchen table and the anesthesia used is a bottle of Old Crow whiskey, poured into the patient using a funnel. Along with removing the ski pole, the good doctor also found an alarm clock, pocketknife, and several other extraneous items. A sign appeared saying the film is "Banned in Albuquerque." In the end "Skijacker Dick" was apprehended by the sheriff and placed behind bars as he attempted to hitchhike away from the Ski Valley. Crime doesn't pay after all.

With the skiing and filming together with the more traditional Christmas festivities, our extended family had a most joyful holiday. Mary and I spliced the film together; it ran about 25 minutes and became a family classic.

Meanwhile, the routine of business continued into 1973.

Chuck Shirran, owner of Parker's Café located diagonally across the street, came in and asked, if we would be willing to loan him money to remodel his commercial kitchen and expand into the pool hall next door to the restaurant. I told him we would be happy to work with him on the financing. I didn't recall we'd ever had any loans with him, but given his stature in the community and the fact he had always been a good depositor, I was sure we could work out a loan arrangement with him.

A couple months later I noticed the expansion had been completed and the kitchen remodeling was also finished. Chuck was bending over his menu planning work papers. He was a meticulous planner. For example, when he had a turkey dinner as the "Sunday Special," it was a given that homemade turkey soup would be a featured offering on Monday and perhaps the Tuesday lunchtime menu as well. It was this careful planning and next to zero waste that made this little restaurant, with good food and inexpensive prices, successful.

"Chuck, I thought you wanted a loan for this remodel project, but it looks to be done. Is there something we can help you with?" I asked.

Chuck looked at me pleasantly, but without a smile he was not a particularly given to smiles and said, "Oh, I managed to find enough money lying around to complete the renovations without borrowing. I seem to be having another good year here. Maybe next time I'll be in to see you. Thanks for your interest."

I shared the story with Gerald Williams, and his response was, "Funny, I've had that conversation with Chuck, I'll bet half a dozen times. He always seems to FIND the money. Do you suppose he mines those booth seat cracks and finances his improvements from that source?"

It was during that winter that my friend from Boulder, Wynn Kinsley and his wife Faith came up to visit us in their dark green, almost black, right hand drive, Rolls Royce. Wynn and Faith operated a quality men's clothing store in Boulder. Many of the goods they stocked were imported from

England. It would be fair to say they were anglophiles; hence the Rolls. Wynn told me they bought the car in 1960; the car was a 1955 Silver Cloud in pristine condition. Upon arrival, they asked if I could locate a garage space for their prized car, since it was expected to be a cold night. I made a couple of phone calls and was able to find a garage at a nearby gas station for the night.

Wynn, who preferred to be called a haberdasher, brought a bottle of quality Ballintine's scotch whiskey. As he "built" the drinks he told us he was possibly interested in purchasing a small hobby ranch and was thinking of moving to our community. In our part of Wyoming, bankers were always attempting to recruit new residents, so I was glad to have this old friend interested in Greybull. I knew Wynn was interested in the history of the west and was surprisingly knowledgeable about the cattle business from his readings. We also learned Wynn had worked summers as a teenager at a cattle ranch near Wheatland, Wyoming. Mary and I decided to take our guests out to Bluejacket's Restaurant.

Since neither Mary nor I had ever ridden in a Rolls before, we accepted Wynn's offer to drive. I sat in the seat where the driver normally sits and kept grabbing for the non- existent left-hand side steering wheel during the whole 20-mile journey. Jim Bluejacket, a Native American, greeted us courteously and took our orders. We all ordered which we enjoyed in the ambiance of the rustic log constructed dining room. On the drive home Wynn kept trying to recall Jim's name, "Was it 'Charlie Eagle Feathers'?"

After thoroughly researching the prospects of moving from Boulder to Greybull, Wyoming, Wynn and Faith decided to stay put doing what they knew best, the haberdashery business.

Not too many weeks later I received a call from Jim Bluejacket, who unknown to me was in the hospital trying to recover from some aliment. "Bert," he said, "I got a notice in the mail that my note is due and I'm here at South Big Horn County Hospital and can't get down there to take care of it. Would you mind coming out with an extension agreement for me to sign? I'll give you a check for the interest and a reduction."

"Sure Jim. I'm rather busy today. How about if I come out tonight and we can take care of business in a more leisurely fashion?" I answered.

"Sounds good to me. Visiting hours start at 7:00 p.m." he replied. At about seven that evening, I arrived at the hospital and was directed to Jim's room. Jim was sitting upright, looking paler than his usual tan Native American complexion. He greeted me and we quickly took care of Jim's banking business and started to talk on a more personal level.

"Jim," I inquired, "How did you land in Greybull, Wyoming?"

Jim gave a kind of grim smile - he was obviously in pain - and said, "I was born here. My father worked at the Standard Oil refinery in the teens, when it was going strong. Maybe you've heard about my dad; they called him 'Big Jim.' He was actually from Oklahoma, but was recruited by Standard Oil, because he was one hell of a baseball player. He could hit, throw, field and run."

"Why would Standard Oil be seeking baseball players?" I asked.

"In those days, big corporate employers all had semi-pro teams, and played the guys who worked down at those refineries in Casper, Billings and Denver," he said.

"He was a ringer then," I replied.

"Exactly," Jim said, "I really appreciate your coming out here. I just hate having past-due obligations."

"Happy to help. I have always liked the way you have been prompt taking care if your loans with us. You look tired, I'll be going and let you get some rest," I replied.

Jim cracked a smile, unusual for this stoic Indian, "Well, I'm just a poor, dumb, but honest Indian."

Spring was now upon us and I was approached by Harry Bishop from Lovell. Harry was in the insurance business, but had applied to us for a ranch loan. I took his financial statement and it looked decent. He showed a pretty good net worth, modest debt. Apparently, what happened was Harry had inherited a good-sized ranch from an uncle and decided to change professions. As we visited I realized that he really didn't have a whole lot of ranching experience, just working occasionally summers as a youth for his Uncle Hiram.

I told him that we would make an inspection of his spread before deciding. I told him I'd get one of my rancher board members to accompany me. I called Herman Mayland and he readily agreed to join me in this inspection. On the 30-mile trip to Harry's place, Herman looked over the file I had built. Herman said, "I knew old Hiram, not a bad old guy. Always seemed to make a good living out of that place. I'm kind of surprised Harry would come knocking on our door for this loan; Hiram always did business with the Pearsons at the First National in Lovell. I wonder if the Pearsons have already turned this guy down."

"I suspect that might well be the case. In fact that was one of the main reasons I wanted you to look at this deal with me. The Pearsons have always taken good care of folks in the north end of the county. I'm always suspicious of Lovell folks coming to us looking for money," I said.

We arrived at the ranch and Harry was there to greet us. "Where are the cattle?" I asked.

Harry pointed to the other side of the house, barns and other out buildings and said, "They're all in the corral, should make it easy to count. You can check the machinery here too, before we go look at the rest of the place."

Herman and I walked over to the corral and started to count. I couldn't help notice that all his farm machinery: tractors, windrowers, balers and everything else was in with the cattle. That was a great way for livestock to break a leg, tripping over all that hardware, I thought. We counted the Hereford herd and the number was almost identical with the number Harry had reflected on his financial statement, just a couple short. Probably hiding behind some equipment somewhere, I thought. Herman started asking some specific questions about the water situation on the place.

We all got into my Jeep and proceeded to look over the mountain pastures and range. It was a pretty place, with a backdrop view of Yellowtail Lake. Since it was May, the pasture all looked quite green. Harry indicated he would be turning the cattle out within the week. We returned Harry to his ranch house and Herman and I started on the trek home. Herman asked, "What do you think?"

"I don't like the way the cattle are corralled in with the machinery. He's just inviting an animal to break its leg. I don't think I'm interested in this deal," I said.

Herman said, "That's bad husbandry alright, but it is not the worst of it. This guy doesn't know where the hell his water is. You know in this country you must irrigate to have a crop and pasture. Unless you have time to irrigate this place for Harry every day, I'd stay away from this guy."

We declined that loan, but we were able to accommodate many farm and merchant customers and the bank growth seemed to be on course. Mary and I continued our monthly trips to Salt Lake City to Dr. Clarissa and the chemotherapy treatments. Towards the end of May we made one more trip, as she became weaker and weaker. She was in pain and I was now giving her a hefty shot of morphine at bedtime every night so she could sleep. She called me "Dr. No" because I had no license. We contemplated whether to attend the Wyoming Bankers Association Convention in Jackson Hole during the second week of June.

We decided to attend. The Monday of the convention week, Dr. Peter Frank called me at work and asked if I could come to his office that morning during what he described as "paperwork time" so we could talk. When I arrived the office was devoid of patients and his nurse ushered me into Pete's inner sanctum. Pete was sitting there smoking his pipe; the aromatic tobacco immediately perked up my senses. Pete said, "I've been dreading this conversation, with you, but I think you need to be aware Mary's cancer has spread though out her entire body. I've talked to Dr. Clarissa, and he feels she should continue the treatments. I guess he doesn't feel it hurts to keep trying, but in point of fact she is dying."

Stunned and yet at the same time not entirely surprised, I asked, "Any idea how much time she has left?"

Pete leaned back and took another puff on his pipe and said, "Of course it is hard to predict, but my guess is two, maybe three months."

"Mary and I were planning on attending the Wyoming Bankers Convention in Jackson this week. We would be leaving Wednesday morning, be back Friday evening. Do you think it is OK?" I asked.

Pete took another draw on his pipe and answered, "If Mary feels up to it, by all means go. She has a couple of months. If she can still find some joy in life, I'd recommend it."

Bright and early Wednesday morning were took off for Jackson, arriving at 1:30 p.m. Mary was tired and wanted to take a nap. I was hungry and decided to find a drink and a sandwich. As I passed through the bar at the Grand Teton Lodge, I noticed a gathering of Jack Pearson, Vern Bower,

Bob Nelson, Sam Allen and Wayne Messenger, all C.E.O.s of the banks surrounding us, sitting around a table having drinks. I walked up to them and asked in a jovial way, "Looks like a meeting of the Big Horn Basin Bankers Association, how come I wasn't invited?"

They all kind of glared at me, finally Sam Allen said, "You remember the Big Horn Canning Company loan, which you declined to participate in with us, when you first went to Greybull?"

"Sure," I answered.

"Well," Sam continued, "you were right in not trusting old Goppert. He isn't going to pay, since there is no personal guaranty, which you had insisted on. Now we are discussing liquidation and how much we should be charging off on the loan. You wise young devil, you!"

"Oh, I guess I'm glad to be left out of this discussion," I said, and turned to find a sandwich and visit with some of the other attendees.

Mary was awake when I returned to our room. We leisurely got dressed in our party duds. Just before we left for the cocktail hour she said, "Dr. No, I need a shot of morphine. Don't give me the full load. I want just enough to take the edge off. I don't want to pass out. I want to visit with all of our friends."

I did as she asked and we marched off to the party. Mary was soon engaged in a conversation with her friend Joan Naramore from Gillette, who was also dying of cancer. They had met at several earlier bankers meeting over the past six years. Since they were both similarly afflicted, they had become close friends in recent months. We had a fine time at the convention and Mary was in good spirits when we returned on Friday. The following morning was the parade for Greybull's annual celebration of our community's history, "The Days of 49." Instead of a float for the parade we were able line up a vehicle for each of the decades the bank had been in business: a 1917 Ford Model T touring car, a 1928 International flatbed truck, a 1935 Ford humpback sedan, Collingwood's '46 Chevy beet truck, Frank Cortez's '50 Kaiser, a '65 Pontiac sedan and finally my new 1973 Pontiac convertible.

Mary took the kids, Oliver age 4 and Martha 22 months, watched and waived as we cruised by. The following day, Sunday, started out pretty normally. We had a light lunch as we were invited to Bud Mr. "Chisel me out of a half a percent" Duggan and Faye Duggan's for dinner that evening. Mary got up out of her chair with great effort to do the lunch dishes.

"Mary, why don't you let me do the dishes. You look very tired." I suggested.

"No!" she barked, "I like to feel useful."

By the time she finished her chores in the kitchen, she plunked down, on the sofa, exhausted. "You're hurting, I can tell. Do you want a shot?"

"It's worse than that. Call Pete," She ordered.

I complied and Dr. Frank instructed me to bring her to the hospital, which I did. I also called the Duggans to cancel our dinner engagement. When we got to the hospital, Pete Frank gave her something to completely sedate her, so she could sleep. The following morning, Monday, about nine, Pete called me at work, "Bert, can you come down to my office, we need to talk."

I drove down to Basin to Dr. Frank's office and we sat down in his smoke filled office. He began, "I know I told you last week I thought she had another two or three months, but I was wrong. She's in the final stages of dying. I've never seen anyone that endured pain so well. She'll be gone in the next 24 to 48 hours."

I was too stunned to even respond. I stopped by the hospital for a visit on the way back to work. She was hooked up to a bunch of tubes and was barely able to talk. She asked, "Do you remember Jim and Katie are on their way up from New Mexico today?" Katie was her favorite cousin and husband, plus their three girls. I told her I would make a motel reservation for them and she would see them this evening, assuming they were on schedule. By evening she slipped a little more, but did seem to enjoy and appreciate Jim and Katie's visit. While they were visiting, I called our respective families to give them the bad news. My parents said they would take off in the morning; Dr. Cramer, who was in the process of closing his medical practice, as he was scheduled to retire the end of the month, promised to be up as soon as he could book a flight.

The following morning, I took the children to Mrs. Reilly's, and then went out to see Mary in the morning. By my next visit about noon, she was just barely lucid. I told her I'd be in later in the afternoon. When I got back, around 5:00 p.m., she was unconscious. All I could think to do was hold her hand and tell her I loved her. I felt a very slight grasp of her hand as I held it. After an hour I went over to Reilly's to retrieve the children. My mom and dad arrived from Boulder as I was trying to put together some supper for the kids and me, although I wasn't very hungry. We talked briefly, when the phone rang. It was the hospital. Mary was gone.

Fifteen

Life Goes On

The following morning, the phone rang about 9 a.m. "This is Sharon Bullard from the Internal Revenue Office in Worland."

"Why in the world would you be calling me?"

"Mr. Harris; this is Mr. Harris, correct?"

"Yes, I am Bert Harris, again why are you calling me?" I responded, my annoyance quite evident in the tone of my voice.

"Mr. Harris, you and your wife have been selected for a 'Taxpayer Compliance Audit'. I am calling to set up and appointment so Agent Withersby can go over your financial records, "she said, firmly.

"Look lady, my wife just died last night and I have a lot on my mind and many things to do, and think about. I don't have time to entertain agent, what's his name?" I exploded.

"Oh, dear, I had no idea," Ms. Bullard sputtered.

She was beginning to sound like she might actually be a human being and that calmed me down. "Look, could you call back in a couple of months after things have settled down."

"Yes, yes, of course, I'll get back to you this fall and we can set up a date. I'll mail you a list of the documents the agent will need to see." she said.

"Thanks, for your understanding. I'll look for your list."

Dad was sitting a few feet away solemnly, contemplatively sipping his morning coffee, "What the hell was that all about?"

"Damned I.R.S. calls today, of all days, to audit my income taxes. Once I told her what was going on she was decent enough and agreed to put it off until fall," I said.

"Well, Bert, we have things to do. I thought we'd go down to Atwood's. I'll give you what moral support I can, to make the arrangements for Mary's funeral. Your mother will look after the children," Dad offered.

Del Atwood, my friend and frequent golf partner, greeted us and expressed his condolences. We selected a beautiful oak coffin. The process caused the reality of Mary's death to hit me again, a kind of double wallop. We talked about a number of issues, foremost on my mind at the moment, was should the kids attend the service. Del recommended that attend the service as it would help them cope with the loss of their mother.

We decided to hold the service on Saturday morning, since this gave our many friends and relatives three days travel time to get to Greybull.

Saturday was a bright sunny day. St. Andrew's Episcopal Church was packed, about 50 mourners were seated in Harris Hall, and addition to the church, built as a memorial to my late grandmother many years earlier by my grandfather. A speaker system had been set up, so the he services could be heard by everyone. In the brief six years we had been in Greybull, Mary had touched so many lives in the community. It was quite heartwarming for our family to see so many people at the service.

Martha, wearing a red and white checked dress trimmed in white walked by the coffin and asked, "Why is mommy in a big box?"

Even though she wasn't yet two years old, it was clear she understood something serious was going on. After the service, our friends and neighbors had brought an extensive lunch to the house. St. Andrew's was without a priest at this time. I called upon our good friend, Bob Thompson who was the former pastor at St. Andrew's to officiate. At the reception, he took Oliver out into the front yard, where they sat on the curb and he managed to consul and counsel him. I don't know what was said, but Oliver seemed to understand.

As I was wondering how I was going to deal with the children, Diana Collingwood came up to me, gave me a hug and offered her services as housekeeper and nanny for the summer. I accepted on the spot.

Diana arrived at 8:00 A.M. Monday morning. She was clad in blue jeans and a red-checkered blouse; her long blond hair neatly combed and her blues eyes sparkled. The kids greeted her happily and I walked to work where things had piled up, although Bob King and Jack Linderman seemed to have their respective sides of the bank covered. I told Diana I'd be home for lunch.

When I arrived home, Diana had a light lunch ready for the four of us. After the children were finished, Diana and I put together a food shopping list, which I thought that I'd get taken care of later that afternoon, before coming home. It dawned on me that my cooking skills were limited. Somehow, I had never in all my years managed to do any real cooking. My mother never allowed me to cook and my college roommate, John Welsh, enjoyed cooking and was pretty good at it too. Bank examiner roommate, Ted Ernst, also liked to cook. Mary was a real master of the culinary arts, and I was resigned not to trespass in the kitchen. With all these talented chefs around, I was content to be assigned dishwashing detail.

I could see this would have to change, and fast. To be on the safe side, on my first trip to the Safeway Store, I purchased three Swanson's TV dinners, just in case. The first meal I remember fixing was fried chicken at noon one Sunday. Diana's mother Charlene gave me step-by-step instructions over the phone. We had a large upright freezer, so I wouldn't need to go grocery shopping too often. My little family settled into something of a routine that summer: work in the morning, lunch back home at noon with Diana and the children. Then back to work in the afternoon until about 5 p.m. When I got home, the house was clean, the beds all made and most important, the kids seemed happy. Martha would wake up screaming for mommy some nights, or when she saw the orange Jeep. I sold it right away, so Martha and Oliver weren't tormented by seeing the thing around.

On Martha's second birthday, July 23rd, Diana prepared a little celebration, so I figured I would leave work by 4 p.m. to properly observe the event. The lobby of the bank in those days closed at 3:00 p.m., giving me time to clear my desk and finish up with the afternoon customers. About 3:30p.m, Becky Lawton, a perky, petite, blond gal, who was now our secretary and receptionist, said there was an elderly white haired gentleman, who was most insistent on seeing me. She said she didn't know the man, which was surprising, since Becky had lived in Greybull long enough to know all the regular customers. She ushered in a spry, slender, white- haired man, into my office.

The old gent's face looked vaguely familiar and I said, "Sir, what can I do for you."

He stammered a minute and said, "I am your uncle Robert, great uncle Robert Burton."

I had received a very thoughtful letter of condolences from Uncle Robert and Aunt Ruth a couple of weeks after Mary died. Uncle Robert by this time was in his early nineties and it had been over twenty years since the last time I had seen him. My father was not at all fond of his mother's brother, so although Robert genuinely tried to keep the family connected; dad never encouraged it. I was quite astonished to have the man dad liked to refer to as "Crazy Uncle Robert" drop in on me. Eccentric probably better describes him.

"Wow, this is a surprise. What brings you to Wyoming? I responded.

"Well Bert, Bernie and Anne, Ruth and I were on our way to Yellowstone National Park and after learning of your dear wife's passing, I wanted to stop by and say hello and express my sympathy for you and your children in person,." Robert explained.

"Today is Martha's second birthday, and Diana, my housekeeper and nanny, is planning a little party. Cake and ice cream, that kind of thing. I think you should join us. I was just cleaning off my desk to leave."

"Be happy to," Robert said.

We arrived at the house about 4:00 p.m. There on the dining room table Diana had made a charming cake, which looked for all the world to be a frost cover teddy bear. Several children from the neighborhood were playing parlor games, which Diana was leading. I made the introductions and shortly thereafter ice cream and cake were served. It was a very nice celebration, which everyone seemed to enjoy. Uncle Robert and his entourage joined us for supper and then took off for Cody, where they had made reservations for the night. The next morning I was back at work, where I picked up an interesting story.

Perhaps some readers will remember the rising gasoline prices and lines at the gas station during the 1970s. While Greybull suffered from the higher prices, we didn't really suffer from shortages, in part due to one local man, Larry Catlin. Larry owned and operated Gordon Refinery, a small fully integrated oil company. By that, I mean they owned their own production, refining facilities, and a string of about 20 gas stations in surrounding communities. The tiny refinery was located just south of town, adjacent to the Greybull River. Larry was a favorite customer of our tellers, because his deposits, mostly cash, were neatly bundled and easy to work; plus Larry was quick witted and a pleasant customer to wait on.

One of the tellers, Jeanne Copp, asked Larry if the present gas crisis would affect Gordon Refinery's ability to provide fuel to us.

Larry replied, "Oh no, we should be just fine. That is, as long as the Greybull River keeps flowing."

Larry's little joke, suggesting he watered the gasoline.

We had a number of patrons directly and indirectly involved in the oil business. Dave Lindsay's company, Frontier Mud Products, was having a good year and came in periodically with invoices for an advance on an accounts receivable line of credit we provided for him. Dave's first wife had also died of cancer a number of years earlier and he could identify with my situation. Dave took me under his wing and became a mentor to me. We had many conversations as the months unfolded. I asked Dave what made his unique drilling fluids successful.

Dave said, "Well, that's a secret. I always keep a patent pending."

"Why not just go ahead and get a patent," I asked.

He replied, "The problem is twofold. One reason is I am always trying to improve my product. The other, more importantly, is once a patent is granted my secrets are published and revealed, so a competitor could copy it."

"Why don't they just try to break down the product and figure it out," I said.

"Cucumber juice!"

"Cucumber juice, what the hell do you mean by that?" I responded.

Dave smiled broadly, "The cucumber juice is to throw inquisitive minds off the trail. It has nothing to do with what makes the concoction work, doesn't react with it or change the product's effectiveness. But it does confuse nosey competitors."

"What else have you got going on?" I inquired.

"Well, since you ask, I have an idea for a new product, a plant food, if you will. I'm trying to put together a little company to manufacture and market it. Can you make it to a meeting with me and some guys next Tuesday evening at my place at seven?"

"Assuming I can get a babysitter, I'll be there."

Sixteen

Moving Right Along

By 1974, the bank had nearly tripled in asset size. During the previous year I had realized that our capital ratios were becoming strained and to resolve this problem we issued and sold $300,000 in capital notes. Bob Waller's bank, The Midland National Bank of Billings bought the notes, which were due to mature in December 1981. Capital was on the mind of the regulatory agencies in Washington, as well.

As it happened, Brenton Leavitt, a Greybull native whose mother resided across the street and had been one of the ladies in Mary's bridge club, was in charge of bank supervision at the Federal Reserve Board in Washington. Mr. Leavitt's home was at the "Watergate" in the District of Columbia. District of Columbia residents were not able to vote at this time, in order to vote, Mr. Leavitt claimed his legal residence to be his mom's home in Greybull, Wyoming. As a part of maneuvers to be a bona fide Wyoming resident he did his personal banking with us, at The First National Bank of Greybull.

Brenton enjoyed his frequent visits to Greybull to see his mother and Brother Richard, a redhead; well, what hair he had left was red. Richard was a rancher, with a place up Horse Creek, not far from Wally and Martin Mayland's Bear Creek Ranch, up against the western slope of the Big Horn Mountains. The Leavitt brothers always seemed to be quite close and it was a frequent sight to see them walking, in unison, about town together. Richard and Brenton, were both fairly tall and bald and had a peculiar dislike of trees. Yes, trees, this is not a typo. Both brothers were quite vocal about this, so I asked Brenton, why? One day I asked Brenton why he had such an aversion to trees.

He answered quite simply. "So I can see out. All those damned trees in Washington, drive me nuts, because I can't see out. Trees spoil my view."

He was a true Wyomingite in that he especially enjoyed the "wide open spaces".

When an article appeared in *Forbes* magazine about the Fed's concern about bank capitalization, in particular the nation's major institutions in New York City and other money centers, Brent Leavitt moved to center stage in the national financial press. J. C. Quigg, the retired superintendent of Greybull's school system, was quite astute about investments and finance and was also an avid reader of *Forbes*, read the article; he accosted me on my walk home from the bank one day at noon and asked if we had been "Leavittized". This was the expression used in the magazine if Mr. Leavitt had called on your bank to discuss your particular bank's capital inadequacy.

I replied, with pride, "No, Mr. Quigg, as a matter of fact, Mr. Leavitt does his personal banking with us."

When Brenton was in town, we often invited him to attend our board meetings, if his trip coincided with our regular meeting day; then he would join us for dinner at Five Sisters Restaurant out at Shell. After Betty Leavitt died, Brenton's mom died, Brenton took over the house and lived there after he retired. Occasionally, I'd have him over to my house for "Happy Hour", thereby greatly broadening my knowledge and view of the banking world. Of course, my main focus had to be The First National Bank of Greybull. With the addition of the capital notes, we were situated to embark on another, although smaller expansion and remodel program. I was concerned about the cramped space for our accounting function, which I realized when we moved into our remodeled quarters. In addition, with growth in the insurance agency, it was clear that we needed more space so we didn't have to sit on each other's laps.

The board and I determined that converting the second floor to bank use would be the most economical and simplest strategy. This area contained about two-thirds the floor space of the main floor. The upstairs had once been an apartment, in recent times, however, it had become mostly a collector of dust and long irrelevant old bank records.

Remembering my previous experience with Bank Building Corporation, I decided a local architect would be more suitable, and found one, Al Lauber, who was located in Worland, and he was happy to take on the task. By this time, I was much more confident in my judgment.

Since our building had originally been two buildings, there was a two feet thick masonry wall between two sections. The east side of the building we decided to make into a large bookkeeping and accounting section. For this we needed a records vault, to insure that vital bank records would survive, should we have a fire.

On the west side of the building, we planned a Board of Directors Room, with a large table, which freed up our old board-conference room for staff and customer meetings. For our general contractor, we selected Calvin Wardell's, Wardell Construction, which was a customer, we had attracted because of our ability in the insurance agency to get him contractor's bonds. Mr. Wardell's specialty was building Mormon churches, all over the country. His expertise was in building commercial buildings. Wardell was a local man and I had always felt guilty that we weren't able to use a local contractor on our first building project, but at the time there we had no customer contractors with commercial building experience.

Charlene, joined by Louise, had successfully grown the insurance agency to more than twice its original size. We were surprised one day, when Herb Miller, who owned the Marshall Agency, down the street came into my office one day to and said: "I want to sell you my insurance agency."

I couldn't have been more shocked, because there had been a certain rivalry between the two insurance agencies, which started during World War II. While Gerald Williams was serving the nation on a warship in the Pacific, Bert Marshall, who didn't join the military during the war, was busy trying to steal Gerald's insurance business, which greatly annoyed Priscilla Williams. My own relationship, with Herb Miller who had fairly recently bought the Marshall Agency, by the time I showed up on the scene, had always been cordial enough and he had been a good depositor. I tried and apparently succeeded in keeping a friendly, professional relationship with Mr. Miller.

I asked why he wanted to sell and he said, "As you know, I'm a retired Air Force Officer. I receive a good pension. To tell the truth, I'm bored with the business and want to do something else."

By something else, I was thinking, he meant fishing or playing lots of golf. I was in for quite surprise, but I will come back to that later. We negotiated a deal, where I paid him some cash up front then the rest, and a non-compete agreement payable monthly and enjoy a tax deduction, to boot. We set a date to close the deal, which was deliberately set on a Friday, so Charlene, Louise and I could merge the accounting systems over the weekend. We discovered, unhappily, that we used two very different accounting methods with the insurance companies we represented, as opposed to the method Herb used with his companies.

Saturday of that weekend, we puttered and struggled with the two different accounting methods used, without a solution. Sunday, we met again, wondering how the hell, we would be able to get up and running by Monday morning. Finally, I said, "I'll be damned if I understand insurance company accounting, but I do understand bank accounting. Why, don't we pretend this is a bank, use a bank like general ledger system."

Charlene said, "OK, how is that going to help us?"

"Well, by setting up an account receivable, every time we issue a policy, we account for what the customer owes us. On the liability side, we set up an accounts payable for the insurance company issuing the policy. We'll then drop the commission portion into income, at such as time as we are billed by U.F.& G., or whatever company, issues the policy and the commission figure is determined. That way it won't matter, which billing method the company uses, Account Current, or the statement method."

Charlene and Louise both smiled and we eagerly set to work and by early afternoon, we had an easy to understand accounting system, which was less labor intensive than if we had used only the company generated statements, Herb used. Thanks to the Marshall Agency purchase we doubled our volume once again, but only needed to hire one clerical person to keep up with the increased workload.

Much to my surprise, a few months later Herb and Jay Wilkerson came in and wanted to buy Lee's Grocery store, we put together a financing package and they were soon in business. However, soon they were struggling. Jay had been the meat cutter, or butcher if you prefer, at the Safeway store, and was considered by many to be the most skilled meat vender in our corner of the world. He was also very frugal. In fact it turned out that he could pinch a penny until you could hear Lincoln scream.

Herb on the other hand, knew next to nothing about the grocery business, other than the fact that he appeared to be well fed. He quickly learned that running a grocery store was nothing like flying a plane for the Air Force. He was accustomed to the insurance business, where the company did your pricing for you. Moreover, agents, never, ever, deviated from this routine. Sales, specials, never happen in the insurance business. In short order the two guys were in trouble, because of inflexible pricing and failure to adequately promote, or advertise their business. They came in and asked if I had any ideas or knew someone who could help them.

I immediately thought of SCORE, Service Corps of Retired Executives, which is a volunteer organization of retired business people. Although it is not mandatory to be retired SCORE members help people with a wide variety of business problems. I called the SBA office, the sponsor of SCORE, located in Casper and asked them to send some help to the J & H Grocery Store.

They responded rather quickly and sent a gentleman, by the name of Ed Long. I had met him, briefly and knew he was a competent, no nonsense kind of guy. Mr. Long, who was in reality quite short, had a background in accounting and was thoroughly versed in the grocery business. He set up an appointment with Herb and Jay for 8:00 AM on a Friday morning. According to the guys, Ed Long showed up at 8 o'clock on the button.

While I was a lunch, Mr. Long stopped by the bank and left me a note stating he had spent the entire morning with Jay and Herb. I hadn't been back from lunch more than ten minutes, when a very bedraggled Jay and Herb came into my office. They looked like a pair of whipped puppies. I said, "Well, how did it go with Ed Long?"

"Where the devil, did you find that mean little son of a bitch?" Jay shot back.

"Well, like promised, I called the SBA in Casper for a SCORE volunteer to come up and talk to you; they sent Ed Long. Was he impolite?" I replied.

Herb chimed in, "No, I guess I can't say that, but he hammered away, at everything we were doing wrong. He went on for four hours, on and on.

The only thing he liked was the way Jay cuts meat. Everything else, from accounting, produce management, marketing, advertising, pricing, using lost leaders effectively, seems like we were doing everything wrong."

"Well, did you get anything out of the experience."

"Oh, yes, Jay and I were taking notes like crazy during the entire visit. There were many ideas we will put right to use today." Replied Herb.

Finally, Jay said, "Funny, though, you know, the nasty little bastard was right on every point."

The guys left determined to do better and I think in fact made many key improvements, but when an offer to sell the building at a good price they opted to get out, a couple years later.

On the home front, the kids were getting along fine under Marcella's supervision. Oliver was bored and largely ignored. He had just missed the fifth birthday cut-off to start Kindergarten, but was primed to start learning to read from watching Big Bird, Ernie and Bert on Sesame Street on television. At breakfast, we would read from the cereal boxes, or whatever else was available; at night I always tried to read the kids a story from the small library of children's books we had accumulated since their arrival.

On weekends we tried to have some fun. When I could find a female friend to take Martha, we would go swimming. Taking a little girl into the men's locker room never seemed like a good idea to me. I took Oliver skiing, which allowed me to ski too. He quickly learned the "snowplow" method. The first trip down from the top of the mountain, he giggled joyously, all the way down. Sunday meals I tried to make special, as well. Fried chicken and steak were our Sunday favorites. I was learning to cook. During the week I'd usually put together crock-pot meals, which were quick, easily assembled, in the morning, and ready to eat when I got home from work. After a day at the office, I was ready for a martini; certainly not slaving over a meal. I even managed to entertain a girlfriend or two with my cooking and began to develop some confidence in the meals I was preparing.

Since it was easier to stay home with the kids, I decided to do some entertaining at home. The first guests I invited for dinner were my next-door neighbors Dan and Jean Hawkins, who had been helpful in many, many ways, when Mary was ill and throughout my ordeal. At the time of Mary's death, they opened up the guest room in their home to my out of town family, lent us a twin engine plane, complete with pilot to gather incoming mourners from the Billings airport. I wanted to reciprocate in some small way, so in the spring, after I gained some trust in my culinary skills, I decided to have them over for dinner one evening.

I decided to prepare beef stroganoff over noodles with green beans and bought a bottle of a fine red Bordeaux wine. By six, I was scheduled to be ready for my guests. Jean called a few minutes earlier to say Dan was called last minute to rescue an injured climber at the base of Cloud Peak in the Big Horn Mountains with a helicopter. Dan was a virtuoso helicopter pilot: if a mission could be safely accomplished, with a chopper, then Dan could do it. Gene Powers, had flow up there, but since his aviation specialty was fixed wing, not whirly-birds, he looked at the ledge where the climber lay and decided he wasn't up to the challenge and radioed down for "Hawkeye", as Dan was affectionately known. Dan took off with the Bell Jet Ranger and successfully made the tricky rescue and brought the guy directly to the hospital. As a result, the Hawkins were about an hour and a half late, for dinner.

I had managed to keep the meal warm, without drying it out, but was still somewhat apprehensive about my cooking. Dan was famished and we decide to enjoy the Bordeaux with the meal instead of having a cocktail hour. Dan plunged into the Stroganoff, and polished off three helpings and said and as he finished the last of it, "Boy, this is good!" It was a great confidence builder for my cooking.

With the summer on its way my life was looking brighter. I decided to terminate Marcella, since Diana Collingwood was looking for a summer job and I knew both the kids and I would be much happier with her running the household. Summer brought a number of curious happenings.

A young man, Jack Orton, came into the bank wanting to finance a car wash.

As I listened to Orton's story I realized that this was to be a very grand car wash, like one might see in a much larger town. I asked, "How much will it cost? How much equity would he invest in the project?"

Orton replied, "Well, I think I might be able to scrape up $5000. The set up for the car wash from the E-Z Car Wash Systems is $55,000. Then I think I can pick up a couple of lots over on Railroad Avenue for $10,000. Another $10,000 for site preparation and water, electrical and sewer hookups, so all totaled about $75,000, which I'd need to borrow, since I'd need my money for incidentals. I'd charge the going rate, like they get in Billings, say five bucks."

"Any idea how many car washes a week you'd need to sell to pay for this car wash emporium? "I inquired.

Young Orton replied enthusiastically, "I figure, I need 500 car washes a week, which would let me breakeven. It is a really wonderful car wash."

I thought a minute and said, "Here are a couple of things you need to think about. First, there are two 'wand' type car washes in town, where you can do it yourself for a dollar's worth of quarters. But ever more important, there are only 1000 or so passenger cars in town so half the people in town will need to wash their car every week for your project to breakeven. How likely is that?"

I paused and continued, "I'm pretty particular about my vehicles and I don't wash them that often."

Orton stared at me in disbelief, pushed the SBA application he had requested back towards me, got up and said. "My God, I never thought of that."

Orton got up and left. At the end of the summer, a dozen, or more German tourists showed up in our bank lobby. Vickie came into my office and said, "These folks want to exchange German Marks for Dollars. How do we do that?"

"Vickie, send one of them in and let me talk to their leader." I replied.

A blustery, ruddy, round faced German gentleman came into my office and said, "Ve need to exchange Marks for Dollars."

I replied, "What is going on here, this isn't a typical request?"

"Oh, I suppose it isn't. Ve have two busloads of tourists from Germany and one of our Mercedes Benz buses broke down. It will take several days to get the parts here. In fact, Ve will be here about a week and ve need American Dollars." The man replied in heavily accented German.

"OK, now I understand. Let me make a phone call to determine the exchange rate and we will be glad to accommodate your group." I said.

"Danke, Danke," he said.

"Let me also call Eileen Diener at the 'Chamber of Commerce' and let her know you folks will be here for a few days. I'm sure she'll want to entertain you, so your people will enjoy our community to the greatest extent possible." I added.

I made a call to First National Bank of Denver, which was the nearest bank to us with an International Department. They explained that the current exchange rate was 3.90 Marks for one U.S. Dollar, but cautioned me that the rate fluctuated some each hour and that I should build in some margin, since they would only credit our account, when they had the Marks in hand. I took their advice and set an exchange rate of 3.95 Marks for a U.S. Dollar, which insured we would come out a little ahead on the transactions. Since there were two busloads of tourists, we exchanged several thousands of Marks for our Dollars. For the effort, we earned, to our surprise, $362 for the week on foreign exchange. This meant Alma needed to establish a new income account, but it wasn't to be our last foreign exchange income.

Eileen from the Chamber of Commerce office rounded up several volunteers to give our community's German visitors tours of what we had to see of possible interest to tourists. One of the points of interest in Greybull was nearby Sheep Mountain, which is a fascinating geological site. The Big Horn River runs north through town and over geologic time cutting through Sheep Mountain, as the mountain rose over millions of years. The result was Sheep Mountain was sliced, as though it was an onion, revealing half a dozen or more periods of layers of different geological epochs, identified by various colorful bands of reds, purple, browns and yellow rocks. The tourists were also treated to our first of the season Greybull "Buffalos" football game.

Because it was late August and the weather was mild, I decided to bundle up the kids and attend the game and sort of act as a co-host. As it turned out, I sat next to a charming blond young German lady, so the evening turned out to be quite pleasant. Monday noon, Diana said she had heard a funny story about her rancher neighbors Stan and Mary Flitner's, seven year old son Danny.

"Diana, today is the kind of day I could use a funny story, let's hear it." I said.

Diana grinned broadly and said, "You know Stan and Mary are, well kind of straight laced, don't use a lot of bad language, so on the first day of school, on the bus some kid lets fly with the infamous "F" word. Danny didn't know what the word meant, since it wasn't something he had heard before. The bus driver got mad, reprimanded the foul-mouthed kid, and even made him walk part of the way home. Little Danny went home and asked his parents what the "F" word meant. Stan tells him, 'it's like animals breeding, mating, you know, it happens here all the time.'"

Danny shook his head and said, 'Oh, is that all?'"

We both had a good laugh and I said, "I've been wonder what to do once you go start bank to school next week. Any ideas?"

As usual Diana came through for me, "You know, Gen Overgaag, used to work as a secretary at Hawkins and Powers. I understand she is looking for a job, she is good with children. I'll bet she would do it for you."

"Sure I know Gen, I'll give her a call this afternoon." I replied.

I called Gen and the housekeeper nanny position was filled that afternoon.

Just before closing an elder gentleman came into my office, it was Homer Renner. Mr. Renner, was a colorful old friend and patient of my Grandfather. I remembered driving out to visit the Renner's with my Grandparents one sunny, Sunday afternoon during the summer of 1955. Mr. Renner was quite excited and wanted to show Granddad his new water well: "a Wyoming rancher's gold mine". After years of being water starved, he was talked into drilling a fairly deep well into the "Madison formation" and hit a gusher, which shot 20 feet or more into the air.

After many years of tough conditions he now had a water bonanza, which allowed him to raise lots more feed and raise a couple hundred more cattle. When we arrived old Homer wanted to show us his place. The ranch was approximately three miles wide, four miles long and the terrain was quite rough. The property was a box canyon, which didn't require much fencing. We all piled into Homer's faded blue, 49 Buick sedan and took off on what was barely a road.

The Buick bounced merrily, on its coil springs, located adjacent to each of the wheels; the shock absorbers had long since worn out and all four tires were rarely on this cow path at once. It was hard to see how Homer managed to control the old Buick, with all the bouncing, but somehow he managed; he even referred, to this deeply rutted trail, as a "good Road." After we had had a plentiful and tasty Sunday dinner, with Mr. and Mrs. Renner, we took off for Basin and I remarked to Granddad. "Boy that was some ride on that bumpy road. Why does Mr. Renner call it a 'good road?"

Granddad smiled, "Well you need to understand Homer. His definition of a 'good road' is one you can get over and a bad road is one you can't. Simple isn't it?"

Remembering this adventure, with Mr. Renner, nearly 20 years earlier, I greeted Homer. "Nice to see you again; it has been a while. What can I do for you?"

The craggy faced old man removed his rumpled Setson hat, "Ever since I learned of your wife's passing a year ago, I been wanting to let you know I've been thinking about you, but I don't get to Greybull all that often, but I've been trading with Ed Blackburn, over at the International dealership, and thought I'd stop by and invite you and the children to dinner Sunday. I guess you know my misses passed away a few years ago, but I manage and can even cook halfway decently, too. Been raising some mighty fine beef since we brought in the Madison well."

"Mr. Renner, the kids and I would love to visit you. It has been a while, since I've been to your place."

"How about one o'clock. Bert, you can just call me Homer, everybody does. Gotta a piece of paper and I'll draw you a little map." Homer said.

I handed him a yellow legal pad, I keep handy to write down my inspirations and for occasions like this. Homer drew a simple map and handed it back to me and said. "See you at one on Sunday."

Homer got up to leave and as he was leaving he greeted Ed Blackburn and left. Ed came in and said, "Didn't know you knew old Homer, does his banking in Worland, I think."

"Well," I replied, "Homer was a friend of my Granddad's and I met him years ago. I can't say I know him very well, but have visited his place up at Tensleep a couple of times. It's a beauty."

Ed smiled, "I sold the old boy a brand, spanking new International Scout a couple of weeks ago. You'll never guess what he did with it?"

I shook my head and said, "No idea."

"Well," Ed replied, "he wanted a blue one, but all I had in stock was a white one and a brown one, so he said OK and bought the white one, since it had all the equipment he wanted and we settled on a price and he took off with the white Scout. Today, he comes in for the 1,000 mile checkup and he painted it blue. I don't mean, had it professionally painted blue, like with a spray gun. No, not Homer he goes down to Thompson's in Basin and buy a gallon bucket of blue paint, I'm not sure it is even an exterior paint. Homer brushed on the blue paint. Looks like hell, but I guess Homer is happy with it."

Following Homer's precise directions, Oliver, Martha and I arrived for Sunday dinner at Homer's house. We drove up to Homer's ranch; it is quite picturesque, just like a place where a John Wayne cowboy flick might have been filmed. Except for the entry way, the west end, the well irrigated pasture and crop land is surrounded by high, layered rock walls, the rocks are various colors, but predominately reddish orange, with stripes of yellow, white and dark purple rock, with occasional trees perched here and there. Homer's house was at the highest spot accessible by motor vehicle. The road wasn't much improved over my earlier visits and I was glad I had my little red and white Jeep Commando.

The kids didn't seem to mind the bouncing around, in fact they even started to giggle with amusement. When we pulled up in front of Homer's modest single story ranch house, I looked back on the peaceful sight with the green irrigated pastures and the contented Hereford cattle grazing below. In front of the house was Homer's new blue Scout, with its crude brushed on blue paint job; streaks of the original white shown through the streaky paint. Homer emerged from the little house and welcomed us, "You're right on time and I've got a dandy roast in the oven."

"Homer," I said, "you really have a beautiful spot here. These are my children, Oliver and Martha."

The old rancher smiled broadly and bent over to shake hands with the kids, then me. "Welcome, come on in."

Upon entering I was struck, how neat and orderly and clean, the place was. Not what I what I would have expected from the old gent, who had been more or less a bachelor for the past ten years or so. Posted on the walls were several placards, which expressed Homer's Atheistic view of life, like: "A family that preys together stays together."

I don't think I had ever known an avowed Atheist before, but had always pictured them as unfeeling cold people, but such was not the case with Homer Renner, who was obviously as kind and good hearted a human being, as I had ever known. We sat down to a delicious roast beef dinner cooked to a medium rare perfection, along with roasted potatoes, carrots and peas. Homer even had an apple pie for desert.

All of this kindness made me wonder, if he was looking to borrow some money, but no Homer was simply being a compassionate human being. During the course of the conversation, unprompted by me, he stated that everything was paid for and he hadn't borrowed any money for many years. After dinner we went outside and enjoyed the view on this late summer day.

Back at work on Monday morning Thelma Kost came in my office to see me. "Bert" she said, "My nephew, Jim Kost, has moved his business up to Basin from Denver, taken over the old 'John Deere' building. It's an interesting business; he publishes a magazine called 'Aviation Mechanics Journal'. Anyway he sells the magazine all over the world and receives lots of foreign checks, drawn on banks all over and in different currencies. The Security State Bank does not want to process them for him, can we help?"

I said, "I'm thinking I can work out something with First National in Denver, like we did with our German visitors back in August. Possibly we could do it with Citibank in New York, but the mail connections aren't very good for sending a cash letter to New York; however, we get overnight service to Denver. Why don't you have Jim come over at his convenience and, in the meantime, I'll see what can be worked out with a correspondent."

By the next morning I had called First National in Denver and my contact there indicated there would be no problem processing Jim's foreign checks, so I was ready for Jim when he arrived to discuss the matter. Quickly, I assured Jim that we could handle his international checks, "Jim", I asked, "Basin's main correspondent is First of Denver, the same bank I plan to use, why aren't they providing this service for you?"

Jim reply, "I don't know, I guess they don't want to bother."

I said, "You do understand, we'll need to charge an exchange fee, since we have currency fluctuations to deal with?"

"Oh, I expected that and am happy to pay a reasonable fee. I can see it is extra trouble for you." Jim said.

"Well, then let's get started." I said and called Becky Lawton, our bouncy, blond new accounts gal to bring signature cards and other documents needed for a commercial checking account.

Becky sat down with him and guided him though the new account process and, after a few minutes of filling out forms, asked he wanted to make an initial deposit this day.

Jim reached for his attaché case, opened it up; it was stuffed with checks from all over the globe. He said, "I have been accumulating these, for a couple of weeks, wondering what the hell I was going to do with them. I sure as the devil don't want to give them back."

"Jim, tell me how many different countries do you have subscribers? I asked.

He replied, "Last count was 31, just like Baskin Robbins Ice Cream. Even had an order for a subscription from the Soviet Union, but I didn't accept that."

"Why not take some of the Commies money?" I asked.

Grinning widely, Jim said, "I told the bastards, that when they, started having free elections and capitalism, I'd sell them, "Aviation Mechanics Journal."

Stunned, I replied, "You didn't?"

He shot back, "Sure as heck did, it was fun too!"

"Well, I guess they're not going to start World War III, over it." I said, barely able to restrain my laughter.

Customer contacts are what always made banking fun for me. I especially liked the farm and ranch people, because of their hard work ethic and sense of humor. This developed a constant stream of amusing stories. One such story was from Tom Van Gelder, who was the proprietor of the Greybull Elevator Company. The company bought and processed grain, in the case of our farms beer barley; they also sold farm supplies including a limited inventory of milking equipment. Tom a large, strapping, good-looking man with an acute sense of humor came in one day and said, "Bert, I had the funniest thing happen this morning. You know Karl Schneider, farms out west of town?"

"Sure, been a regular customer here for many years, what's he been up to lately?" I replied.

"Well, just as I was opening up this morning, he comes bursting in the door and wants to buy a whole bunch of milking equipment, come to about

$5000. I said, 'Karl, why all this milking hardware, you only have two or three cows?'" Tom said.

"That doesn't, sound like Karl, he's not incline to go wild on equipment purchases." I commented.

Tom replied, "Right, frugal guy. Well, this morning he said he went out to milk his three cows. The milking goes fine, with this patient old Guernsey, then he gets to this cankerous old Holstein, they tend to be temperamental anyway, this old girl has mastitis too, making her even more irritable. Karl's in a hurry so he sits down, on the milking stool, and starts. Just after he gets the pail wet, she sticks her front dirty foot in it and of course, Karl has to stop, clean the milk bucket out. He puts hobblers on her front feet and starts milking again. He's got the pail, better than half full, when Blackie kicks over the damn thing with her rear foot; Karl luckily has another set of hobblers, puts them on the old cow's rear feet. Cow lets out a loud, belligerent moo and with a newly cleaned bucket, Karl starts milking in earnest, just as he gets the pail wet, what do you think happened?"

"No idea." I said in anticipation.

Tom goes on, "Well sir, the ornery old cow, whacks him in the face with her wet, manure laden tail, right in the face, knocks his glasses off, Karl loses his balance and falls off the three legged rickety stool. By this time Karl is furious, grabs some baling twine, ties it around the cow's tail and hoists it up and proceeds to tie it to the top of the stall divider. Irma, comes in about now, wondering, why Karl is late for breakfast. Finally, Karl, says to me, 'If you can convince Irma, I was just milking the damned cow, I don't need all this equipment.'"

"Quite a story, Tom. Were you able to talk him out of buying the milking gear?" I said unable to restraint my laughter.

Tom started to laugh too and when he had quieted down said. "Yeah."

1974 was another good year for our agricultural customers and that, of course, helped our local merchants as well. With the holidays approaching I needed to prepare for Christmas at home. With the children now three and six, I decided it would be less disruptive to spend Christmas Eve at home and let the kids open their presents in their own home, thereby avoid a logistic problem. I had decided to spoil them royally. It seemed the least I could do, since in spite of their pestering I wasn't moving forward finding them a new "mommy", as they frequent cried out for.

Brother Frank was scheduled to get married shortly after Christmas in Denver, so I planned to drive south Christmas day. I quickly realized I didn't have a suitable dress for Martha, but was able to enlist Charlene and Diana to select something, on their shopping junkets, to Billings. I gave Charlene my dusty Hart Albin department store credit card and they came back with a lovely little red with white trim dress for Frank and Katie's big day.

The wedding was held in Denver at Robert and Kathryn Hill, Katie's parents' home in Denver with Bob Thompson, my Episcopal Minister friend, who had been so helpful to the family, when Mary died. In the middle of the wedding liturgy, Frank managed to muff one of his lines, I suppose from nervousness grooms all suffer, but recovered nicely, by saying: "Moving right along." This seemed to both sum up the event, as well as my year in general.

The reception was held at a nice place, so I don't remember the name of it. What I vividly recalled was Martha, in her little red dress sampling the adult, spiked punch, which was caught on film by Katie's friend and wedding photographer, Mary Anne Tindal. The happy couple took off on their wedding trip in Frank's green Jeep, named Lulu. Oliver, Martha and I returned to Greybull, to close out the year at home. I found being at the bank at the end of the year was necessary, as there were many details that needed to be attended to, like making sure the year end accruals were correct. There was also the matter of Mockler's New Year's Eve Party, which had been a tradition in recent years. This year was, as it turns out, was to be special.

The party was held at Mockler's spacious Tudor styled home, a little different for Basin, Wyoming and a goodly variety of friends were in attendance including Red O'Neill, the Big Horn County Chairman of the Democratic Party, who always registered as a Republican. Curious to be sure, but not without reason. Big Horn County, may well be the most Republican county in Wyoming. The last non-Republican Presidential candidate the county had voted for was Teddy Roosevelt, when he ran under the Bull Moose Banner. The local elections are all decided in the Republican primary and Red didn't want to disenfranchise himself, which registering as a Democrat might have done. Red O'Neill was not; however, the highlight for me at this particular New Year's Eve gathering.

At the stroke of midnight I happened to be standing with, conveniently under the Mistletoe, with Jo Rawlings and we exchanged kisses. Jo is a lovely dark hair beauty, who I knew slightly from Mockler parties in past years and I had been able to assist her, as a customer, when I was able to arrange a home loan for Jo and her husband Mike. Little did I know, how this lady would become a part of my future?

Seventeen

The Sun Shines Through

With the new year dawning and winter's snowy grip upon our corner of the world, my thoughts turned to, what else, but skiing. Our local ski area, Antelope Butte Ski Area, had a new lodge building and something more than the garage, where lunch had been prepared and served in a sort of makeshift kitchen. After the ski day was done, the picnic tables, where the lunch crowd ate, had to be stacked in order to make room for the operator's snow removal equipment.

After a long, but exhilarating, day of skiing I decided to have a beer before beginning the trek down the mountain. The young lady behind the counter, looked me over suspiciously, then asked to see my identification. By now I was 36 years old and it had been several years since I had been asked for my ID. Obediently, I reached into my wallet and produced my driver's license.

With great care the young gal inspected my license and exclaimed, "Wow, I thought you were old enough, but I didn't think you were, THAT OLD!"

With that said, she handed me a Coors beer, as I had requested.

After taking Saturday off to go skiing, I had bank work to do on Sunday. I had made an appointment to do a farm visit that Sunday afternoon, with Ralph Kafka, a livestock grower located out at Burlington, 20 miles west of town. Ralph, was a tall, slender, shy, gray haired, old bachelor, who ranched in partnership with Bob Bryerson. Ralph's main source of income came from working, as a construction superintendent for Morrison Knudson, or "MK", as it was known around the globe. When Ralph was away, most recently working on the Alaska pipeline on the North Slope project, Bob and his family managed the ranch.

Since it was a Sunday farm visit, I took Oliver and Martha along. I had recently taken deliver, on a new dark green Pontiac convertible, which was to be the last year convertibles were to be offered, thanks to Ralph Nader inspired safety standards. The car was also equipped with an irritating, shrill buzzer that sounded loudly, if the engine was running and the seat belts weren't buckled. The obnoxious buzzer went off in protest, when the motor was running, even though the car wasn't in gear. I had dubbed the annoying device, "Ralph", in Mr. Nader's honor. The children, picked up on this moniker, for the noisy warning sound immediately.

On this bitter cold below zero January day, I pulled into Mr. Kafka's farm yard, left the engine running to keep heater going full blast in order to keep the interior of the car warm. I ran the window down to greet Ralph, as he walked up to the driver's side door. As he reached the car, I unbuckled my seatbelt, which set off the Nader inspired warning alarm. The kids began yelling, with great glee, "Shut up Ralph, Shut up Ralph."

With a puzzled expression on his face, Ralph Kafka said, "I haven't said anything?"

I shut off the motor and explained my children's outburst to Mr. Kafka. Then he grinned and said, "Damned cold out here, let's go inside. I can rustle up some hot chocolate for kids. I'm ready for a cup of coffee myself. I need to warm up, been out feeding and making sure the animals are OK in this brutal cold weather."

I asked, "Where is Bob?"

"Oh, Bob and his tribe, went to town, some kind of doings at church, you know, Sunday afternoon and all." He answered, as he ushered us into the modest ranch house.

Adjacent to the kitchen, the house had a good-sized living room and lying on the couch was half a dozen or so recently born lambs, snoozing comfortably. As soon as we entered the room, the little white lambs were awakened and began jumping, on the furniture, and running around the room, with joyous reckless abandon. Oliver and especially, Martha were delighted, as they proceed to play chase, with the newborns.

"A little early for lambing isn't it?" I inquired.

"Yes, it wasn't planned. Old Buck, our Columbia ram, broke through the fence and got in with some of the ewes early. Can't keep a good ram down; you know. Awful cold, for those little ones to be outside, even in the sheep shed. We hate losing any livestock. I do whatever it takes to prevent that." He said with a good-natured chuckle.

True to his word, Ralph fixed the kids some hot chocolate and they enjoyed playing with the baby lambs, who seemed to enjoy the attention. After we had warmed up, Ralph and I went out to the corrals and I made a quick inventory of the livestock and farm machinery, owned by Ralph and Bob. I told Ralph, I would have their documents for their operating line of credit, ready for signatures Tuesday and I'd look forward to seeing them then. I said, "Thanks, for the hospitality and business. Oh, yeah, sorry about the buzzer business."

Back at work the next day, I set Dottie Bernard, who had graduated from secretary to document preparation specialist, to work preparing the loan documents for Ralph and Bob. I focused on working with customers. Mondays always seemed to be our busiest day, as folks seemed to spend their weekends conjuring up new projects that required financing. Charlene, whose desk was adjacent to mine, saw one of her insured, Harry Manning, come staggering out of the "Hanging Tree Bar" across the street. Quickly, she grabbed her coat and headed for the front door.

"Where the dickens are you going, Charlene, in such a hurry?" I asked.

"That damned Harry, is fix'n to drive home drunk and I'm going to drive him home, so he don't hurt anyone," she answered, as she flew by.

"Talk about a full service insurance agent," I said to myself.

That winter I decided to remodel my house, to accommodate my present circumstances. I had developed a good working relationship with Al Lauber, the architect, who had done the design work for our bank upstairs remodeling and expansion project. I had resigned myself to being "Mr. Mom" and was thinking the odds of finding a suitable mate in Greybull were not too encouraging. Even though mom reminded me, as recently as Christmas, that she had met Dad at the train station in Greybull, Wyoming, so many years ago.

Nonetheless, I wasn't convinced and had it firmly planted in my head that a live in housekeeper- nanny would solve a number of my household problems. I made some sketches of what I wanted for Al to serve as the architect's guiding inspiration. The house was to have a number of features to make life for me and the children more enjoyable.

First was quarters for a live-in housekeeper-nanny, which would include a full bath, bedroom and sitting room upstairs. Another full bath for the children's portion of the house, leaving the existing bath for my exclusive use. I also, planned for a study, lined with bookcases off the master bedroom. Then a fireproof closet, entirely made of non-combustible materials on the south end of the study, for my stamp collection and other treasures, and to the north a painting studio, with a glass ceiling to let in natural light for my painting activities, which was at the time one of my main recreational outlets.

I planned to add a wood-burning fireplace in the living room and also a log burning Franklin stove in the new family room, which was also to be a dining room. I have always like the looks of stone work and decided I would do the stone masonry construction myself. At the bank we had customer, Richard Cosgrove, who was trying to launch a quarry business. A couple of years early, I had bought a load of stone, a gorgeous dolomite, or "young marble," geologically speaking, with colorful streaks of red, purple, and orange running through the tan rock. The stone replaced the dilapidated fence grape arbor between our yard and Hawkins.

Poor Richard was struggling, but I couldn't justify making him a bank loan, until such a time as he was able to attract some investors, get some equity in the business, and cleanup his credit report. As I anticipated the project, I made Richard a proposition. I would purchase from him quarrying rights for sufficient stone to do my house project for $1000. I further agreed to quarry the stone and haul it to the job site myself. This way he had no cash or labor outlay. Richard was happy to get the cash, without giving up anything more than some stone, which he had in great abundance.

I contracted with a couple of local carpenters, Butch Rimer and Art Sylvester, to do most of the construction and the work commenced by spring. I traded off my Jeep Commando for an ugly used, mustard colored, four wheel drive, three quarter ton Chevy pickup and I began quarrying and hauling stone the 80 mile round trip. By spring the project was rolling along in high gear.

I had recently been appointed as a director of the Wyoming Girl Scout Council. I was roped into this community service relationship by my friend Dick Corbridge, the senior Trust Officer at First National Bank of Casper, who I known for many years. Dick explained to me that, as one might expect, the council board was composed almost entirely of women, with Dick being the lone exception. Sherri Carlisle, the Executive Director, was looking for someone with a financial background in addition to Dick, who being a lawyer by training, had a less practical view of finances. Never in my wildest dreams did I ever think, I would become a Girl Scout. Council director, luckily, did not need to pass a physical examination.

I had hopes of meeting some charming ladies, but alas, these gals were all married and at least 10 years my senior. One of the women, who happened to be from the nearby town of Worland was Christiana Gee. Christiana and her husband Tom, were the owners of the Washakie Hotel, which had always been a good place to eat and stay, thanks to Tom's skills as a restaurateur. I knew the Washakie Hotel from my days as a bank examiner, when I had been a periodic guest. Christiana was a native of Denmark and kept in close contact with her family in Copenhagen.

Discovering my plight as a "Mr. Mom", at one of the council meetings, she suggested and volunteered to find a "nice young Danish girl", who would like the opportunity to come to America to work as a nanny. Within a few weeks, she had lined up, such a woman in the person of Anna Ertmann, apparently a neighbor of her sister, in Copenhagen. Arrangements were made, and by June, Anna arrived. We put the rush on the carpenters and by the time Anna arrived we had livable lodging for her. But, I seem to be getting a little ahead of my story.

In April, just before the Federal Income Tax deadline, Vic Peterson came into my office, gleefully waiving his Federal Tax return, the ultimate report on an enterprise's success. A year and a half earlier, we had financed the development of Vic's riverside property into a K.O.A. Campground, using an SBA guaranteed loan, which had become one of my offensive weapons for assisting customers developing new businesses. For Vic's loan, we had based the repayment entirely on projections, which are often, only varying degrees of educated, guesses. All too frequently, the results missed the mark by a wide mark, possibly in either direction. No so, with Vic Peterson.

"Vic, what's going on?" I inquired.

With great excitement, he laid both the tax return and projections he'd made for the loan on my desk, "Bert, look at this!" Vic exclaimed.

Comparing the projections, which had estimated a profit for the year at $7000, then I looked at the Federal Income Tax return. Net profit for 1974 was $7049. It was the first and as it turned out, the only time in my banking life that projections were so precisely on the money.

"Great Scott, Vic! You really nailed those projections. I never saw them come this close before. Congratulations" I said and shook hands with him enthusiastically. 1974 was not only a good year for local businesses, but also for our agricultural customers and friends. This enabled them to improve their property as well. Charlene and her husband Don, a hard working farmer built a new shop building and decided to have "shop" warming party, harkening back to the old tradition of a barn raising or housewarming celebrations.

The party was turning out to be a noisy, joyous event. About 10:30 as I was listening to Don Collingwood's observation about his disdain for chewing tobacco. He said, "I'd rather put cow dung in my mouth than goddamned chewing tobacco."

Suddenly, I felt the cold chill of pieces of ice being dumped down my back, via the collar of my shirt. I reacted, without thinking and punched Ron Dalin, the perpetrator, squarely in the nose. Hardly, the image of the genial, mild mannered local bank president I wished to project. Ron began bleeding profusely and was madder than a nest of angry hornets. I apologized, for I knew I was totally wrong, to react so violently, to this harmless prank. It didn't seem to help. He was still fuming. I decided it was time to leave and took off, on the ten-mile drive home. Soon, I noticed headlights, in my rearview mirror, following me all the way home and guessed it was Ron Dalin. It was!

I was driving my Chevy pickup, as I had let Anna have my Pontiac, for some errands she was running with the children. Ron, who is a big brawny 6'3" guy, pulled up behind me. My thought was, "Oh shit, this huge joker is going to beat the living be-Jesus out of me."

We both got out of our respective pickup trucks and I once again, offered an apology, "Ron, I'm really sorry, but I grew up in New Jersey and I have had to defend myself on numerous occasions. Ever since some kid pulled a switchblade on me back in the eighth grade, my instinct has been to retaliate and ask questions later. I reacted, before I thought."

By this time he had calmed down and said, "I never dreamed that you would even respond. I have this idea that your family had just bought you the bank like you had a silver spoon in your mouth from birth. You're more of a man, than I thought."

"Ron, let me tell you about the bank. I was a bank examiner and Jerry Williams offered me an opportunity to buy the shares over a period time. I had $15,000 that I had saved during those years by living on my examiner's expense account; my apartment was a $50 a month dump, I used to keep my stuff in and address for my mail. Luckily, I was able to save most of my salary. I have had to poor boy the whole bank deal," I replied.

Remembering his wife Donna was an employee at the bank Ron asked, "You aren't going to fire Donna over this, are you?"

"God no, Ron. Donna is an excellent employee and I want to keep her. For my part I'd like to forget the whole incident. Remember I was totally in the wrong here. No hard feelings?" I replied.

We stood talking for another 15 minutes, shook hands and parted friends. The following morning still feeling embarrassed, I drove out to Don and Charlene's, to apologize for making an ass of myself. When I arrived Don's Brother Bud, and his wife, Connie, were visiting and enjoying a morning coffee break, with the prior night's hosts. Embarrassed, I apologized profusely to Don and Charlene.

Connie, who was also a bank employee and of course was at the previous night's festivities, said, "Bert look at it this way, Ron was drunk and out of control and several of us wanted to punch him in the kisser, but you actually got to do it !"

Monday morning, I reassured Donna, that all was forgiven and reminded her that her station at the bank was certainly not in jeopardy, after all I was at least as out of line as Ron.

Donna smiled broadly and said, "Ron was still worried, but I told him, I thought you would treat me fairly. Thanks!"

In spite of the construction mess at home and the frequent servings of "Cream of Sawdust Soup" the kids and I, with Anna's help faired quite well. Anna was good with the children and a respectable cook; however, she had one characteristic that drove me nuts she insisted on arguing about virtually every topic imaginable. Her pet subject was why didn't I invite a labor union to organize my employees? I tried to explain to her that, we only had 12 or so non-officer employees. Not only that being in a fairly remote area of Wyoming, there were only two unions present in our county: The Brotherhood of Railroad Workers and the United Mine Workers, representing one of the bentonite local plants. Neither in my mind, were equipped or of a mind to deal with a measly ten, or twelve, clerical workers at the bank.

Anna, in truth was quite pretty, tall, slender, bright smile, and not a bad personality, until she started to tout the glories of labor unions. I asked her why the passion for labor unions? She told me her father was something of a Danish version of John L. Lewis, less the bushy eyebrows. When she asked if she could have a week off to visit her uncle, who lived up in Calgary, Alberta, Canada, I was very happy to get rid of her for a week in spite of the obvious inconvenience. Martha was by this time three years old and enjoyed mixing with other children at Vi Reilly's. Oliver was of course attending school, so he could report in at Mrs. Reilly's and play in the neighborhood after school. I drove Anna to the airport in Billings, where she caught a direct flight to Calgary.

A week later, I picked her up driving my ugly Chevy pickup. At the same time I had volunteered to pick up in Billings some T-bars for the ski area's lift, at a machine shop, where their hydraulics had been rebuilt. My good friend Lee Kunkle, the manager, needed the help and after all that is what friends are for? Anna was chagrined, to say the least, that I didn't arrive in the Pontiac, which she had become quite fond. On the way home I inquired, "How did it go with your uncle?"

"Oh, I guess it was alright, but you know, he insists on arguing all the time, just like the rest of the family," she answered.

"Really," I said, thinking to myself, I know exactly, what you are saying.

As the months progressed, I let Anna take the Pontiac for the weekend, so I would get some peace and enjoy time with the children. I also was busy with the stone masonry project on the house, either quarrying rock or putting up the stone itself. My excellent friend and kindred spirit, Lee Kunkle, offered to help in my quest to finish the project, as his time allowed. He said, "I'll mix the mortar and keep you supplied with stone, but on one condition."

"What might that be?" I inquired.

"I'd like a highball, after were done working each day," he said.

"Bourbon and Ditch, right? What kind of whiskey?" I answered.

"Black Jack, if you please," he replied.

"With pleasure, this is the best deal, since the Dutch bought the island of Manhattan, from the Indians for $24.00. You will have earned a drink and more," I said.

That fall cattle prices were inordinately high and guys were falling all over themselves to get into the cattle business or expand their herds. In the euphoria of the moment, Wally and Martin, Jr. Mayland came in and requested a loan to buy 400 'pairs' at $800 each; that is, mother cows with calves at their side.

"Guys, this is way over our bank's legal lending limit. I'd have to go to a correspondent; we already have sold an over line on your sheep operating line. I'll run it by Bob Bryans, at First of Casper, but to be honest I think it is a bad idea at this time, especially since you don't have the pasture and would have to buy feed too," I argued.

"Well, let us know," Wally replied.

I called Bryans and he was in accord, with my analysis of the situation. The purchase price of the cattle was at a record breaking high and it was hard to image that prices would remain so high. Wally and Martin were in the next day and asked in a demanding tone, "Well, are we going to get the money?"

"No. I appreciate you have been really good customers, but this is a bad deal. A risk I am unwilling to accept and neither is Bryans. I'm sorry, but I can't help you this time," I replied.

"Why, you dirty rotten son of a bitch!" Came Wally's fervent response.

"Here we thought you were our friend and banker; you bastard." Martin, who was usually the quiet one, added.

"Well like I said, I'm sorry I can't help you this time," I replied, in resignation.

The good news to this little story is the farmers and ranchers, who were selling livestock, but especially cattle did well that fall. The house was progressing, but not finished, by any stretch of the imagination. I decided not to renew Anna's visa and put her on a plane back to Denmark. I was in a quandary as to how I was going to resolve the nanny housekeeper issue. For the time being, I decided to piece it together using Vi Reilly and neighborhood teenagers, when Vi wasn't available.

I had invited my family to Greybull for the holidays, as Mom and Dad, were curious about the house project's progress. I had also invited a lady friend from my youth in New Jersey along with her two kids. The living room space was livable, but the walls were bare and the carpeting hadn't been laid. One weekend the kids and I took my acrylic paints, along with half empty cans of paint that had been left remaining after several decorating projects over the past eight years. We painted Christmas pictures, like a nativity scene, Christmas trees, Santa Claus's, sleighs and reindeer on the living room walls. Oliver remarked, "This is great fun and we know we wouldn't get to do this ever again."

I am not sure whether we got more paint on the walls or ourselves, but we did have a wonderful time decorating for Christmas. It was about this time I received an unexpected pleasant surprise. Jo Rawlings called and said, "Bert, I keep hearing about the remodeling work you are doing on your home. I have always been fascinated with houses, architecture, that sort of thing. Would it be possible for me to see your home?"

"Sure, I'm not doing anything tonight and it is early. You could come over tonight if you'd like." I responded.

Jo replied, "That sounds perfect, I'll be over in fifteen minutes. See you then."

She arrived right on schedule and I asked, "Where is Mike?"

"Oh, we are separated and I have filed for a divorce. Haven't you heard?" Jo said.

I replied, "I guess I might have heard that in the form of a rumor. I tend to not pay much attention to rumors. You can't believe the rumors about me that circulate. Like, I was 'in love' with my housekeeper, Anna, from Denmark. I can't stand the woman. I used to give her the keys to my Pontiac, weekends, just so I didn't have to be around her weekends. Sent her back to Denmark, you know."

Jo smiled and said, "Funny, I don't think I had heard that rumor. Anyway, I'm really curious to see, the house. How about a tour?"

"Right this way. The living room construction is done, but not the decorating, so I let the kids just have fun with it," I said.

She eyed our artwork, probably thinking I had taken total leave of my senses. Then we walked around the house, which was still in disarray. The kitchen was functional, but not done. The family room/dining room was roughed in, and the stonework on the west wall wasn't yet started. The kids' rooms were in working order, but again not yet decorated. The house was enclosed, but much work remained to be done. I showed Jo the pictures I'd taken to chart progress of the project.

We sat down and talked about life in general. Suddenly, it was 10:30 and she said, "I didn't realize it was this late. I need to go. Must go to work at Dr. Doerr's in the morning."

"Well, this has been fun, I'll call you after the holidays," I said and kissed her goodnight. There did seem to be a spark of something going on.

The following morning, as the kids and I were eating cereal and reading together the description of the contents of the Cheerios box, right down to the niacin, riboflavin and whole grain oats. Martha said, "We like her."

I said, "She's very nice. I wondered why you two were behaving so well."

School was out for the Christmas holidays and Linda Gleason, from up the street arrived to look after the kids for the day. This was the first time I had used this fifteen-year-old babysitter, but I had used her elder sister, Jenny, knew her family, so I figured she would be OK.

Boy, was I ever wrong. About the third day the kids didn't say much except they had been playing outside, and didn't seem very happy after the day with Linda. Winter had set in and an inversion had settled cold temperatures, around zero, in the Big Horn Basin of Wyoming, where we lived. It seemed odd that the kids would want to play outside on this cold December day for very long. After putting Oliver and Martha to bed, I caught up on reading the mail and paying a couple of bills. When I went to bed I couldn't help but notice the aroma of perfume on my pillow. It seems to me it was a scent called "musk", which Diana had worn, but she hadn't been in the house in over a year, as she had graduated from Greybull High School and taken a job in Billings. So to paraphrase the three little bears, "Someone had been lying on my bed!"

Suddenly, I was beginning to put the picture together. Perhaps Linda was entertaining a boyfriend in my bed. I asked at breakfast Oliver and Martha, if my hunch was correct. Oliver said, "Yes, and you know what else?"

"What?" I asked.

Oliver blurted out, "She locked us out in the cold. She is mean."

Martha added, "We don't like her."

"Neither do I," I reassured the children.

I made a quick call to my old reliable friend, Vi Reilly, and asked her to take the kids for the day. Luckily she assented. Then I called Linda and let her know she was fired. She didn't ask why; she knew damned well why.

The Christmas holidays went off as scheduled. We started opening gifts Christmas Eve, but the kids examined each gift with great interest and then played with it some. It took until the noon Christmas Day before we plowed through their haul. After the holidays I heard a lady in town was starting a little pre-school, so I enrolled Martha in it and she seemed to enjoy it. Oliver, now a first grader was going to school for the whole day, getting out at three and reporting to Vi Reilly's house after school. Life and banking started humming along and I started concentrating on banking problems.

As I grew the bank, one of the problems was funding our loan demand, which was seasonal due to the needs of our agricultural customers, as well as some of the commercial clients, who had similar cash cycles. A large part of the problem was due to the fact that we weren't allowed to pay as much for time deposits as our savings and loan competition, Big Horn Federal Savings and Loan Association. As interest rates began to rise due to inflationary pressures in the economy, our in ability to compete for funds became more acute. I had been appointed to the American Bankers Association, Agricultural Bankers Executive Committee.

This was a group of bankers I had a lot in common with and I found that we were all having the same kinds of funding problems. Our bank, as were all National Banks, were members of the Federal Reserve System and theoretically had access to the Fed discount window, but by this time the Fed had become preoccupied with monetary policy, controlling inflation by tinkering with interest rates and more or less blind to the needs of small agricultural banks like mine.

Gradually, member banks starting leaving the system. Many National Banks converted to state charters, and state banks, where Federal Reserve membership was voluntary, thereby being able to exit the system. The Board of Governors of the Fed wondered why the primary reason in many states was the onerous reserve requirements mandated by the Fed. This was not an issue in Wyoming since the Wyoming state chartered banks were subject to tying up even more investable funds in reserves, than if they were Fed members.

What rankled my banker compatriots, more than anything was the Fed's attitude that we were somehow a "bad bank" if we used the Fed discount window. The irony of this for The First National Bank of Greybull and many other banks was the access to the discount window was a godsend during the 1920s and 1930s, and the primary reason why, we became member banks. Now it was some sort of sin to use the window. The Federal Reserve Board asked the Agricultural Executive Committee members to make suggestions as to how the Federal Reserve Board might stem the tide of exodus from the Fed by the smaller member banks.

I was asked to give testimony before the Fed Board in Washington. I explained to them that the situation at our bank and many other banks as to loan demand was while our loan deposit ratio was about 50% during the winter months after crop and livestock sales were taking place. As spring came on our farm and ranch customers drew down their deposits and started to borrowing money for their operations. By midsummer, our loan deposit ratio was 80% or greater and we were often forced to sell securities, often at a loss, to avoid the humbling experience of being a "bad bank" and applying for a loan at the Fed Discount Window. Several others spoke and I was chosen to serve on a committee to suggest ways to address the problem.

I was invited to attend a meeting with Fed officials and an equal number of agricultural banks in Pittsburgh, Pennsylvania. Why one would choose Pittsburgh, the steel capital of America, for this particular meeting, remains a mystery to me, but on a dreary March day the meeting was held and our little band of ten bankers and Fed folks hammered out the foundation for the Fed's new seasonal borrowing privilege. Once more the Fed was fulfilling the part of its original mission to assist country banks like mine. When I returned home I was surprised by a visit from Wally and Martin Mayland, Jr. By this time cattle prices had dropped dramatically; pairs were now selling for $400.00.

Wally took off his Stetson and looked me straight in the eye and said, "Martin and I want the thank you for turning us down last fall on that loan. You saved our asses. We would have gone broke if we had bought those cattle."

I replied, "Thanks for coming in and saying that. I appreciate it. Ready to set up your line of credit for the sheep operation?"

They said, "Yes."

We went back to work. By this time the interior of the house was pretty well completed including the decorative finishing touches. Of course, I still had years to go to complete the exterior stonework, but I was making progress. Since my housekeeper-nanny situation was in a kind of week-by-week situation. I enlisted my mom and dad to look after the children, when I took a trip to attend a banking seminar in Fort Lauderdale, Florida. The seminar was about time management, which I was coming to see was important to me. By this time Jo and I were seeing each other frequently. As it happened Jo's mom, Feb Breault, was visiting her from Hudson, Wisconsin at the same time of my folks visit. We all went to dinner at Bluejacket's, then a school play at Greybull High School together and got acquainted. Something happened at the conference.

It was a peculiar situation. I seemed to be the only single person at the Florida event. Everyone had his or her spouse with them. Except for me, not a solitary bachelor for week in attendance; I felt like a fish out of water. So I decided to propose to Jo even though we hadn't been going together that long, we had known each other for about five years. We also had some common interests like art, architecture; besides she was quite lovely and a cheerful personality. After I had met Jo's mom, I remember my father's words of wisdom, when I was dating a young lady, whose mother Dad found decidedly unattractive, "Before you propose to a lady, take a good look at her mother, because that's likely how she will look when she gets older."

Recalling the good looks of both my mom and her mother, I realized this advice couldn't be too far off the mark. Mrs. Breault, was a very attractive lady in her 60s and I thought if Jo looked that good at that age I would indeed be very lucky. After our parents had left for their home, Jo and her son Chad came over for dinner. I suspect it was spaghetti and meatballs, an easy meal to prepare and one the kids were sure to enjoy. It was as if the stars were all lined up. The evening began with Oliver and Martha cornering me, as we watched Chad climb a tree in my front yard. Jo was watching Chad, hoping, praying that he wouldn't fall out of the tree as he climbed higher and higher.

Martha said, "Daddy, we really like Jo, we think you should marry her. Then we would have a mommy."

Oliver nodded in agreement, "She's nice."

That evening after dinner, after the kids had gone to sleep I took advantage of our mutually romantic mood and I proposed. She said yes!

It was about this time after two years or so I finally earned my private pilot's license. Vic Leonard, my first instructor had taken a job as a corporate pilot for Admiral Beverage Company in Worland and my new instructor was Rowe Yates. Yates soled me a year earlier and as I accomplished the written test, and the various solo flights, he began final preparation me to take my check ride. He wanted me to have quite a bit of instrument flying under my belt. We went up and I was "under the hood", unable to look out of the windshield for any visual reference and I was totally relying on my instruments. Rowe's instructions to me went something like this: "Ascend to 7,000 feet, turn left 30 degrees, right 170 degrees, descend to 6500 feet, left 90 degrees." On and on like this so after an hour of this, unable to see anything except the Cherokee's gauges. I had not the slightest goddamned notion of where we were or what time it was. Instrument flying can be quite tedious.

"Descend to 6,000, heading 330," he said.

I obeyed, then he said, "Hold the heading and descend 5,500."

Then he ordered me to descend to 5,000, then 4500. I'm thinking "Where the hell are we? There are mountains all around us. What the hell is going on?" Then he said, "Descend to 4000, set up a glide, throttle back, maintain heading 330."

"Jesus Christ the Greybull Airport runway is 3,950 feet. Can't see a damn thing," I'm thinking.

He said, "Throttle back to idle, nose up, don't let it stall, maintain heading of 330 and keep up your airspeed to 65 knots, just above stall."

We drifted through 4,000, then lower, to 3,975. I am still under the hood, can't see a damned thing. Then nose up and I heard the rear wheels of the Cherokee squeal as we hit the pavement of the runway. Finally, Rowe says, "you can lift the hood."

I complied and saw the familiar runway 33 of the Greybull Airport. I had just made a "zero-zero landing", completely on instruments. Rowe said, "I like my students to do a couple of these landings before they get their private licenses. That way if they ever have old man weather close in on them, they know how the make an all instrument landing. Piece of cake if you've done these before!"

So I was off to take my license test with Jack Elgin over in Cody. The test was easy enough, he had me do a stall recovery, simulate an emergency landing, and then he said, "You know what you're doing. You pass."

I rushed home excitedly and found Jo had come over with her sons, Michael and Chad. I said, "OK, who wants to be my first passenger."

There was a moment of poignant silence. Then, Michael, who was thirteen, said, "I'll go."

Jo said she would start supper and Chad went off with Oliver to find some First Grader sized excitement. They were just seven months apart in age. So off we went up for a half hour spin in the Cherokee. It takes a little bravery to be an amateur pilot's first passenger. I will always admire Michael for his faith, confidence in my piloting ability, or perhaps it was naïveté. In more way than one I would be flying off in new directions.

Eighteen

New Directions

Not only was I flying off in airplanes, but of greater importance, Jo and I were married on May 29, 1976. It was good to shedding my "Mr. Mom" persona and I was quite happy. We were joined in matrimony in a civil ceremony presided over by our good friend, Justice of the Peace, Gary Hartman. The nuptial celebration took place in the recently completed living room of my house. It was a small gathering, with my brother Frank and his wife Katie, my parents, former brother in-law Dick Cramer and his wife Carrie. All of our children were present, except Michael, who was off with his father, across the Big Horn Mountains in Gillette.

Katie, my sister in-law, who was well acquainted with my spoiled, rambunctious, but well-loved children, took Jo aside and advised, "It's not too late to run. You don't have to do this."

Luckily, Jo had the self-confidence to take on the children and me and didn't disappointment me on that fateful day. Compared to my first trip to the alter, when I wasn't able to keep a meal down, I was quite relaxed and busy, working on a stone "Growie" box by the front entryway to the house, on the morning of the ceremony. While the interior of the house was completed, decorated and functioning in top form, the exterior was still a couple of years away from completion.

Our honeymoon consisted of taking the kids to the Wyoming Bankers Convention at Jackson Lake Lodge in Grand Teton National Park. Instead of playing golf with my fellow bankers, Jo and I found entertaining things to do with the kids. I was never any good at golf anyway, so it was a painless decision. We decided to take a trail ride as a family.

I had never been on a tourist type horseback trail ride before. The kids, Jo and I were excited about the prospects of riding horses in view of the spectacular Grand Teton Mountains, on this perfect sunny June day. If they had previously ridden horses before, their experience was quite limited. I, on the other hand, had ridden horses numerous times and was, was at least able to ride with some degree of confidence. We were all decked out in red patterned western style shirts, blue jeans and cowboy boots, and proceeded to mount our respective animals.

My particular horse was a good-sized dark brown gelding with a black mane. The horse seemed amiable enough as I mounted him. He was a bit out of line with the rest of the horses, so I nudged him gently in the ribs, pointed him in the direction of the other 15 horses in the procession. Nothing happened. "What kind of horse is this?" I wondered to myself.

In the meantime, Oliver, Chad, Martha, and Jo were sitting on their horses, smiling and enjoying the moment and scenery. Finally, Marvin, the wrangler, our erstwhile leader, had everyone in the group aboard their mounts and we were ready to ride. I nudged my no named horse, in order to get him in line. He gave forth with a little snort, but stoically remained in place, like a stone statue. Finally, Marvin mounted his great white steed, motioned us with his right hand to follow, something like John Wayne in cavalry movies. Suddenly, my no name nag started to amble behind another brown gelding.

Then it came to me, these horses were not trained to be ridden, but rather they were programed, trained to follow like a bunch of sheep. As we rode along, "No Name" just plodded along behind another horse, no matter what the rider's desire might be. The ride was fun and we all enjoyed it, even after I realized it was more like getting on a bus, than actually riding on a genuine horse.

I enjoyed being at home with Jo and the children. After the kids were in bed and asleep we would enjoy a game of Scrabble. As players we were evenly matched, so it was always a challenge and yet relaxing at the same time. It became a tradition in our marriage.

During the remodeling construction, when the house was somewhat open, a large rather good-looking grey and white tomcat came to live in the crawl space under the front portion of the house. At first we didn't realize it. What we did notice was that Scratches, our own black cat, seemed to be eating increasing quantities of her food from the bowls we kept in the basement, near her litter box.

One day, while feeding Scratches Martha happened to see the grey and white cat, jump up into a lowboy dresser I used to keep tools in and then dart into the darkness of the crawl space. That explained why our cat's food was disappearing at an increased rate. We named the cat "Howard Hughes" since he was such a recluse. Mr. Hughes lived in the crawl space for several months as we tried to figure out a way to get him out. It was during this time that the real billionaire Howard Hughes died and Oliver, who by this time was reading very well saw the headline on the front page of the Billings Gazette, the daily paper we received. At breakfast that morning he saw the article and asked me, "Dad, that's not our Howard Hughes?"

I replied, "No, our Howard Hughes still resides in the basement."

That night, we decided Mr. Hughes overstayed his welcome, so we decided to leave a trail of food for him to follow out of the house.

We tried several times, but each time we either scared him back into hiding or he just wasn't hungry. Finally, during an engrossing Scrabble match, Mr. Hughes found his way to freedom. I never saw him again, although the kids reported occasional sightings around the neighborhood.

Being married also meant that I was able to again more actively participate in community happenings. Shortly after Jo and I were Married, I was elected as President of the Greybull Area Chamber of Commerce. Since the "Chamber" board meetings were at noon, I had continued this pursuit through my "Mr. Mom" stage. In this capacity it was part of my responsibility to host visiting dignitaries on their occasional visits to Greybull. One morning I received a phone call from Eileen Diener, our Chamber of Commerce Manager, informing me that Governor Stan Hathaway would be visiting our town that afternoon. He was scheduled to land at the airport about four.

We decided that a cocktail party reception by the Chamber board would be appropriate. Eileen suggested my house would be a great place, since most of the members hadn't been in it since the remodeling had taken place. The whole town was curious about the transformation that had occurred. That sounded OK to me and I called Jo, "Governor Hathaway is coming for cocktails, along with the Chamber of Commerce board at four o'clock. Be ready."

Jo replied, "Just how many people should I prepare for?"

"Oh, I suppose twenty to twenty-five, I guess," I said.

Jo went into action. One of her first calls was to Meredith, wife of Doug Crouse, the current President of our bank competitor in Basin. Doug was the son of Del Crouse, my longtime friend from bank examining days. Del was now pretty much retired and had assumed the mantel of Chairman of the Board of the Security State Bank of Basin. By the time four o'clock rolled around, Jo had arrangements well in hand: Hors d'oeuvres prepared, glasses ready, a quick trip to the liquor store to restock our supplies. We were ready to party. Jo, in the role of hostess at this impromptu party, was great success.

The Governor's plane must have had a tail wind, as he arrived quite early. Jo had just prepared for a fire in the new fireplace, this chilly November day, when the doorbell rang. She greeted Stan Hathaway, a wise, genial, and somewhat portly gentleman, at the door and tossed a match in the fireplace, as she walked back towards the kitchen to tend to the hors d' oeuvres tray, leaving Stan alone in the room. Suddenly, the living room started to fill with smoke; the damper had not been opened. Hathaway, immediately recognized the problem and opened the damper, as though it was something he did routinely, just as Jo entered the smoke filled din of our living room, with the goodies tray. I followed with the Governor's, Scotch and soda.

Quickly, we opened the windows and the last of the smoke was just disappearing as the guests began to arrive. The gathering went off without a further incident and we all had a fine time, chatting with Governor Stan. The party was not political, although, when one's guest is your state's popular governor, politics is not far from everyone's mind.

As for political activity, I was persuaded by Frank Copp, our teller Jeanne Copp's husband, our town's Mayor to run for a vacant seat on the town council. Frank and I were pretty much of the same accord, with regard to local issues. In Greybull each of the four councilmen is assigned a department: Parks and Recreation, Streets and Alleys, Water, and the Police Department.

His honor the mayor asked me to serve as the Police Commissioner, which in many ways is the easiest assignment. It also had a rather small budget, which was historically the primary issue.

This year was no different. The Town's insurance rates had gone up again, as the town police for the third consecutive year in a row had totally wrecked the town's only police car. It was almost like the cops were running a single car destruction derby, reminiscent of the old Keystone Cops in the days of silent movies. Core Chevrolet, the Chevrolet, Pontiac, and Buick dealer, located across the street from the Town Hall happened to have a couple of former Big Horn County Sheriff's office Pontiac patrol cars, that had been traded in on new models on their lot. The cars were equipped for police work. Although they had about 70,000 miles apiece on them, virtually all road miles, as our county is roughly the size of New Jersey. Yet there were only about 11,000 residents at the time. The cars were well maintained and really in great shape.

I suggested to the council, that rather than buy new cars, which seemed destined to be wrecked and pay terrifically high premiums, we should buy the two former sheriff office cars, save the collision piece of the insurance bill and self-insure the cars. I had talked to Jim Core at the dealership and they were anxious to move these two dogs, since most used car buyers don't want them; plus in the lingo of auto dealers these units had been on the lot too long and were beginning to "grow whiskers."

The town bought the two units for less than the collision insurance costs on a new car. Miraculously, the cops stopped having total destruction accidents, and now the town owned two patrol cars. The extra car often served as a decoy, which when thoughtfully placed acted as a deterrent for minor pilfering that goes on in some neighborhoods. Another problem I had to deal with was that of Police Chief Mandy Mohr.

Mr. Mohr had some kind of a feud with Mayor Frank Copp and therefore vociferously backed Don Clucas for Mayor. In truth, I had no issues with either mayoralty candidate, but had worked with Mayor Copp, in a previous stint on the council before Mary died, and therefore was aligned with him. Immediately after the election, Mayor Copp fired Mandy Mohr and I received a phone call from Mrs. Mohr, wanting to know why I hadn't prevented her husband's termination as chief.

I explained to her the appointment of police chief was entirely at the mayor's discretion and that the deed was done before I had even taken the oath of office. That of course didn't satisfy her, but it was the only explanation, I had to offer. I saved her the philosophical debate, as to the wisdom of backing the Mayor's challenger, since its' logic would be of little interest to her anyway. It would not be the last time I would hear from Mrs. Mohr on city matters. The Mayor appointed Elvin "Al" Saul, as the new police chief, but retained the other cops, as they were guys content to do their job and not get mixed up in politics. One of the policemen was, a gregarious, rotund patrolman, by the name of Don Neuman. Mr. Neuman was a neighbor of mine and had a young son, Don Junior.

Donnie, as he was called, was a precocious five year old. One day, while he was cruising the sidewalks of the neighborhood on his little red tricycle, he noticed an older boy about 10 years old on two-wheeler leaning up against my Pontiac Convertible. Little Donnie perceived the boy as something of a local "tough" and said to him, "I hope you realize that car belongs to the Police Commissioner. I wouldn't do that if I were you."

The words must have worked for the older boy pedaled away in silence. No damage was done to the car. During the summer of 1978 Lee Kunkle had been working all summer to prepare the ski area for winter. At the end of the summer Lee, his wife Caroline, Jo and I decided to utilize the ski lodge for a party for our mutual friends, especially those interested in skiing. It was during the party that Lee and I happened to go to the men's lavatory at the same time. As we were standing there washing our hands, we both realized we were carrying our respective wife's combs, lipstick and other female paraphernalia. Lee turned to me and said, "Damn, I hope I'm not caught dead with you someday."

All I could say was, "Right!"

The party was a great success and we went home and as near a Jo and I could determine it was the night our daughter, Juli, was conceived. Of course we didn't know it at the time. About the time Jo was able to confirm and announce that we were expecting, I received and urgent phone call from my brother Frank.

He said, "Mom took Dad to St. Joseph's Hospital in Denver. He has a number of ailments, any one of which could kill him: heart condition, chronic asthma, or cancer coming back. Right now he seems to be having a great deal of trouble breathing."

I replied, "I'll see if I can fly down Saturday, stay overnight then fly home Sunday. Jo and I are scheduled to leave for Hawaii and the American Bankers Association convention in Honolulu on Wednesday."

Frank said, "I'm sure Mom will appreciate it. Oma, our maternal grandmother, isn't doing very well, either. She never recovered from that fall she took last summer and seems to be fading fast. She must be 91 or 92 by now."

"Frank," I said, "weather providing, I'll fly down first thing Saturday morning. As soon as I'm in radio contact with the Boulder Airport I'll ask them to call you and you can come out to the airport to fetch me."

"All right then, I'll see you Saturday," Frank replied.

The weather was perfect, a crystal clear flying day and I even had a bit of a tail wind so was able to make the trip in about three hours in the Piper Cherokee I was flying at the time. We went to the folk's house and Mom was tearful. She had just received a call from her sister in New Jersey; Oma had passed away that morning.

"Are you going back to Hackensack for the funeral services?" I inquired.

"No." Mom said, "I need to stay here with your father, I can't do anything for Mama, but I can be of some comfort to your dad."

After a simple lunch we drove into Denver to St. Joseph's Hospital to see Dad. He was breathing with great difficulty, he seemed to rise out of his elevated hospital bed for each breath. First Mom told Dad of Oma's death. He gasped and inquired, barely audible, "Are you going back for the services?"

"No, I don't think so. My place right now is here with you," she said softly.

I said, "I have some good and exciting news. Jo and I are expecting, end of May the doctor says."

Dad tried to smile and wheezed with difficulty as he said, "I hope it is a redheaded girl."

It was plain he was pleased by the news, in spite of his discomfort and difficult breathing. On the way back to Boulder Frank said, "He's a tough old bird. He'll probably pull through."

Mother wasn't so sure. We went to visit him again on Sunday and watched as he fought valiantly for each breath of air. We didn't say much. Not really much to say.

"All one can do is hope and pray," I thought to myself as I flew back home to Greybull.

The following morning, about 7:30 as I was preparing to go to work, Mom called to say Dad had passed away about 5:30 that morning. We cancelled the trip to Hawaii and drove to Boulder to be with the family for the services, which took place on Friday. My Uncle Werner, who had just been to Oma's funeral was there to be with us. I introduced him to the children.

"Kids this is your great uncle Werner."

They duly shook hands with him and turning to me he said, "great uncle, makes me sound so old."

Thinking fast I said, "I use the statement qualitatively speaking, you have been a wonderful uncle."

Placated he smiled, reached for a cigarette and lite it. Martha, now age seven and never shy about her feelings, said, "Don't you know smoking is bad for you?"

Embarrassed Uncle Werner put out the cigarette and promised to quit. Which, incidentally, he did. Mother had decided to have Dad's remains cremated and we would have them interred in the cemetery in the family plot in Basin, next to his parents. Dad was very fond of his native state of Wyoming and it seemed appropriate. We would do it in December when the family gathered in Greybull for the Christmas holidays.

In November, after a mild Indian summer, winter's fury descended upon the Big Horn Basin and we were deluged with something like two feet of snow. And guess who I heard from? My old friend Mrs. Mohr. Normally Greybull only gets a few inches of snow in an entire winter, this winter we were inundated and Mrs. Mohr was on the warpath. The town crew was swamped and did their best, working extra-long hours to handle the situation with two ancient, short wheel based dump trucks, leftovers retired from the Wyoming Highway Department many years earlier.

The Mohr's owned and operated the Yellowstone Motel, which they like to advertise as Greybull's finest. It was a very nice motel and had the "Best Western" franchise. One row of rooms faced west on to a city street.

The town crew carefully plowed the snow in such a way that all the motel guests could access their rooms from the street, without interference from the great snow piles created by the plowing. But to Mrs. Mohr's chagrin the drifts were piled up smack dab in front of her kitchen window. This huge mountain of snow blocked her view of the street.

She called me to complain. "Bert," she said, "Is this some kind of vendetta by Frank Copp?"

"Hazel, this is the biggest snow storm the town has ever seen. The town doesn't have the equipment to haul all the offending snow away. The town guys are doing the best they can with the limited number of snow removal pieces they have to work with. I could see your being angry, if your guests had been plowed in, or the rooms on the west side of the motel were blocked. Neither of these things happened. The blocking of your kitchen window view was certainly not deliberate, and to my mind a minor annoyance in light of the special pains taken by the crew to keep your business accessible for your customers." I said.

For a change she seem placated and replied, "Yes, I see what you mean. Thanks for your time and have a good day, Bert." She answered and hung up the receiver.

The 1978 Christmas Holidays rolled around and we had scheduled Dad's interment for the 27th of December with Del Atwood, my good friend and the local funeral director. The Big Horn Basin had an inversion so it was a bitter cold and blustery the day. The two feet of snow was still in place and even more had fallen the day prior to the services. We formed a small procession. Atwood's hearse got stuck; I got stuck. Wheels spinning and enduring the twenty-below-zero weather, we did finally manage to bury Dad's ashes in the soil of his beloved Wyoming.

As Dad had fought valiantly for his life in the end, I could imagine Dad, my loving father and mentor laughing uproariously as he view us from above as we endeavored to bury his remains. It was fitting and typical for my father, who in spite of his struggles with ill health, loved life and was not to be removed from it without a heroic fight to the very end. Life for the family goes on.

On May the morning of May 22nd 1979 at about five, I was sleeping soundly, when I felt a wetness creeping onto my side of the bed. A split second later Jo nudged me and said, "My water just broke. We called Howard Willson, our family doctor and he instructed us to me him at the hospital. Howard examined Jo and said, "The baby isn't ready to come just yet. You're not nearly dilated enough."

"Should we check her in?" I asked.

Dr. Willson responded. "No, let's wait until evening, unless contractions start to come. I'll plan on inducing her if nothing is going on."

Jo said, "Good, I have laundry to do and a couple of local errands to run."

I took Jo home where she did her chores and I went to work. I went home at the usual time, about 5 PM. We had a quiet dinner, when the contractions started. Once again we called Dr. Willson and he instructed us to meet him at the hospital. He examined her, dilation was slow and he proceeded to start the inducement process; things began to happen. For the first time I was invited to participate in the birth process. I was excited and pleased to be present and to cheer, or at least encourage Jo along with the delivery.

Pretty soon the head came out and Howard said, "It's a redhead."

Some more pushing and synchronized breathing on Jo's part and after a few minutes the baby was out and Jo asked, "What is it?"

To which Dr. Willson replied, "It's a redhead."

Exhausted as she was Jo asked emphatically, "Damn it Howard, is it a boy or a girl?"

Howard looked a little puzzled, "Oh, it's a girl. I forgot to mention that; didn't I?"

Jo smiled broadly and said, "A girl, just what we wanted. Is she okay?"

"She looks to be perfect." Howard answered as he cut the umbilical cord.

Now Julie Alaine had entered our lives, a redheaded girl as Dad had hoped for. Julie was to be welcomed by the entire family. She was to become our common denominator and all the other children were to enjoy her presence.

In small towns everyone is ultimately tied at the hip in one way or another. This became apparent one day when Darlene Claycomb our proof operator came into my office to report something fishy going on. She came to us from the Wyoming National Bank of Casper, with high recommendations from her supervisor. Darlene came bursting into my office with an advice from our Billings correspondent, Midland National Bank, noting that our cash letter to them had been $50.00 short.

Darlene waived the slip of paper at me and proclaimed, "I've been a proof operator, for years and I don't make this kind of mistake."

"What are you talking about?" I answered.

`She calmed down a bit and said, "Well, what has happened is a $50.00 check seems to have been run through proof twice."

"And you can prove this?" I replied.

"You bet!" She shot back, instantly, "I compared the microfilm pictures we take of each cash letter, against the proof tape. There was a $50.00 item run through in the morning work, but a picture of it was missing when I looked at the film; then a $50.00 traveler's check, with teller stamp #3, as in the afternoon work. The $50.00 missing item was in the middle of a batch of cashed checks from number three also." She replied.

"Hmmm," I murmured, "teller number three, would be Jeanne."

Darlene replied, "yes, I'm afraid so."

I thought a minute, this could be a tricky situation, since Jeanne was Mayor Copp's wife. There was also a chance of a greater defalcation."

Finally, I said, "Darlene, this could be something much bigger. I believe I want to have her over and short account audited and check this out in more detail, before I confront Jeanne. You've done a nice job of researching this out. Let's just keep this between the two of us, until I have an outside person check this out. I sure don't want to accuse anyone until we know exactly what we are dealing with."

Darlene answered, "I understand completely, you can depend on me."

"Thanks." I answered.

After I thought a few minutes about the situation, I remembered my old examiner friend Verne Sorheim, had left the American National Bank of Cheyenne, where he had been the Auditor due to illness. I called him and asked if he felt well enough to take on this little auditing project for me. Verne said he was available and would drive up to Greybull the following Monday.

Verne arrived in time for lunch, so we had the opportunity to discuss the ramifications of the situation in a leisurely manner. For dessert Verne ordered a scoop of vanilla ice cream, with to quote his exact words to the waitress, "A dime's worth of chocolate sauce on the top."

Then, with his thumb and forefinger, he made a little he made a circle with his hand, leaving a hole roughly the size of a dime. That was one of the characteristics about Verne, I always liked, especially, when it came to performing detailed auditing work; he was always very meticulous. The waitress came back, with a scope of ice cream, with tiny spot of chocolate syrup on top, exactly the size and shape of a dime. Verne grinned, a little disappointed I think there was so little of the chocolate topping, and said, "Well, I got precisely, what I asked for didn't I?"

He left the waitress a generous tip. After lunch he set to work and by five the following day he had completed an exhaustive study of Jeanne's long and short account for the past her many years working as a teller. What he discovered was quite remarkable. Jeanne, who had been a teller with First National for over 20 years had a remarkably clean track record for 17 years; a couple of dollars either way for an entire year, which would be normal teller activity. Then, starting three years earlier, the records showed she was out in excess of $1000 each year, always short, never long. Gerald Williams was always concerned this could happen and had advised me to watch her, due to her tendency, to live beyond her means.

Verne and I sat down with Jeanne and went over the findings of Verne's audit. Verne had neatly and in great detail laid out all the transactions. We both felt badly about it, since Jeanne was not only a very likeable person, but had been a long time, an over 20-year veteran, of our bank.

I asked, looking directly at Jeanne, "Is there anything you would like to say?"

Jeanne gave me a stern kind of look and said, "Bert, I don't understand, why you are trying to frame me."

She offered no explanation of why the dramatic increases in shortages had occurred in the last three years. I was more than a little stunned and said, "Jeanne, I have always liked you as a person and also the excellent way you treat customers. However, I can't refute these facts, which is why I asked Mr. Sorheim, to do an independent audit. I really hate having to confront you with this evidence and also to terminate your employment here, but our bonding company requires it under these circumstances."

She mumbled a dejected, "Oh."

I went on, "Jeanne, here is what I will do for you. First, I'll give you a month's severance pay and I won't turn the loss over to the bonding company. Even more important to you, I won't press criminal charges, which the bonding company would likely demand, and all the mess that would entail for both of us."

Tears welled up in her eyes and she repeated, "You framed me."

I told her, "I'm sorry you feel that way, but I think we both know the truth here. Good luck to you in the future."

Within a few weeks Jeanne was hired as a receptionist a Dr. Rogers' medical office, and I suspect she did well in that capacity, like I said she did have a pleasant demeanor. I had expected some repercussions with her husband Frank at the town council level; however, we continued to work in harmony, until the end of his term, when he didn't seek re-election. At the next election the town elected Herb Asp. Herb had recently retired and turned his masonry contracting business over to his son-in-law. Herb was able to give his job as mayor all of his attention, which had not been possible for Frank Copp and other mayors, who had jobs to maintain. Being mayor became his full time job and he enthusiastically tackled many projects.

Herb had steel grey hair, with a husky physique and startling, bright blue eyes. One of the things that came to pass during the Asp administration and my term on the town council was to address was the town's lack of zoning. Greybull had zero zoning and as a result, there were all sorts of situations like auto body shops in otherwise residential neighborhoods and homes on what otherwise would logically be commercial districts. The council proposed to grandfather, existing properties, but once the business or purpose changed then the property was to revert to the primary characteristic for the neighborhood. This situation would catch up with me later at the bank, but it was a fair plan designed to work with people who had invested in a property and or businesses that were otherwise out of sync, with the zoning plan for that particular neighborhood.

It was during all this community zoning debate that Martha's class was studying about how democracy works. I was anticipating a lively debate about the zoning issue. So I invited Martha to come to the meeting with me to observe. I pointed out the various members of the council and said to her,

"Mr. Asp is the Mayor. He sits at the head of the council table and runs the meeting. He is the one with the bright blue eyes."

As expected the debate, with vehement objections coming from the opposition, most of whom hadn't bother to read the actual proposed zoning ordinance, we had proposed. There were also passionate pleas from supporters of the propose law, who emphatically embraced the council's initiative. Fortunately, once the opponents of the proposed zoning rules, understood, that the status quo would be maintained and no one was being asked to give up their business or tear down a building; they were in a more agreeable frame of mind by the end of the evening.

It was a longer than usual meeting. That summer evening and as Martha and I walked homeward, I asked, "Martha, what did you think of the meeting?"

She looked at me with a serious expression on her face and replied, "You are right, the Mayor does have pretty blue eyes."

Bank presidents are frequently called on to participate in local politics and at times state politics also. As mentioned earlier, Big Horn County has been a Republican stronghold ever since it's' formation in the early days of the twentieth century and I was frequently called up to support Republican candidates and was occasionally invited to Republican events. One such event took place in Cody, the county seat of Park County. The keynote speaker was the famous aviator, Army Air Corps General Jimmy Doolittle. By a stroke of good fortune, I happened to wind up setting opposite the General at the dinner table.

The discussions in the room and on the podium soon degenerated into discussions of political interest to Park County residents. Being a fairly, newly minted private pilot I was delighted to have the opportunity to engage Doolittle in a conversation about airplanes and aviation in general. By this time all others at the table, all from Park County, had left to join in a heated discussion of Park County political intrigues, which were of no interest to the General and I, at least, not when we could talk about airplanes. I had Jimmy Doolittle all to myself for two hours.

During the course of the conversation, I mentioned that my dad had been a great admirer of his, after seeing him perform an outside loop, a very dangerous maneuver, and at that time attempted by very few pilots, who lived to tell about. This took place about 1933 in Rio de Janeiro, Brazil at an air show. Doolittle remembered the event vividly and said, "And now let me tell you the rest of the story."

I was enthralled and said, "Do go on."

Jimmy Doolittle continued, "About two weeks after the air show, I was still in Rio and was invited to a friend's home for dinner. After dinner, they proceeded to show home movies. I absolutely hate home movies, and as I had more than enough for dinner, I quickly dozed off. All of a sudden, everyone in the room began to yell, 'oh, oh, oh, my God!' Jarred from my little nap, I gazed at the screen in disbelief and shouted, 'that crazy bastard is going to kill himself!' Then, of course, I realized the crazy bastard was me."

I had to laugh out loud. Jimmy Doolittle was one of the most interesting people I have ever met. He went on the tell me of various other exploits as a pilot including the famed Tokyo Raid and the fact that the first plane he ever flew was a World War I, Curtis Jenny and more recently he had been type rated in a Boeing 707 while he was Chairman of Pan American World Airways. Among his achievements was he was the first pilot, back in the 1920s to take off and land solely on instruments; in addition, he was the first person to earn a PHD in Aeronautical Engineering. He was indeed, master of the calculated risk.

Speaking of flying, Jo and I were invited to a dinner party at the home of Gene and Louise Powers. Gene was the other half of Hawkins & Powers Aviation. Gene had just return from Alaska, where they had a contract to fly fresh fish, including Alaska King Crab, from Anchorage to Los Angeles and other cities on the west coast. He explained, "We go out into the Aleutians using our C119 cargo planes, which we can land on the beaches, pick up the fisherman's catch then fly to Anchorage, transfer the load to our KC97, turbo propped freighters, then on to the west coast with the freshly caught fish."

I asked, "How did you get that contract?"

Gene answered, "That's the funny part. The outfit that previously had the contract was using retired airline Boeing 707s, which use a lot more fuel than our KC97s. The 707s make the trip in five hours, where as our KC97s make the same trip in seven hours. But you know the fish don't seem to mind at all."

We all got a good chuckle out of that and enjoyed a delicious dinner of fresh Alaskan King Crab Legs, which Louise had prepared.

As the 1970s moved on inflation moved ever up ward and we faced challenges and more intense competitive pressures from not only our savings and loan competitor, who were allowed by law to pay a quarter to half a percentage more on time deposits than commercial banks, but also from Production Credit Associations (P.C.A.), which funded their loans to farmers and ranch through the Farm Credit Systems, Federal Intermediate Credit Bank, which issued bonds and notes at Federal Agency rates, perhaps a quarter percent higher than U.S. Treasury securities. It also allowed them to charge their customers based on a blended rate; this of course was much more palatable to agricultural customers, who depended on borrowed money for their operations. At The First National Bank of Greybull, I was determined the meet this challenge head-on.

Nineteen

Meeting the Competition

As a bank examiner a dozen years earlier, I had seen in Arnie Trautwein's Cheyenne National Bank an Agricultural Credit Corporation, which Arnie had named High Plains Agricultural Credit Corporation (HPAC). I had wondered what this peculiar subsidiary was and why Mr. Trautwein had created it. I asked and he explained that HPAC was used to fund agricultural loans, which Cheyenne National, being a fairly new bank, didn't have the deposits to fund. The farm and ranch loans made by HPAC were funded by the Federal Intermediate Credit Bank (FICB) in Omaha. Our board made the decision to explore the possibilities of an FICB funded agricultural credit corporation and I made a trip to Omaha to visit with FICB.

The trip to Omaha didn't go quite as planned and the FICB people didn't exactly welcome me with open arms. A cantankerous old bureaucrat laid out in detail all the hoops I would be required to jump through to get an agricultural credit corporation launched. The good news was they didn't close the door on my proposed Agricultural Credit Corporation either. Our bank had a correspondent relationship with Omaha National since our beginnings in 1907. While in Omaha I went over to see my friend, John Clements, our Omaha National Bank representative and explained the difficulties I was having putting my proposed Valley Agricultural Credit Corporation (Valley) together. John listened patiently, as I explained the problem.

FICB wanted Valley to have at least a year operational tract record, before they would allow us to access FICB funding resources. This ignored the fact that our bank had been active in lending to farmers and ranchers in our community for over 70 years. In the meantime, we would have to set up a wholly owned subsidiary and make loans in it, separate from the bank's portfolio. Capitalizing the equity part was easy enough. We could transfer some of the bank's agricultural loans to Valley, which was little more than a bookkeeping entry. The problem was it didn't generate the loanable capital I needed to fund my agricultural borrower's needs, which of course was the whole reason for the establishment of Valley. John pondered the question and said, "I have a solution for you."

Interested I said, "Tell me more."

John answered, "Suppose the Omaha National Bank sets up a line of credit for Valley, we could fund it at prime, until such a time, as FICB is ready to fund you."

I replied, "That would be the perfect solution and would be less cumbersome than trying to sell participations for funding purposes, since few of our agricultural credits exceed our legal lending limit; in fact most of our farm loans are relative small. Our problem is funding, not large loans."

John smiled and said, "I'll get my loan committee to approve $750,000 line of credit. Then I can come out to Wyoming in the summer, I love to visit Wyoming anyway, and do an inspection of your records to monitor the quality of the loans; I'm sure our guys will want that. Then we can go out to dinner at Five Sisters for their famous juicy steaks. I'll get back to you in a couple of days. That way you can start making loans in Valley for the new season right way."

"That sounds perfect! Many Thanks,"

Summer came and John, true to his word came to check our loans out. He was accompanied by Bill Joe, a boisterous sales guy and would be womanizer from the trust department. After the inspection, we all went out to eat at Five Sisters on a beautiful, balmy summer evening. Our waitress was Kathryn Flitner, a gorgeous, well-tanned, sophisticated brunette, who was working as a server evenings. Kathryn was a student at Dartmouth College in New Hampshire and was at home for the summer, living with her parents the Dave Flitners, a local ranching family. Bill was smitten immediately, not only by the young lady's striking beauty, but also her elegance and yet outgoing personality.

Throughout happy hour, the dinner, and dessert Bill aggressively pursued conversation with the lovely Kathryn. Pushing the dialog further he said, "Do you work here full time?"

Tired of Bill's obnoxious badgering, the woman of his dreams, replied, "No during the day, I work on my father's ranch, shoveling shit."

With that Bill choked on his drink and quickly lost interest, exactly as Kathryn had intended. John was annoyed and embarrassed by Bill's antics and decided to play a practical joke on him on the way home, when they stopped in Lusk, Wyoming. John called me on the phone and related the story, "Bert, you used to come Lusk as an examiner?"

"Right," I replied.

John said, "When in Lusk, do you remember the big yellow house on the main drag."

"Sure," I replied. "It was a whorehouse run by a benevolent madam. Max Bird over at the Stockman's National Bank told us about it. He said the old girl, used some of her earnings to give scholarships to deserving local high school kids, who were University of Wyoming bound. A kind of Lusk legend. What about it?"

John started to chuckle and said, "On the way home we were scheduled to stop and visit Gene Lenz at the Lusk State Bank, we do some ranch over lines with them, Well, anyway when we pulled into Lusk, I told Bill the Yellow House was a really nice bed and breakfast place with excellent breakfasts and to see if they might have a couple of rooms for us. Bill having never been to Lusk wasn't aware of the 'Yellow House Legend', so he goes up to the door thinking it's a B & B. The old madam, dressed in a sluttish red dress with her wrinkly old boobs on full display, she must be over seventy, answers the door. She's painted up like a madam from the movies. Anyway she says to Bill, 'you're a little early in the day ain't ya?' Bill still doesn't get it and says he's looking for a couple of rooms for night. Finally, the old broad catches on and says, 'Sonny, we rent rooms complete with ladies for about an hour at $20 a clip.' Bill catches on and hightails it out of there back to the car."

Laughing, I said, "What did he say?"

John, replied, "he said, 'God damn you, Clements, you set me up, didn't you.' Of course he was right and I just laughed."

Within a year we had satisfied FICB's requirements and we were able to obtain funding through them. This also allowed us to match rates without Production Credit Association (PCA) competitor, by using the same index. Not only that there were a couple of other benefits. By indexing to the FICB interest scale, we were able to lower rates, while protecting our margins. An unexpected benefit turned out to be that, while PCA required their members to purchase PCA stock equal to10% of their line of credit, which we didn't need, since the bank had already capitalized Valley. This was really appreciated by our frugal farmer clientele.

With the matter of funding agricultural loans solved, I decided to take on our savings and loan competitor by offering mortgage home loans to our customers. Here to for, we had sent nearly all of our home loan applicants over to the competition. Bob King, who I mentioned earlier had a good deal of banking experience with larger institutions, suggested we make home loans, documented to Fannie Mae (Federal National Mortgage Association) specifications. By doing this we could sell the loans to investors wishing to geographically diversify their home loan portfolios. Our strategy would be to retain the servicing, that is collection of the payments, hence earning fee income as opposed to be solely depend on volatile interest rate spreads, on long term loans funded by short term deposits. We would then earn a servicing fee and our customer could deal with us for any issues that might arise during the life of the loan. With this in mind we needed to get some of our people up to speed, which involved some training.

On one such training trip we flew to Casper. Joining me was Connie Collingwood, who was to manage the operations side of our new mortgage banking venture and Judy Colwell, our mortgage lender. I decided to take along Randy Sullivan, a Hawkins and Powers slurry bomber pilot, because I was working on an Instrument Rating and wanted to get some instruction and flying time under the "hood", which requires a check pilot.

Randy is quite short, and always retained a sense of humor about it. His wife Marilyn, was a good six inches taller, was one of Charlene's associates in the insurance agency. Randy, was a highly experience pilot, chatted with Connie and Judy as we flew over the Big Horn Mountains, directly over the

"Hole in the Wall" country, west of Kaycee, where Butch Cassidy and the Sundance Kid hid out during the outlaw days of the old west. Connie asked Randy, "Do you do much instrument flying?"

Randy came back with, "I fly on instruments all the time, can't see out the windshield, you know!"

The seminar proved a useful learning experience for Connie and Judy and we developed a growing home loan servicing portfolio. On a quiet summer day as I was contemplating what I might do to build the bank I was interrupted about 11:00 AM by Becky Lawton, our receptionist and my secretary. "There is a lady out front says she is Barbara Walters, and wants to see you. She doesn't look anything like the lady on TV. May I send her back?"

"Sure go ahead and send her back." I said.

I thought for a moment and realized that it could only be Barbara Walter formerly Barbara Trott. Barbara was a large blond gal who had grown up in my neighborhood in New Jersey years ago. Barbara had married Alvin Walter, her across the street neighbor, shortly after graduating from Hackensack High School. I remembered Barbara clearly from the eighth grade, when she invited me to a dance at the Women's Club, where she had been taking dancing lessons. In those days I was short for my age and was an insensitive thirteen year old, so I refused. She was not up to my standards of beauty at the time, which were unrealistically high, given I was a bumbling bashful eighth grader, who was totally afraid of girls.

Her mother called my mother. I think they knew each other from PTA, or some other subversive organization. When Dad came home that night he took me aside and said that I shouldn't be hurting Barbara's feelings and it wouldn't hurt me to go to the dance with her; he even hinted that if I behaved myself in gentleman like manner, he might give me his 1941 Ford, which he reckoned he would be replacing by the time I was old enough to drive. So I took Barbara to the dance and it proved not to be too painful. Okay, I actually had a good time.

Barbara ambled into my office and greeted me, "Hi, how are you? Haven't seen you in years, Al and I with the kids are on our way Yellowstone National Park. Got your address from Bob and Judy Busam, who I understand you keep up with."

I replied, "Yes I get a Christmas card every year from Bob and Judy. It's getting on towards lunchtime. Let me call my wife Jo and see what kind of lunch we can rustle up."

I called Jo and she put together a nice lunch. Our kids seemed to enjoy their children and we had a good time visiting, catching up and remembered our youthful days.

With our strong loan demand, we were always on the lookout for ways to build our deposit base as well as service income revenues. Wyoming attracts a good number of out of state hunters. One Indian summer like October day, a tall, dignified, white haired gentleman, who immediately reminded me of Colonel Saunders of Kentucky Fried Chicken fame, came into the bank to cash a check. He identified himself as Jefferson Davis and gave me, in addition to the usual driver's license and credit cards, his business card, which read: Jefferson Davis, President, Air Force Federal Credit Union, Beaufort, South Carolina.

It was a quiet October day, a day or two before the hunting season began; Mr. Davis had come a few days early to get in position for the hunt. Since he was essentially in the banking business too, he started a conversation, "what's your loan demand like?"

I answered, "We have lots of loan requests; we serve of course farmers, ranchers, business people, home loans, and the usual consumer financing for cars and so forth. Our banking competitors don't like main street commercial loans very much. They prefer to do the agricultural loans. Many of the merchants down in Basin, come to us for the borrowing requirements, we are usually quite fully loaned, at least until sugar beet payday in November, when our agricultural customers pay down."

Davis seemed interested and drawled in his thick southern accent, "Our customers are Air Force folks and they mostly buy cars, consumer items. For the most part, they are savers. Consequently, we always surplus funds, looking for an investment. How long has your bank been in business?"

I replied, "Our bank was founded in 1907. C. J. Williams. His son, Gerald Williams, who was the President before me, is our Co-Chairman."

Davis then drawled, "Old as Methuselah, I don't have a lot of confidence in some of these upstart institutions. Would you be interested in some CD money?"

"Sure, we can always use deposits." I said and quoted our CD rates, which were somewhat higher than banks in his region.

"Sounds good, I'll wire you $500,000, when I get back home." He said.

What started as a transaction to cash a check for $200, had turned into a very large deposit relationship. The story doesn't end there. Soon we started get calls and large deposits from his credit union buddies across the south.

We were also concerned about small, local depositors. One day Cleo Brown, who was a kind of junk and scrap dealer, came into close his account. Although it wasn't a large account, I never liked to lose demand deposit accounts. Moreover, Mr. Brown, a likable, colorful old cowboy in his youth, had a son who was an excellent commercial customer. I asked Mr. Brown, "Why are you closing your account; I hope you are not mad at us."

"Oh no, I'm not at all mad, but I have a terrible time keeping my checkbook straight. So I keep an account here and one down in Basin. When one gets messed up and I get confused, I stop using it. Then I use the other account until it is all fouled up. Seems like I rotate every five or six months. Been banking that way for years." He said.

I resisted laughing and smiled at the old gent, we shook hands and I said, "I'm glad to know you're not mad at us."

He grinned and said, "I'll be back in about six months. See you then."

"OK" I replied, and sure enough he was back in six months.

On the subject of small accounts one such customer was Joe Cortez. Joe was a Basque sheepherder and went on a whiskey binge during his periodic visits to town. He visited a big-busted redheaded lady nick-named Babe. The story went around that she and her girlfriend, nick named Toots performed certain services, which I will leave to the reader's imagination. Every Monday morning after Joe had gone back to the mountain to tend his sheep, Babe would come into the bank and deposit Joe's money for him. In addition, to personal services, she was also the steward of his finances and performed these duties worthy of any fiduciary. If you are wondering if I knew the lady, I did. Not professionally I hasten to add.

Babe and Toots catered our local Rotary Club lunches on Tuesdays. The ladies were decent enough cooks and for years did a super job for the club too. Babe was also an avid sports fan. She attended all the home games and cheered the loudest and most enthusiastically, as anyone in the crowd. No wonder, when I became Police Commissioner, Dave Lindsay, warned me: "whatever you do, don't close down Babe and Toots."

These gals never requested loans and I'm sure that we never could have received approval for SBA financing for them. Our bank pursued SBA loans, with vigor. Gerald Williams was a strong advocate of the program and over the years we developed a certain expertise in making these loans. SBA loans allow small banks like ours to make larger loans than our legal lending limit would normally allow us with more generous repayment terms. We made several so called 502 loans, which were designed to make loans for facilities. One of our goals was to make loans either for facilities needed in the community or foster economic growth.

A community problem we were able to solve with a 502 SBA loan was a grocery store crisis. Our main grocery store was a small 6500 square feet, Safeway Store, a national chain.

Safeway in their infinite corporate wisdom decided that stores of less than 20,000 feet were no longer economical. What Greybull could reasonably support was a store half that size. We had a couple of "Ma and Pa" operations. As it happened all the proprietors reached retirement age at about the same time and none had family members interested in continuing the family business. We were about to go from four stores to none, when Ron Fiene and Annette Clifton came into the bank and wanted to talk grocery store financing. Greybull needed a grocery store. Jay Wilkerson and Herb Miller, the youngest folks in the grocery business, had closed when they sold their building to be used as an office for a land title company.

Ron and Annette worked at the Safeway store, which had given notice they would be closing, their smaller operations. Ron was about 25 years old and Annette, perhaps 10 years older. I remembered Ron, from when he was an inquisitive high school student, and I had given a talk to his class about how banks function. He asked a bunch of probing questions, almost to the point of being an obnoxious wise guy. Ron was stocky man, perhaps six feet tall, with a great shock of unruly dark brown hair. Annette was a trim blond gal, who wore fairly thick-framed glasses, which seemed to me detracted from her otherwise good looks.

Ron began, "Annette and I have been working at Safeway and it is driving us nuts, we think we could run a much better store and want to start a new one."

News travels fast in a small town, so I already knew the Safeway store was slated to close. I said, "Tell me why the two of you think you can do better?"

Ron shot right back, "My present responsibility at Safeway is produce manager. Part of the job is to spray water on the vegetables and fruits to keep them fresh. The other day, we were busy and I wasn't able to get to freshening up the vegetables, before my shift was done. So, I punched out on the clock, so as not to work any overtime. Then I went over to take care of the veggies. The union shop steward, comes over to me and chews my ass out for trying to do a good job. This annoyed Annette and me no end."

"Interesting," I said, "are you thinking of renting the Safeway Building?"

Ron replied, "No. There are several problems with that building. I have been studying information from Associated Grocers (AG). They provide volume-buying discounts to make small stores, especially in small communities, which allows us to be competitive. Annette and I are thinking we'd like to build a ten or eleven thousand square foot store, which is the size AG says communities our size will support. There aren't any buildings available in town that size. Another problem is there is virtually no parking at the Safeway location, since it is right on Greybull Avenue, next to the Post Office."

I answered, "Sounds like a big project that would take quite a bit of money to put together. Can you come in with some equity money?"

Ron said, "As you know my Dad died recently and left me some money and Annette has savings to put into the project as well. Here is a business plan we have put together using AG information and projections. They really did quite a bit of work on this for us."

"Ron, Annette, let my study this and see if I can't find a way to make this happen for you. After all Greybull needs a grocery store; we all have to eat, Don't we?" I replied.

I pondered the store problem and called Larry McDonald at Wyoming Industrial Development Corporation (WIDC), since it was evident it was going to take a great deal more lending capacity than we in Greybull had by ourselves. The plan we put together was involved, but at the same time sound and practical.

The financing package we put together was complicated. WIDC would own, build and inject the equity into the project. Using the SBA 502 program our bank and our friendly competitor, Big Horn Federal Savings & Loan, would participate 50/50 in a first mortgage. Then SBA would take the second position. Ron and Annette would have the right of first refusal to purchase the building in the future. Our bank also made an SBA guaranteed loan for the furniture, fixtures, equipment, working capital and inventory, utilizing the cash equity Ron and Annette had provided.

The store, named Ron's Food Farm, was a huge success and Ron and Annette proved to be able managers. It was about this time, when Ron's opened, that my wife's sister Susan's sixteen-year-old daughter Connie Patterson came to live with us. Juli was a baby and with our other kids, Jo had her hands full. Connie it seems had a romantic entanglement, with a young man who her parents vehemently disapproved and wanted her to get far away from the troublesome young man.

As I remember Connie hadn't been to Wyoming and pictured it as the wild and wooly west as depicted in the western TV shows. On her first trip to Ron's Food Farm she was impressed with this nice shiny new clean store with good selection. Connie, who had a way with words, promptly dubbed it: "Ron's Fat Food Farm." A name that lives on to this day in our family, as I'm sure we all gained a few pounds resulting from the cuisine Jo was able to prepare from the groceries purchased at Ron's. More than eating though, Connie hadn't given up on her interest in boys.

Connie was enrolled as a junior at the Greybull High School and by February, became enchanted with a young man named Jerry and they began dating. One cold, blustery Wednesday evening about 8PM, she announced that she and Jerry were going out for a coke. They had done this before and Jo and I didn't think too much of it as she was usually back home by 9:30 or so. But not this particular evening; by 10 PM, we became concerned, by eleven we were really worried. I went out cruising around town, looking for Jerry's car, but no luck. Midnight came and no Connie, by this time Jo was frantic. Jo called the highway patrol and they reported no accidents, but promised to watch out for Jerry's car, an older blue Oldsmobile.

The evening passed hour by hour and we heard nothing. Finally, at seven the following morning Connie called and reported they were in Wendover, Nevada, over 400 miles from Greybull. Jo asked, "What the hell is going on? We have been very worried, you know."

Meekly, Connie replied, "Jerry and I decided to get married, but when we got to Nevada, we discovered that you need to be 18 to get married without parental permission."

Jo said, "so now what?"

"We're on our way home. We will see you when we get back to Greybull." She replied.

They arrived back in town in the late afternoon, tired, but none the worse for the adventure. Jo asked, "If she had anything she wanted to say?"

To which Connie replied, "We are really sorry, we caused you all of this worry. On the drive back we decided getting married was a bad idea!"

"Thank God!" Jo and I said in unison.

Interestingly enough Jerry and Connie didn't date after that. The irony of this little story is that Connie and Jerry could have driven to Montana, the border is just 50 miles north from Greybull, where sixteen year olds can get married without their parents' consent. Connie finished the year in Greybull, then return to Stillwater, Minnesota to graduate with her class there.

While we were doing a number of things to improve the quality and range of services offered our customers, we were also focusing on realigning our income stream to earn more money from fees and obtain less reliance on interest spreads. There had been for years a general rise in interest rates, which increased both our cost of money, and put unrelenting pressure on us to keep our rates as economical as possible for our customers. As one of the speakers at an American Bankers Association seminar succinctly stated, "It is one thing to charge a farmer 15% interest, but it is quite another for him to be able to pay it."

While pondering all of this I received a phone call from my cousin, I believe she would be a third cousin to be technically correct. My Cousin, Ruth Ranges Wilson, was employed in the cash management department of the First National State Bank in Newark, New Jersey. Her boss Bob Mervine, was looking for a bank to serve as a "remote disbursement facility" for several of their large corporate customers. Mr. Mervine flew out to meet with us and check our operations capability out.

At the time the manager of our backroom operations was Nancy Booth, who had a stellar mind for numbers and was an efficiency minded bank officer. Mr. Mervine looked over the town as well as our operational setup. Our accounting operations were as organized and productive as was possible with the technology available at the time. Mr. Mervine was sufficiently impressed that he was prepared to go to meet with Wayne Martin, the manager of the Denver Branch of the Federal Reserve Bank to explain the set up.

The following week we were in Denver explaining the fail safe set up we had for the wire transferring Federal Funds that is collected Federal Reserve deposits, to settle for the New Jersey checks which we were to receive each day. The set up included a backup system to transfer Fed Funds from the Bank of America in San Francisco in the event the First National State's Fed in New York had closed for the day when we needed to make settlement. Mr. Martin wasn't thrilled with our arrangement, but neither did he interpose any official objection. After we conducted our business, Mr. Martin, who I had known and had a pleasant relationship with for years, invited us for a tour of the Denver Branch's facilities.

The tour included a trip to the money vault, some five stories below street level in the bowels of the earth. When we got down to vault, through all kinds of security guards, we were escorted under the watchful eye of the guards to the various money rooms. Here, several electric forklifts were whisking around with money baled as though it was a farmer's hay, between the various rooms in the Fed's great cavernous vaults. I couldn't help but be reminded of Scrooge McDuck's money bin depicted in Donald Duck comics. Within a couple of weeks we were up and running with our remote disbursement arrangement for Cousin Ruth and Mervine's bank.

Jo and I were preparing to attend a banking seminar in New York City within the next month and I said we could spend at day with cousin Ruth and Mr. Mervine in Newark. A few days before we took off for the east coast, we attend a Chamber of Commerce function and happened to sit with Jim and Ginny Core, our local Chevrolet dealer who had just return from an auto dealers convention in the "Big Apple."

As they were sharing their New York adventure with us they warned us about New York cabbies. Ginny began, "We were in this Checker cab, cars, trucks and buses whizzing around everywhere and the cabby turns to us, instead of looking where the hell he is going, says, 'Where are you folks from?'"

Jim chimes in, "We are nervous as hell, as the driver charges through a damned red light, barely missing a Yellow Cab."

Ginny said, "We live in Greybull, Wyoming."

Jim continues, "Upon hearing that the cabby turns around, as he nearly misses a bus, and says, 'GREYBULL, WYOMING, that's just west of Shell Canyon. I've never been so scared in my life. The road is nothing but a shelf built on the side of a cliff.' Finally he starts looking where he is going as we pull up in front of our hotel."

Ginny laughs, "Riding in that clown's cab is as scared as we've ever been."

Jim adds, "We'll take peaceful, scenic Shell Canyon, any day over New York City."

I said, "We'll take your advice and avoid New York taxi cabs."

As it turned out we rented a car and I did my own driving. We accepted my Aunt Gerda and Uncle Irv's invitation to stay with them in Edison, which under ordinary conditions is about an hour from downtown Newark. First National State Bank in Newark had a beautiful multi-story building located in the inner city of Newark. This fine gleaming white edifice was a stark contrast to its' surroundings, which immediately reminded of the eastern sector of Berlin in the years after the end of World War II, which I had visited on a vacation in 1964. Devastated, burned out buildings everywhere, with dejected homeless people wandering about. We parked in the bank's secure parking facility and went inside to meet with Ruth and Bob Mervine.

All over the cash management department were bumper stickers which read, "We are Greybull Boosters." We were surprised by the Greybull Booster decorations. Bob quickly explained that Eliene Diener at the Chamber of Commerce office had given him a handful of them on his visit to Greybull. We had a cordial meeting and we discussed a few fine points for the purpose of streamlining the operations. The return trip to Edison turn out to be an adventure, since during the four hours we were conducting our business at First National State Bank, a serious snow storm had begun.

In fact by the time we had started our trek to Edison four or five inches of snow had fallen. The streets and roads were unplowed and cars were sliding every which way; the visibility was even worse as we made our way to Edison on the New Jersey Turnpike, a limited access toll road. Not only were the snow plows behind schedule, but the roads were plugged up with cars running out of gas, because of the long waits, waiting for the travelers ahead to move, and infrequent gas stations on the Turnpike.

Since I had at that point been an avid skier for many years, I was not to be intimidated by snowstorms. But this storm was different. I never thought so many cars could run out of gas from idling on the highway. At one point we sat there waiting for an hour. The couple in the car next to us rolled their window down. Apparently, they just wanted to chat, to while away the time while waiting for the traffic ahead to get moving. They were just friendly folks wanting to talk about the weather, which of course there was plenty to talk about. Finally after four hours or more we arrived at Aunt Gerda and Uncle Irv's house in Edison, about three hours later than our planned arrival.

The Federal Reserve eventually regulated remote disbursement services out of existence and we of course shut down the operation. It was my goal and vision to provide an ever-increasing variety of services to improve earnings and get away for our inherent dependence on interest rate spreads. This was of special significance in the ever-increasing rising of the general levels of interest rates in the U.S. economy in the 1970s and 1980s.

Twenty

Taxes, Troubles, and Transition

At the beginning of 1978, I searched for ways to diversify our earnings, so we would become less dependent on net interest margins. In addition to the aforementioned ventures into mortgage lending, forming of an agricultural credit corporation, we also set up a leasing company and a trust department. The trust department took a bit of negotiating with our regulatory agency, but we were able to win the battle, by hiring a competent and experienced trust man to guide us. We managed to breakeven within the first year but it was not a very profitable venture. None of these efforts changed the vexing tax issues I was encountering with 60% ownership interest I was forced to pay the interest on my bank stock loan with after tax dollars.

By incorporating the insurance agency, I placed 25% of my bank ownership in a holding company that was not forced to meet Federal Reserve regulations. This was because the agency insurance corporation was a for profit corporation and didn't controlling ownership. I was obligated to pay the interest for the remaining 35% with after tax income; that is I received no deductions for interest payments over $10,000, since the IRS regarded this as "passive income." This argument would hold water if I had used borrowed money to hold for example public owned companies like General Electric or Bank of America. It is true in these instances that I would sit in my easy chair and watch management earn money for me. However, in my case, ownership in The First National Bank of Greybull was a means of me buying a job. I was hardly a passive participant, as envisioned by the Internal Revenue Service.

My old bank examiner buddy, Jerry Swords of Kansas City, had become a consultant who assisted bankers informing bank holding companies, which allows banks to form one bank holding companies. A bank holding company can be formed if a holder owns 80% of the bank's stock.

Jerry Swords, and his wife who is also named Geri, were regular attendees at the Wyoming Bankers Convention in Jackson Hole. On several occasions Jerry, Geri and his troop of five children would visit me in Greybull after a few days of taking in the delights of Yellowstone National Park as well the Tetons. Jerry and family did not visit me to talk bank holding companies, but rather to use our restroom facilities. While his family was tending to the business of the bladder, Jerry and I would chitchat about banking issues of the day. Jerry would also educate me about the benefits of forming a one bank holding company.

Buying the additional stock for me was problematic for two reasons; first of all most of our minority stockholders had owned the stock for 40 years or more, so their capital gains taxes would be painful. Moreover, because of my need to service my bank stock loan our dividends were quite generous, especially considering the low basis of many of the long time, elderly stockholders. I decided another strategy was needed.

Jo and I decided to get into the rental property business. My wife, Jo is a self-described "real estate person," who on occasion will say, "I never saw a house I didn't like." Meaning of course, she saw the potential, not necessarily the status quo, in a great variety of homes. With Jo's flair for decorating and willingness to take on the cleaning and some management tasks, coupled with the enjoyment I found in carpentry and other handyman tasks, we bought several local properties.

One of the places we bought was a structure built shortly after World War II ended and named the "El Rio Motel" in honor of the Big Horn River a couple of blocks away, although the building didn't enjoy a view of the river. The motel was located on a residential street, at an inconvenient location for tourists passing through town. A subsequent owner had converted it into apartments, dubbed the "El Rio Apartments." At the time we purchased it, the building needed a good cleaning and a number of relatively minor repairs. The individual units were small and we marketed them to low-income people. Our niece, Connie Paterson, assisted with the house-cleaning chores and promptly labeled the place, "El Dumpo." Not that our tenants weren't decent enough folks.

One of our renters was Angel Lopez, a farm worker. One bitter cold winter morning, the temperature was right at 25 below zero when Mr. Lopez appeared at our door. Jo was at home alone, with baby Juli in her arms. She invited Mr. Lopez into the foyer and out of the penetrating cold. Angel Lopez spoke very little English, saying nothing he proceeded to remove his coveralls, then a sweatshirt, after that a vest, next off came a heavy sweater, soon he was removing a pair of quilted snow pants. Jo thought, "My God, what the hell is going on here? Am I safe with this guy in the house?" Finally, Angel silently got down to his faded blue jeans and pulled out a roll of bills out of his pocket and peeled off $100, the amount of the rent for his tiny apartment and handed the wad of bills to Jo.

Then quietly he began the process of reassembling his wardrobe, step by step. Jo said, "thank you!"

Angel, smiled faintly and said, "da nada." (Spanish for you are welcome)

Times of high interest rates frequently lead to problem loans. One problem asset in our portfolio was an S.B.A. loan made to Fun Valley, Inc., which was initially a publicly held corporation with over 300 shareholders, with not one person owning more than 1%. The controlling shares were eventually sold to a parade of stockholders, who promised to develop the property with a lodge and other amenities, but eventually got discouraged due to oppressive Forest Service interference. The last of these principal shareholders was Ken Andersen, an ambitious, energetic, and hardworking young contractor.

We knew Ken fairly well. While he was working his way through college, we made him a construction loan to build a modest speculative home on a city lot he had acquired for $1000. Although I am not a fan of financing spec homes, Greybull was growing at the time and needed housing so I figured if Ken could lessen the housing shortage by one house. Ken did an excellent job. The project came in under budget and the house was sold shortly before completion. When Ken came to us was the ski area project, we decide to go for an S.B.A. loan.

Once again Ken delivered and built the new lodge within budget. For the first time one of the owners actually delivered on promises to develop the property. Then the Forest Service got in the middle of the business, by limiting the rate increases on lift tickets and also insisting various and sundry improvements. One of which was insisting on guard railing where the T-Bar path crosses Granite Creek. A T-Bar tows the skier up the hill, rather than providing a ride like a chairlift. This was totally unnecessary, since the whole area is filled with snow in winter. Where the T-bar crosses the creek is not detectable in winter. Some bureaucrat sitting in an office in Washington wouldn't know this. Moreover, the railing would have been perfectly situated for a skier to catch his or her skis, fall or even break a leg. Our arguments fell on deaf ears in Washington.

Fortunately, Roger Williams, our Tree Department assistant district ranger, himself an avid skier, immediately saw the problem and managed to get the Forest Service to drop the requirement. Eventually, Mr. Andersen gave up on the ski business. The bank attempted to secure management. To allow the ski area to close could have resulted in the cancelling of the lease granted by the Forest Service.

My good friend, Lee Kunkle took on the job for one season, working year round to maintain, improve and manage the facility. Later, Jo with the financial backing of Jim Kost ran it one season. However, the property always seemed to need more money than it was certainly prudent to lend or invest in equity due to the Forest Service's iron fisted control on lift ticket rates. Rarely, did Fun Valley, Inc. generate a positive cash flow, much less turn a profit.

It was obvious that what the ski area needed was an owner with deep pockets and a vision for the future, which might include expanding the lodge to include a motel facility that could generate revenues year round, especially in the summer, which made perfect sense since the ski area was located on U.S. Highway 14, an important road leading into Yellowstone National Park. A couple of other improvements like a chair lift to the top of Antelope Butte, which would quadruple the length of the skiing trails on the mountain. This had a least the potential of attracting skiers from out of state, since Antelope Butte would then have over a 1000-foot vertical height;

the trails would offer something for beginning to expert skiers. All of this development obviously would take a great deal of money.

Jim Kost who was now on the bank's board and doing quite well, had a friend, Gary Furstenfeld, a Chicago based real estate investor. Gary had succeeded in rescuing Westinghouse Commercial Credit from a lending disaster by purchasing a distressed large motel property located near O'Hare International Airport and turning it into a profitable venture. Westinghouse gave Gary a four million dollar loan commitment to use anyway at his discretion for a development project of his choosing. Gary and his wife Kay, a Wyoming native from across the mountain, came out to Wyoming to visit Kost and look over the ski area situation. After carefully studying the project, he drew up plans to include the oft dreamed about chairlift to the top of the mountain and a 40 unit motel.

Gary then returned to present the plans to the Forest Service and made an appointment to explain his vision along with detailed drawings. This would have been in the early fall and Gary was hoping to obtain Forest Service approval in time to start construction once the snow melted on the mountain in May. By this time our Forest Service Ranger was Kevin Manson, who knew next to nothing about business and envisioned every dollar of revenues the ski area took in as money that could be used to finance non-revenue producing Forest Service projects, oblivious to the fact Fun Valley had a staff of employees in season, along with a multitude of operating expenses.

Mr. Manson informed Gary Furstenfeld it would take the Forest Service five years to study the project plans. Incensed, Gary gave him the finger and left without a word. The Forest Service had blocked both every opportunity to make a profit and to develop the ski area as well.

I mention this frustrating series of events, because every lender who assumes any risk at all, will at some point have a significant lending disaster; this would be in all likelihood the dumbest loan I ever made.

As interest rates escalated, a number of farmers in our community decided to call it quits and a number of farm auctions were held. Our local auctioneer Hugo Ward presided at one of the auctions I attended. Auctions are peculiar events, sometimes people walk away with terrific bargains, other times the competitive zeal of the moment causes people to pay outlandish prices for some items. At this sale there were graphic examples of both.

I was in the market for a reliable old pickup truck, having sold my old Chevrolet truck after the stone project was completed. So I bid on four year old Ford, red and cream, F250 with the big V-8 engine, automatic transmission, defects being it used a little oil and a somewhat bashed in side panel. I bought it for $725, a fraction of the book value. A little while later Hugo offered a wire cage contraption for raising multiple chickens. This poultry apartment dwelling was rusty, smelly, and encrusted with, well, simply stated I'd call it "chicken shit". A more decorous word would fail to describe this evil, odorous, piece of hardware.

He started with, "let's start the bidding off at $50.00."

To Hugo's surprise, Harvey Manning jumped right on it, "fifty dollars."

His neighbor, Lewis Schultz, with whom he had a long-standing feud, countered with, "sixty."

Without a moment's hesitation Manning came back with, "seventy."

Hugo tilted his hat on the back of his head, and scratched his brow, pointed to Lew Schultz.

Before Hugo could open his mouth, Schultz barked back, "eighty."

Not to be out done and thinking he could end it right there, Marvin Manning, jumped the bid, "one hundred dollars."

Lew Schultz, not be out bid, shouted back, "one hundred twenty five dollars."

Hugo shook his head and pointed over to Harvey Manning, before he could say anything, a red faced Harvey Manning responded, "One hundred fifty dollars!"

Lew immediately, yelled, "Two hundred!"

By this time it was like Hugo, the auctioneer wasn't even there. Harvey bellowed, "Three hundred!"

Lew Schultz roared, "Damn you Manning, FOUR HUNDRED DOLLARS!"

Finally, Manning meekly turned to Hugo and said, "I'm done."

Hugo banged his gavel on the podium and said, "Sold to Lew Schultz for four hundred dollars."

I was standing next to Tom Van Gelder at the time and he remarked, "I could have sold him a brand new shiny one for three hundred."

Farm sales and high interest rates meant that our loan portfolio quality was deteriorating and we were taking significantly more loan losses, or at least pumping up of our reserve for loan losses to meet the increasing possibility of impending credit losses. We were forced to cut dividends, and shortly thereafter eliminate them. This was compounded by the Administrator of National Banks demanded we replace our maturing capital notes, which the bank paid the interest on out of the banks revenues, with equity capital stock, which I would have to pay interest on the debt incurred to make the injection out of my depleted pockets. Selling the bank became the only solution to the problem. I began seeking suitors.

For us, life was not all bad news, Juli was now talking and making some interest observations. One day a neighbor, asked her one day what I did at the bank and since her connection with the bank was the lollipops, or "suckers" as she called them, she said, "my daddy makes suckers."

I was on the American Bankers Association Agricultural Bankers Committee and during the summer of 1981 we had a meeting at The Grand Hotel on Mackinaw Island in Michigan. The resort site for a number of movies, and a great place for a family vacation, so we decided to take Oliver, Martha and Juli along. Jo's boys, Michael and Chad were to be spending this part of the summer with their father. In the morning I attended the meetings, and Jo kept the kids busy with the fun activities offered by the island. Afternoons we had the opportunity for family adventures.

The island bans all except emergency motor vehicles, which prompted us to rent bicycles. Juli was only two so I rented a bike with a child's rear mounted seat and we proceeded to cycle around the circle drive, which takes you next to the water all the way around the island. The older two kids were by this time accomplished riders, and had no trouble keeping up. In fact were able to lead the way. I brought up the rear, with Jo periodically drifting back to check on Juli's wellbeing. About half way around the island Juli was fast asleep leaning out of her seat. Of course, she was belted in and in no danger falling. We didn't need to wake her, as she slept, until it was time to return the bikes to the rental shop.

After Mackinaw Island, we drove across part of Ontario to Niagara Falls and viewed the falls from the Canadian side. Juli had never seen so much water and exclaimed, "my God look at all that water."

From there we were off to West Chester, Pennsylvania to visit my boyhood friend Pete Brakman and his family. Our original plan was to travel to Washington, D. C. As we traveled, cross country, avoiding the Interstate Highway System in favor of the pastoral farming communities in western New York state. Jo said, "I don't want to go to a big city, I want to visit cute little villages."

As we cruised across western New York and took in the beauty of the dairy farms, lakes and country towns, I said, "well, we wouldn't find cute little villages in Washington, but I know where to find what you're looking for."

Jo rolled her lovely brown eyes approvingly and replied, "What are you thinking?"

I replied, "I'm thinking New Hampshire. I know just the kind of spot you're dreaming of, Snowville, New Hampshire. I spent a few weeks in the summer there on a couple occasions with our Hackensack neighbors, the McKenzies."

We spent a few days with Pete and his family, checked out the Amish farms in nearby Lancaster and were on our way northeast to Snowville, with intermittent stops in Hackensack, New Jersey, where I was born, showing the kids the house I grew up in, then on to Mystic Seaport, Connecticut, and the old colonial village at Sturbridge, Massachusetts. Arriving in Snowville, we lucked out and found a charming Bed and Breakfast, appropriately dubbed the Snowville Inn.

Snowville turned out to be remarkably unchanged, virtually the same as I remembered in from 30 years earlier. We looked up the senior McKenzies, who had retired there. Mac and Barbara were available for dinner and we ate at an excellent seafood place in nearby Conway. I observed how little things had changed during my thirty-year absence. The old Snowville post office was still there and run by Mrs. Headley, who looked to me, a twelve year old, with her pure white hair looked to be pushing 100; she was now in her 90s. The birch log tree house Sandy McKenzie and I had built was still there thirty years later.

Those summers we swam in Crystal Lake, named for its' remarkably clear water, with a white sand bottom, which emphasized the water's clarity. We took the children swimming in Crystal Lake; the water was clear and pristine as ever. I looked across the lake, where there had been a summer camp for girls. My God, they still had the same 48' Chevy truck, which must have at least been repainted, looking just like it did 30 years earlier.

After the summer vacation it was time to get back to work and the serious business of selling the bank, as much I hated the thought. We talked to a few possible buyers. The most attractive proposal, an all cash buy out came from Bob Ferrill at the Bank of Commerce, across the mountain in Sheridan, 100 miles east of us. I was comfortable working with Bob as I had known him from both Wyoming Banker's Association and serving on the Wyoming Industrial Development Corporation (WIDC) board with him for many years.

Bob was the President of WIDC and invited me to join the board after our bank had lead the way by making WIDC's first loan. I remembered with fondness the first board meeting. There were several interesting investment propositions on the agenda that meeting. Bob turned to me and said, "now isn't this more enjoyable than making car loans all day?"

I had to agree, it was fun to be able make loans and other investments, which were different from the ordinary routine of the banking business. I was looking forward to working with Bob and the rest of his team. We settled on a price and immediately Bob and Bill Ruggamer began attending and participating in our board and loan committee meeting. One of the most interesting parts of the transition was the psychological tests they ran on each officer and employee.

They were called "Personalysis Tests" and were based on Dr. Eric Berne's book, I'm OK, You're OK. The test quantifies an individual's psychological makeup into their adult, parent and child personalities. Instead of defining characteristics in words which might be offensive, the person is described as being, for example high red. The color red represents tendency to be authoritarian. A bossy person might get the maximum points of red, six points in the adult or workplace personality. Adolf Hitler no doubt would have been a six pointer. On the other hand motivation in the child personality, or what the person wants for his or herself satisfaction might reflect something entirely different.

My own Personalysis came out pretty much as I would expected. In the workplace I like to be in charge, five points of red. I am not much of a detail person in my adult person, but in my child I can get into detail. Thelma Kost on the other hand, we all knew would be high red, in fact she scored six points of red. No surprise there; around the bank she was often referred to a "Sargent" or "Boss Lady." However, in her child personality, what motivated her was she wanted to be loved. Six points of green in the child.

What no one understood about Thelma was she needed, in fact required quite a bit of stroking. Because she was so bossy, that never occurred to any of us who, worked with her. Thelma had been with the bank since before I arrived. She was capable, intelligent, hardworking, and most of the time was pleasant enough to work with. But she could also be overbearing, easily offended and her personality could be quite prickly, if she wasn't happy. There were times that I was tempted to dismiss her, because getting along with her wasn't always easy.

Fortunately, I always concluded that her overall competence and super work ethic outweighed those times I felt frustration with her. The last six or seven months I worked with her were a joy, because at last I understood what made her tick. How I wished I had the Personalysis tool the day I arrived in Greybull.

After the results of the test were revealed to the staff, I went home and told Jo about it. That night we were scheduled to have dinner with the guys who gave the test. The dinner conversation mostly dwelled on the Personalysis test. Jo was also fascinated so I asked what it would cost to have Jo take the test. The one hundred bucks, paid out of my pocket of course, turned out to be a great investment for me. I learned some things about my wife that I never realized.

In the adult personality Jo is very outgoing, meets people well and is as personally charming as she is just plain good looking. In spite of her outward charm, she is deep down not a little shy, but very shy and reserved. By this time we had been married better than five years and it never dawned on me that her outgoing facade, did not overshadow her reluctance to meet new people and a basic shyness.

By this time we were looking at what we should be doing for our next act as it were. After a conversation with my director Bruce Kennedy, I focused on the point that after being in charge for past 15 years I would not be too happy losing my authority, especially in situations when I would have to go to committee or the guys from Sheridan, when dealing with long established customers. While Bob Ferrill and I were compatible, I didn't care for Bill Ruggamer, who Jim Kost once described as a "Hitler Youth." Jo and I decided to look around and perhaps relocate to somewhere else.

Jo was looking at an issue of Country Living magazine, the real estate sampler section. Jo's interest in real estate is never far from her mind. A property in Wilmington, Vermont caught her eye. We were in need of a break so we decided to take a long weekend. Flying out of Billings to Hartford, Connecticut, we then rented a car for the weekend and drove up to Wilmington, which is in southern Vermont between Brattleboro and Bennington.

The house was a twenty-five-room affair, built about 1940, by a wealthy family from Boston according the real estate salesman. The house sat on hillside eight-acre lot with a terrific view of the surrounding Green Mountains of Vermont. It was within in fifteen minutes of three really top-notch ski area. The place had a swimming pool, tennis court, a small barn where evidently a previous owner had kept a horse or two and quite a bit of woods as well. All of this for the seductive price of $175,000.

Jo's idea was to make it into a bed & breakfast. There were plenty of rooms for both our family and a dozen or so guest rooms. We thought we could attract skiers in winter, colored leaf tourists in the fall and perhaps utilize the tennis court for a tennis clinic when the weather was fine. While we both enjoy the game of tennis neither of us would have been skilled enough to attempt to be tennis pros.

We talked to the Vermont National Bank about financing and it appeared we would be able to swing a deal. There were of course other considerations, like how would our Wyoming "Cowboys & Girls" adapt to Vermont. We didn't have family or friends here I had a friendship with a couple of Vermont bankers from St. Albans and Burlington, both at the extreme north end of the state. Jo's family was in Wisconsin, mine in Colorado, and my business connections were all in Wyoming and Rocky Mountain states. In the end we decided to stay in Wyoming.

The problem with staying in Greybull, was what would I do for a living, although it did look like I would come away from the sale of the bank with enough in investments and contracts on sale of my local assets to survive? I was 43 at the time, so I wasn't ready to retire.

One important issue was school for the kids. Considering the small population and limited resources of the local school district, we felt that the school system was pretty decent. Yet our children had divergent educational needs, so a larger town was key. This boiled down to either Cheyenne or Casper.

We selected Casper for a variety of reasons. Casper was more centrally located as well as in our opinion more cosmopolitan. Not only that, we had a number of good friends residing in Casper and from a business perspective, the possibility of landing a job at a bank in Casper seemed more likely. In fact I did quite a bit of networking and was fairly close to a CEO position at Guaranty Federal Savings & Loan, which was struggling with asset- liability problems. The chronic problem of the whole industry was their assets were mainly long term fixed rate home loans. Borrowers were naturally hanging on to their low rate loans, while the bank was paying ever increasing high rates on the deposits which funded these same loans.

As it turned out I didn't get that job and that was a blessing in disguise as some of the board members were making, from what I read in the papers, speculative loans, which brought down the institution within a couple of years. Meanwhile, we went ahead and bought a home in Casper.

Our good friends Larry and Ann McDonald lived on a two-acre parcel on Skyline Road; they told us about a house in their neighborhood, which was the first house we looked at. Jo and I made several trips to Casper to look at houses, but nothing appealed to us as much as the house on Incline Road, around the corner from Larry and Ann. By this time Jo's son Michael had graduated from high school and was up in Gillette where his dad was living and working on a ranch for the summer, before going to Northwest Community College in Powell. We had the four younger children and as it happened the McDonalds also had four children, close to our kids in age. The kids would have some friends in the neighborhood.

Twenty One

Glenrock

In June of 1982 we moved to our new home on Incline Road, a stone's throw west of the Casper city limits. The house was a yellow Dutch Colonial style house, gambrel roof, second floor dormers in front: a classic style. Jo was happy to have a home to decorate in her taste. The kids: Juli age 3, Martha about to turn 11, Chad and Oliver both13, although seven months apart, all quickly adjusted to the new neighborhood and schools. Michael, now 18, was off to Gillette having graduated from Basin High School and working at a ranch near Gillette. We even bought a new dog, an Old English Sheep Dog. Thinking we were being clever, we named him Winston Churchill. However, when the AKC registration came back to us, we were surprised to learn his official name was Winston Churchill, 23rd.

I didn't have a job, but had started to do some consulting with banks and small businesses. Although the income stream was irregular, earning anywhere from $700 to $7000 in a month, the projects I took on were varied and interesting. I figure I would take on anything I was confident I wouldn't screw up. The biggest problem was, as a lawyer friend of mine put it, "keeping the funnel full." I did have investment income, which kept the wolf away from the door. After about twenty months or so I did land a banking job.

One of my old bank examiner friends, Bart Neville, was now President of the Wyoming National Bank of East Casper. We called him "Black Bart" in honor of his piercing dark eyes, not his demeanor, which was wise, kindly, and cheerful. Bart hired me to do his annual budget and growth forecasting. The project took a couple of days and was welcomed work.

It was through Bart that I landed the position as president of the Security Bank of Glenrock. Bart happened to be talking with Donn Dorset, President of the Bank of Casper, which was owned by Energy Banks, which also owned the Glenrock bank. At first I was asked to work there as a consultant. The bank had been recently chartered in 1982, but had managed to get itself into a great deal of trouble rather quickly, with the result the first president and operations officer were dismissed and the bank was without leadership.

I went down to Glenrock to try to come up with a turnaround solution. The bank had a new attractive building conveniently located between the post office and Glenrock's only hardware store. The staff were decent, likable, competent people, but totally lacking in either banking experience or education. It quickly dawned on me that I had more hands on banking experience than the sum of all seven employees. The bank's problems were centered in three areas: deficit earnings from operations, too many bad loans and a critical liquidity problem.

The bank's liquidity was entirely dependent up being able to purchase Federal Funds on a daily basis. The term Federal Funds refers to deposits with collected balances with the district Federal Reserve Bank, in this bank's case the Denver branch. To purchase Fed Funds is a polite way of saying they were borrowing daily from their correspondent bank, in this case The First National Bank of Denver. Typically, a country bank such as Security might buy Fed Funds to meet Federal Reserve deposit account reserves held at the Federal Reserve Bank as required by Fed membership rules. This practice usually would be to avoid cashing in liquid investment securities for short periods of time.

In the case of Security Bank, not only were they borrowing reserve requirements, but also borrowing to pay for incoming customer checks, in banking parlance cash letters, and in fact funding lending activities; the bank had no liquid investment securities to sell. The folks at First National Bank of Denver were oblivious to this and had not a clue of the bank's precarious situation. Until, I called them one day to let them know I was working to alleviate the problem.

Our account officer was an attractive young brunette, whom I'll call Nancy. After I had outlined the problem, Nancy said over the phone, "We are going to need to call your Federal Funds line of credit."

I responded, "Nancy, I don't think you really want to that, because if we can't meet tomorrow's cash letter; the party is over and the next calls will be to Dwight Bonham, the Wyoming State (bank) Examiner; his next call will be to the FDIC to liquidate us. You folks have the bank stock loan on the Security Bank stock. You'll take a double hit both on the Fed Funds, which we can't repay except by borrowing tomorrow, as well as the bank stock loan. Besides, I am confident I can work this out for our mutual benefit."

There was a silence at the other end of the line for a moment. I said, "Nancy, are you there?"

Softly she said, "Yes. How can you solve this problem?"

I replied, "We can bid aggressively for some jumbo certificate of deposit money; we can advertise for deposits. For all practical purposes, we don't have any money to lend. I might have a loan or two here that we can participate out to our sister bank in Casper. Let's not panic. We need to raise about $600,000 to get out of your debt on the Federal Funds side. We have other problems too, but liquidity is the first priority."

Nancy said, "Call me next week and let me know how things are going. I'll try to keep management off your back. I expect I'll be up to see you within a month."

I said, "Thanks for working with us. I'll get busy right away. Good bye."

She said, "Goodbye and good luck."

As soon as I got off the phone I motioned to our secretary-receptionist, Joy Sorenson, to come into the office. "Joy," I said, "We need to do some serious advertising. When does the Glenrock Paper publish? Thursday? I need to see Mr. Reed about an ad, see if you can round him up."

Joy nodded and punched in the newspaper's phone number. That afternoon Nerwin Reed, the owner, publisher and main guy at the Glenrock Independent came ambling in. He was of medium height and had greyish white hair. His face was a pasty white; he appeared to be very ill. He had a cigarette hanging out of his mouth and reeked of tobacco. I had never met him before, we shook hands and I greeted him cordially as he sat down at my desk. Joy came in and sat down next to him. I said, "I understand the paper comes out on Thursday, this will be just in time for my Friday the thirteenth promotion."

Mr. Reed looked at me quizzically, as I took out a legal pad and sketched in what I had in mind. I said, "For starters $100,000 - 13 month Certificates 13% interest, and gifts for opening lesser CDs with 13-month maturities. We have lots of safe deposit boxes, $13.00 for a one year lease on the small box, when accompanied by any deposit account."

Mr. Reed gave a slight smile and said, "Yes, I can put something together for you. I'll have a proof over first thing in the morning."

Joy said, "I get it, we're going the thirteen them to death on Friday the Thirteenth."

"Bingo, Joy!" I said, "Let's hope this works."

Thirteen percent in light of interest rates seems extraordinarily today, but at the time, the prime lending rate was north of 15%, and the rate was only somewhat higher than competitors, besides we needed deposits immediately. To make sure it worked, I made a few phone calls to people I thought might place a few bucks with us. Liquidity was not the only issue at hand. We had many delinquent loans and the bank parking lot looked more like a used car lot from all the repossessed cars we had. When I arrived in Glenrock, the bank had a full time collector named Barbara Ireland. Sitting on her desk were two large drawers of the delinquent notes. Barbara called and wrote collection letters to all of these errant borrowers. Considering the small size of the bank's total loan portfolio, there was an ungodly volume of past due paper.

I pulled out some of the larger loans that were past due as well as current to work myself. One loan was technically current, but obviously trouble was a five-year "bullet loan" requiring no amortization, with only quarterly interest payments. The problem was it was supposedly collateralized by accounts receivable, which should have been paid a year earlier to the borrower. This meant either the borrower didn't get paid; for sure, he hadn't paid us.

"Yikes." I yelled out to no one in particular.

Colleen Randorff, the bank's newly designated operations office, was standing outside the door to my office. She said, "What's going on?"

I said, "I can't believe the way this loan is structured."

Colleen smiled and said, "Well, Dan Singer was one hell of a tennis player, didn't really know squat about lending or banking in general from all I can tell. Can I talk to you about some of my problems?"

"Colleen, sure that's why I'm here," I said, "to try to solve some problems around here."

Colleen said, "Well, after Dan and Jim the cashier were fired, I was promoted from bookkeeper to Cashier and I have been trying to reconcile our correspondent accounts. They are all screwed up. Take the Central Bank account; we clear our Bank Americard deposits, well now it's called Visa, through them. It's way off. I don't think anyone ever bothered to reconcile it since the bank opened two years ago."

I shook my head, "Wow, any idea how far off it might be?"

Colleen looked at me dolefully and said, "Right now it looks like about $10,000, but I am hopeful I can whittle it down to a more respectable figure."

"How about the other accounts? I guess there are just two more with any activity, First National of Denver and the Denver Federal Reserve." I inquired.

Colleen responded, "I keep careful tabs on the First National, since we remit to them our daily cash letter (depositor's checks to clear) and they are our main account. A few old items are shown as exceptions, a couple of hundred bucks. As for the Federal Reserve, we receive a daily statement from them and I monitor it carefully, we can't afford any penalties, we still aren't making any money."

"Well, hang in there Colleen, I believe we can turn this ship around. It looks like to me we'll need to write off some of these old items. We could spend a lot of your valuable time chasing these errors down and in the end would take the hit anyway." I said.

I began digging more deeply into the loan files. One of the loans that got my attention was a $110,000 loan, fully advanced for the construction of a home out on Langley Road in Rolling Hills, about five miles north of town. The file indicated the borrower was one Edward Langley, an engineer at Glenrock Coal, which was a wholly owned subsidiary of Pacific Power & Light. PP&L operated a large generating facility just east of town. All well and good, the man had a good paying job. Strange though, there were no inspections of the construction progress, which, since the loan was fully advanced should be virtually complete.

Late one afternoon I drove out to the Langley project and discovered to my alarm, the Langleys were living in the basement of the yet to be competed home. The house was nothing but a shell, steel at that; it looked more like an industrial building than a home. I knocked on the door and Mr. Langley answered the door. After introducing myself I got down to business and asked the vexing question, "Since the house is obviously incomplete, what happened to the rest of the construction money?"

Mr. Langley looked at me with a puzzled look and said, "Didn't Dan tell you? We used the money to start the Rolling Hills General Store; it's a convenience store."

"Oh," I replied, "I passed it on the way our here. The store doesn't appear to have any gas pumps. Incidentally, I've never met or had a conversation with Dan."

Mr. Langley look downcast and said, "Well, we didn't have enough money for that." I responded, "What was the plan? The $110,000 you owe is the bank's legal lending limit, plus I notice there haven't been any interest payments made on the note, over $15,000 of interest has already accrued; when it matures in a couple of months, the total will be about $19,000."

Mr. Langley said, "I think Dan was planning to sell a participation. Is that the right term? Anyway sell a piece of the loan to another bank, but had no takers."

I said, "Then Dan was terminated and the situation has just sat since then. Correct?"

Langley responded, "That's about the size of it."

I said, "Mr. Langley, with the loan being fully disbursed and the house needing completion, plus there is nearly one year's interest accrued, there is no way anyone would be willing to participate in this deal. I realize the loan terms don't call for periodic interest payments, so it isn't in technical or legal default. Any chance you could pay the interest?"

Mr. Langley said, "No, I don't have much cash, just enough for groceries and utilities. You know living expenses."

I shook my head and replied, "That was what I expected. Dan wasn't thinking when he made this loan. He should have required monthly interest payments on the loan and withheld disbursements pending the construction progress. The convenience store loan should have been a separate deal."

Langley came back, "Mr. Harris, we did everything Dan asked."

I replied, "Ed. May I call you Ed?"

He nodded affirmatively. I resumed my thought, "I don't blame you, but what is important now is for us to work together and see if we can't come up with a solution. Generally, we need to put an SBA loan together for the store and try to generate some proceeds which can be applied to the construction loan. What we have now is a half-baked convenience store, with the most important key to success, fuel services, missing. And we have a house that is nowhere near completion. I'll get a letter out to you, as to information I'll need to work something out."

The Friday the Thirteenth promotion worked amazingly well. We pulled in quite a few new accounts, including three or four jumbo $100,000 certificates of deposit. Within a week we had our Federal Funds purchased account down to about $100,000, which was at least manageable and within a few weeks we became net sellers of Federal Funds. Friday the thirteenth turned out to be our lucky day.

By the time the directors meeting rolled around, I had successfully had solved the liquidity crisis. I went through the delinquent loans, which Barbara Ireland had been working on vigorously. Most of the loans had recent payments and in many cases customers, at Barbara's urging were making accelerated payments and headed towards current status. I pointed out that we had a dozen or so repossessed cars and light trucks, plus a good-sized recreational travel trailer, and a big Kenworth truck tractor. The next challenging question: earnings?

The central problem was a lack of deposits with which to fund earning assets. I pointed out that the bank was well positioned to make higher yield consumer loans for automobiles and other personal type assets. Glenrock being a blue-collar community had a population of folks with good jobs at the power plant and in the extractive mineral industries, mainly coal and oil. I recommended the bank concentrate of installment loans, which allows the bank spread its' risk, earn a better yield, as compared to business or agricultural loans.

There was little agricultural activity near Glenrock, except for a few large operations the bank didn't have the capacity to serve. I recommended that the commercial loans we should go after be generally limited to SBA guaranteed loans. Guaranteed portions of SBA loans could be either participated out, or used to collateralized public fund deposits.

It was at this point that the board named me president. The date was May first. That wasn't the only stroke of good fortune to occur that day. I learned that in a contest I had entered at East Ridge Mall in Casper, I turned out to be the winner. Greiner Ford, the Casper dealer, had a crushed car on display, the person who correctly identifying the car, was to win a decent freshly painted 1969 Ford Torino two door fastback; a classic little old lady's car driven only to church on Sundays. The crushed car was a 1965 Mercury Breeze-Way sedan, which I had figured out to be from the remains of the rear window assembly.

The timing was perfect as Chad was about to turn 15, the legal age in Wyoming to get a learner's permit, on June 16th. I turned the car over to him. Both boys were interested in cars and I set them to work cleaning up and in most cases repairing minor dents to get the most dollars out of the bank's numerous repossessed vehicles. Since I was into the auto restoration hobby at this point in my life, I had a better than average workshop garage which proved very useful.

Not long after my appointment as president, I received a phone call from Phil Schmidt; he was in charge of Federal Reserve member bank supervision for our district to ask some questions about our latest call report, which reflected our enormous Federal Funds purchased account. It was obvious from the call report, which is the bank's published balance sheet that we had critical liquidity problems and it was hard to miss our deteriorating capital accounts as well, due to operating and those loan losses previous management had acknowledge; to be sure there were more to come.

He asked what was going on and I explained that I had just been named president. Then I outline the steps I had taken to eliminate the Federal Funds borrowings, and get my arms around the bank's disproportionate volume of problem loans. Of course he was expecting to be talking to prior management. He said, "I can see you have your hands full and here I have a Consumer Compliance Examiner scheduled to pay you a visit on Monday."

"Hmmm," I said, "Well, I guess we'll just have to deal with him."

"No," Mr. Schmidt said, "I'll reschedule him in a couple of months, when you've had a chance to get on top of things. I'll call you in a month or so to see how things are going. Call me if I can be helpful to you."

I thanked him profusely, the consumer compliance examinations are a nuisance and a minor event compared to the main regulatory purpose, keeping banks solvent. I had heard the Federal Reserve was good to work with and I wasn't disappointed.

As stated earlier we had decent enough employees, the problem was they were lacking in experience. Colleen Randorff was a whiz with numbers and conscientious worker. Joy Sorenson was an attractive, slender blond with a pleasant outgoing personality and also a good worker. Brenda Harvey was a tall slender brunette, who handled new accounts, processed loan applications and documents. She and I shared a common malady, asthma. On her desk she had a sign picturing a frog on it that read, "Please don't smoke, or I might croak."

Starting with Nerwin Reed, I had noticed that Glenrock seemed to be a town of smokers. I allowed customers to light up in my office, since people are often nervous, or at least uncomfortable when they come into my office either to request a loan or discuss problems with an existing debt, more often the case in my first months in Glenrock. One day when I was obviously having trouble breathing Bonita Hunt, a real estate broker, came into my office smoking a cigarette. She saw the big tan pottery ashtray on my desk. She immediately put out her Parliament in the ashtray and said, "That is really dumb, Bert. Here you are plainly having difficulty breathing and you invite me, with that damned ashtray, and people like me to smoke in your office. You really need to get rid of that damn thing."

I did and it was never to reappear. "Many thanks for the excellent advice." I replied.

At the following board meeting I got a little better acquainted with the board members. Dick Sedar was the Chairman. Mr. Sedar own a bowling alley, called Sunrise Lanes and also in the same building a package liquor store. Mr. Sedar was a bit on the crusty side and didn't seem to have more than a rudimentary knowledge of what makes a bank tick. He was also a State Senator, who was running for re-election that year of 1984.

Another Board member was Patrick Meenan, a jovial gentleman who had been successful in the radio broadcasting business; he was also for Casper. Dr. Pippen, a likeable man and a dentist too; he did some endodontic work, it may have been his specially; he was also from Casper. Then there was Janice Cardine, who was the wife of Joseph Cardine, who was a justice on the Wyoming Supreme court and also a Casper resident. She frequently missed meetings and when she did attend rarely spoke. Pete Greiner, owner of Greiner Ford in Casper was also a member, but not an especially good contributor.

Bank boards of directors are typically made up of successful people, mainly from the business and professional community. These folks fit that mold quite well. What struck me was every board member was also from Casper. There was not a single resident of Glenrock or person with a business connection in Glenrock. It struck me as odd, and also poor public relations. Small wonder the bank had attracted less than the needed deposit basis for profitable operations. Local directors bring many positives to a directorship. They are knowledgeable about the goings on in the community. Invaluable, on loan committees for they generally will have a fair and wise assessment of would be borrowers. They are also often wonderful when it comes to steering business, both deposits and loans to the bank. As I recall none of the board members carried any significant deposits in the bank, which after all are the lifeblood of any bank. Perhaps one of the directors had a loan with Security Bank. Although these folks were decent up standing citizens and brought a good mix of experience to the board they were sadly lacking in their ability to be cheerleaders for the bank, which it so desperately needed. I suggested to the board that we find a way to bring on board some Glenrock directors.

I was pleasantly surprised when I brought up the idea of getting some Glenrock business people on board as members, that they all agreed it was a good idea. I began to put together a list of a few select people who were customers or at least friendly to us. The first person I proposed was Jean Taylor Harper. Ms. Harper and her husband Robert, known locally as Pug, owned an oil field service company called Taylor Welding, which had been started by her father, Gordon Taylor Senior, years earlier. Jean drove around an impressive looking Cadillac and was to some extent regarded as a local "Mrs. Got-Rocks." In point of fact she wasn't really all that wealthy, but she was a native, well known and respected in the community and was excited about the potential the bank had, if it became a "Glenrock Bank."

Another board member I was able to bring on board was Daniel Johnston, a CPA. He was the town's only Certified Public Accountant. He had been doing a little business with us and of course was in contact with many business people and as well as individuals. Dan and his wife Carol were among my early Glenrock acquaintances. As I recall Carol knew my wife from the Merle Norman store Jo had bought a while earlier. Dan had a good head for numbers and an analytical mind. CPAs often make excellent board members.

The last person I was able to corral into service on the board was Arnie Sybrant, a general practice dentist. Arnie and I hit it off immediately since we were both car restoration buffs. He was working on a 1953 MG-TD and doing a meticulous job too. Since Arnie had lived and practiced in Glenrock for a few years he was known and respected. The addition of these three people gave Security Bank a "Glenrock" face and we began to build deposits and take on a few new loan customers, from established business people.

One of the accounts I was able to snare from the competition was the Glenrock Garage, the local Ford dealer. Glenrock Ford was owned by Ted Lewis, a spry 82 year old. Mr. Lewis was the oldest individual in the nation holding a Ford franchise. He had been a dealer since 1932, and had a complete set of Ford shop manuals going back to Model T days. I quickly struck up a friendship with Ted and he generously allowed me to use his shop manual library for my restoration projects. Mr. Lewis didn't sell many vehicles, but was diligent in taking care of the town's Ford service needs.

At 82, Ted still happily would crawl under an ailing car to check out a problem and make a repair. What he didn't like was to have his evenings interrupted by some customer was automatic door locks, locking their keys in the ignition. He was able to partially solve this problem at least with the cars he sold off the showroom floor by never ordering cars for stock with the automatic door latches. That didn't stop the evening phone calls; however, his listing in the phone book was, "Lewis, T.V." Citizens would call him thinking he was a TV repairman. I think that bugged him even more than the door latch calls. Ted had a single employee, Esteban Rodriguez; he was a competent mechanic, whose occasional visits to the bank I always enjoyed.

One couldn't help like him, since he was always smiling.

One day Esteban, or Steve as he liked to be called in America, came in with a bright smile on his face to tell me, "I just came back from the Ford fuel injector training school in Denver."

He reached in a manila folder to show me his gold embossed certificate and said. "Mr. Harris, I learn all about fuel injectors, spent a whole week there."

"So what was the main lesson you learned?" I asked.

"I learn," he said looking pensively. "You leave them alone."

Some months later Steve came in just beaming, I don't think I have ever seen a grown man look so happy. "What's up Steve, you look like you're having a good day." I said.

"Mr. Harris, this is the happiest day of my life." he paused, a moment for effect and said, "Today, I become a United States Citizen!"

"Wonderful, congratulations!" I said.

Several members of our staff overheard Steve's big news and joined in the celebration. It caused all of us there the pause for a moment and appreciate the great joys of being a U. S. Citizen. With our liquidity restore to a safe level and at least some sort of idea of the possible solutions for of loan problems we were in a position to grow the bank.

Twenty Two

Growing the Bank

With my arms around the liquidity and asset problems I was prepared to tackle the daunting task of growing the bank into an institution with a sufficient deposit base to generate an operating profit. This is not to say the loan problems had gone away, but they were in large measure confined to a few larger loans, like the Langley loan, which I was hopeful could be restructured into something workable for both the bank and the customer.

The bank had a Glenrock face now we had local people on the board. Our Glenrock directors were enthusiastic and brought in their friends and business connected people and at last we were growing deposits. The delinquent loans after a few months shrunk from two large drawers of loans to about a third of a single drawer all thanks the Barbara Ireland's tenacious efforts. With a significant increase in deposits we were once more in the hunt for quality installment loans.

I thought Barbara would be highly trainable as a lender. There is nothing that teaches one about being cautious when extending credit as having to collect bad loans. Besides, Barbara had essentially worked herself out of a full time job; I decided to her offer a position, with a significant raise as a loan officer complete with a title.

To my amazement Barbara turned me down, saying only, "I like what I'm doing and don't want to make loans."

"Barbara," I countered, "there aren't enough delinquent loans now to keep you busy, even for half a day. Besides I really need consumer loan officer, I'm confident that you would do a good job. You'd still get to work collections, too."

She was adamant. "Absolutely not. I like what I'm doing."

"Damn it, Barbara, we just can't afford to pay you for sitting around." I said, thinking she spends more time doing her nails than working.

Again she repeated, "No way am I going to be a loan officer."

For the moment I left the situation alone, as I tried to come up with a way to retain this very able employee. After conferring with a couple of the local board members, I decided to let her go.

This started something of a chain reaction. Once I fired Barbara, Joy quit in protest. I guess she thought I had fired her out of meanness. Never before or since, have I ever fired a person for refusing a promotion. I turned to my local directors, especially Jean Harper for some ideas.

She suggested her brother, Gordon Taylor, Jr., who had just sold his insurance agency might be interested in working as a loan officer, so a meeting was arranged and Gordon I were able to come to an agreement as to how we would train him. I was pleased to have him aboard since he carried with him an old established Glenrock name, which the bank badly needed. It was about this time Brenda announced an elder gentleman, Mr. Barkley, wanted to see me.

Mr. Barkley wanted to borrow $100, which he would repay in two weeks when his social security check came in. I suggested that perhaps for the same cost $7.50 minimum charge that stretching it into two or three payments, might be a better arrangement for him.

"Oh no," Mr. Barkley replied, "that wouldn't be necessary, I'll take care of it on the third of the month when my social security check comes in."

I didn't argue the point and made him the loan. As promised 15 days later he came in and repaid the note, insisting again that he could only talk to me. I thanked him and suggested that he talk to Gordon if he needed another loan.

The secretary problem was still unresolved. Again Jean Harper came to my rescue and asked if I knew Kathy Miller. I was well acquainted with Kathy, who I first met when she worked at the First National Bank of Lander, back when I was an Assistant National Bank Examiner. Later, about the time I received my commission as a full-fledged National Bank Examiner, she was working at the First National Bank of Casper as Bob Bryan's secretary. I had known her as Kathy Reeves in those days and knew from Bob Bryans she was excellent. She was also terrific looking, tall, blond, with a statuesque figure and an enchanting personality.

I was still a bachelor in those days and we saw each other socially. We became friends and one winter evening she allowed me to use her garage to repair minor damage to my car, which I had done on one of my frequent skiing weekends. Apparently, I didn't ring her romantic bell and she starting seeing and eventually marrying John Miller, who owned the successful restaurant and bar in Glenrock, The Four Aces. I'm sure John was far more sophisticated and mature than I at the time. I was transferred to New Mexico and met and married Mary. By the time I return to Casper she was Mrs. John Miller, but still working for Bob Bryans.

Nevertheless Kathy was always friendly towards me and when I offered her the position at the Security Bank, she accepted. She was excellent and at last our team was coming together. Well not quite. About that time Colleen Randorff announced she was leaving for, "greener pastures" as I recall she put it. I don't recall where she went. This time Gordon and Jean came up with an excellent suggestion in Lois Grant.

Lois must have been about 40, never married, had worked as a supervisor at Williams Market, Glenrock's only grocery store. I was told she was a whizz with numbers, which proved to be spot on. She quickly made the adjustment from the grocery store to managing the tellers and bookkeeping operations of the bank. As a means of breaking the ice with her and getting acquainted, I asked her if she was any relation to General and later President Grant. She seemed to be a little embarrassed by the question. "Well I am a descendent of Ulysses Grant's brother."

I asked her why the shyness to talk about her heritage and famous relative. She explained, "Everything she understood was he wasn't a very good president and also drank too much."

I was amazed and said, "He was a great general and while his administration was tainted by corrupt underlings, Grant was obviously personally honest."

And I added, "He was an interesting man and for what it's worth was a good husband. In fact," I went on. "I have a fascinating set of books about him by famed Civil War historians, Lloyd Lewis and Bruce Catton. I'll lend them to you and I'll bet you'll change your mind about General Grant."

She took me up on the offer and revised her opinion about her illustrious relative. Meanwhile, she turned out to be excellent as the bank's fiscal and operations officer. With Lois's addition, the operations side of the bank was running smoothly. What wasn't running so well was the bank's car which I drove home and delivered our computer processing work to the Bank of Casper, then in the morning I would pick up the print out from the previous day's business. Apparently, Dan Singer had a similar arrangement as he also lived in Casper.

The car was an AMC Eagle, a fancy leather upholstered version of the old AMC Hornet, with four-wheel drive. Although it didn't have a lot miles on it was becoming increasingly hard to start and wasn't running smoothly. When I took to a repair shop, they determined that the timing gear was made of some composite material rather than steel and was worn causing the timing to be slightly off and getting worse. One of the great mysteries to me was why an AMC Eagle in the first place, when we had Ford dealer, Pete Greiner, on our board of directors. I suggested trading it off on a Ford Bronco II bought from either Greiner or Ted Lewis at the Glenrock Garage our customer and local Ford dealer.

The board agreed with me and I first offered to have Ted Lewis order us a vehicle, since he didn't have one in stock. Ted said, ordering one would take a while and he wasn't turned on by the Eagle as a trade in. He said, "I'll tell you what why don't you buy the car from Pete Greiner, he probably has one in stock that will suit you and I'll happily service it and do the warranty work if it needs any here."

We bought a "Plain Jane" tan Bronco II with four wheel drive and stick shift from Pete. Ted provided the service which was handy for us, although other than routine oil changes the vehicle didn't need much. Of course some of the employees couldn't drive a stick shift or were uncomfortable with a manual shift. Since I was the primary driver, I was happy with it. This purchase underlines one of my principles of community banking. One always should do business with a customer whenever possible.

The bank transcended into a kind of rhythm as our lives began to smooth out. Mr. Barkley became a part of our routine and visited us about the middle of the month to borrow $100 and pay it off plus the $7.50 minimum charge faithfully with each social security check. He was always very chatty talking to either Brenda or I. Each time we offered him the option of making small payments, so he could blend the $100 into his cash flow for the same minimum charge. No he insisted on paying off the note on Social Security payday.

Brenda and I talked about it after seven months as this peculiar pattern persisted. It dawned on us that money was not the object of the loan at all. The old gentlemen, a lonely widower, just wanted to talk someone; he always insisted in a gentle sort of a way on a conversation two or three times as long as the transaction would take for the ordinary borrower. The pattern continued as long as I was in Glenrock.

Our larger, thorny loan problems persisted and we did work diligently to clear them off the books, often resulting in a loss. About the time I thought I had things cleared to straighten out the Langley situation, Mr. Langley came in announced, "I have found the Lord!"

I wasn't sure what he was driving at and said, "What does this have to do with the Security Bank?"

"It means we are leaving town and moving to South America, Peru to be exact. We will be missionaries. How can I settle up with you?" He replied.

Stunned, I said, "you mean you're quitting your job, abandoning the Rolling Hills store, and are just taking off for Peru?"

"Exactly," he replied. "I'll give you deeds to the properties, we are leaving on Friday."

"Wow, seems like rather rash decision." I said. "I'll tell you what, today is Tuesday, I'll call Jim Anest our attorney and have him draw up quit claim deeds, and hopefully we can have the paperwork done late tomorrow or first thing Thursday. Have you already resigned at Glenrock Coal?"

"Yes!" he said, "The Lord has spoken to us, we must do this."

"Okay, I'll call you as soon as the paperwork is ready. You and Eloise can come in and sign the documents. Well Ed, I had hoped we could work this out for you, but I do appreciate your willingness to give us deeds in lieu of foreclosure. It does allow us to get right on top of solving the problems this creates for the bank. Perhaps you know a judicial foreclosure takes nine months in Wyoming." I gave my little speech as calmly as I could.

Truth be told, I was angry and would have liked to punch him in the nose. I supposed I would go to hell for my thought. My frustration and boiling temper must have shown, because he said, "I'm sorry for the trouble I have caused you, but it is the Lord's work we will be doing."

"Okay, Ed, I'll call as soon as the papers are ready." I said.

I called Jim Anest on the phone and explained the situation. Jim told me he'd drive down immediately, since he wasn't especially busy and had some other business in Glenrock that he could take care of at the same time. He arrived in about an hour, by this time I had Kathy dig out the file and I had a chance to go over it. It really wasn't going to be difficult, since a quitclaim deed and a simple bill of sale for the chattels at the store was all we needed.

Jim walked in the door and was smiling broadly. You could tell he was on the verge of laughing. I said, "Jim what are you so happy about. I trust you're not finding humor in the Ed Langley mess."

"Oh, no I wasn't thinking about that at all. As you know I do some public defender work for the Natrona County court. The judge has assigned me this case, in fact it is the third or fourth time I have had to defend this joker. His name is Marvin and he is a flaming homosexual and every time he falls in love, that's what he calls it, he attacks the guy before he even has determined if he is a fellow gay. The result is the offended straight fights back and in this case files charges and prosecutes him for assault and battery. Then I make a deal to get the offended man to drop the charges."

"What's so funny about that?" I said.

Jim smiled again and said, "Like I said, the judge has assigned me this guy three or four times now. This plaintiff is adamant to pursue the case. And I'm getting really tired of old Marvin, so I says to him: 'Marvin, the judge and the county attorney are wanting to throw the book at you, you're looking at a stretch in the pen in Rawlins, where they keep all the state's nastiest bad guys.' He looks at me and says quite innocently, 'Mr. Anest what should I do about it?' I said to him, 'God damn it, Marvin you gotta stop being a queer!'"

Then he started laughing, as did I. Finally, I said, "You didn't? Political correctness to the wind?"

Jim Anest said proudly, "I did! He tells me he'll try to be more selective before he makes a pass at another guy, but I'm afraid he is going to be sent Rawlins this time, unless I can get the injured party to drop the charges; however, he is not in a forgiving mood."

Jim had brought some standardized Mills Company forms with him and we had Kathy type them up so we were ready for the Langley signing the following day and the deed was done without ceremony the following afternoon.

By this time we were making a few consumer loans, when my friend and former Greybull director Jim Kost asked me if I would finance a year-old red Porsche 911SC convertible. Jim was in the tall clover it seemed and had a personal income approaching $1,000,000, but the tax burden caught him short of cash. I was surprised at his choice of vehicles since he always seemed to go for more sedate Lincolns and lately Mercedes, but I figured he wanted a toy.

Shortly after the first payment was paid, he called me and said he wanted to sell the car. "Well," he said, "one of my magazine editors, Jerry Williams, is a former racer on the sports car circuit and he asked why I bought the car. I told him it was a gift for Krista, her 16th birthday, you know. She thought the car was cute."

"Jim, are you nuts, turning a 16 year old loose with performance car like that?" I said.

"Those were Jerry's thoughts." He replied. "What he said was, 'Jim, have you ever driven a supercharged Porsche?' I said no. Then he says, "that car will do 150 miles an hour, zero to 60 in 5 seconds. Totally lethal in the hands of a beginning teenage driver.' Then I thought my God I got to sell this thing."

I shook my head and said, "I see what is going on here, no market in Basin for it, and you want me to sell it down here. I'm not sure Casper is much better. I'll store it in my garage and we'll drive it now and then, blow the cobwebs out. Just to be on the safe side I'll run an ad in Hemings Motor News too."

Jim said, "That sounds like a plan. Go ahead a drive it, you might as well enjoy having it around."

"Upon think about it, Freddie Wiggins one of the guys at our competitor, First National likes sports cars and the rumor around town is he has inherited some money that's burning a hole in his pocket. I'll call him, see if he interested."

Jim arranged to deliver the car and I tucked it away in our garage, carefully covering it with a car cover to keep it clean. I called Freddie and drove the car down to Glenrock so he could try it out. He was eager, I had decide to ride with people trying it out as a precaution. The car had a very heavy clutch, which made shifting more difficult than the average manual shift vehicle. Freddie tried it out and it was evident as he ground gears, this car wasn't for him.

However, my ad placed in Hemings got replies and I described the car to a fellow in Milwaukee, who wanted it. He flew into Casper with a cashier's check for the asking price. Drove it, liked it, and quickly drove off eastward in a matter of a couple of hours. Jim Kost wasn't my only link with the past encountered while at Glenrock.

The Wall Street Journal is must reading for every banker. This particular morning I picked up the Journal and right in the center of the front page was an article about a Texas banker, my old fellow examiner and friend Sammy Spikes, who had been convicted of a Ponzi scheme of sorts. He bought some desert land in north Texas, seduced an appraiser to give him an excessively high value to the property and borrowed the maximum allowable on it; then gotten an even higher appraisal and borrowed an even greater sum.

When the lending bank realized the land was worth only a fraction of the amount their loan, Sammy's house of cards fell in and he was convicted of fraud. He was sentenced to several years in a minimum-security executive prison in West Texas. The irony of all this was it was exactly what he told us he was going to do that night 20 years earlier at that charming Mexican restaurant in Las Cruces, New Mexico. We all thought it was quite funny, I suppose the Margaritas had added to the humor of the idea, but none of us ever dreamed Sammy was serious.

One of the things that I tried to do to grow the bank was to cold call on all the businesses in town to introduce myself. I also made a point of eating lunch at one Glenrock's eatery, with a customer or potential customer if possible, otherwise by alone. One day at noon I was eating at the counter of The Four Aces, when Gary Reed, the son of Nerwin Reed of newspaper fame, sat down next to me. Gary owned and managed the hardware store next the bank and we started talking. Finally, he said, "Say, I notice Barbara isn't working for you anymore, what happened?"

"Odd situation with Barbara, she was a reliable employee and was doing good job for us, but had worked her way out of job as a collector. I offered her a promotion, she turned me down and wound up leaving. Never had anyone turn down a promotion before." I replied.

Jerry said, "Funny, she worked for me too, but when I asked her to do something different, she refused and I had to let her go."

Most of our people were willing to do what was necessary to make Security Bank viable. Two of the people I haven't mentioned are Tommy Silsbey and Deanna Halsey. Tommy was pretty blond with an athletic build. Tommy was excellent, when we needed a teller she was a good one and always treated the customers in a helpful and friendly manner. Tommy drove to work in a red Pontiac Ferro, which she had named Geraldine in honor of Geraldine Ferraro, the 1984 Democratic vice presidential nominee. When you needed any task done, Tommy would do it with a smile.

Likewise Deanna Halsey was always the willing worker. Deanna was a tough, sturdy gal who had a strong facial resemblance to her grandfather the famous WWII admiral Bill "Bull" Halsey.

One of the things that spurred our growth was the failure of the First National Bank of Glenrock. The bank had been founded in 1963 and had been a charter investigation the Mr. Van Dyke and I had conducted. The bank's deposits were assumed by one of the Casper banks. Wyoming law didn't permit branch banking at this point so we were the only bank and it brought us a rush of customers. Quickly, our deposits reach a level and our operations became profitable, but we still had bad loans to workout.

One of the problems I inherited was a large Kenworth truck tractor. The truck had sat for a long time on our lot since before my arrival, but no takers due to the fact it wasn't in running condition. That was until the jovial Kenneth Mohr strolled in one day. Kenny, as he liked to be called, made me a proposition. The deal was if we would finance the purchase of a rebuilt Cummins engine for the truck, he would buy it and put it to work.

At the time Kenny was an out of work truck driver. I suspect the reason might have been due to health issues; he was grossly overweight. My wild guess was he weighed over 350 pounds. I insisted we write the loan with life and accident and health insurance, which added over $3000 to the principal of the loan. Ordinarily, I see this insurance as something as a customer rip-off, which I tend to avoid. Kathy Miller, whose banking ethics paralleled mine, reasonably questioned this decision. She said, "Why the A & H insurance, it adds so much to the loan Kenny will have to repay?"

I said, "Kathy, look at the man. He is terribly obese, a heart attack, just waiting to happen."

Kathy's response was, "Bert, just because your grandfather was a doctor, doesn't give you a license to practice medicine."

I had to chuckle at her observation, but I kept the A & H insurance on the loan. And as I understand it my diagnosis was correct, Mr. Mohr's health problems precluded him paying the loan and it was the insurance that ultimately retired the debt, after I was gone.

In spite of all the hard and devoted work my staff put in, Security Bank was far from being out of trouble. The Federal Reserve our federal bank supervisory agency had the board execute a "Memorandum of Understanding" which stated all the things we needed to do to save the bank. One of the key components we needed to address was capital, which had been eroded away by operating losses stemming from a lack of deposit base to fund sufficient loans and investments for the bank to operate at profit. By mid-1985, the bank was earning an operating profit but there were still loan losses to be absorbed. The other issue was the loan losses reserves were inadequate to sustain the hit the bank would be taking from the Langley and other loans made during the first two years of the bank's existence.

With these factors in mind I went around to a number of Glenrock's leading and wealthier citizens and received commitments of sufficient monies to inject into the Security's capital accounts. I started a special account to collect the money to purchase the stock. But to my amazement the majority of the board and principal stockholders, led by Mr. Sedar didn't want to grant stock for the local money being injected in the bank for fear they would lose control.

Mr. Sedar routinely voted no for motions he didn't comprehend, blocked my efforts to raise capital by his unwillingness to issue investors stock in exchange for the money they were willing to invest. In addition, he voted against the transfer from operating earnings in to the reserve for loan losses as mandated by the Federal Reserve.

Because of the liability as the bank's CEO, I went ahead and made the transfer from operating earnings to the reserve for loan losses, in spite of Mr. Sedar's objections by the December 31st deadline imposed by the Federal Reserve Examiners. There was nothing I could do about the refusal to issue stock to my investors, which obviously was beyond my control. Naively, I thought that they would recognize this was a solution to the bank's pressing capital problem. Of course, I thought that perhaps they were willing to cough up the money themselves, but I had seen no indication of that.

As Christmas approached I asked and received permission from the board to have a party for the employees at the Paisley Shawl, a bed and breakfast, which also operating a classy restaurant. We had recently put together an SBA loan for the owners Margaret and Paul Dahl, so it seemed like the right place to have the party, which was in lieu of any kind of bonus which we could ill afford. I felt that it was a relatively inexpensive way of thanking the staff for their efforts during the past year.

At the January board meeting which took place January 26, 1986, Mr. Sedar decided to fire me. I have to say I felt betrayed. In less than two years I resolved the liquidity crisis, put together solutions for many of the bank's problem loans. In addition, I had provided the leadership to grown the bank's deposit basis to the point where it was earning a comfortable operating profit and had rounded up investors to put in the equity capital, including a substantial personal investment which I had pledged. When I emerged from the board meeting, Brenda excitedly asked, "Did you hear, did you hear the news?"

I was focused on my own troubles and said, "What are you talking about?"

She said, "The Challenger rocket into space has crashed and everyone was killed."

"Jesus Christ," I said, "This really is a bad day. Dick Sedar has just fired me."

"Oh, my God, I am so sorry," she replied.

The board left in silence and I proceeded to clean out my desk. Lois came in and said she would cut me a check for my salary plus, several weeks of vacation time I had accrued. Gordon drove me home in the bank car, along with the personal belongings from my office. I was about to start an entirely new chapter in my life.

Twenty Three

A Dumb Decision

After being fired by Mr. Sedar for - as I saw it- doing all the right things, I developed a burning desire to be independent and started looking around for a business to purchase. One afternoon in February returning from a trip to Boulder visiting family, Jo, the kids and I, stopped at the Frontier Mall in Cheyenne. We had checked out the various stores and were walking through a very charming store called "Yesterdays.""

The store was filled with reproduction antique furniture, attractive decorations, and gift items. As we browsed, we were greeted by Wayne Klassen, the owner. Mr. Klassen was affable and apparently not very busy. During the course of the conversation we learned that the store was for sale. The reason he gave for its availability was he wanted to focus on a larger Fort Collins operation and on an idea they had for franchising a sort of mini-version of the store. This piqued our interest and I asked for copies of tax returns, which he promptly furnished.

The business was reporting profitable operations to the I-R-S., indicating we could make a modest living out of it, which was a good sign. After talking it over, we made the decision to buy the business and move to Cheyenne. I suppose I looked at buying a business pretty much like I would view a business loan application; I liked the numbers and the vastly superior gross profit margins, as compared to a bank's, once the basic fixed costs were met. The Klassens provided a helpful little manual with all the things we needed to know about the business. What they couldn't tell me was whether or not I would enjoy the business.

The lesson I learned within a couple of weeks was that Yesterdays' was not my cup of tea; I was bored. In the banking business people were constantly coming in with something on their minds. While the store had pleasant surroundings, there were hours upon hours of no activity. When someone did come in, more often then not they were more in the mood to reminisce about the oak hutches, tables, or grandfather clocks that we had on display than they were actually interested in buying something. A customer would say, "That's just like the clock Grandfather Olafson had in his living room," then wander out without buying a thing. It was rare for us to make a sale.

On many days we sold next to nothing. I recall one day our total sales amounted to only two dollars, for a bottle of furniture polish. It drove me nuts. The contrast with banking where the interest kept on earning, clickety-click- clickety- click was immediately evident. At the bank there were always files to work on, or telephone calls to make. It seemed weird to me to be idle. I actually looked forward to receiving somewhat damaged goods that I could repair, because it gave me something to do. Of course, Yesterdays' wasn't all bad.

One of the things I liked was the staff we inherited from the Klassens. There were five people, four gentlemen, all World War II veterans and the fifth was a pleasant lady named Dorothy, who seemed to spend more money with us than she earned working for us. Luckily, her husband was a successful State Farm insurance agent in Cheyenne. Johnnie Grant, Klassen's store manager, was a WWII Army Air Corps pilot who flew a B-24 in the Pacific Theater of operations. Johnnie and his wife Irma had run his own business for many years.

Dick Morson was a gregarious former hardware salesman who served in the Navy in the Pacific Theater during the war. His tales of experiences in the Battle of the Coral Sea; his telling was positively riveting. Then there was Phil, who had enlisted in the Marine Corps at age sixteen. He had been raised by an aunt and an uncle who were only too pleased to have him get out of the house and getting on with his own life. He served on Bougainville Island in the Pacific. Phil had had long a career as a dealers' representative with General Motors Acceptance Corporation (GM) and had been required to drive GM vehicles. He celebrated his retirement by buying a new Ford pickup as a statement of freedom.

Last, there was Jerry who had served in the Army Air Corps. His career was in accounting and he was a very frugal man. He never talked much about his war experiences and generally was quiet. He didn't have a whole lot of personality, although when working with customers he was knowledgeable and carried his weight as a salesman. These employees were the best part of the Yesterdays' adventure.

Like in any other business there were always problems to solve at Yesterdays'. One of the main problems was inventory turnover. The Klassens were skilled at maximizing inventory turnover to, five or six times a year, well above the industry average. This is not to say that every piece sold. One particular piece in the store was a green velour upholstered chair. I thought it was an attractive piece, but from what Wayne Klassen told me it had been around awhile. He explained that it was used as a display piece, so people could check out the quality of the furniture and order something in fabric more to their liking. We didn't have the space to display much upholstered furniture, so the green chair just sat there month after month.

I was getting tired of looking at it and thought we needed to get rid of that chair and get a new display piece. A frequent, nearly weekly visitor was a gentleman named Leo. Leo. A Looky Lu as our primary wholesaler call people who just looked but didn't buy, would come in the store, sit in the chair and say, "Oh boy, I like this."

The problem was he would never step up to the cash register and buy it, though all of us tried to sell him the chair. One day as Leo was lounging in the chair in complete comfort, I said, "Leo, suppose instead of paying the $495 price on the tag, I could give it to you for $250?"

Leo rose out of the chair and said, "You betcha, at that price I can't resist."

Within minutes Leo had written me a check for the $250 plus sales tax and arranged delivery. The question that arose in my mind was how do I replace this piece with something that will turnover more rapidly? Our primary wholesaler in Denver from which we purchased many of our goods was Charter Oak. Donald Watson, the owner, was assisted by his two sons and a charming young lady named, Ginnie. I made weekly trips to Denver in a tired old Chevrolet Hi Cube van which we had purchased with the rest of the business's assets. Don had been after me to buy a platform rocker to display. I didn't care for the either the appearance or the comfort of the chair and had resisted making the purchase.

Yet Don had been telling me they were selling these chairs in great volume at their five metro Denver stores. I figured it couldn't be any slower a mover than the infamous green chair, so I bought one for $250. It was an oak chair with a blue-patterned seat and backrest. I put in on the floor at $495 and to my amazement it had sold without any price negotiation by my next trip to Charter Oak a week later. I decided to buy two more in different colors. Within a week they, too, were sold. Finally, we settled on an inventory level of six and found it profitable and practical to purchase them directly from the manufacturer. It was at this point that I realized that just because I didn't like an item didn't mean a customer wouldn't.

I wasn't in the furniture business very long when I got a call from Patrick, the guy that Dick Sedar had selected to succeed me as president at Security Bank. He said, "Bert, I need help."

I told him there wasn't much I could do, but that I would be happy to answer any questions he might have. Luckily, it was a slow and boring day at Yesterdays' and we talked at length. He asked some specific questions about various customers and banking in general. The guy had been a collector for a consumer finance company, and, as I was later to learn that was the extent of his knowledge of finance and banking.

This poor job appointment further illustrated Dick Sedar's total lack of understanding of the banking business to me.

By this time there were relatively few collection issues that required a tough collector. Barbara Ireland had pretty well taken care of most of the problems with delinquent car and small personal loan accounts whittled down to a respectable level. The greater loan problems were ones like the Langley properties, and others that required a more sophisticated and creative approach beyond badgering the borrower for payments. From my conversation with Patrick, it was apparent that the coalition of people in the community to raise additional capital had fallen apart which was based on my remaining as the CEO. The bank's primary vexing problem was unsolved if not ignored by Mr. Sedar and the Casper board members who owned the controlling shares.

Patrick thanked me for my time and I hung up the phone. I didn't talk to him again. After all I had a furniture store to run and pesky customers with whom I had to deal. The customer I remember most vividly was Mrs. Olson. She came in the store and bought an oak table, which was one of the best-quality pieces we had to offer. They were manufactured in Fort Collins, Colorado by Antique Images, which was owned by Phil Marker. The workmanship was superb and we sold several items from that manufacturer every week. They were made of solid oak with no veneer and weren't prone to cracking unlike tables manufactured in humid climates.

For Mrs. Olson we had put together a set consisting of an oak hutch, a table and a set of six chairs, a very nice order for us. We made the delivery, but a few days later I got a phone call from Mrs. Olson. She complained, "I don't like the grain of the wood on the table."

I drove out to Mrs. Olson's house, fearful that there was something faulty in the manufacture of the table, although knowing it was one made by Phil Marker I doubted that was the problem. Mrs. Olson, who was obviously in a grumpy mood, ushered me into the dining room and said, "See?" as she pointed to the tabletop.

I could see nothing whatsoever wrong with the tabletop. When I questioned her further I found out that what was bugging her was that the grain patterns were of a non-uniform width. This grain pattern reflected a year with more or less moisture than was typical, as compared with uniform narrower widths from dry years. I tried to point out that there was nothing defective in the manufacture of the table. She said, "I wasn't complaining about the quality of the construction of the table. I don't like the grain pattern."

Finally, I said, "I'll exchange the top for you; we have a number of them in stock in our warehouse."

What I wanted to say was, "Why don't you talk to the tree about this?"

We had her inspect a number of tabletops, and after looking at several she finally selected one that had in her opinion, "A friendly and satisfactory grain."

I told my wife, Jo, about this and knowing she had a discerning eye would surely notice any flaws. Jo looked it over and said, "Well, I like it just fine. Let's take it home."

We did just that and it has been our dining room table for over twenty years and my wonderful wife has never complained once about the grain. Like I said earlier it was the boredom of the furniture business, I hated. About 3:00 o'clock on a slow Friday afternoon, with not a customer in sight I received a phone call from my old examiner buddy and former roommate, Ted Ernst.

Ted said, "Do you have a moment to talk?"

I said, "Things this afternoon couldn't be slower, I have lots of time. What's on your mind?"

Ted by this time was Senior Vice President and Quality Control Officer at Wyoming National Banks, a statewide holding company. Ted said, "We have a bunch of problem loans at our Cheyenne bank. Jim Saunders, our workout guy is very good, but he needs some help, would you be interested is working for us for a while until we get our arms around the problems?"

"Yes, Ted I am bored stiff in the furniture store here. I have a staff of good people who can mind the store while I'm downtown. Besides they are looking for more hours. I would be very interested."

Ted said, "When can you start?"

"Would eight o'clock Monday morning be soon enough?" I replied.

Ted said, "That's great, you must be really bored."

We agreed on a wage. I got together with Johnnie and we rearranged the schedule. The guys were happy with the new schedule and I was happy to be back in banking doing something interesting and enjoyable. Eight o'clock Monday morning I arrived the Wyoming National Bank of Cheyenne. Since that was the bank I had my business account with, it was very convenient too. I could deposit my daily receipts when I went to work. From my days as an examiner and also serving on various Wyoming Banker's Association committees, I knew and was friendly with a number of the people who worked there.

However, I had never met Jim Saunders, my new boss before. Jim was a burly, greying gentleman, five years my junior. His expertise as a loan work-out specialist became immediately clear. While many of the banking people I have met with his credentials are pretty much humorless cutthroat kinds of guys, Jim had a sublime sense of humor. While he could be tough as a negotiator, he also had a heart. When making a decision he would often say,

"My heart says to do this, but my head says I need to solve the bank's issue and make the tough decision."

I won't tell you that we hit it off immediately, but it didn't take long before we became friends. Jim was a constant tease. When we would go out for lunch he would point to me and say to the server, "I want you to take extra good care of my father."

One of the first assignments he gave me was to workout was that a company called Easy Storage, run by Vincent LaRosa. The business consisted of several hundred storage units, which had been built over a number years in five stages, with five separate financings. The central piece of the property was a large warehouse with loading docks, which for many years had been leased to a national trucking company. The original loan made twelve years earlier, by The First National Bank of Laramie, was now three years away from being paid off, but still demanding a hefty monthly payment. This loan was followed by successive loans at approximately three-year intervals.

Vincent had been making his payments in a timely manner when the lease contract with the trucking company, unexpectedly failed to renew their lease. The economy in Wyoming in the 1980s was in the doldrums and Vincent was unable to find a new tenant. Our junior loans went delinquent, although Vincent paid what he was able, when he could. The storage unit business continued to prosper. After doing a thorough analysis, I visited Vincent and his wife and suggested a restructure based on the income derived from the storage units alone. I told the LaRosas that I would present the proposal to our Special Assets Committee on Friday.

Bob Ostland was the chairman of the committee, but the dominant personality was Bob Miracle, who was the President and Chairman of the Wyoming National Bancorporation. I knew Mr. Miracle from my days as a bank examiner and had a friendly relationship with him. The Special Asset Committee meetings were held over the telephone by conference call. The meetings would start out by Jim Saunders calling out the names of the errant borrower and then the progress, problem, and solution if one had been developed would be discussed and approved or disapproved. Jim Saunders announced the name, "Vincent LaRosa - Easy Storage."

Bob Miracle, who was on the phone line speaking from Casper said, "Vincent LaRosa, that no good deadbeat."

Saunders interrupted before Miracle could finish his tirade, "Bob, look at the proposal we have sent up to you and let Bert explain problem and his solution."

I explained why the loan had fallen behind due to the warehouse lease terminating and went into my idea, if we packaged all the loans into one, paying off The First National Bank of Laramie's first and second mortgages which were rapidly approaching maturity, we could put the whole loan back on a repayment schedule Vincent could easily make from the steady income coming from the rental of the storage units alone.

There was a silence emanating from the Casper committee members, then Bob Miracle spoke, "Well, all of a sudden this is a good loan."

Saunders shot back, "Yeah, Bob that's what Bert's been trying to tell you."

My routine became get up in the morning go to work at the bank, grab a little supper, then go to store and work evenings until closing time usually until 9:00 PM. Since we were in a mall our hours were chosen by the management of Frontier Mall, we had no voice in the matter. Daughter Martha joked, "Dad, there is an opening at the Mini-Mart on Dell Range Boulevard for the graveyard shift from ten to seven in the morning. This way you wouldn't have to bother going to bed."

I drew my enjoyment from life and sanity from my work at the bank. It also helped that Jim Saunders and I got along well, and I also liked Mike Franck a young man who worked with us and did a lot of the collection follow-up calls. Mike had been a collection man at Ford Motor Credit following up on delinquent car purchasers around the state of Wyoming. The three of us usually went to lunch together and it was at one of these lunch hours Mike told the following story:

Mike had under his supervision several loans made to Native Americans who resided on the Shoshoni Indian Reservation near Riverton, Wyoming. Including a over loan sixty days delinquent on a pickup truck to a large husky Indian named, George Great Bear. It seems George had a reputation for being tough, violent, and very angry about nearly everything. On a routine trip to Riverton, Mike was told that George Great Bear was looking for him. Mike is a tall slender guy with little muscle and a greater desire to leave Riverton, without injury. When he arrived in town, one of his Indian clients told Mike that Mr. Great Bear was looking for him. To Mike this was frightening and he had no desire to meet with him face to face.

Yet one day while Mike was eating lunch at a local restaurant, George Great Bear came into the same eatery and cornered him. George said, "You Ford?"

Reluctantly, Mike said, "yes."

Scowling, Great Bear began to undo his jacket and reached for something. At this point Mike is thinking he is reaching for a gun or knife and is going to kill me right on the spot. Mike is trembling. George pulls out a roll of bills and proceeds to count out the money and says, "One hundred, two hundred, three hundred, four hundred, and five hundred that should be enough for four payments."

Astonished, Mike says, "That's enough for four payments, puts you one ahead. Thanks George."

Then without another world George Great Bear strode out of the restaurant, and Mike uttered a sigh of relief. On another luncheon outing we noticed that each of us had worn light gray pinstriped suits complete with vest, white shirt and a red tie. This was totally unrehearsed or planned. When we got off the elevator into the main banking lobby we looked like a musical trio instead of three bankers headed out for lunch. Fred Pannell, the bank's agricultural lead loan officer noticed our attire and said, "Where the hell are you guys going, dressed like overgrown triplets?"

Saunders looked at him with a dead serious expression. "Didn't you get the president's memo?"

Fred shook his head and went back to work. Fred had the habit of wearing, a least by my taste, the ugliest ties on the face of the earth. I had received from my brother-in-law, Dick Cramer a tie I was sure was the most unsophisticated tie ever. Dick and I had a tradition of giving each other the most outlandish ties we could find as a kind of joke at Christmas time. One of the ties depicted a farmer driving a tractor on golden fields, with a red barn and a brilliant green sky in the background.

If I wore this silk tie with a vest, only the pretty emerald green of the sky could be seen and went nicely with a brown three-piece suit I frequently wore to work. One day I wore the tie to work and knowing how Fred appreciated, nay loved ugly ties, I thought I'd show Fred the tie. I walked over to Fred's desk and unbuttoned my vest and said, "Hey, Fred check this out."

Fred gasped in amazement and said, "My God, it is beautiful."

I said, "You mean you actually like this?"

Fred responded, "Like it? I love it. Would you consider selling it? If so how much?"

I said, "For you my friend, how does fifteen bucks sound?

"Sold!" Fred said and reached in his pocket for the cash.

"I'll get it to you after the lobby closes," I replied.

So Fred became the proud owner of this hideous tie and wore it frequently, never covering it up with a vest as I had done. It was about this time Saunders assigned me an account to work for Elaine's Gift Shop. It was a block or so from the bank. I had no idea what to expect, except from the file it was apparent she was struggling to meet her payments and someone had failed to perfect the Financing Statement and Security Agreements. Saunders chuckled as I prepared to walk out the door to see the infamous Elaine Wickersham, "Good luck with that one." He said.

Elaine was a gushy, overly made up lady I would guess to be in her fifties. She wore brightly colored flowered print blouse, which showed off her ample bosom. She welcomed me in a throaty, sexy voice, I could now see what Saunders had on his mind. She was provocative in both her appearance and behavior. I got right down to business and pointed out she was a couple of payments in arrears and I offered to lower her payments, which was really a carrot so I could reset the loan and prepare corrected collateral documents.

She said, "Well that would help to lower the payments, but I can give you a couple of payments today."

Instead of taking the money out of the cash register, she reached between her breasts and pulled out some sweaty bills and gave them to me without counting them. It was several hundred dollars, enough to bring the loan tor current status, although the next month's payment was due in another week. When I got back to the bank, Saunders said, "Did you have to take it out in trade?"

I reached in my pocket and pulled out the bills and a copy of the receipt I had given Elaine. I said, "No, I collected the cash. She is current for now, but next week another one is due. I did agree to rewrite it, lower he payments a little, but we can redo the documents, which are flawed."

I worked with a number of clients until a month before Christmas, when the bank determined had done what was expected of me and Jim and Mike would be able to carry on. The worked out well since, The Christmas season was our busy time and the mall would be requiring we stay open longer hours. The store did well that Holiday season. Meanwhile, I decided to make the best of the retail business. By this time we had disposed of our Casper house but Jo still owned the Merle Norman store and we had purchased a house in Cheyenne.

Twenty Four

Making Lemonade

I still wasn't happy about being in the furniture business but was learning. As stated earlier, I still liked the potential for profits. So I decided to make the best of it and try to develop it into a larger more profitable enterprise. Jo still owned her Merle Norman cosmetics store which was located at the East Ridge Mall in Casper, but was now running by remote control by our niece Connie Patterson, as on location manager. Connie had lived with us for a year back in Greybull. Connie's marriage had ended when Roger, her husband, was discovered to be growing marijuana in the backyard. Connie was a loose ends, but this time she was helping us out, as much as we were helping her.

One day when Jo was up in Casper tending to Merle Norman business, she called me and said, "How much money to you have in the Yesterday's checking account?"

I said, quickly looking at my checkbook balance, "about $8,500, why do you ask?

She said, "Dale is going out of business, selling everything cheap."

Dale Myers had a similar store our Yesterdays' store at the East Ridge Mall called the Oak Leaf, just around the corner from Jo's Merle Norman store. He bought most of his goods from Charter Oak in Denver and carried many of the same furniture items we did in Cheyenne. I asked, "What happened?"

"Well," Jo replied, "he is a little light in the loafers, you know and he has decided to come out of the closet. He has been parading up and down the corridors of the mall here hold hands with his paramour. That's when he is not in Denver hanging out with his gay friends. Anyway, he has wrecked his business from a PR point here in Casper, and is spending money extravagantly in Denver enjoying the gay lifestyle in the big city."

I said, "How cheap is cheap?"

Jo replied, "It looks to me like half of wholesale on the same nice oak items we buy from Charter Oak. We can make some serious money on those items."

"Okay," I replied, "you can have up to $8000. I'll get up there with a check and the truck tomorrow morning."

Jo rushed over to select the items and told Donna, his manager I'd be up before noon to settle with them and a truck to take delivery. In essence we bought new furniture we could retail for about $30,000 for the $8000 expended. A few days later, we bought some more merchandise and then Dale's store, the Oak Leaf closed finally. Within a week I got a call from the manager at East Ridge Mall, wanting to know if we would be interested in taking over the location with a Yesterdays' store.

I told the guy I wouldn't be interested if the rent was anything like we were paying at Frontier Mall in Cheyenne. The guy explained under the complicated terms of their leases with their major tenants like Sears, Penney's, The Bon, and Target they needed to maintain a minimum number of small stores, which given the slumping Wyoming economy, they were having difficulty keeping independent stores. He said, "How does $500 monthly, no long term lease, sound?"

This was substantially less than we were paying in Cheyenne, where the Common Area Maintenance was over $1200 alone. So we made the decision to open the store and hire Donna Pickering; Donna was a pleasant middle-aged woman, who knew the business and was needing a job, since the Oak Leaf had closed. She had been frustrated by Dale's lack of attention to business and welcomed us. It was a good fit. We had sufficient merchandise in our warehouse to stock the store, which was about half the size of our Cheyenne store.

The only thing we needed was another truck and I went looking in Casper for another "High Cube Van." I found a 78 Ford van at a used truck dealer. The van had an interesting history; the previous owner had been Roseanne Cash, Johnny Cash's singer-daughter. Like her father she traveled the country and used it to haul band instruments. The truck's box was four feet longer than our Chevy and appeared to be in better condition; it even had air conditioning, a feature all of us that drove the truck really enjoyed. Apparently, the truck had broken down in Casper and Roseanne need to replace it quickly, not having time to wait for it to be repaired.

Our 78 Chevy ran well, but was tacky looking and got horrible gas mileage; the Ford used half as much gas, although both had similar sized engines 350 & 351 V-8s respectively. Probably the most annoying thing about the Chevy was the speedometer didn't work. With the many wide-open spaces in the state of Wyoming the temptation to put the pedal to metal was irresistible. Our son Oliver was driving on the lonely stretch of highway between Medicine Bow and Casper, about 80 miles of uninhabited desert, except of course the local population of rabbits and antelope.

Not knowing how fast he was going he was stopped by the Wyoming Highway Patrol, clocked at 80 miles per hour. The policeman said, "Do you know how fast you were going?"

Oliver accurately responded, "No sir, the speedometer is broken."

The cop said, "Son, I clocked you at better than 80 miles per hour."

Astonished Oliver said, "I had no idea this old crate would go that fast."

The policeman replied, "Son, to tell you the truth, I wouldn't have thought it would either, I'll tell you what, I'll just give you a warning ticket. Be careful."

Perhaps the non-functioning speedometer was at least a part of the reason the Chevy got such lousy mileage. The Ford's speedometer was in good working order and with the air conditioning quickly became the favored truck. Shortly after the acquisition of new truck, Rubin Cano, a young man we had hired as a part time delivery person, and I were making a delivery out in Rawlins of a large oak roll top desk. It was a heavy piece of furniture and required two people to handle, even when taken apart, which was necessary to get into many homes.

The house was quite small and it was obvious it would be a tight squeeze to get the huge desk through the narrow doors. The family had a precocious little four-year-old boy who was intensely interested in the proceedings. He asked, "What are your names?"

From the toys spread around the home's living room, the kid was evidently a fan of Sesame Street so I said, "I'm Bert and this is my pal Ernie."

"Bert and Ernie," he repeated. "I like that."

But the illusion was shattered, when I said, "Rubin, is this thing going to clear okay?"

Rubin replied, "Yeah, it looks like we got a couple of inches to spare."

The little boy frowned and looked at me and said, "I'll bet you aren't named Bert either."

I tried to explain I was just kidding and that my name really was Bert. But he just wasn't buying it. "You lied to me," he said emphatically.

I tell the reader this story because this was one of the few humorous moments I encountered in the furniture business. I relayed the story to Ginnie at Charter Oak on my next trip to Denver. She laughed and dragged out a new item they had bought on a trial basis and she shared with me the single joke I heard in the furniture business.

It was a hideous combination of hat stand and chair. The finish was a foreboding dark oak and the design had odd proportions. Ginnie brightened and said, "It's a special model they make especially for blind people."

Not long after the opening of the Casper store, we received a phone call from United Bank of Colorado and told us the Klassens were in default on their loan and were on the verge of declaring bankruptcy and would we be interested in liquidating their store in Fort Collins. I drove down and was more than curious as to what had gone wrong. The banker told me that there were all strange things going on in the Klassen's life. They suspected Wayne was drinking heavily and Sue was perhaps trying to support a cocaine habit. He said, "Mr. Harris did you ever notice Mrs. Klassen has a constantly runny nose?"

I confessed I had noticed but assumed she just had allergies, since I a few of my own. I said, "I guess I thought she had hay fever. What I did notice was she always wore these funny little knickers. They were kind of unique to Sue. I couldn't help but wonder where one would buy them since I had never seen any other women wear these garments."

I made the banker a proposal that we would liquidate the inventory for them, provided we could split the proceeds down the middle with them so we could pay our employees and store overhead. I said that I would need to work out a rental arrangement with the Fort Collins Fashion Mall before I could commit to a deal. The store by this time was locked up and the mall manager took me in to do an inventory. There was a great deal of inventory and it looked like getting the bank their money back would be no problem.

Then I inquired what terms for the short term might be available and also out of curiosity whether a longer lease might be possible, since we knew that sales wise Fort Collins was a better market than either Cheyenne or Casper. To my surprise we learned that the store location was about to blitzed for a hallway to a new addition they were adding to the mall, but once construction project was completed in a year, they might be interested in leasing us space. We needed to complete the liquidation by the end of December 1987.

This meant that if we wanted to stay in Fort Collins we would need to find a location. I wasn't too thrilled about a mall location, where mall management dictated hours, holidays and at least in the case of CBL (Costa Nostra Bastards & Leeches?), the company we leased from in Cheyenne, charged excessive uncontrolled common area fees. While the anchor tenant's fees were contractually controlled, there were no restrictions on what independents such as ourselves might be assessed. After mulling the idea over we decided to put in a store in Fort Collins in a strip mall right on College Avenue, Fort Collin's main north-south street.

The Klassens had copyrighted the Yesterdays' name in Colorado. We decided rather than deal with them and to escape any reputation problems that might have resulted from their difficulties, we would operate in Colorado under the name Victorian Oak. This would tell the public we hoped that we sold reproduction oak furniture, much of it from the Victorian Era. The store next door was an upscale grocery store and in the same strip mall there was a Red Lobster and a Chinese Restaurant, which we thought might develop good foot traffic.

We opened the store in January 1988 with a capable young man Jim Gilbert as a full manager and a couple of retired gentlemen for sales people. One of the salesman was Ed Maynard, who was a brother in law of Dick Morson. Ed was a WWII Army Air Corps pilot, later a MATS (Military Air Transport System) pilot. After a career in the military, he piloted airliners on international flights. Ed had lots of great flying stores, which being an amateur pilot myself, I enjoyed immensely. His best story was when flying a MATS plane from Shannon, Ireland to Reykjavik, Iceland.

He was three quarters the way to Keflavik International Airport, when he radioed their control tower that he wanted to land there and requested airport conditions. Keflavik came back that due to high winds they were closing the airport. Ed came back that he didn't have enough fuel in the DC-6 to return to Shannon. Realizing his predicament, the Keflavik tower advised him they would keep the airport open for him. They advised that there was heavy cloud cover, along with excessive winds, over the airport. The ceiling was 200 feet, just enough for standard minimums for an instrument landing. He was approved for a straight in landing approach.

Ed carefully planned his landing and sure enough when broke out of the clouds at 200 feet the visibility was clear. However, there was no runway in front of him. As he looked to the right he saw the runway and realized the strong winds had twisted the plane around so that he was flying sideways. He would need to make a tricky crosswind landing by side slipping using right rudder, left ailerons to make the land. Experienced pilot that he was, he was able to straighten out the plane just in time to make a safe landing. Airport emergency vehicles were there to greet him, but he had pulled it off safely.

February is always the slowest day in the furniture business and 1988 was no exception. For one thing it has fewer days and it being winter there was no particular reason to purchase furniture. Our breakeven point for a month at the Cheyenne store was $30,000 and by the 26th of the month our sales were just over $20,000. I was working the store alone to save money. I was getting ready to close at about quarter to 9:00 PM, after a day when we had sold less than $200 worth of merchandise.

In marches a well-dressed gentleman and began selecting office furniture, the finest roll top desk we had in stock, several oak filling cabinets, chairs, a table and hutch. The whole order came to over $10,000; we were going to make our numbers after all. Desperate to make the sale I oozed all the charm I could muster. In the process, I had a nice visit with our important customer. It was well after 9:30 by the time I completed filling out the sales slip and made delivery arrangements. Dr. Allen Atwell, M.D. wrote out a check for the whole order on the spot. It was nearly 10:00 by the time I got home that evening. Jo said, "Why are you so late?"

I said, "You'll never guess what happened this evening. Dr. Atwell came in and bought $10,000 worth of furniture for his new office. We are going to make our numbers in February after all."

Jo started to smile and said, "What kind of a doctor did you say he was?"

"Oh, he told me he was an O. B. GYN, why do you ask?" I said.

Jo replied, "I think I have just found a new gynecologist."

Jo sold the Merle Norman store so we could concentrate our efforts on the furniture business. The rest of the year we limped along making our sales numbers only some months. Basically we were staying afloat waiting for the last quarter- the Christmas season when we would finally be solidly in the black. At the beginning of October Don Watson at Charter Oak announced they would be selling the business to a younger guy named Douglas Greene. Shortly after the transaction was completed, Doug Greene announced that he would no longer sell to us. To make matters even worse Greene open a Charter Oak store across the street from us in Fort Collins.

This was devastating news since we relied heavily on Charter Oak as our main supplier of several key items like roll top desks and chairs. It turned out we had to buy at retail back orders for items like chairs. Buying direct from the manufacturer often takes a great deal of capital since for many of the furniture lines we carried and bought from Charter Oak, required that we order six months in advance of delivery. In our case, because we were new in the business would need to pay at the time we ordered, tying up huge amounts of capital we didn't have. After a discussion with Jim Saunders, who was now my banker, we decided to liquidate the business, first Fort Collins, next Casper and finally in the last week of 1988 consolidate everything left in Cheyenne. After Christmas we planned a big auction on December 31st to clear out remaining every piece of our inventory.

In the month leading up to the end of the year we arranged with our mattress supplier in Denver to park a semitrailer loaded with mattresses behind the store to give it the full look. I asked Jim Saunders if they could give me a letter of credit for $5000 in favor of the manufacturer to finance the mattress inventory. I was doubtful they would approved it, but Saunders and Bob Miracle said they were happy to help us because of the honorable way we had handled out business with them under these difficult circumstances.

Once we started advertising a Going out of Business Sale, our sales jumped skyward, even though we didn't initially lower our prices. It is a peculiar thing about human nature, once people think they smell blood, they get out their wallets. We had our bank loan paid off a couple of weeks before the end of December. We sold the mattresses at a 20% markup over cost, which allowed us to offer the best mattress deal in Cheyenne and we actually sold over $15,000 in mattresses during the course of our liquidation. We made pre arrangements to sell our trucks to a couple of suppliers in Fort Collins to be delivered in January.

For the past couple of years we had been renting a four-car garage as a warehouse in a residential neighborhood, which was located behind the home of Donald Unrein. Mr. Unrein was a sales representative for Beatrice Foods during the week. His hobby was being auctioneer, whenever he could sandwich a sale in. We hired Don to do our final liquidation sale; it was a great success and we literally cleaned out the store.

As Oliver and I made our final delivery on December 31st. I was surprised by Oliver's comment, "Dad, I going to miss this business. I particularly liked working for Donna who gave me the responsibility for deliveries."

Oliver had worked summers and holidays in Casper for UPS and Yesterdays' as his schedule permitted. He made a point that even though the Yesterdays' adventure hadn't been altogether a rousing success it had brought us close together as a family all working together. Now it was time to get back into banking or at least get back to work.

Twenty Five

Minnesota Bound

After liquidating Yesterdays' both Jo and I started looking for jobs in earnest. In January 1990, the banking prospects were not very good, although I had a good network of banking people throughout the State of Wyoming.

The Wyoming economy was weak and a number of banks, including some very old established institutions failed and their deposits and selected assets were assumed by stronger banks. Interestingly enough the number of failures in the 1980s exceeded those in the 1930s. Included in that number of dubious distinction was the Security Bank of Glenrock. I learned from Gordon Taylor that Patrick got into a fistfight in the bank's lobby with one of Mr. Sedar's pet customers and he was fired. Gordon left to take a position as Wyoming State Insurance Commissioner. The bank continued to flounder and the board was unable to raise the funds to recapitalize the bank and it was closed.

I made a lot of phone calls and visits but nothing turned up. I turned my networking efforts to include the greater Denver area. One day I had several appointments in Denver and decided to call Alan Kris, a fellow I had known as a bank examiner twenty years earlier. Alan and I had had at least one heated discussion about examining techniques; we certainly weren't close friends. I wasn't sure he would even see me, but since I had an appointment with an employment service across the street I thought I'd give him a try. Al was president of the First National Bank of Southeast Denver, a neighborhood bank and no relation to the old downtown bank which was part of the First Interstate System and currently bore that name.

Al said he would be happy to see me and we had a good visit. He said, he wished he had a slot for me since he thought well of the job I had done as an examiner. It proved to me both the value of networking and that one can be surprised who your friends really are. It was about this time that Jo said she would like to go home to Hudson, Wisconsin for the wedding of Scott Anderson one of her sister Sandra's kids. Since neither one of us were having any luck finding jobs to apply for in Wyoming, she said, "I think I'll look for a job, while I'm home. The economy in Minnesota is bound to be better than here."

I thought that was a good idea and stayed in Cheyenne to look after Juli and Martha who were in school. Jo was able to book an MLT round trip flight for $149, but the catch was she needed to stay for two weeks. This gave her lots of time to look for work. By the time she returned she had landed a position with Eastern Heights State Bank in Woodbury, Minnesota. This bank was at the time a subsidiary of 3M and meant from there you could potentially transfer to other jobs within the 3M organization.

Jo started her new job about the 15th of March and bought a townhouse in Woodbury, Minnesota close to her new job. I set about to sell the Cheyenne house, pack up, and rent a Ryder truck. Martha was a senior at Cheyenne East High School and arranged to stay with a girlfriend's family until her graduation at the end of May. I managed to arrange for the sale of our Cheyenne house to one of my friends at Wyoming National Bank in Cheyenne.

We were set to close on the townhouse May 1, 1989. I drove the Ryder truck, while Martha followed me in my car, a twelve-year-old Mercedes we had bought several years earlier. Martha then flew back to Cheyenne to finish high school. While starting her new job as a new accounts and receptionist at Eastern Heights, Jo had rented temporary apartment over in River Falls, Wisconsin. When we arrived a week before the closing, it was pouring rain and rained daily for the first week. Juli said to me, "Daddy, I'm worried."

I said trying to reassure her, "What are you worried about, we are all together."

She said, "Daddy, I am worried about flooding, I have never seen so much rain."

I told her that everything would be okay, since they typically get three or four times the rain we received in Wyoming. I assured her the rivers and streams could handle all the water. She seemed relieved. On May first we closed on our new home. The Ryder truck was packed solidly to the ceiling. In fact when I stopped at the Nebraska weigh station, the truck was two tons over weight; however, since I wasn't a commercial trucker he let me off. Jo hired a local moving company called Two Guys and a Truck to help us unload.

They assured her that it would only take a couple of hours. Jo said, "You have no idea how much stuff my husband can get on a truck."

Four and a half hours later the truck was unloaded of all of our worldly goods. There had been some benefits of being in the furniture business for three years, among them how to load and pack a truck. Not only that there was no broken furniture or anything else for that matter. As much I hated to give up my Wyoming license plates with the cowboy on the bucking horse, they were about to expire, so I immediately bought Minnesota tags for my car.

We began to get settled and within a couple of days later our new telephone was installed. The first phone call I received was from Jim Saunders who asked, "Would you be interested in coming to Casper and help me workout some problem loans, mostly here in Casper, but also throughout the Wyoming National Bank system?"

Anxious to start rebuilding my banking credibility and realizing I was running low on unemployment payments, I accepted Jim's offer. So by the following Monday morning I was back in Wyoming and working at Wyoming National Bank; this time in Casper. Jim was in process of moving up to Casper and had rented a home in the city's Sunrise neighborhood.

I rented an inexpensive apartment on Hyview Dr. The neighborhood wasn't awful, but obvious wasn't affluent either. Across the street one of my neighbors had a very tired 1968 Chevrolet. It was badly rusted and banged up. Each fender was a different color and its bumper sticker read: "Thank You for not laughing at my car."

"Sorry buddy, I couldn't but help laugh at your bumper sticker, not you, nothing personal, you understand." I said to myself, for I was now experiencing hard times in a way I had never had before.

The Special Assets Department (SAD), a politically correct way of saying problem loan unit was my assignment. As I understood it Mike Franck was working in Cheyenne and Jim had come up to Casper to mastermind the SAD enterprise for the whole system. Funny, the SAD acronym seemed to fit, quite accurately what was really going on better than our official name.

Saunders set me to work on a variety of projects, including the liquidation of a plumbing and heating contractor, arranging repossession for a few stray defaulted car loans. Luckily, this was mostly telephone work. I restructured a couple of loans and it became something of a routine job. One day I was surprise by a phone call from Don Unrein, the gentleman I had rented the warehouse from in Cheyenne. Don said, "I'm going to be in Casper Friday, let's have lunch."

"That sounds good." I replied, hoping he would pick someplace inexpensive.

He said, "Let's meet a Benham's at 11:30."

Benham's is the classiest and most expensive restaurant in Casper. I said, "Benham's is a little pricey for my budget."

"Oh, that's okay, I'll treat." Don said, "Benham's is one of Beatrice's best customers and corporate requires me to spend a couple of hundred each month with them. You'll be helping me meet that goal."

So we met a Benham's had a great meal; the best since the last meal I'd had of Jo's excellent cooking. During the conversation Don said, "I felt so sorry for you the day of the auction."

"Oh," I replied, "You need not be, getting out of the furniture business was one of the happiest days of my life."

Although I was away from Jo and Juli and I missed them, Oliver was in Laramie working towards an Electrical Engineering degree and by fall Martha was also enrolled at the University of Wyoming. Chad was serving in the military in Denver at Lowry Air Force Base, and Michael had taken off for California.

In addition to Saunders, our SAD crew included Roger Trupp, who like Saunders had a lot of commercial banking experience. Our department was housed in an old office building that had once provided office space for the Amoco Oil Company production unit, but now housed assorted functions of Wyoming National Bank Corporation, SAD, including personnel, legal and the holding company's sole investment officer, Hans Nelson.

Hans Nelson was a three combat tour veteran of Viet Nam, with Purple Hearts to match. He was a real "Rambo" kind of guy, always interesting to be around. Hans like me was an avid history buff and lunches with Saunders, Roger Trupp, and Hans Nelson were frequent, always fun and interesting. Hans had a repertoire of great stories like the one when he nearly got court-martialed.

In the thick of battle Captain Hans Nelson had a badly wounded man. A General landed with a helicopter, which could potentially take the injured man to a medical unit for urgently needed medical attention. However, the General refused to be inconvenienced. Hans argued with the General to help save the soldier's life to no avail. Finally, Hans took his 45 caliber automatic pistol to the General's head and ordered the pompous Brigadier General to ferry the injured man to the nearest medical unit. The General complied and the man survived.

Not so with Captain Nelson's military career. He was brought before a military tribunal and court martial trail. Although he wasn't thrown out of the Army, his rank was frozen at Captain. With his 20 years in service, he retired and studied investments to become Wyoming National's only investment officer. Hans believed in the KISS principle - "Keep it simple stupid."

Hans used a simple ladder approach to the purchase of securities, which consists of buying bonds, primarily treasuries and municipals securities with uniform maturities so that every year a specific volume of bonds would mature and be replaced with a similar number of new bonds distributed maturity-wise up the ladder, not to exceed ten years. Often he would buy if available bonds deeply discounted from face or par value. Therefore, there was almost always profits within the investment account which could be sold to augment bank earns or liquidity if needed. With this strategy in place Wyoming National had a consistently profitable bond portfolio, which to some extend off set loan problems caused mainly by the weak Wyoming economy.

When the National Bank Examiners arrived, Hans was criticized for having an overly simplistic investment philosophy. Hans Nelson in his typical confrontational style said to the eager youthful examiner, "Tell me do you consider Citibank, J. P. Morgan, and Chase to have sophisticated investment strategies?"

These banks all used variations of the so call "Dumbbell System," which consists of heavy emphasis on short term bonds within a year and a somewhat equal volume of bonds with maturities out with 20 to 30 years and few with maturities in between. With wildly fluctuating interest rates, the market values of these long bonds dropped precipitously and when the banks sold them significant losses were suffered. This ongoing saga was frequently reported in the Wall Street Journal at the time.

The ardent young bank examiner, responded quickly, "Yes, of course those banks are highly sophisticated."

Hans came back triumphantly, "Then how come they are taking heavy losses and we are actually taking profits in our bond account. I'm not sure I want to be highly sophisticated."

Saying nothing, tail between his legs the examiner strode off with a copy of a Wall Street Journal covering the latest episode in the ongoing investment loss story in hand, which Hans had just handed him. It was about lunchtime, so Saunders was rounding up the four of us to go to lunch at a Chinese restaurant down the street called the Peking Duck, affectionately known in our family as dubbed by my 10-year-old daughter Juli the "Pink King." Saunders says to Janice the tall dark haired legal secretary, "Have you seen Roger?"

Janice replied, "I think I just saw him go into the comparison room."

When Roger emerged from the men's room the four of us walked down to the "Pink King" and got a table. Roger recently had a heart attack; his cardiologist had put him on a strict diet, instructed him to quit smoking and to stop putting salt on his food. Roger asked, "What about pepper?"

The doctor replied, "Roger, you can have all the pepper you want."

Roger who was not a great fan of Asian cuisine ordered Moo Gao Pan, and immediately seasoned it with lots of pepper. In fact the whole plate was literally black with pepper. I shook my head doubtfully as I watched Roger dig in, wondering if the meal was now even edible.

Roger's face turned red as he devoured the meal and he said, "Man, this shit is good."

One of the great things I always liked about working for Saunders in addition to what I learned about working out of problem loans and negotiating deals, was his unfailing sense of humor. One day we decided to play a little practical joke on Russ Fennel. Russ was a neat, fastidious man who was the operations man at the Cheyenne bank. It was this attention to detail that made him an excellent operations man, but it also manifested itself in his personal dress and the particular in the way he cared for his car, which happened to be an immaculately kept dark blue Lincoln Town Car.

Saunders wrote a note and stuck in under the windshield wiper of the Lincoln. It read: "Sorry I bumped into your car, see me. Hans Nelson."

In fact Hans hadn't bumped into the car and knew nothing of the prank. He was amazed when Russ, who couldn't find the damage, because there was none confronted him, "Hans, I got your note, where did you bump my car?"

Rambo guy that he was, Hans retorted, "I didn't bump into your goddamn car, Fennel."

Russ reached in his pocket to produce the note about the time Saunders, Roger Trupp and I stared laughing, when Russ and Hans both realized it had all been a joke on them.

Russ said, "I guess that explains why I couldn't find any damage."

Speaking of damaged automobiles, Saunders' pride and joy was a 1927 Hupmobile four-door sedan. Jim and his wife Colleen were newlyweds in 1965 and looking for furniture near their native Cincinnati and answered an ad placed by an elderly lady for household goods. The furniture was piled high in an old 19th century carriage house. Surrounded by piles of old furnishings and other household goods was the black Hupp, which had only 26,000 miles on it, perfect dark green mohair upholstery, and 1936 Ohio license plates. The fenders were pocked with numerous little round dents from the years of having all kinds of stuff heaped upon it.

Noting Jim's interest in the car, she wanted to know if he would be interested in purchasing the ancient automobile. Jim explained while he could see the car was in very good condition for its age, they were newly married and couldn't make such a purchase. She came back, "Would you take it off my hands for $50.00?"

Minutes later they had acquired the Hupmobile and some assorted furniture. Quickly, Jim had the old car running sweetly. As Jim traveled from one banking job to another he had always included the Hupp as part of the household goods to be included in the moving package. At a stop in Fort Collins, Colorado after sanding it down Jim took it to a local auto body repairman to have it painted. The body was a cream color and the fenders were dark brown. The problem was no one had bothered to straighten out the multitude of dents on the fenders. Wyoming National had moved the car to Casper from Fort Collins in advance of Colleen's arrival, where she stayed with their two daughters until the school year was over.

Since it wasn't practical for me to go back to Minnesota on weekends or Saunders to go to Fort Collins, we hung out together and started eyeing the old Hupp. The guy who had done the painting had done a good job of laying on the paint, but the fenders looked shabby. I said to Jim, "What a shame no one took the time to straighten out the dents in the fenders."

Jim said, "Do you know anything about auto body work?"

I explained that my son Oliver and I had restored a number of cars, and I had some expertise as a body, fender repairman, and painter. So we started redoing the fenders and I repainted them so they looked quite presentable. After that success, Jim says. "Now the body looks kind of crappy, I suppose we should tackle that."

We then repainted the body the same cream color. Of course it would have been easier to have redone the body first and fenders last, but it all turned out okay. At least I wasn't bored on weekends. During the summer break at the University, Oliver took a job working construction for Ed Rate, erecting steel buildings primarily for oilfield service companies like Haliburton, Schlumberger, and smaller local outfits.

By now he had driven his 55 Ford sedan delivery for a number years and decided to modernize. He had replaced it with a four cylinder 1979 Ford Mustang. The engine was weak so he decided to replace in with a low mileage turbo charged-inter-cooled SVO engine, which he found in a Hemings Motor News advertisement. The seller was located in New Hampshire and the engine arrived the last week of June. With the fourth of July weekend upon us we decided to tackle the engine swap that weekend. In 1989 the Fourth occurred on a Tuesday. Ed Rate had generously allow us to use his shop facilities, which was complete with a hoist.

On Saturday we removed the engine. Sunday we installed the new engine. I had to work Monday, leaving Oliver to do the tricky part, merging new wiring system including installing new electric fuel pump in gas tank with the old setup on Monday. I managed to obtain a wiring diagram from Bob Tripenny Casper's Lincoln Mercury dealer, where we had bought a couple of cars and knew socially, as well. By the Fourth of July little was left to be done, and by noon it was time to start it up. It started immediately without the slightest hesitation.

We decided to test drive it and celebrate by going to lunch at a nearby Hardee's. The Mustang performed flawlessly en route. When we arrived at Hardee's Doug Laatch and several other of Oliver's high school buddies were also having lunch so we joined them. I said, "The amazing thing was that it started with the first twist of the key."

Doug said, "That's the trouble with Oliver, engines always start immediately for Oliver after he has worked on them."

During these days away from home in Minnesota, Jo and I talked on the phone at least every week. On one of periodic phone conversations that fall Jo said there had been an ad in the St. Paul Pioneer Press there had been a classified ad for a "Managing Agent" for the Resolution Trust Corporation (RTC) which was being staffed to deal with the numerous failed savings and loan associations, which became known as the "Savings and Loan Crisis." She said, "The job description is you, experienced bank CEO and workout specialist."

I responded to the ad with a complete resume and references which included board members from Greybull, Stanley Hunt, the Wyoming State Examiner, who had seen me at my best in Glenrock, Jim Saunders, and Jack Thomas who had been my boss when I was a bank examiner.

Now I waited for an answer. One of last the projects I took on at Wyoming National was assembling a bunch of various and sundry items for an auction sale. The sale was to be held down in Torrington and was mainly a farm equipment, which included trucks and some the hardware from the plumbing and heating company I was charged with liquidating. Since it was held on a Saturday, I called Oliver and suggested it might be interesting to come along since he was living in Laramie going to the University of Wyoming, a 135 miles away, not far by Wyoming standards. There were hundreds of items on sale including a nearly new computer driven IBM automotive diagnostic system, which had cost over $5,000 less than a year earlier.

Oliver decided to bid on it and bought it for only $50.00. I said, "How high were you willing to go?"

He said, "I only had $60 dollars to spend, but I figured it was worth a shot. With all of these farmers walking around I figured this definitely wasn't a computer crowd. I just got lucky."

As the Thanksgiving Weekend approached I was notified by the RTC in Minneapolis that I would be granted an interview. Craig Nulliner, the director agreed to talk to me the day following Thanksgiving. Since my employment arrangement with Wyoming National was a temporary one, I knew I needed to find other work and it needed to be in the Twin Cities, as Jo had what appeared to be a secure job with 3M. This was no secret to any of the people at Wyoming National and I was pleasantly surprised when Bob Ostland the Chairman of our Special Assets Committee offered to give me airline tickets to home.

He explained the bank bought blocks of tickets from Frontier Airlines, which had expiration dates on them and he thought they had more than they could use before the expiration date. I was delighted since money in my present situation was in short supply. The interview went well with Mr. Nulliner and I learned that in particular that Stan Hunt the Wyoming State (bank) Examiner had given me an especially good recommendation, which given the ultimate fate of the Security Bank might hurt my chances. Now it was a matter of waiting for the final word, did I have a new job or not?

In the last few weeks with Wyoming National I couldn't help but think of some of the people I had known from that institution in the past, including Fred Goodstein longtime director and major stockholder. Fred was a wise, amiable man, who was reputed to be for all of my years in Wyoming to be the state's wealthiest citizen. Fred was charismatic and I felt lucky to get to know him. In his later years when asked, what his favorite business was he responded that it was the junk business, because, "people pay you to haul it away, and then you sell it."

During World War II Fred owned a company called, American Pipe and Supply, which catered to oilfield enterprises. On day a man from Midwest, a small town 40 miles north of Casper came into Fred's office with an offer to sell him some pipe located in Midwest for a very cheap price.

Fred took him up on the offer. One of his assistants said, "Mr. Goodstein, you already own the pipe he wants to sell you."

Fred replied, "I know that, but I can't send a truck up to fetch it for that price."

Another Fred Goodstein story I liked was when his only daughter was about to get married. Her beau was from a fair wealthily California family. The young man's father owned a small manufacturing company which he was quite proud of. The old man was decidedly a "blowhard" and went on and on bragging about his accomplishments and company, which was worth perhaps twenty million. By the end of the two-hour tour Fred's daughter had enough. When he asked what she thought of it, she responded, "I can write you a check for it." And she could, but it wasn't enough to stop the marriage; they did marry.

In the December I was working with a limited budget for Christmas. I bought for Juli a dollhouse kit from a craft store, which I figured I would assemble when I got home. During the evenings and weekends I handmade furniture for the dollhouse so she would have some packages to open. The Friday before my departure the bank had a dinner in my honor at Benham's restaurant, hosted by Bob Miracle and Bob Ostland and I was commended for the work I had done there.

A week later, Oliver, Martha, who were both students at the University of Wyoming, and I formed a two-car parade to Minnesota to celebrate our first Christmas in Minnesota. We drove through the night and arrived a few days before Christmas. Shortly, after getting my batteries charged, Jo sent Juli and me out to purchase a Christmas tree. This was just three days before the big day so the pickings were slim, just like my budget. We picked out a scrawny little tree; the cheapest on the lot. After all it was a Christmas tree and we had a good holiday, as I contemplated: would I hear positive news from RTC or otherwise find a decent job in Minnesota?

Twenty Six

RTC

As the new year of 1990 dawned, I began looking in earnest for a job. However, within the first week, I received formal notice that I had been selected for a position as Managing Agent, by the Resolution Trust Corporation (RTC). The RTC was in fact an extension of the FDIC and was managed at the upper echelons by senior, experienced FDIC executives. Craig Nulliner was such a person and was the Director of the RTC Minneapolis Consolidated Office. I was instructed to report to the RTC offices, located in an impressive building in Eagan, Minnesota, on January eleventh, 1990.

The name of the office was a puzzlement to me since it was located in Eagan, several miles away from Minneapolis, geographically speaking it was more like a suburb of St. Paul. Perhaps if it was necessary to name in honor of a major city, St. Paul seems like the more logical namesake. On the other hand with a name like St. Paul, one might draw some sort of religious connotation. Political correctness might explain the choice name of Minneapolis Consolidated Office. All in all, I was very happy to have the job.

At the appointed hour I arrived and went through the new hire ritual. My immediate supervisor was Jerry Brandt, who I discovered had a similar background to my own. Jerry had a banking background much like my own, having been a president of a couple of community banks over in Wisconsin. Another fellow I met that morning was Robert (Bob) Scott, who like Jerry and me were former community bank CEOs. In Bob's case he had been the president of a couple of independent agricultural banks in Iowa. Jerry assigned Bob and me to work at the Durand Federal Savings and Loan conservatorship, which was located in Durand, Wisconsin, roughly 60 miles from my home in Woodbury.

The drive between home and Durand is mostly on a winding and hilly road, which passes by many dairy farms with their red barns and sometimes blue silos. When covered with snow, it reminded me very much of Vermont, which I had visited a couple of times recently in the winter in quest of skiing adventures. The managing agent at Durand was a big burly guy named Patrick Sheehan. After a cup of coffee Bob and I each were handed a stack of problem loan files, with instructions to figure out some sort of solution. They were as I recall run of the mill routine delinquent commercial real estate loans. The question posed was could they be restructured into something that would allow the owner to repay the loan or would foreclosure be necessary?

Usually Bob and I would have lunch as well as coffee breaks together. One day, I think it was a Monday, Bob hadn't yet arrived from his drive north to Durand from his home in Iowa, and I went out for lunch at a quaint little eatery a block or so from the bank. As it was the lunch hour and I had plenty of work to do, I elected to sit on the one remaining stool at the counter. The gentleman seated to my right was a fairly newly appointed Durand policeman.

His name deserves to be memorialized, but I'm sorry to say I have forgotten it. We began to chat and he proceeded to tell me about the first arrest he ever made for some relatively minor offense. The policeman told me that when it came time to recite the villain his "Miranda Rights" he totally drew a blank. He said, "Instead, I proceeded to recite to him Lincoln's Gettysburg Address, you know, 'Four score and seven years ago out forefathers brought forth on this continent a new nation, etc. etc.'"

Finally, about half way through Lincoln's classic speech the policeman said he recalled the correct words for the Miranda Rights. Within a few weeks Bob and I both received instructions to report to the office in Eagan the following Monday at 8:00 AM, We would be doing an "intervention" that afternoon at the bank's closing time and our lives as a Managing Agent would begin. Bob was sent to Fairmont, Minnesota and I was assigned to Equitable Federal Savings & Loan Association in Columbus, Nebraska.

As managing agent we were the de facto Chief Executive Officers of the S & L in conservatorship. The process works like this: the old institution is formally declared insolvent and closed, then the assets and deposit liabilities are transferred to a newly chartered institution, with a name very similar, but not precisely identical to the failed institution. During the conservatorship period, the institution carried on business as usual as to the deposit side. On the lending side next to nothing was done, but we could restructure loans. In the case of Equitable S & L at Columbus. I was "delegated authority" to restructure loans up to $750,000 on my own signature. The conservatorship would last until a new buyer could be found for the deposit base and selected good quality assets.

About two dozen of us RTC employees, flew down from Minneapolis to Omaha via Northwest Airlines, then drove the 85 miles west to Columbus. At closing time were all marched into Equitable's main office and seized control of Equitable Federal Savings & Loan Association of Columbus. In conservatorship the new name was Equitable Savings & Loan of Columbus, F.A. (Federal Association). This process is called "Intervention."

Interventions by their very nature are often confusing, and difficult for all concerned, especially for the S & L's personnel. Our team included Dave MacMillan, our attorney and his legal secretary Barbara Nelson, who I would be working closely with for the next year. A number of accountants and others to inventory all the assets of the institution. In addition, my credit specialist Lyle Hanson would be with me for most of the coming year. All of these folks, except for Jerry Brandt, my immediate supervisor, I had just met for the first time that morning at the office in Eagan.

Events got off to a ragged start, as several team members went to the wrong Equitable Federal Savings & Loan. They invaded Equitable of Fremont, which had a branch office a few blocks away from Equitable of Columbus. The folks at the Fremont Branch were puzzled by this since RTC had already intervened in their institution a couple of weeks earlier. The error was quickly recognized and within 30 minutes our legal crew arrived at the correct institution.

My first duty was to gather all of Equitable's officers and employees together and explain what was going on. It was a good news-bad news message I had to deliver. The good news was that we were not going to terminate any employees and asked for their assistance and cooperation in liquidating Equitable's assets, which was to be our primary focus. I told them that immediately the deposit function would continue in a normal fashion. We would review interest rates paid and keep them within a competitive range so as to keep the deposit base together to the greatest extent possible. This again was in my discretionary authority.

Loans would be a different situation. Very few loans would be granted, mainly limited to loans secured by deposits. Initially, we were allowed to make a few loans to finance the sale of foreclosed real estate we had in our portfolios. We were also going to restructure existing defaulted loans in order to cash flow existing debt if at all possible.

The bad news was obviously, that the old Equitable as they had known it was insolvent and essentially bankrupt. The RTC then repudiated all of the old Equitable's non-deposit obligations. This included contracts for everything except those essential to the operation of the conservatorship, such as the telephone and other utilities. Bills for past advertising, equipment service contracts and subscriptions were all denied.

Intervention is a delicate situation, since it is essential to secure the institution personnel's cooperation. In the case of Equitable there would be Lyle and I and about 30 staff members from the old institution. Obviously, we would be depending on them to do most of the work. I wanted to have a harmonious relationship with them in order to most effectively do my job. In short, RTC really needed their help and goodwill. I mustered up all the good manners my mother and dad had instilled in me and my introductory talk was a success.

At a branch of another institution in Swedesburg, Nebraska, the RTC personnel were very arrogant and treated the failed institution people without sensitivity and respect. The morning after intervention the head teller said to the RTC agent that overnight she had forgotten the combination to the vault, even though she had always remembered it for the previous five years. Because of her "alleged forgetfulness" RTC had to have the Mosler

Safe people come and drill the lock, which delayed getting at the cash as well as all the essential records.

Our intervention got started at 3 PM and we finally finished the immediate work that needed to be accomplished about 8 PM. Fortunately we had established a good working relationship with Equitable's staff. We asked Mr. Gonka, the president, to recommend a restaurant where we could get a drink and good meal; we were tired, hungry and needing to relax a bit as the following day would also be a long one.

Mr. Gonka suggested a steakhouse on the east side of town, which he assured us would meet our needs and served "World Famous Nebraska Beef." The restaurant staff arranged a large table for us so all 20 of us could sit together. All of us ordered drinks, which we felt we had earned. As we were enjoying our libations the waitress took our orders. With one exception, all of us ordered from the numerous beef steak offerings on the menu. The deviation from this pattern was my credit specialist, Lyle Hanson, who ordered trout.

While we were waiting for our meals and getting to know each other. Barbara Nelson told us about her recent visit from the Fuller Brush Man. As she explained to him, she had just gotten married and was short of cash, but emphasized that she loved their products. She said to him, "Why don't you stop back in six months when we're better settled and I'm in a position to buy some of your wares."

As Barbara finished her story the waitress began to deliver our orders. Each of us was treated to glorious cuts of Nebraska's finest beef, juicy, flavorful, and cooked to perfection. That is except for Lyle's trout, which was a miserable, freezer burned excuse for a fillet of trout. Lyle peered at it through his thick glasses and said, "I guess they were saving it for the Fuller Brush Man."

He nibbled at the fish, as the rest of us dove into our superb steak dinners. Dave MacMillan dubbed Lyle "Trout" as his official RTC nickname. For me, that was good news, at least I knew the guy that I would be working with for the coming months had a sense of humor.

During the first week various members of the RTC crew went about their duties. One of the guys I hit it off with was Ron Snyder. I am not sure his job title was, but his job was to go around and inventory all, and I do mean all, of Equitable's assets. Equitable had a single branch located on U.S. Highway 30 in a fairly new building. Like many S & L properties, both of Equitable's locations were located on former gas station sites.

At the Highway Branch, Ron and I went into the basement and smelled the strong unmistakable odor of gasoline. It seemed like if one were to light a match the whole place would blow up. This was a problem, I would be required to deal with if at all possible.

While Snyder and I were exploring the basement, we discovered an unused Mr. Coffee brewing pot, just gathering dust. Remembering how much Lyle enjoyed a cup of coffee, we decided to bring it downtown to him. On the way we stopped at Wal-Mart for a few items, when Snyder had a brainstorm for a practical joke on Lyle.

We purchased out of own pockets a couple of goldfish and filled the coffee pot with uncontaminated water and the fish. By the time we got downtown it was well after our usual 5 PM quitting time. So we placed the coffee maker, complete with the two gold fish merrily swimming around and around on Lyle's credenza.

The following morning Snyder, Lyle, myself, and others all had coffee in the employee lounge while I outlined the tasks to be accomplished for the day. Snyder casually said to Lyle, "Hey, Trout we found a Mr. Coffee brewer at the branch and put it by your desk for you."

About 10:00 A.M. I was meeting with Chuck Gonka, the former president of Equitable. As managing agent I was the de facto CEO of the newly created institution. Just as we finished the pleasantries, Lyle came barging into the conference room and said, "Who put the goldfish in my coffee pot?"

Immediately, I started laughing and at this point Lyle knew I was at least one of the culprits. It had taken him two hours to notice the fish. I suppose Snyder and I should have realized that he wouldn't see the goldfish right away since Lyle worn Coke bottle thick glasses and obviously had some vision issues.

Then Lyle said, "What the hell am I going to do about with that damned fish?"

I said, "We got you covered on that one. Steve Wolf, a residential mortgage lender, said. "I'll take the goldfish home and give it to my ten year old son. He'll surely enjoy them."

Lyle the said to me, "Okay, now you guys have had your fun. Now I can enjoy my coffee?"

After this interlude, Mr. Gonka and I got down to business. He said, "Until recently, I was the Senior VP and as such was charged with developing loans designed to improve our earnings. The Federal Home Loan Bank Board, our supervisory agency had recommended that we buy some participations in large construction projects, which have both a bunch of big front-end fees and high interest rates. They sent me down to Texas to look over several deals, which I did."

I said, "Those would be the four $2,000,000 participations, plus there is one large project for a shopping center in Omaha."

Mr. Gonka said, "Right, I wrote a report on each. The total loan on each project was over $30 Million. Of course we are only small players in the deal. If you read my reports to the board, I said, 'There is little equity, no tenants, and I cannot recommend them.' The board overruled me and we made the loans anyway. It is all in the in minutes. Damn it, I tried to stop them, but this is what FHLBB said we needed to do to make up for our ever increasing cost of funds, shrinking interest margins, as compared with our long term fixed rate home loans, which of course are substantially below current market rates. That's why we are broke. Our locally generated home loans and consumer portfolios are 98% performing as originally agreed."

I shook my head in agreement. I said, "There are only a few local problem loans, Lyle and I will need to work. For most of them I have the authority to restructure on the spot. Meanwhile, we'll start liquidating assets as favorably as we can."

I explained the repudiation process to him, including some of the service contracts on some of the equipment, like Pitney Bowes on the copier and postage meter. Mr. Gonka said, "The Pitney Bowes rep is a customer; he'll be mad."

"Well that can't be helped, Pitney Bowes contracts are notoriously overpriced. At least that was my experience at the last bank I was CEO of."

No sooner than the repudiation notices gone out, when I received a phone call from some guy at the "Mad Dog Collection Agency" about a subscription to some publication, which had only been partly paid for. The caller said, "Don't you realize your credit reputation will be destroyed if you don't pay this bill? It's only $450."

I told "Mad Dog" that essentially Equitable was bankrupt and RTC was the receiver and as such out duty was to deny all claims, except those of the depositors."

Again he reiterated that our entire credit reputation would be destroyed."

I asked him, "Does the word *bankruptcy* ring a bell with you?"

Again he repeated, "Your credit reputation will be destroyed."

I gave up and hung up on him.

While Lyle, or Trout as he was generally referred to, had a funny sense of humor, we spent little off duty time together, rarely did we have lunch together. Except for the night of the intervention never shared evening meals. Where he disappeared to was a mystery to me.

We stayed at the New World Inn, a Christopher Columbus theme motel, which appeared to have been built in a style similar to the Holiday Inns of the 1960s. It had several things going for it, besides being the best Columbus had to offer. The rooms were comfortable and were equipped with a TV with multiple channels. The restaurant was not fancy, but offered decent meals at a fair price and there was lounge.

I enjoy a before dinner cocktail and frequented the lounge every evening. There was live music virtually every night featuring a musician, who looked and sounded much like Kenny Rogers to me. After work I would go in and listen to the music while sipping my nightly libation. Kenny, as I thought of him, although his real name was Jim as I recall would play and sing a song and if you could name the tune, or in the case of an instrumental, the composer, Kenny would give you a chit for a free drink. Luckily, he played many tunes I knew and I won many free drinks.

Jim also got to know me and as my time in Columbus progressed, we frequently would have supper together. To my not very good ear, I thought Jim was every bit as good as Kenny Rogers and wondered why a guy with his obvious talent wasn't able to make a better living.

On the whole, on the job, Lyle and I got along well. He was a competent as a credit man and I frequent asked for his input on cases I was working. We did have one client we had a disagreement with. The guy, I'll call him Harry Saltzman, had a furniture store and three rental houses in addition to a commercial loan, collateralized by inventory and fixtures. He was in default on the rental property loans, but current on the commercial loan. I told Harry I would accept a deed-in-lieu of foreclosure on the rental property loans, if he would refinance the business loan elsewhere.

Since at the time there was a decent local market for homes and credit wasn't difficult to get to for a reasonably well-qualified buyer. On the other hand my analysis of the business loan showed he was liquidating inventory to pay his loan. The business was not cash flowing, since the inventory was our collateral, from a potential loss potential perspective it was a bigger risk than selling off the real estate would be since we would have the expense of the foreclosure process. Lyle on the other hand want to foreclose out the real estate, which would have in my mind sabotaged Harry's chance of getting the commercial loan paid by another lender. Harry was able to get financing from one of the local banks and I was able to sell off the rental houses easily and without loss.

After about six months the mystery of Lyle's disappearance evenings was solved. Normally, on Monday morning Lyle and I would share a car and drive together for the drive from the Omaha Airport to Columbus. However, on this particular Monday Lyle was to work at Columbus with me until Wednesday, then planning drive over to Nebraska City to spend the rest of the week assisting Harvey Orndorff at his institution, since our work load had decreased and we no longer needed him full time at Equitable. Although I had expect to see Lyle the following morning in Columbus, he had failed to show up. As I wondered why he hadn't showed up, midmorning I received a phone call from him. He said, "Bert, I need your help!"

"What's the matter?" I asked.

"I am in jail in Fremont for a DWI," he said.

In that instant, I knew where he has been disappearing to after work evenings. I replied, "How can I help?"

"I need $200 bail money to get out of jail. I need you to come to Fremont to bail me out." He pleaded.

"Okay, I'll take a long lunch hour, work late tonight." I replied.

I cashed a personal check for $200 to loan him, since they wouldn't take a personal check at the Fremont County Jail. Having spent the night in their captivity, he was deemed sober enough to drive his rental car. Lyle thanked me profusely and promptly rounded up the $200 to repay me.

By the time Christmas 1990 rolled around, things for our family were looking up. I had decent employment that promised to be stable for a couple of years. I took the week off and once more Jo set Juli and me off to find a Christmas tree. Remembering the sparsely branched tree of the previous year, Juli said, "Daddy, this year could we get a tree with branches on it?

Juli picked out a beautiful fully foliated tree and we had a happy Christmas, with three of out Children, Juli, Martha and Oliver. Chad was in the Air Force, serving in Saudi Arabia during the Gulf War Conflict and Michael was far away in California.

After a busy week early in 1991, all of us working in the eight failed eastern Nebraska S & Ls gathered in Omaha for lunch prior to taking our flight home to Minneapolis. RTC management encouraged us to do this to exchange experiences for the week; you might say learning from each other. This week Joe Wilson, the liquidator-in charge of the Occidental Savings & Loan Association, asked us to come a little early as he wanted us to help him with a problem he was having with his acquiring institution. They were procrastinating in submitting a bid for Occidental's main office building. It was as especially attractive structure, which was suitable for more than just a financial institution. It was obvious they were trying to negotiate at better deal; they were hopeful of buying it for a price far below the recent appraised value RTC had received on the building.

Joe's ploy was for us go in pretending we were businessmen looking for a new Omaha office location looking over the premises and hence encourage the acquirers to come up with a bid in line with the appraised value. Harvey Orndorff, the managing agent from our conservatorship in Nebraska City, was a tall, distinguished looking white hair gentleman posed as the interested businessman. Lyle posed as his administrative assistant. I arrived early and had a chance to scout out the premises and was elected to show Harvey and Lyle around the property. I said to Harvey, "Here is the perfect corner office with a view and lots of space, plus right next door a super office for Lyle."

Harvey acted very impressed and said within earshot of the acquiring bank's manager, "Yeah, let's get back to the office and work up bid for Joe."

Our little ruse worked and early Monday morning Joe had a strong, serious bid for the building from the acquirer. Shortly thereafter Joe called all of us to let us know the plan had worked.

After I had been at Columbus for nearly a year, my workload had lightened as I sold off nearly all of the assets I had jurisdiction over. I decided to invite Jo and Juli down during Juli's spring break from school. The New World Inn is very family friendly with a giant covered area, which includes a good-sized swimming pool. We allowed Juli to bring her friend, Sarah Place a fellow sixth grader along, so she wouldn't be bored. We drove down in our black 1983 Mercury Grand Marquis, which was now seven years old, comfortable, and very reliable. The extra time was on my clock, not RTC's.

While Jo, Juli and Sarah enjoyed the pool at the New World Inn, I tended to my duties at Equitable. Lyle, by now was full time with Harvey Orndorff at the Nebraska City institution. As the week progressed to our surprise, the New World Inn filled up with all kinds of secretive acting people. These folks turned out to be the advance team for Vice President Dan Quayle's visit. The Vice President was also staying at the New World Inn. It was exciting for the girls in particular to stay at the same hotel and get to see the nation's Vice President.

On Friday just as we were departing, Vice President Quayle was also leaving Columbus. In fact we were the first civilian car behind the Veep's entourage of black official government vehicles. Since our car was also black, it appeared that we were a part of the parade. Juli and Sarah thought it was great fun, even though our positioning was purely a matter of dumb luck.

The following week as I prepared for Equitable for the final resolution, that is the sale of deposit base and bankable assets to the purchaser, we were visited by a team of high priced *experts* from Smith Barney. Their function was to evaluate the assets and determine the estimated loss to the FDIC Insurance Fund. There were five people, who looked over all of the remaining assets of Equitable. I had sold off or liquidated most of the various undesirable assets, except for the five large, $2,000,000 participations, which were under the management of RTC personnel at the lead institutions. Four of these institutions were located in Texas. At the end of the week the Smith Barney leader asked me, "What do you think the loss will be to the fund?"

Without hesitation, I replied, "I'd say the loss will be $10,000,000."

The Smith Barney guy said, "That's amazing; our figure is $9,950,000."

I said, "You forget I have been living with Equitable and its' problems for over a year now. I can't help but wonder why RTC leadership didn't just ask me, instead of hiring you guys."

The gentleman from Smith Barney shook his head and replied, "I see your point."

A week or so later we learned that Conservative Savings & Loan of Omaha would be the acquiring institution. During the past year many Equitable employees found other jobs. Steve Wolf joined Edward Jones & Company. Bill Flint, our very able operations man, was employed by the First National Bank of Columbus. Conservative picked up a number of the Equitable employees. Cindy Bryant, a descendent of William Jennings Bryant *Boy Orator of the Plains* and perennial presidential candidate was not selected by Conservative and only later found another job. I thought Conservative missed a gem of an employee. Cindy was very able and a joy to work with as were most of the people at Equitable.

The Monday morning following the "Final Resolution" at Columbus I reported into the RTC office in Eagan. I happened to join Graig Nulliner on the elevator to the RTC offices. Craig was, the district director and the gentleman who hired me 15 months earlier. Craig said, "you certainly picked the bones clean out at Columbus."

I smiled and thanked him for the complement. Then he said, "Whatever happened to that branch with the gas leak?"

I chuckled a little and said, "We had an engineer look at that situation. It turned out that Equitable had properly removed the old fuel storage tanks from the former gas station. The smelly fumes were coming from the gas station across the street. Their gas tanks were leaking into the aquifer located under both properties. Luckily it is the gas station's owner and oil company supplier that are responsible for resolving the problem."

I continued, "Equitable was an institution that was pretty clean, except getting misled by the Federal Home Loan Bank Board into those jumbo office building projects in Texas.

For my next assignment, I had asked my new boss, Linda Henning to be placed in Minnesota. I explained that I had only16 months earlier moved to Minnesota and would like to see more of the state if that was possible. Linda thoughtfully assigned me to Lakeland Federal Savings in Detroit Lakes, where intervention had already occurred. Dave Paulson was the Managing Agent/Liquidator-in-Charge. Detroit Lakes is about 50 miles east of Fargo, North Dakota and notably north of Columbus, Nebraska.

While spring had come to Nebraska, and the promises of spring were evident in the Twin Cities, it was still winter in Detroit Lakes. I was surprised to see over one foot of snow on the ground and the lakes appeared solidly frozen, owning to well below freezing temperatures. Dave was staying at a Bed & Breakfast which sat on a hill overlooking Big Detroit Lake. Our hosts were genial folks and were a typical husband and wife B & B team. The husband worked at a job downtown and the wife managed the B & B.

My first trip out to Detroit Lakes was by flying on Northwest Airline from the Minneapolis-St. Paul Airport to Fargo, North Dakota. Then I rented a car for the one-hour drive to Detroit Lakes, Depending on Airport delays this took four to five hours. Dave pointed out that it could be easily driven in four hours from my home in Woodbury, which is southeast of St. Paul, even if I wasn't driving a Porsche 944, like Dave's.

Dave was a single man, but very much interested in the ladies. We typically ate breakfast and lunch together, but he always disappeared evenings. It seemed he always had a date. I was puzzled how he could always find a date. And it seem that he was dating a variety of women. It was obvious he wasn't dating any of the gals at Lakeland. One day while we were lunching at Sven & Ole's very good Italian-Pizza restaurant I asked him, "How is it you always manage to find a dinner date every evening?"

He laughed and said, "Oh, it's easy. I advertise in the local paper's personal column. Works like a charm."

The loans causing this institution's insolvency were not unlike those at Equitable. The primary difference was they were on commercial properties located in Arizona, rather than Texas. Same deal, big front end fees, high construction period interest rates, and few, if any tenants for the finished projects.

The deal I recall most vividly was a loan on a shopping center Lakeland made directly to the borrower. Lakeland's former CEO liked to winter in Arizona and solicited different loans in the Phoenix and Tucson areas, while basking in the Arizona sun.

Like so many properties financed by S & L's, The Sunrise Strip Mall was built on a former gas station site. Unlike Equitable's offices, no one had bothered to remove the old leaking fuel tanks. No effort other than filling the offending gas tanks with sand were made to deal with the faulty gas tanks and contaminated soil. All of this information was fully disclosed in the RTC's offering literature. In addition, this deficiency and expense to remediate was discounted by the RTC's professional appraisers, who valued the property at $1,200,000.

On a Wednesday morning, I received an offer for the property for $1.3 million from a Californian named Mr. Gold. This was over the delegated authority granted to Dave or me. Therefore it was necessary to submit a case to a committee at the office in Eagan. This was despite that it was clearly a good deal for the RTC; that is the United States Taxpayers.

Mr. Gold, the bidder, owned a string of flower and gift shops. He used them as the anchor tenants for strip malls he owned. More impressive, he was making a cash offer. The only condition was, we had to accept or reject his offer by close of business the following Monday. He stated he was looking at comparable property and RTC needed to decide otherwise he would purchase the other property.

Rapidly, I prepared a case for the so-called credit committee and faxed it to the office in Eagan, in order that it could be presented at the scheduled Friday morning meeting. Since my flower shop guy offered one hundred grand over our appraisal and wasn't asking for RTC to provide financing, I figured approval would be a "no brainer" decision.

Wrong! To my amazement I received a call from Mike McGown, a knowledgeable credit man I had worked with on other cases, exceeding my delegated authority of $750,000 out at Columbus. Mike said, "Sorry, the committee has decided to decline Mr. Gold's offer."

Amazed, I said, "Mike, are you kidding me? This is a really good deal!"

Mike said, "You're right. I voted for it, but you know how the committee works."

I said, "Run that how the committee works by me again."

Mike replied, "I forgot you haven't had a case declined before, have you?"

I said, "No, tell me how they could possibly failed to see this as one hell of a good deal for the taxpayers."

Mike responded, "The committee consists of all the Grade 14 or higher people in the office. Many of these folks have no credit experience whatever. They're guys like Dexter from purchasing, several lawyers, and techy computer guys. Today they had the credit people out numbered. They automatically decline deals they don't understand."

"I'll be damned!" I said, "How do I get this approved? I need to have this authorized by Monday, or Mr. Gold, my flower guy walks."

Mike McGown said, "Why don't we take this to Bob Fish, you know he just replaced Craig Nulliner as the district director. I don't know Bob, but I'm told he is an excellent credit man and has the authority to reverse a committee decision."

"That sounds like our best shot. I'd hate to see Mr. Gold buy a non RTC property."

I had briefly met Mr. Fish, when he introduced himself at a staff meeting. It was a "hello, how are you?" kind of conversation. From what I understood, his apparent management style was to come into the office promptly at 8:00 o'clock, and shut the door. He would emerge at noon for lunch, back at one, shut the door and remain in seclusion until quitting time. He was obviously very reclusive.

Never the less Mike, not without some trepidation, knocked on the door of Bob Fish's inner sanctum and was admitted. By 3:00 PM Bob Fish called me to inform me that he had overridden the committee's verdict and approved the deal. I immediately, called Mr. Gold and let him know we had a deal. We were able to close the sale by the end of the following week.

As spring the of 1991 blossomed into summer, I received a phone call from Linda Henning, my supervisor informing me I was being reassigned to Westland Federal Savings & Loan, located in Rawlins, Wyoming.

She explained that this was an experimental program called, Accelerated Resolution. In a way it was a sort of covert operation. I was to go out there alone and prepare Westland for resolution, without going through a conservatorship, as was usual in the case at Equitable-Columbus and all other previous RTC institutions up to this point.

Linda explained that I was to keep a low profile, since in this instance RTC was not assuming official control of the S & L. In a manner of speaking, I was to prepare Westland for burial, prior to its ultimate demise and closing.

I explained to Linda, that I was well acquainted in Wyoming. Quoting Governor Mike Sullivan who famously stated, Wyoming is a small town with long streets, everyone knows everybody."

I was well known in Wyoming banking circles.

Linda didn't see this as an impediment. She and the powers in charge at the Minneapolis Office liked the idea that I was familiar with Wyoming people having been a resident for most to my adult life, 29 years to be exact.

The commute to Rawlins takes the better part of the day. I took an early, 7:00 AM flight out of the Minneapolis-St. Paul Airport to Denver, then either I could drive from Denver to Rawlins, about 225 miles, or four hours, or change planes in Denver, fly to Casper, then drive 120 miles to Rawlins. This meant on that Monday, the first day on the site, I didn't arrive at Westland until 2:00 PM Mountain Time, or 3:00 PM Minnesota time. About all I had time to do was to get acquainted with the Westland staff and outline to management the purpose of my visit.

People showing up in a suit and tie in Rawlins is a bit of an oddity in itself. I almost had to be from the "Feds." Tuesday when I went out for lunch I happened to meet Karen Clark, who was now the Cashier, or chief financial officer, of the Rawlins National Bank, which was located directly across the street from Westland's main office. I knew Karen from half a dozen or more visits to the Rawlins National Bank, back when I was a National Bank Examiner. Tall, pretty, blond, she was an attractive, bright woman, and easy to recall.

I tried to pass my presence at Westland, as I told her, "I'm just here helping out."

Karen was smart and figured out immediately what was going on. Many people in the Wyoming banking industry knew, I was now working for the

Resolution Trust Corporation. I went right to work to get my arms around Westland's problems.

The primary issue was the typical S & L difficulty of holding old low rate mortgages funded by ever increasing high cost deposits, hence they were losing money at an alarming rate. Their capital accounts were exhausted. Thankfully, there were few really serious asset problems. At least they hadn't fallen into the trap of buying participations with high front-end fees and high interest rates on speculative projects in Texas, Arizona and elsewhere. Had it not been for the disparity between their cost of funds and their low yielding mortgage loan portfolio, they would have remained solvent.

The one asset problem I recall was a conventional home loan to a local couple, which was nearly four payments in arrears. I looked over the file and saw that Willard and Agnes Gardner had lots of toys: boats, snowmobiles, camper trailers, and a fancy pickup truck. The good news was Willard had a good job and had been employed at the Amoco Production Company for the past 20 years. I called them up and Agnes answered the phone. I invited them to come in and discuss their situation with me. "Mrs. Gardner would you and your husband come in at talk to me about your delinquent mortgage loan? I'd like to find a mutually agreeable solution for you."

Agnes was alarmed, that her husband had allowed the payments to go this far delinquent. They were in the office promptly at the appointed hour, 1:00 PM the next day, and we had what I like to call a, "come to Jesus meeting."

I explained to the Gardners that Westland was under strict supervision by the Feds, leaving out that Westland would be placed in receivership within a week or two. I didn't want to blow my cover, but with Karen Clark and other acquaintances and friends of mine in all likelihood it was already blown. I emphasized that once the loan became four payments delinquent the foreclosure proceedings would begin. I said, "Picture a steamroller at the top of a steep hill. It has no brakes. The only thing keeping it from rolling down the hill and flattening everything in its path is a wooden chock. Once that hunk of wood is removed, nothing can stop it. This is the way it will be with the foreclosure proceedings. There will be no way to stop it, short of paying off the mortgage in full, once it begins."

Agnes starred at her husband and said, "God damn it, Willard you need to sell some stuff, like your damned toys, and get this taken care of!"

I said, "I can give you two weeks to get this current, I mean four payments, otherwise I'll be forced by the Feds to start the foreclosure proceedings. Once started I will NOT be able to reverse course."

This was of course not a bluff, because I knew that once Westland was closed, any delinquent loan would be property of the receivership and the foreclosure would be automatic. Agnes glared at Willard, who by now realized he was in big trouble, not only with Westland and had even more trouble with his wife. They left the office and within a week had sold their boat and trailer, which was more than enough to bring the loan to current status.

In the meantime, the word was on the street that I was from the RTC and people began lining up to withdraw their deposits, not only that they demanded cash and were unwilling to accept even a cashier's check. On the day the run started, by 3:00 PM when the bank closed for the day, we were down to a paltry $23,000 cash on hand, much of it in coins. I knew we were in trouble.

I dashed across the street to see Karen Clark and Tom Wagonette, Rawlins National's president. I said, "I'm in big trouble, we are having a run, and I have only $23,000 cash on hand."

Karen and Tom looked at each other and Tom said, "We can let you have $100,000 from our vault cash and order more from the Fed in Denver. Under the circumstances, we'll get them to send an armored truck, so they can be here early in the morning. How much do you think you will need?"

I replied, "$500,000 should do the trick. I can't tell you how much, I appreciate your helping me out! Thank you, thank you, thank you!"

By this time, Karen and Tom were well aware of my mission at Westland, as they had been asked to submit a proposal for the acquisition of Westland Federal. They had been invited to submit a proposal for the purchase of select assets and assumption of deposit liabilities of the failing institution.

The following morning, we opened and after an hour, we had burned through most of the $100,000 in cash acquired courtesy of the Rawlins National Bank, The money from the Federal Reserve Bank in Denver arrived in the nick of time, and we were able to calm depositors' nerves. I should point out that Rawlins National was a Federal Reserve member bank, while Westland Federal was not, since at this time savings and loans did not have access to Fed services. We did have bank deposits sufficient to repay Rawlins National.

Within a couple of weeks the Rawlins National Bank was announced to be the winner of the competition for Westland Federal's deposits and bankable assets. We then went through the final resolution of Westland and I remained in Rawlins for the next couple of months, disposing of the assets not included in the transaction with Rawlins National.

One of my duties as Liquidator-in-Charge was to prepare a weekly report to the Minneapolis Office of the receiverships ten largest, measured by dollar value, assets needing to be disposed of. In the case of Westland the list was rather comical.

The bank's largest asset was Westland's main office building, which was of no use to Rawlins National, the acquirer. They had a more suitable building across the street. Next was the building for their branch in Hanna, Wyoming. Rawlins National indicated they would purchase it to continue to serve their newly acquired customers. There were several inexpensive houses they had acquired through foreclosure. Rounding out the ninth place was a modest collection of jewelry thought to be worth perhaps $1000. Finally, there was a tired, optimistically valued 1975 Ford pickup truck, which I hoped would bring $500.

Once Westland had gone through the resolution process, my duties were not pressing, as there wasn't much to do. I had time to have lunch with my friend and fellow pilot, John France the retired President of Rawlins National Bank. John and I shared a number of common interests and best of all John had a quick wit and a terrific sense of humor. In addition, I reconnected with my high school buddy, John Gilman, who was a local artist residing in nearby Saratoga.

After concluding my duties at the Westland receivership, I was transferred to The Benj Franklin Savings & Loan Association receivership in Portland, Oregon in October of 1991. This institution had already passed through conservatorship into the receivership phase. The acquiring institution was the Bank of America, based in San Francisco, acquiring the Benj's 89 branch locations. Because it was a large institution, we had a staff of about ten RTC credit specialists, all working on the numerous troubled assets retained by the receivership.

The Liquidator-in-Charge was Mike Kriston, a short stocky gentleman with excellent credit and workout credentials. Because of the size of the Benj, there were many, many problem assets requiring resolution. These were Mike's great interest and focus. As he zeroed in on the multitude of asset problems, he gave little attention to the administrative issues and had gotten crossways with Deborah Mueller of Internal Review. Deb was a bureaucratic, by the book kind of person; Mike on the other hand was her polar opposite. She and Mike were constantly at each other's throats, as Mike resisted her dogmatic approach to this large and complex institution's numerous and challenging problems. Mike's animosity and frustration for Ms. Mueller was expressed vigorously at every coffee and lunch break I spent with him.

The Supervising Managing Agent, John Johnson for this institution, I had previously had only met briefly. He recruited me for this assignment because I had both a banking administration background and also had experience as a National Bank Examiner. John explained to me on the occasion of our first visit, my job was to handle getting along with Ms. Mueller. He said, "Bert, your job will be to keep Mike away from Debby to the best of your ability. Plus, Mike will undoubtedly have you work some credit cases as well. This arrangement will allow Mike to focus on his specialty, solving loan problems,"

Johnson and I had similar career histories having been the CEOs and principal owners of small independent banks, in my case in Wyoming, and his bank being located in Owatonna, Minnesota. We also had a love of flying, airplanes, and similar aviation resumes. On and off the job, we had lots to talk about.

In addition to running interference between Mike Kriston and Deb Mueller, I was given several credit resolution projects. The most interesting task was to resolve a capital note problem, which was issued by the Old Stone Bank in Rhode Island. Although the name sounded like Old Stone was commercial bank, in fact a few years earlier it had switched to a Savings and Loan charter, to take advantage of the more lenient regulatory climate prevalent at the time.

The Benj had purchased for its investment portfolio $15,000,000 of Old Stone's capital notes, which was a substitute for shareholder equity in the association. Old Stone offered to settle the obligation for $7,500,000. The transaction for the Benj was strictly cash to get out of an unattractive a asset. For Old Stone Bank it eliminated a liability and they would as a result boost their stockholder equity by $7.5 Million.

The question I needed to resolve was this only a good deal for Old Stone Bank. I made a call to the top guy at the Office of Thrift Supervision (OTS) in Boston. This gentleman turned out to be a contemporary of my old boss when I was a National Bank Examiner, my friend and mentor, Jack Thomas. I asked about the condition of Old Stone and learned it was weak, even precarious but the OTS was hopeful if it could be saved. The proposed transaction was a key piece of the solution to saving Old Stone.

The offer turned out to be a win-win for both the Benj receivership and Old Stone. I submitted a case to the Minneapolis Consolidated Office. Simply stated was if we didn't accept the offer and held out for the $15,000,000 to be paid at maturity, seven years away, the failure of Old Stone would leave us with nothing, zero. By accepting the proposal we immediately recovered half the Benj's investment and perhaps help save Old Stone from failing. This time the credit committee was dominated by people who understood the benefits to the taxpayers and it was promptly approved.

Mike Kriston was pleased too, as he was working on some other sticky transactions involving the precarious, Old Stone Bank, whose solution was made possible, provided Old Stone Bank remained a viable institution. It was about this time Mike had a curious experience with the Hertz Rent a Car people. Because of his short stature, he preferred small cars and every week for months rented a small Ford Escort, although we were authorized to rent midsized cars. On this particular week Mike's Escort had a flat tire. Mike called Hertz and let them know they needed to come and repair the tire.

Mike was expecting to just get the tire fixed, but Hertz was embarrassed, since Mike had been renting a car nearly every week for over one year. They told him they would deliver another car to him. To gain favor with Mike, they replaced the Escort with a gigantic new Lincoln Town Car. Even though he could barely see over the steering wheel, Mike didn't complain as he appreciated the thoughtful gesture, as he wallowed around in the Lincoln's spacious interior.

In order to maximize holiday time and still keep the receivership adequately staffed for the 1991-1992 holiday season, the local guys worked the days which led up to Christmas, which fell on a Wednesday that year. This allowed the Minnesota guys and Mike whose home was Seattle, Washington to take the days leading up to Christmas off. Then we returned late on Christmas day and stayed out New Year's Day for what amounted to be a ten-day stay in Portland.

Since I was to spend a weekend in Portland, I thought it would be interesting to explore the State of Oregon, which I had never visited beyond the City of Portland. In particular I decided I would like to visit Oregon's scenic coast. I used my Frequent Flyer Miles to get a full sized car, which I thought would be more comfortable, since I am six feet tall. Before leaving for the Christmas holiday I put in an order with Jennifer, the lady at National Car Rentals. Jennifer asked, "Would a Pontiac Bonneville be satisfactory?"

"Yes," I said that would be perfect."

Upon arriving in Portland late Christmas day, a National employee I didn't know greeted me. She handed me the keys and said, "Merry Christmas, your car is located in slot E-7, see you in 10 days. Have a great stay in Portland."

I walked down the ramp to get my car. Tired, I focused on finding the parking spot E-7. I opened the door, sat down in the posh leather seat, and inserted the key in the ignition. As the engine started, I looked out the windshield and to my surprise, I saw the distinctive Cadillac crest ornament at end of the long hood. My friend Jennifer had arranged a Cadillac Eldorado for my upgrade.

The amusing part of this and Mike Kriston's rental Lincoln, was RTC, government policy, was they expected us to drive modest, humble looking automobiles, even though in both instances there was no extra cost to the taxpayers. The joke among us RTC travelers was, "we were to request cars with a few dents and scratches so we would appear even more humble."

The counter people at the rental car agencies, which incidentally were selected by the RTC travel specialists, were trying to please customers since we rented cars from the same rental car companies, week after week.

My arrival in Portland was in October a couple of weeks before the rainy season began. The rainy season in Oregon seems like it rains every day until the end of April, when the dry season begins. To my delight I was to get another opportunity to see the sights of Oregon. Chester Morrison, one of the credit specialists and I were assigned by Mike to check out on the foreclosed properties, referred to as OREO, in the Benj's portfolio at various branches scattered about Oregon. The acronym stands for Other Real Estate Owed, nothing to do with cookies.

Chester was a widower, who had been an officer at the Bank of New England, which had gone down in a scandal-ridden failure. Both Chet's wife's passing and the collapse of his employer happened with a few months of each other. His first RTC assignment had been at a savings and loan in Iowa, where he spent a year. He fell in love with the desk clerk at the hotel where he was staying. In order to retain his relationship, they were married and she traveled with him to the greatest extent possible.

The lady's attraction to Chet, was not only his charming personality, but also his wry sense of humor, which got us briefly into a little trouble on our trip. Our trek around Oregon took the better part of a working week. The last night out we stayed at a place called the Seaside Motel in Oceanside. Chester started visiting with the desk clerk and said, "We are Federal Agents looking for bad guys, wanted for fraud in the savings and loan mess."

The lady looked acted nervously and said, "Specifically, just who might you be looking for?"

Chester, sensing her discomfort and that he had evidently struck a nerve, said, "We are not in a position to reveal the culprit's name just yet."

Then she confessed, "My brother, Gary Seymour, must be who you are looking for here. He defaulted on a mortgage loan at Oceanside Savings."

Chet then, says, "I'll bet that's our guy."

At this point she started to cry, "Oh, please don't arrest him, he lost his job and couldn't make his payments. He is really very honest and wouldn't do anything illegal."

Finally, Chester realized he had pushed his little joke too far, said magnanimously, "Okay, we'll leave Gary alone." He never confessed this was just a joke that had gone too far.

As an aside to the adventures in Oregon and the Benj Franklin Federal Savings & Loan Association, the Bank of America, the acquiring institution paid a substantial premium, several million dollars to assume the deposit liabilities and acquire the bank quality assets. Years later I read in the financial press, that the shareholders of the Benj, were actually paid a liquidating dividend. In the end the taxpayers suffered no loss, thanks to the RTC team at the Benj.

The Bank of America-San Francisco personnel, who serviced the liquidation loan portfolio, proved to be excellent, professional bankers to work with. I couldn't help think if there was ever a large bank I would like to work for it would be the Bank of America. For me it was ironic that the two best acquiring institutions I interfaced with would be the largest, Bank of America and the Rawlins National Bank in Wyoming.

Twenty Seven

Going Postal

In July of 1992 the Benj Franklin receivership was consolidated into the Minneapolis RTC office, where we worked on the problem assets from cubes. I worked with John Johnson and Mike McGown on a variety of projects from different institutions. As the volume of this worked slowed down I was assigned to work in Kansas City Consolidated Office. The Minneapolis office was being merged into the Kansas City Office.

This time I was working in the Office of Subsidiary Management (OSM) for Bob Martin. Savings & Loans frequently had subsidiaries in which they were allow engage in a number activities that they were not permitted to do directly. This loophole in the law when one thinks about is really foolish since an insolvent subsidiary can impair the financial health of the principal institution. However, presuming the "Corporate Veil" wasn't pierced, losses could be limited to the extent of the subsidiary's investment, if the subsidiary went broke.

The result of this legal structure was that virtually all S & L's had at least one subsidiary. The larger institutions often had ten or more corporate offspring. OSM's job was to dismantle these corporations. The complicating factor is that the corporation charters are issued by the various states and each state has very different laws for dismantling them, or terminating their corporate existence.

For example in California and Texas, they *must* be formally dissolved. If not formally dismantled the state imposed fees continue and are personal liabilities of the officers and directors. Whereas in other states like Colorado and Wyoming, failure to pay the annual fees automatically kills the corporations after a specified period of time. At the Kansas City Consolidated Office (KCCO) Office of Subsidiary Management we worked with corporations chartered in 41 different states.

The technique employed was to liquidate the corporation's assets, passing the cash generated upstream to the parent S & L institution. The process varied depending in which state the subsidiary was chartered. My last couple of weeks at RTC was working with Bob Martin, the gentleman in charge of OSM, liquidating various assets so the corporation could be terminate. Hence the people at OSM were known as the "Terminators."

At the end of October 1992. When MCO was closed my job was also ended. As it turned out this would be only temporary. By now I was 54 years old and had long since realized while employers according to the law cannot discriminate against job seekers because of age, they do. As a practical matter employers copiously avoid hiring older workers. One friend of mine, who was also 54, used to leave off the first 10 years of his work experience on his resume and left out college and high school graduation dates.

This technique in my case wouldn't work unless you were gullible enough to believe my first job out of high school was that of a bank president, which is not likely or believable. In addition, this approach would also mean I'd have to leave out my valuable experience as a National Bank Examiner, which was generally a selling point to would be employers in banking.

Since I wasn't anticipating finding a new job quickly, I decided to apply for work as a "Christmas Casual" at the St. Paul post office. This job would stretch my unemployment compensation dollars further if needed. After demonstrating I could lift fifty pounds, prove I could read, and answering a few questions I was hired to work at the Minneapolis-St. Paul Airport Mail Facility. Not too tough!

I elected to work the graveyard shift from 10:30 in the evening until 7:00 in the morning. This gave me the opportunity during the day to schedule job interviews for a more permanent job and it also paid better than the day shifts. The first night on the job I was told to report to a man named John. I never did learn his last name. John explained to myself and another casual named John Maloney, who would become my post office buddy, how the sorting room at the Airport Mail Facility worked. Along with a half dozen "Christmas Casuals, we were assigned to work the "spider."

The spider is a sorting device consisting of several roller boards. The guy at the top of the spider, we never knew his actual name, looked like Jeff Chandler to Maloney and I. Jeff Chandler would sort the packages by airline and destination. We would place the packages in large baskets marked by the airline, like NWA for Norwest and, DEN for destination Denver, and also the flight numbers.

Jeff Chandler's spider had a blue light above it. The other spider had a red light overhead and was manned by guy who looked like Festus on the old Gun Smoke TV Show. Of course we referred to him as Festus. His real name? Who knows?

One very cold night, twenty below zero, a bunch of us were called to load into the baskets a huge pile of Christmas packages. The pile was over twenty feet high in this unheated lean-to that was open at both ends. Inside the sorting room it was cold, but tolerable if you wore a sweatshirt and warm gloves, but the lean-to was North Pole frigid. Due to the extreme, bitter cold, we all worked quickly and were anxious to get back inside.

At last we were down to the last basket, my supervisor, John says, "Harris, wheel this basket over to the blue light (Jeff Chandler)."

"Okay," I said eager to get inside.

I pushed the cart over to the blue light. Jeff Chandler glared at me and said, "No, no this goes over to the red light."

I shoved the basket over to the red light and Festus says, "Jesus Christ, this goes over to the blue light."

Being a new guy, I pushed the cart over to the red light as instructed. "Damn it, didn't I tell you this goes over the red light." Said Jeff Chandler."

Obediently, I returned to the red light and Festus says, "For Christ's sake, didn't I just tell you this goes over to the blue light."

Bewildered, I said, "Hold it right there, the guy at the blue light says to bring it here, and you say it goes over there. Something doesn't make sense."

Festus walked all around the postal mail cart, carefully looking over several different packages. Calming down now, he said, "Ah ha, I see the problem some of the boxes go here and some go over to the blue light."

Festus put all the parcels needing to go on the red light on his work ramp. Then said, "okay, all these can go over to the blue light."

When I returned to the blue light, Jeff saw the packages were in his domain and silently removed them from the cart. I went back to loading when one of my co-workers, as big fat guy, whose great belly swayed as he tossed a package clearly marked *Fragile* in three inch high letter into the most distant cart, where landed with a reverberating thump.. I said, "Damn it, Mike, you probably busted some little kid's Christmas present."

Mike said, "Hell pretending we're in an NBA basketball game is the fun part of the job."

All kinds of things get broken at the Airport Mail Facility (AMF), like bottles of booze, which people are not supposed to mail in the first place. The room smells of liquor for days after a few bottles are broken. Surprisingly at least to me, it is not illegal to ship live animals, such as chickens in the mail. The chickens obviously, don't like to travel this way. For when they are postal travelers, you can hear their cries of, "AUCK, BUCK, BUCK AUC, BUCK, BUCK, AUCK, AUCK," all over the sorting room until they are loaded on to their flight.

Apparently, John, my supervisory, thought I was good help and I was invited to keep working at AMF, even after the Christmas Holidays and on into February, when I received a phone call from Bob Martin at OSM in Kansas City, inviting me to return, since he now had the funding for an additional person to help terminate subs. Joyfully, I accepted the offer.

Twenty Eight

Terminator

On the third Monday of February 1993, I reported to Bob Martin and the Office of Subsidiary Management (OSM). Several of us from the Minneapolis Office were working at OSM. There must have been a total of twenty or more from the Minneapolis Office now working in Kansas City. Among them was my old friend, Bob Scott, who I had worked with at my first RTC assignment in Durand, Wisconsin. Since RTC didn't provide for our living expenses, we were looking for inexpensive lodging, Bob and I found a clean but cheap motel several miles from downtown, Kansas City. A couple of days into our new digs, a huge twenty-inch snowstorm buried the city in a deep wet blanket of snow.

Being accustomed to driving in severe winter conditions, I had no problem making it to the OSM office at 4900 Main Street on time. Most of the locals stayed home, but we hardy Minnesotans were all present. To our surprise Lanis Yarborough from the Baton Rouge, Louisiana office also made it in. Bob Martin, our leader, said to Lanis, "How did you manage to make it in? You don't get snow in Louisiana, do you?"

Lanis drawled, "Well, I figured if I was going to live here, I'd better learn how to drive in this stuff, just in case I run out of something important like, beer."

Lanis was in charge of one of the more interesting cases at OSM. The RTC, like the rest of the nation, had a love affair and irrepressible faith in computer technology, once data was entered into a data base, getting even the most obvious errors corrected, was not so easy, especially when it came to property owned by the RTC or one of its subsidiary corporations, which came under the jurisdiction of OSM. Everyone with even a scant knowledge of American history knows Franklin Delano Roosevelt's vacation home at Campobello, off the island of New Brunswick was in Canada. While it is easy to forgive a person for not remembering which of Canada's Maritime Provinces, it is hard to understand how anyone would not know that Campobello was definitely not in the state of California.

Yet that is exactly what happened. One of RTC's computer data entry people erroneously placed a development property a savings and loan subsidiary was attempting to develop on the island of Campobello, New Brunswick, Canada, presumed it was in California. This is in spite of the inspiration behind the development was trying to capture customers, with the allure of Campobello's natural beauty, but also the historical connection with FDR, long regarded as one of our great presidents. Even if you didn't agree or buy into Roosevelt's politics, it is impossible to ignore him as one of the most fascinating occupants of the White House.

Apparently, computer technicians are not at all versed in American history, since it took months of cajoling from Lanis Yarborough, our asset specialist on the case to finally get the matter resolved on and Campobello back in New Brunswick where it belongs. As Lanis put it, "Only the RTC could move an island from Canada's Maritime Provinces to California, and back to Canada, with a couple of strokes on a computer keyboard."

Working out of Kansas City, I was assigned to work a number of projects in Oklahoma, where I got to visit a number of my old haunts from my assistant bank examiner days in Oklahoma. One of the RTC-OSM properties was the Abundant Life Building in Tulsa. It was on Boston Avenue and I passed it when every day I went to our examiners' office in the National Bank of Tulsa Building. In 1961-1962 it appeared to me to be fairly new. A gleaming white edifice, decorated with gold colored diamond shapes. The building had no windows I could see. I had never heard of Reverend Roberts or his vision for the building.

From the name, *Abundant Life Building,* I assumed it to be the headquarters for a life insurance company. By 1994, when I encountered it again, it was now real estate owned by the subsidiary of one of our failed S&L's based in the Sooner State. My task was to do an inspection of the building and prepare a report and figure out what it would take resolve its problems. The main issue was it was loaded with poisonous asbestos. What RTC would need to do to sell it?

RTC had listed the building with a Tulsa realtor. I met Abigail Allison, the agent, for the grand tour. Ms. Allison showed up with a big flashlight, with a five-inch diameter lens, powered by four or five "D" batteries. The entryway consisted of double wide thick, perhaps bulletproof, glass doors. The *Abundant Life Building* evidently been unoccupied for a number of years. The first thing that caught my eye was a decorative plant rooted on the inside of the building in a planter was searching for moisture and sunlight. It had grown through the space between the right hand door several feet outside, jamming the right hand door shut.

Once inside the building, which except for the glass in the entryway, the lack of windows became foreboding. The place was dark and dank as a cave. My observation 33 years earlier had been correct; there were no windows. The furniture had all been removed, although there were miscellaneous pieces of junk scattered about. Since there was no electricity, we relied entirely on Abigail's giant flashlight. On the second floor, there was not even a skylight. It was mostly a large room and it was evident the roof had been leaking profusely in numerous places. A few minuscule shafts of light slipped through the porous ceiling. The place smelled musty from the water that had seeped in over the years. It was rather spooky and I began to suspect Abigail's choice of this extraordinary flashlight, might also be a potential defensive weapon. When the inspection tour was over; I was glad to get back into the sunlight. The place needed a roof. I thought some windows, and of course all the damning asbestos needed to be removed.

Asbestos contamination was of great concern and the RTC went to extraordinary lengths to remedy these problems. One of the properties that fell into the hands of one of our OSM corporations was a couple small vacant lots near Sapulpa, Oklahoma. The report we had was that someone had dumped an unquantified amount of asbestos material on the lot. I went and took a look at it. There wasn't much material there. It appeared to me that a half-ton pickup truck, would be more than sufficient to haul the asbestos to a sanitary landfill.

Instead of rounding up a local handy man with a pickup truck to haul the material away, RTC protocol required that we get some kind of a certified environmental contractor to do the work. This meant soliciting bids visa via RTC's contracting department. When I added up all the costs in my head it appeared to me that RTC could have purchased a fairly decent pickup with what it cost for hauling what amounted to pickup up load of asbestos to an approved dump site.

Another familiar place I returned to was Coweta, Oklahoma. What had been sleepy, poverty stricken community, was now a pleasant, if not thriving suburb of Tulsa. The First National Bank of Coweta was still in business, operating under its original 1912 charter name. Now it had both a respectable deposit base, about $25 Million vs. a mere million when I knew it back in 1961. Now it owned an attractive new red brick building, with drive-in windows and I'm pretty sure indoor plumbing, although I wasn't able to check it out. To me this was rather ironic, when in all the traumatic troubles in the oil based economy in the 1980s, all the major banks in Oklahoma, the sophisticated, "well managed" banks, were up to their eyebrows in bad loans and sought merger partners, and additional capital. Meanwhile, the little bank in Coweta continued to operate without assistance and even appeared to have prospered.

My mission to Coweta was a mobile home park, which was spawned by an S & L subsidiary that wanted to make money lending to folks to purchase mobile homes. One of the recommendations of the Federal Home Loan Bank Board was that S & Ls make "high yielding" loans.

Mobile home loans earn higher interest rates, because compared to a typical home they are flimsy in their construction and tend to depreciate rapidly. Moreover, the buyers of mobile homes are often folks with lower incomes and often less stable jobs. In short, they are a good deal more risky. Another problem I observed with mobile homes is just that, they are mobile and can be towed off to almost anywhere, which the lender discovers when the payments have stopped. The trailer home has been towed off to only God knows where and the lending institution gets stuck with a loss. Fortunately, in my banking career I only made perhaps a half dozen mobile home loans, but in the end regretted every one of them.

In the case of Coweta's mobile home park, I visited it and it was less than half occupied, which explained why the property was in the subsidiary's real estate portfolio. To find out what was going on, I visited some to the occupants of the homes. One pear shaped, plump lady dressed in an unflattering faded green housedress greeted pleasantly me, while holding a tight leash on a huge brown and black Mastiff dog. The dog didn't growl, but seemed to look me over like I might be some kind of a doggie Blue Plate Special. With Mrs. Greenhousedress reining the dog in with both hands, I let the massive Mastiff dog take a good sniff.

He must have smelled our dog, Charlie P. Pomeranian, because at that point he figured out I was a *Dog Person*, and began to lick me like I was his long lost benefactor. The enormous dog sat down quietly, Mrs., Greenhousedress, said, "Well, I'll be damned."

Then she proceeded to unload all of her grievances with the corporation that is the S & L subsidiary, that she had been leasing the mobile home parking space from. The place was unkempt, with weeds all over the place. The sewage line was troublesome and she ended up hiring a plumber, in cooperation with a few of the remaining tenants to resolve the problem. The subsidiary never honored the bill, but the mobile home park residents chipped in and made the obligation good. Other residents repeated her grievances. Obviously, RTC need to clean up the place and find a buyer for the Coweta Mobile Home Park.

Traveling was a major part of my duties. When RTC intervened in an institution, we from OSM traveled to take charge of its subsidiary corporations. I spent a considerable amount of time traveling to airports in taxicabs, in airports and of course flying on airliners. One of the interesting facets of this routine was the men I found driving cabs. Out of Minneapolis I arranged for my Monday morning ride to the airport with Airport Taxi. They were always on time in their maroon, rejuvenated former Minnesota Highway Patrol cars. A couple of the drivers were memorable. One gentlemen, who I rode with frequently, had an excellent stereo system in his car. Playing softly was soothing classical piano music from Debussy, Rachmaninoff, or Mozart. Talking to the cabby, I learned that he was a music studies graduate, but had been unable to find work either as a musician or teaching music. It was at a time of high unemployment in the country.

Another cab driver I encountered was a recent graduate civil engineer, named Albert. He lamented about his inability to find work in his chosen profession. I suggested that he try contacting one of RTC's environmental contractors, which because of the work RTC was placing with them, needed civil-environmental engineers. I gave him one of my business cards, with the name of my contact at the engineering firm.

A few weeks later on a Friday evening, when I returned from one of my many RTC excursions, while I was waiting for a cab to take me home, I heard, "Mr. Harris, Mr. Harris,"

It was Albert. He said, "Mr. Harris, thank you, so much. Your friend hired me. I start Monday."

It seems to me the people in Washington could learn as much by listening to cab drivers as they do from economists. Every economist has a different idea, theory, or solution, since it is hardly an exact science. This was brought home to me in a resounding way, when I was working with a mortgage servicing subsidiary of another Oklahoma failed S & L.

The mortgage servicing business is one I was familiar with, since at The First National Bank of Greybull, we originated home loans and sold them either to savings and loans in other states wishing to geographically diversify their portfolios, or to Fannie Mae or Freddie Mac. What this requires is very good clerical people, who pay close attention to detail and conscientiously work towards accurately processing customers loan payments. The typical servicing portfolio can be profitable with one half of a percent service fee. It works like this: if the customer pays 7-½ % interest, the servicer earns half a percent and the mortgage holder receives the remaining 7%.

I was talking on the phone to the president of one of these mortgage servicers and the guy proceeds to tell me the company is losing money. I asked, "What kind of a service fee are you collecting?"

To my astonishment, he replied, "we're getting 3/4% of a percent."

I responded. "Many servicers earn a nice profit with only half a percent."

He replied. "Well, I'm an economist, P.H.D. in fact, and I don't see how they do it."

I said, "Ah ha, I think I see the problem, you're a theoretical guy. Mortgage servicing is grunt, detail, clerical work. The last thing it needs is a P.H.D. in economics running it. It just needs good, conscientious, people, who can keep the payments and their applications straight."

He hung up the phone. I did some more checking into his mortgage servicer's numbers. All the work was being accomplished by the line people. The economist's salary was superfluous; the profit was all going into his pocket. I'll bet he never processed a single payment and was most likely an unemployable relative of one of the institution's principal officers or directors.

As an economy move, Richard Palmiter, one of the guys, whom I rode back and forth from Kansas City and the Twin Cities and I decided to share an apartment at the Casa Loma. It was, a 1920s era apartment house across the street from 4900 Main Street, where RTC offices were located. It faced on Ward Parkway; which paralleled Brush Creek. Across the creek was the *Plaza,* a 1920's era Art Deco shopping area that had been maintained and refurbished. It was and is one of Kansas City's trendy shopping spots. Best of all it had a number of truly excellent restaurants.

Richard's and my birthdays are just two days apart and with two people The Park Plaza Restaurant gave a free dinner to the birthday person, when accompanied by a friend. Those first weeks of August we ate high on the hog.

More often than not the Minneapolis guys and gals would rent a van or a car for our weekend treks home, which saved wear and tear on our own vehicles. Although sometimes we would use our own cars. At the time I owned a 1982 Ford Mustang, with a souped-up engine. It was the hotrod, I wanted to build in my youth but never could afford to build.

The Mustang had a bored out 302 V-8 engine with a California Highway Patrol Pursuit Car camshaft, 600 cfm Holley four barrel carburetor mounted on an Offenhauser manifold. It cranked out about 300 horsepower and at least theoretically could do 150 mph. It required a light touch on the accelerator, especially under winter driving conditions.

Normally, on the Minneapolis-Kansas City trips we would stop once in Des Moines, Iowa for fuel and grab something to eat. On one memorable trip, the roads were snow packed and I had driven the first leg of the journey. Richard then took the wheel. Going through Des Moines on I-35, the fast lane was snow packed, but slow lane appeared snow free. It was not.

The pavement turned out to be very slippery black ice. As Richard changed lanes, he touched the gas pedal ever so gently. The Mustang turned 90 degrees and we went sailing between two light posts, like we were going for a field goal in a football game. Over the embankment we flew coming to a stop three quarters of the way down the deep snow covered hill. It happened so quickly, I just sat there in the front seat holding my hamburger in one hand and Coke in the other, without dropping my burger or spilling my drink. The engine stalled, but restarted easily.

While we were contemplating what to do next, a grey Chevy Suburban appeared below us. The driver got out and walked up to us and said, "Are you guys okay?"

Richard rolled down the window and said, "We're fine. Just wondering, how we get out of here?"

The man replied, "I saw you fly between those two light posts. Wow, were you guys lucky! Listen if you can get the Mustang the rest of the way down the hill, I've got four-wheel-drive and I can make a path for you to get back on the Interstate."

Richard and I had never left our seats. Richard shifted into low gear, let out the clutch and with the help of gravity and the incline, the car plowed forward through the snow, down the slope to the road the gentleman in the Suburban had made for us. If anyone had called the police, we didn't know about it. We were long gone by the time they might have arrived.

As was typical we talked about everything that might have popped into our heads. Richard, whose expertise was working out problem real estate situations related an amusing story. The wintery snow covered landscape caused him to recall the following story.

One sunny winter's day he was working on disposing of a partially occupied apartment building in Edina, a Minneapolis suburb. Inspecting the property on a sunny winter day, he and a colleague entered what was supposed to be an empty unit. They noticed the French Doors to the third story balcony was ajar. Richard's associate went over to latch the door and looked out and saw, a lovely dark haired, totally naked woman out there taking in the winter rays of sun, calmly, as if this were an everyday occurrence. The temperature was below freezing. With no effort to cover up, she explained her boyfriend was coming back and resided elsewhere in the building. Richard remarked had the door been locked she could have been marooned and ultimately frozen to death.

Other than the stories we shared, the rest of the trip was uneventful. Richard and I arrived at the Casa Loma pretty much at our expected time.

Most of my trips for OSM were made flying out of Kansas City. I made various trips to Texas, Cleveland, Ohio, Washington, D.C. and Chicago, Illinois. The trip to Chicago was in itself pretty routine, but for me the most memorable part was restaurant, across the street from Irving Park Federal S&L. The place was called Cas and Lou's and the bistro had an ambiance right out of Mario Puzo's novel, *The Godfather.*

The cashier and greeter was a friendly, plump, little, grey haired Italian lady, everyone in the place called her Mama. Her ruddy sons, were the waiters and we understood cooked too. Unlike most restaurants, the dining room was carved up into little booths. It was easy to picture Mafia chieftains in a clandestine meeting, plotting their next whack job in one of these booths. The food was excellent and we frequently ate lunch here. We learned the place had been there since the 1920s and indeed had been a meeting spot for underworld characters.

One of my duties was to assemble the data on the status on the hundreds of subsidiary corporations we were charged with terminating. Then I would submit a report to the RTC/FDIC headquarters in Washington. Due to our office in Kansas City's efficiency, we were leading the nation in sub-corporation terminations. As a result of this achievement, I gained the nickname, "The Terminator." I accepted the moniker, with apologies to actor Arnold Schwarzenegger.

Another part of the job was dealing with lawyers. Westland Federal in Rawlins, Wyoming, the institution I have brought into receivership had a couple of subsidiaries, which by the time RTC closed Westland down were dormant and devoid of assets. Rosemary Lorenzo, one of RTC's attorney called me and asked, what I was doing about terminating the corporate life of the two Westland Federal subsidiary corporations. I said, "Rosemary, we don't need to do anything, under Wyoming law, if we fail to file the corporate report and pay the annual fee to the Secretary of State's office, the state will can automatically cancel the corporate charter. I recommend, we just let it die."

Rosemary said, "Bert that sounds too easy. I'll call a Wyoming attorney."

I replied, "Suit yourself."

Rosemary called back the following day to tell me the attorney in Lander, Wyoming she talked to told her she would call her back, once he had researched it. A week later, Rosemary called back and said, "The lawyer in Lander, after researching it agreed with you. We just need to let it die by not filing the annual reports. How come you knew the Wyoming law better than the attorney?"

I said, "Well after spending 29 years in Wyoming and working with numerous Wyoming chartered corporations there, I learned most of the basics of the state's corporate statutes."

As RTC began to wind down, RTC management desired to help us find new careers. They had all of us take the *Myers-Briggs Test.* This is a test that quizzes the takers on their interests and comes up with a conclusion as to the occupation the test taker is best suited for psychologically. Along with everyone else in the Kansas City Office, I took the test. In a week or so the results were back and the lady from personnel called me into give me my results. She said, "Tis is interesting, according to the test you are psychologically best qualified to be a career Navy or Army officer."

I responded, "Now they tell me, I am 56 years old, I can't imagine I could even get in any branch of the military at this time in my life."

Most of us were scurrying around trying to find jobs. One of my colleagues, Oklahoman, Bob Brown, who I knew from some of our evening get-social events had an interview in Oklahoma City, for U.S. Government position. The interview was to take place at the Murrah Federal Office Building on Robinson Avenue downtown. Bob's appointment was a 9:00 AM. Unfortunately, he thought at the moment, he was running late and couldn't find a parking place. Finally, after much searching he found a spot three blocks away. As he walked to the Murrah building, he heard a tremendous KABOOM, and then the sounds of much of the building crashing down. When he walked the remaining couple of blocks to his appointment. He heard the sirens of various police cars, ambulances, and fire engines, all head in the direction Bob was headed. Within a block he could see the emergency vehicles with their flashing lights arriving on the scene. Upon arrival, he asked the first policeman he saw, "Is there any way I can help?"

The cop said, "Mister, the best thing you can do now is stay the hell out of the way, unless you're a doctor or an emergency medical technician."

Bob said, "Sorry, I was just headed for an appointment in the building."

When Bob Brown returned to Kansas City, commented that, "It was the one time in my life that I was thankful to be late for an appointment."

By the spring of 1995, all of us from the outlying offices knew we would be out of a job and began to scramble to find new employment. Like everyone else I sent out numerous resumes. One of them, placed by the McGladrey, Pullen firm in Duluth, Minnesota responded and asked I call them to set up for a personal interview. At this point I didn't know who the potential employer might be. I arranged the meet Ken Buck at their firm's office in Duluth and arranged for a couple of days leave for the interview.

Mr. Buck, was the "head hunter" for the accounting firms executive search unit. Ken and I hit it off well and he said, "John Peyton, the president and principal stockholder of The Pioneer National Bank will be interested in your experience and I'm confident would like to meet you in person."

I told Ken Buck, "I'm very interested, this position is exactly the kind of job I'm seeking."

The job was as executive vice president and chief operating officer of the bank. Mr. Peyton had recently recovered from a kind of stomach cancer and wanted to not be less involved in the day-to-day operations of the bank. In short, he was looking for someone with years of banking leadership and administrative experience. He also liked that I had a great deal of experience making SBA, government guaranteed loans, which was one of my fortes in both Greybull and Glenrock. The downside of the bank was that Mr. Peyton, owned virtually all the bank's shares except for a few outside directors who only owned minimal investments to qualify as directors. A stock option plan would be out of the question.

Meetings with John Peyton and the board were arranged. My meeting with John Peyton went smoothly. Next, I was to meet the board at

Duluth's famous Gitchy Gummi Club, named after the Indian name for Lake Superior. Duluth is at the extreme western end of the largest of the Great Lakes. The "Gitch," as it is referred to locally, is very much like an old fashioned English men's only club. The building itself must have been built early in the century and was in a classic English Tudor style.

The meeting with the entire board, was a bit daunting for me and although I usually am fairly calm in interview situations, I was nervous. I kept harkening back to dealing with, in particular with Dick Sedar at the Glenrock bank. I did feel like Ken Buck was in my corner, when he told me, "Bert, just be yourself, answer the questions. A couple of your stories will illustrate your qualifications, personality and ability. You'll do Okay."

I must have been in there for an hour or more. The board was quiet didn't have many questions. Mr. Peyton pretty well dominated the questioning, but they were fair questions requiring only an honest straight answer. After the meeting, Ken Buck walked me out to my car. I said, "Well, how did I do?"

Ken said, "I'm betting they'll offer you the job. You were one of the two finalists. The other guy was from Norwest (now Wells Fargo). He talked for fifteen minutes, but it seemed like an hour. With you on the other hand they were enthralled. You talked for over an hour, but it went by like fifteen minutes. I'm pretty confident they'll make you a nice offer."

After the meeting I went back to Kansas City to tie up the loose ends at OSM. It was time to reflect on the RTC experience. Even though there were some things, I didn't agree, or understand about how the RTC/FDIC went about things, on the whole the net effect was a job well done and the taxpayers it seems were treated well.

As the RTC began its work, the estimate was this S & L clean up would cost $250 Billion. I hesitate to call it a bailout since the government was merely honor its commitment to the depositors of those failed institutions. When all the receiverships were resolved the cost to the national treasury was $125 Billion. This is in spite of some in the media projecting the cost would run to $500 Billion. All in all I was proud to have been a part of this and made a contribution by my efforts of several million dollars.

Twenty Nine

Pioneering

By the Fourth of July weekend 1995, all of us from the Minnesota delegation to the Kansas City RTC were back home looking for work. Although my interviews for the job at Pioneer National Bank in Duluth had been a month earlier, I still hadn't heard anything from them. I called Ken Buck and he said, "Bert, you are still in the running. Hang in there."

In the meantime, Richard Palmiter called me and said, "Hey, GMAC's mortgage banking unit is looking for some temporary guys to do loan document review. They're located in Bloomington. The hours are odd, noon to 9:00 PM. But what the heck it will give us the morning to look for a more permanent position. The pay is decent and best of all they're looking for guys with our kind of experience."

I replied, "Sounds good to me. I hate being on unemployment. I'll apply."

Both of us were hired on the spot. Since it was summertime, most days we enjoyed our supper break in a tree-covered park on Hyland Lake. Reviewing loan files is perfunctory work, but it turned out to have a few flashes of interest. The reason for the odd hours was the mortgage documents we were reviewing were all jumbo (Over $500,000) loans originated in California. Many of the loans were to various Hollywood celebrities, who for reasons of personal privacy, I cannot reveal the names. It was look into the lifestyles of the rich and famous. Sadly, too many of these folks who were earning millions, were also in debt up to their eyeballs.

When I returned home one evening, Jo said, "You got a letter from the Pioneer Bank in Duluth."

Expecting a rejection, I tentatively opened the letter. To my surprise it was a letter offering me the position of Executive Vice President and Chief Operating Officer. The salary was substantially more than I had been earning at RTC and while I had asked for a three week vacation, they offered me four. I was elated and immediately phoned my acceptance.

I started my new job the first of September and received a warm welcome from John Peyton, the president along with the rest of his staff. My new office was next to Jeannie, the Executive Secretary who I was to share with Mr. Peyton.

As the job at Pioneer was unexpected good fortune, we were not totally prepared to move to Duluth. We had started a major expansion project on our home on Dartford Road in Woodbury, which we had started 15 months earlier. The project involved adding 1000 square feet of living space to our house as well as enlarging the garage. With the help of our nephew, Greg Breault, I had done most of the construction work myself, working on weekends and vacation days. At the time the offer came through from Pioneer we were closed in, but much of the finished detail work was yet to be accomplished.

For the first month I stayed at Manor on the Creek, a bed and breakfast facility in Duluth that had comfortable rooms and an excellent gourmet dining facility. I commuted home to Woodbury to paint and pound nails on weekends. Jo continued working at 3M and was on a fast track to greater responsibilities in the Human Resources Department. I found a basement apartment in an elegant old house on London Road. The place had its own private entrance and best of all looked right out on Lake Superior. I had a great view during daylight hours of the great ore ships going in and out of the Port of Duluth. The great disadvantage to the place became apparent when the snow started to fly. Duluth being on the shore of Lake Superior gets "Lake Effect" snowstorms. That winter it snowed a total of 134 inches.

One morning I woke up, dressed and was ready to go to work. We had a huge snowstorm the night before and I could barely find my car for it was well buried under the snow. London Road is one of Duluth's main arteries and was plowed by the city's efficient crew. Although my car started easily enough, the driveway exodus to London Road was buried under over six feet of snow. Without even a snow shovel, I had no way of getting out and off to work until the landlord's snow removal folks arrived. I called Jeanne and let her know my predicament. It was well into the afternoon before I could get out of the driveway.

My routine became to travel home to Woodbury on weekends leaving midafternoon on Fridays. The roads were frequently sloppy as the Minnesota Highway Department salted the roads. As a result my car, a 1989 Mercury, a synthesized woody, station wagon which served as a truck during frequent trips to the lumberyard on weekends, was white from the salt. I named it *Margarita* in honor of its frequent brine coating. The house project in Woodbury was completed just in time for daughter Juli's high school graduation party and we put it on the market.

In the meantime, Jo and I had spent a number of weekends in Duluth looking for a suitable home. Both Jo and I have always loved fine old homes. There were many wonderful such houses in Duluth. Jo had the idea that we should buy a property, suitable to make into a Bed and Breakfast. The first such house was located on what Duluthians call the eastside of town. True east from the center of the city would put you right into Lake Superior, which was not where we wanted to be. Jo and I put together a business plan but in the end decided to opt for more modest quarters.

I settled into my new duties at Pioneer Bank and enjoyed it from the very first day. It soon became apparent John was very well organized. His management style was that on a typical day he would arrive about 9:00, look over the mail, and visit with selected members of the staff. Shortly, before noon he would go out for lunch and frequently not come back until the following day. The bank was devoid of any major problems and the various departmental people were highly competent. It was a well-managed institution, with an exceptionally clean loan portfolio.

I spent some time with every staff member and things were under tight control, but not to the point of being oppressive. There we two ladies I especially recall Dee, a slender petite gal who assisted customers with their deposit accounting problems. Then there was Dee Dee Westerman, a large framed, buxom woman who the bank's auditor. I had no problem keeping those two people separated in my mind despite the similarity in names.

I particularly liked the lending personnel, Steve Schnaberger, Don Pykonan and Ross Peterson who managed the bank's only branch at the Miller Hill Mall, which was located about five miles from the main office in west Duluth. The bank had no presence downtown, but was in the process of opening on the east side in the Mount Royal Area, which was one of the better residential neighborhoods. Our largest competitors consisted of Norwest Bank (now Wells Fargo) and First Bank, which is now called U S Bank. There were also three other independent banks and Twin City Federal Savings and Loan (TCF); later they converted to a commercial bank with a National charter and are now called TCF Bank, National Association.

John liked to say First Bank was his favorite bank because Pioneer derived many new clients from their disgruntled clients. First Bank was very impersonal, as was Norwest to a lesser extent. Both mega competitors had derogatory monikers like: *First Arrogant Bank and Norworst.* Pioneer's ability to attract new customers from their ranks became especially apparent one day when Steve and I attended a business fair at the DECC, Duluth's community events center. A couple of young men approached us and asked, "Do you guys make SBA loans?"

Since this was the main interest John Peyton had in hiring me, I replied, "You bet, we were very interested. What are you needing to finance?"

The taller of the two men said, "My uncle owns a bar at the Fitzger's Complex, but is wanting to retire. I've worked there for the past eight years and manage it if Uncle is taking some time off. Gene here has worked at the bar for nearly as long as me."

Steve said, "We're very interested in working with you. Why don't you come into the bank tomorrow morning, with your documents and we'll see what we can put together."

The following morning they were at the bank with a complete package of financial statements, business plan, business and personal income tax returns. Their application was very complete; it was obvious they had done their homework. Gene said, "We put this package together for Norwest. They said it would take two weeks to get in-bank approval, before shipping it off to SBA for their okay. How long will it take you guys?"

Steve and I had looked over the package. It was evident that the cash flow was more than adequate to make the payments and they had a parcel of rural real estate offered as extra collateral, plus the guys had a 30% cash equity injection in the project. Smiling Steve and I looked at each other and I said, "We just approved it."

It was obvious that small business loans were Pioneer's niche. In this case we were able to obtain SBA approval and book the loan before Norwest was able to get back to the customers with their answer. Of course all loan applications are not as clean as this one and sometimes even after the most careful underwriting customers fall on difficult times and it is necessary to reset the payments or take other actions. One such case was Ralph's Auto Body Shop.

Ralph's had been profitable for a number of years, even to the point of having to pay substantial income taxes. Then, he started losing money. Ralph was struggling to make his SBA loan payments. I called on him at his body shop and he seemed busy. I asked Ralph, "What do you see as the problem?"

"Well," Ralph replied, "I was making a lot of money, but paying a bunch of taxes, so I changed accountants. She made a number of recommendations, which I followed. I'm not paying any taxes, but cash flow has become tight and that's why I'm behind with you."

I said, "Ralph, saving on taxes is all well and good but you still needed to make a profit. Let me see if I can find a SCORE counselor for you and perhaps they'll be able to help you figure something out a solution. Kinda like keeping your cake and eating it too."

I called the SBA office in Minneapolis and to my surprise I learned the local SCORE (Service Corps of Retired Executives) had disbanded. I sat down with Ralph and acted as his counselor and we were able to get him back on a profitable course. It turned out his accountant had him burning cash needlessly in the name of saving money on taxes and ignored his need to be profitable to meet all his obligations.

The Duluth Chamber of Commerce put together a business symposium for its members, also at the DECC. I happened to sit next to Ed Daum, the Director of Minnesota SBA local office. I commented to Ed that I was surprised and disappointed that there wasn't an SCORE Chapter in Duluth. I said to Ed, "When I was in Wyoming and running a bank, we frequently used SCORE counselors and with great success."

I told him a couple of my SBA stories, which I have previously shared with the reader. Ed then turned to me and said, "Why don't you start a chapter in Duluth. I can see one is definitely needed here."

I replied, "I'll have to talk it over with my boss, John Peyton, as it will obviously be a commitment of some of my time."

First, I talked about it with Jo, who by this time had settled into our new home in Duluth, a stately three-story house old house, situated on a large lot surrounded birch trees. It was built in 1914, by a "mini lumber baron." We called the place "Birch Tree Hollow." Jo volunteered to do all the administrative duties, which meant I could limit my time to presiding at periodic meetings and perhaps a counseling session every month. I explained to John that by Jo doing the administrative piece of the SCORE chapter establishment it would take little time away from my duties at Pioneer Bank. John was okay with this proposal.

John felt and I agreed with him that it was important that I be a participant in community affairs. He sponsored me as a member of his Rotary Club. This was the old Rotary Charter #25 club established in 1911 and met downtown at the Radisson Hotel; the club had something like 250 members. This was in sharp contrast to the Rotary Club of Greybull, which had something like 20 members. I was also asked to join the board of the Duluth Community Theater. At a social function, I had let slip that I had done some acting at Boulder High School as well as at Colorado State University.

That fall they produced a play about the sinking of the ore ship *The Edmund Fitzgerald* which sank in a ferocious storm on Lake Superior November 10, 1975. Gordon Lightfoot made it famous with his song, *The Sinking of the Edmund Fitzgerald.*

I happened to mention this to Ken Buck and learned that his dad was the regular captain of the *Edmund Fitzgerald.* I was fascinated by Ken's dad's knowledge of the affair the killed all 19 men aboard her. According to the senior Mr. Buck, the skipper that fateful night was in a hurry to get launched and failed to batten down the hatches covering the cargo. Once the ship got out into the lake the storm had become violent and the crew was unable to secure the hatches, which took on excessive amounts of water and caused the ship to sink. Again Captain Buck's opinion was the master on *The Edmund Fitzgerald* on that stormy night was sloppy in his ways and never should have left port without the cargo covers being fastened securely.

One of my other community activities was to write a column in the warm, fuzzy newspaper, *Twin Ports People.* My piece was called Banking Issues and featured stories about how the Federal Reserve operated and other topics to relate banking to the general public. At the top of my articles was photo of myself and as a result people would often recognize me on the street and comment on the latest article.

So I became quite recognizable to people in the community. One day, I was wearing a black suit and fairly somber tie. A gentleman came up to me and said, "Reverend, I really appreciated the nice tribute you made at old Arthur Horton's funeral this morning."

I was flabbergasted to say the least since I never, ever dreamed of being mistaken for a minister of the Lord and didn't know the late Mr. Horton. I replied, "Thank you, glad you enjoyed it." And quickly crossed Superior Avenue on my appointment.

In every banker's life there come once or twice a year from bank examiners. Pioneer was a well-run institution, so we had nothing to fear from the National Bank Examiner's periodic visits. On this particular there were only a handful of delinquent consumer loans and perhaps one or two modest sized commercial credits for the examiners to complain about. Steve and Don had these situations under good control. So I was surprised when the examiner wanted to talk about our loan policy. I had never looked it over and since the bank was operating smoothly enough it never seemed worthy of my diverting from my pursuit of SBA loans to study the problem.

The examiner said, "This policy of your bank is obviously copied from a much larger bank. As a matter of fact, it was the policy Steve and Don, both First Bank veterans had come up with, from the time when the bank apparently had no written policy. The examiner said, "It looks like a copy of First Bank's policy." I later confirmed with Steve and Don that this is exactly what it was, word for word, a copy of First Bank's policy.

The examiner said, "This policy had hardly anything with Pioneer's customers."

When I read it over I saw the examiner was absolutely correct. Reflecting further on it I had to agree with him. There were pages of gobble-de-gook about lending to large companies traded on the New York Stock Exchange. As it turned out we did have one line of credit extended to Minnesota Power, which was based in Duluth. Given our small commitment to them, to my knowledge they had never drawn on, John explained that he thought Minnesota Power had asked for the accommodation as a goodwill gesture rather than any need.

I don't recall if the examiners actually wrote us up for this minor infraction, since the quality of the bank's loan portfolio was very good and the written policy was irrelevant as compared with the actual loans being written. It seemed to me the problem was easy enough fix, so I set about rewriting the policy that made, since when considering the nature of our customers' lending requirements. This took some time and I was again diverted from the pursuit of SBA loans.

For months I worked on developing SBA loans, but not every situation is a good fit for an SBA loan and often they take months to develop. My relationship with John Peyton was very cordial for the first twelve months. However, when I returned from a two week vacation the end of August to attend my son, Oliver's wedding in Laramie, Wyoming, where he had just graduated from the University of Wyoming with a degree in Electrical Engineering, John seemed a bit frosty towards me.

On October 31st, 1996, John joined with Jerry Sweetnam called me in the conference room and I was informed that he was letting me go. The reason given was that I hadn't produced, that is booked $1,000,000 in SBA loans, the fees for origination and servicing loans sold in the secondary market would largely pay my salary. I said, "I realize that I haven't booked the million in loans you are looking for, but I seven in the pipeline, and hopefully will develop the volume and income you desire. As nearly as I can tell, I have been well received in the community."

John, however, was adamant; I was gone. John left the room and Jerry said, "John, will pay you a month's salary severance and buy your house for what you paid for it if you wish."

That of course cushioned the blow considerably, but I never the less felt like a damned fool for having taken the job in the first place. Jo had given up an excellent position at 3M and taken a buyout, Juli was enrolled at Superior College in Duluth, and of course we had bought a home that in many respects was the home we had always dreamed of. I was devastated.

As I drove home I noticed a steel structure where one exits I-35 on to Superior Street. The thought flashed through my mind, "If I hit that thing at say 70 miles an hour, I wouldn't have to come home and face Jo and Juli."

Jo was of course very angry and I can't say I blamed her. My resume was beginning to look like I was incompetent and couldn't hold a job. At age 58 I was unemployed, I looked around for something in Duluth, as despite the cold winters, I really enjoyed the people and the community in general and was thinking if I could land something locally Jo would get keep the house we both enjoyed.

In Duluth, I did a bit of networking with the local independent banks and also with investment securities firms. I even applied for a position of CEO of a food company that produced and sold a line of jellies and preserves. The most promising interview was with Merrill Lynch. First they gave me a test to evaluation my knowledge of the investment securities. I scored something like 97% on the test. The guy administering the test was impressed but gave me some very valuable advice, "You will need to start out with a minimum of ten million dollars of accounts if you are maintain the income level you were enjoying at your most recent position."

I made calls to a number of people and only could come with up with half that amount, so on the gentleman's advice declined the offer and decide to pursue work in the Twin Cities. I called on Ed Daum, the district director of the Minnesota SBA office and gave him a copy of my resume. Ed already knew I was knowledgeable and experienced in SBA lending and at my time at Pioneer National Bank had developed a good working relationship with people in his office.

We spent Christmas in Duluth. The "Birch Tree Hollow" house was deep in snow by this time and a picturesque setting for Christmas festivities, but it was glum Christmas, with no real prospects at this point. Jo rented a condo in Woodbury and found a job at the Mortgage Banking subsidiary of Banc One in Bloomington, MN. I rented storage space to keep our furnishings and possessions in Duluth until I could land something.

I received a phone call during all this transition from Bruce Stewart, Vice President of the Bank of America (San Francisco) Community Banking

Division. He said, "I've been talking to Ed Daum to the SBA office in Minneapolis and he tells me you know SBA lending. We want to establish a loan production office in Minnesota; in fact we are doing this in all the major markets nationwide. Would you be interested?"

I practically yelled, "Yes!"

"Great, can you meet me at the Bank of America, Housing Division offices in Coon Rapids on Thursday at 1:00 PM?" Bruce said.

We met as scheduled and he said, "I'll need you to do a phone interview with Bob, my boss. I'd like to hire you. I'll set this up with Bob and get back with you with a time."

We shook hands, and couple of days later I talked with Bob and was offered the position of Government Loan Products Specialist.

Thirty

Life at a Really Big Bank

The first event in my life at the Bank of America was to visit the SBA underwriting office in Las Vegas, Nevada. Lesson number one was the Bank of America was highly compartmentalized. While the run of the mill 7-A SBA loans were processed in Las Vegas, I discovered there was another underwriting office in Sacramento, California that handled large 504 loans as well as numerous other U.S. government guaranteed loans including Farmers Home Administration Rural Development Loans and individual programs sponsored by various states.

The bank had a travel department that made all the arrangements for me. I was housed for the week at the MGM Grand in an elegant room, outfitted me with a rental car, as the office was several miles from the "strip" where casinos, restaurants, and hotels were to be found. The first day I was introduced to Gary, a local GLIP - that's Bank of America talk for Government Loan Product Specialist, which was my designation as well.

Gary grew up in Las Vegas, he explained his dad worked for United Air Lines. As we talked in the car driving down to the "strip," Gary made a sweeping gesture pointed to all the huge hotels and fancy casinos and said, "These magnificent edifices were not built by winners; they were all built on the backs of losers."

Gary and I spent the day make calls on a variety of small businesses, none of which involved directly in gaming, although even Subway sandwich shops in Las Vegas have slot machines. The following day I began to visit with various underwriters, starting with the unit leaders. One of the senior lenders was a guy named Dave. He looked at an application file on his desk, frowned and gasped, "How I hate startups!"

For me that set the tone of things around the B of A; they were not very interested in helping people start a new business, unless it was a really outstanding application. Dave explained to me that they did many restaurant loans, but they much preferred franchises like Subway and McDonald's, but would look at restaurants provided they were well capitalized and highly experienced management. It occurred to me that an Italian restaurant Steve Schnaberger had financed in Duluth as a direct loan because the highly experienced restaurateurs owners had a 50% cash injection, would have only been considered by my current employer as an SBA loan. Their food was excellent and I visited it on my periodic visits to Duluth. In spite of exceeding all the generally accepted standards for restaurant lending, they went broke, a poster child example of why restaurants are among the riskiest loans a lender can make.

I met most of the underwriters, with whom I would be working. First there was a gal, originally from a small community in Nebraska. It seems to me she told me her father was a community banker in that small town. I was hoping to develop some common ground with Jane, but soon found out why she was nicknamed, "Iron Jane." The moniker proved to be accurate, as she proved to be very stubborn and seemed more interested in turning down loans than granting approval. She consistently refused to call the clients to clarify points on the application and would blindly believe anything she read on a credit report.

Months later, in frustration with her obtuse attitude when she adamantly refused to talk to an applicant, I said, "Jane, tell me, do you get paid a bonus for every loan you decline?"

She shrieked, "No!"

That was obvious not the politic thing for me to do, but I was occasionally, able to specifically request another underwriter on deals I thought might be marginal. Another underwriter I met that first week was Brian Astle. By contrast, he and I discovered we had a mutual interest in flying and he had an uncle who had lived in Wyoming. Brian had a similar reputation as Iron Jane and was dubbed "Brian Asshole" by GLIPs in the field. I can't say this was my experience with him. Although a tough underwriter, he was always willing to talk to me and customers as well, not that I was always successful in getting him to my way of thinking.

The funny part of this story is many of the GLIPs routinely referred to him by his unflattering label. Once a newly appointed guy asked me, "Is Brian Asshole, really his name?"

Another underwriter I met that first week was Michael Jackson, not to be confused with the eccentric pop singer of the same name. Shortly after I signed on, underwriter Jackson was dismissed for, "inappropriate behavior involving a female employee." I can offer no details, but it was evidence that Bank of America would hold us to high moral and ethical standards.

The week in Las Vegas was an excellent introduction to the culture and lending policies at the Bank of America. Returning back to Minnesota, my office was to be a cube at the Bank of America Housing office in Coon Rapids, Minnesota. Bank of America Housing was a mobile-home lending unit. I thought to myself, I hope they were having a better experience than my own personal foray into mobile-home loans at Greybull and what I had seen with several S & L subsidiary corporations, which all seemed to turn up excessive volumes of bad paper.

Upon my return home, Bruce Stewart met with me for a day to outline his expectations and my territory, which were the states of Minnesota, North Dakota, South Dakota and I was authorized to do deals in Wisconsin too. The Bank's plan was to have an SBA loan production office in Wisconsin, but at the time they hired me they didn't have a GLIP in place. Bear in mind Bank of America had no depository, brick and mortar branches in any of the states I have mentioned.

The people at Bank of America Housing were cordial and I frequent took coffee or lunch breaks with them. Initially, I spent most of my time out of the office calling on community development companies (CDCs) in hopes of getting referrals. I had no business or banking connections, except at the local bank where I did my personal business. Therefore, most of my potential for business at first was up north in Duluth, since I was well acquainted with the half dozen CDCs in Duluth, plus numerous business owners, and many were friendly towards me. As a result I received a number of viable referrals from them.

The first lead was a couple I had talked to briefly just before I left Pioneer. Their project was on hold, I suppose because no one from Pioneer followed up on it. A redheaded gentleman, Donald Sorenson and his partner, girlfriend I suspect, Patricia Owens were interested in purchasing a bar across the St. Louis River in Superior, Wisconsin. Don, Patty, and I poured over the tax returns presented by the selling owner. They indicated mostly losses, or meager profits; certainly, there was not anything like enough cash flow to service the proposed debt.

"Don, Patty, I don't want to burst your bubble here, but this guy doesn't have what our underwriting people call 'verifiable cash flow.' By that I mean the Federal Income Tax Returns here just show losses or minuscule profits."

Don said, "The guy says he skims lots of money out of the place. Patty and I drove by his home and it's quite palatial. Hell, he just bought a new Corvette and his other car is a late model Cadillac Fleetwood."

"It is a known fact the bar business is largely a cash business and lends itself to skimming, but saying you are skimming wouldn't get you an SBA loan. Remember we are dealing with a tax hungry government's agency. It's pointless to submit even submit this application." I said.

A couple of weeks went by and Don called me and said, "Patty and I have figured this thing out. We've been sitting in the bar at all hours drinking cokes and we know this guy is selling a lot of booze from his financials. Not only is the owner skimming, but we can see so are the employees too. If we can get this bought, we'd have to fire all of them. Old George has set a really bad example for them."

I asked, "Have you two made a comparison, between the liquor bought and drinks sold?"

Don laughed, "Oh yeah, if you compare the drinks sold, with the booze he expensed, he's only getting four or five, maybe six drinks out of a fifth of whiskey. According to our information on the bar business and experience, he should be getting about twenty drinks out of a fifth. You know Patty and I have both have worked and managed bars for years."

I replied, "Well we can try an application with that kind of detailed information. It seems logical for sure, but again I remind you the underwriters are looking for *verifiable cash flow*."

That happened on a Friday and over the weekend I thought I'd verify Don and Patty's concept with my father-in-law, Lloyd Breault, who had been a successful tavern operator in Hudson, Wisconsin for many years. Jo and I went over to visit her folks, as we frequently did. Lloyd had heart and back problems and was in declining health. He would have been about 86 years old at the time and was lying down on the couch, somewhat sedated from his medication. I told Lloyd the situation without reveal the confidential information as to names of either the applicant or the seller. I said, "Lloyd, according to the amount of whiskey the bar purchases as compared with what he sells he's only getting about five drinks out of a fifth bottle of hooch. Does that sound right to you?"

Lloyd sprang to an upright, sitting position, motioning with his fingers open about two inches, and said, "Oh, no a fifth should get you twenty drinks, and that's a nice full jigger of whiskey. That guy is conning the hell out of the IRS."

With that pronouncement, Lloyd laid down back down to his preferred horizontal position. And I had reliable verification of Don and Patty's contention. I inserted this anecdote in my analysis and the application to the underwriters in Las Vegas. In addition, I also pointed out the bar was one of the first one a thirsty person would see once on the Superior side of the bridge, reminding them that Wisconsin permits bars to be open on Sundays while Minnesota strictly forbids it. I wasn't too hopeful, because Dave, the lead underwriter told me that they decline about 80% of the loans submitted. This percentage gave rise to one of my fellow GLIPs to say, "Your odds are better at the casino gaming tables than at the Las Vegas Underwriting Center."

Fortunately, the research, well-documented projections, and otherwise strong application allowed me to get this deal approved. It was shortly after the loan had been approved, I received a call from a young lady in the Las Vegas office's document preparation section. She said with a clearly recognizable accent of black person, "I need the address you want me to send the loan documents to?"

I told her my office address, which was in Coon Rapids, Minnesota. She came unglued and said, "What kind of racist town is you in?"

I said, "You are misunderstanding the name. Coon Rapids refers to the numerous raccoons found inhabiting the town's site at the time the town was settled."

"Oh," she said, "that's better. Are there still RACOONS running around Minnesota?"

"Yes!" I replied, "In fact we used to frequently get them in our yard. Last winter we had an especially big one, maybe 100 pounds worth, peering into our dining room from the back porch."

Since I have made some valuable contacts for the bank while volunteering as a SCORE counselor, I decided to check out the St. Paul SCORE Chapter. The first guy I met was George Emslie and he invited me to participate in one of the seminars put on by the chapter at Century College. This was the Financing Your Business Seminar and my task was talk about the issues lenders could be expected to talk about when applicants apply for a loan. George gave an insightful piece on accounting and financial records. He immediately started stuttering, smiled as he said, "People ask me if I have always stuttered? I tell them no, only since I started talking."

That brought a laugh and added some levity to an otherwise potentially dull subject. In addition to SCORE and the CDCs, I also contacted various economic development organizations. On one of my fairly frequent trips to Duluth, I called on John Pegg at Northstar Community Development Corporation. John said, "I have an interesting deal and I need a bank to work with me on this. The guy is Barry McFadden and he is terribly dyslexic, has tough time with math, and can't do a decent job of filling out a job application. Consequently, he has had a rough time getting a job among other things, resulting in long periods of unemployment."

I said, "I pretty well understand dyslexia. I have a daughter with the same problem, but from your description I don't think her's is nearly as severe. What are Barry's strengths? Why do we want to make him a loan?"

John replied, "As it happens, Barry is an excellent mechanic, because of the dyslexia he remembers how things he has taken apart go together, because he remembers things backwards. Barry wants to purchase a service business for industrial tractors, like forklifts and such. It is very physical work; the seller is getting older and has painful back problems. Barry has worked for him occasionally when he needs extra help. He is young, maybe 35, and in good health. Also, he strikes me as responsible and of good character."

Knowing the first thing the Las Vegas underwriters would look at would be his credit report, I asked, "What's he credit report like."

John said, "It looks like crap. That's due to his extended periods of unemployment. His total debts amount to about $8,000 and he has few assets, mostly tools and an old car. He could, I suppose take bankruptcy, but Barry insists he will get it all paid off if given a chance to make a decent living, after all it is not an insurmountable amount of debt. I like his attitude, integrity and the way he cares about his two children."

"Sounds like a tough deal to make work. How do you propose to structure it?" I inquired.

John smiled and said, "Here's the deal. The total financing will be $40,000 including $5,000 in working capital. We're looking for $20,000 from a bank lender in the form of an SBA loan. North Star will lend him $10,000 with a second lien and the equity piece will come from the State of Minnesota's Disabled Worker Grant Program. I've already cleared this with Paul Moe, the director."

I replied, "I'll give it a try; it sounds like the guy needs to be self-employed. Oh, by the way how does Barry deal with numbers? That's critical for anyone in business."

John Pegg replied, "Barry does fine as long as he has a pocket calculator. He'd be lost without, but is smart enough to know it and carries one with him at all times."

"Good, I'll remember to include that detail in my analysis." I said and sent the application off to underwriting in Las Vegas.

To my surprise Dave was willing to do the deal, in spite of the dismal credit report. But since the Bank of America is an SBA Preferred Lender, meaning they can approve their own deals, Dave said, "I want to run this by the Minneapolis SBA Office and get their concurrence. Bert, I'd like to have you hand deliver this to them. We can't afford to sacrifice our reputation and *Preferred* status on this deal. I want them on board too."

"Okay makes sense to me." I said and was on my way to Minneapolis as soon as I received the application package.

When I arrived at the SBA offices, which are housed in an office complex developed with in the walls of what once was an old warehouse. It has lots of open space and great wooden beams; the interior is architecturally an interesting, original and aesthetically appealing place. Upon arrival, I asked to see Ed Daum. Ed and I visited a few minutes and I had the opportunity to thank him for the referral to Bruce Stewart and recommendation that undoubtedly had a lot to do with my being employed by the Bank of America. Finally, Ed said, "I'd like to have you visit with Mark Latenschalger, he's one of my most experienced lenders."

Ed escorted me to a conference room, and Mark arrived a couple of minutes later. First, he looked at the credit report and frowned. I thought, "Oh nuts that is going to kill the deal, before we even get a discussion started." But to my surprise Mark kept on reading and his frown disappeared. Mark said, "I have a dyslectic cousin and I totally understand this guy's problems. Let me do a work up on this application and I'll see if I can find a way to do this deal."

I said, "Mark, I really appreciate your taking an understanding look at this deal."

Mark called me back a few days later and said, "I think I've figured out a strategy for approving Barry's application, but I need to have Barry have something at risk in the way of collateral. I don't see much on his balance sheet. See what you can come up with and call me."

I said, "There isn't much there, just his tools and an old car."

I relayed this to John Pegg and he replied, "As you know Barry is mechanic and has a pretty decent set of good quality mechanics tools, maybe worth a couple thousand dollar. His car is a 1965 Pontiac GTO, which he restored. It's a muscle car classic. I know he prizes it highly. I've seen it. It's a beauty and psychologically it would be good collateral. Maybe not the usual cash injection standard, but certainly something of value to him. Remember this guy has a lot of pride and this car is worth more than just dollars to him."

I provided a detailed list to Mark at SBA and a few days later we had their Okay to move forward. As I understand it Barry made a success of the business. Another of my Duluth contacts was John Eagleton, who operated a small manufacturing business at the Duluth Airport Industrial Park.

John's finances were pretty well in place, but I thought I'd like to network with him, in hopes he might have a lead for me, since he was active in the Duluth Chamber of Commerce and the business community in general. Upon my arrival we shook hands and John said, "I saw John Peyton the other day, guess what I told him?"

I replied, "I have no idea, what?"

John said, "I told him that letting you go was dumb, and what he should have done is retire and let you run the bank. Bert is very well liked in the business community."

I said, "You didn't."

He said, "I certainly, did. Then Mr. Peyton shook his head and walked away."

It was nice to know I was appreciated in the community. Another project I was working on was a multimillion dollar financing for a new facility for Northstar Ford, a Duluth car dealership. I was able to get this project approved by Sacramento underwriter Ken Galli, which was the start of one of the best underwriter relationships I had at Bank of America.

Just as I was getting accustomed to my office at Bank of America Housing, I learned from Bruce Stewart that the Bank had sold this unit to a finance company and I would be moving. Since the deal happened rather suddenly and I had to leave Coon Rapids right away, I would be working from home until something could be worked out. A few weeks later I was told I would have my office at France Place, an office building in Edina. My spot would be on a floor devoted to small one or two person offices. Telephone answering and receptionist service was provided by a pretty, perky young lady from Texas. Billie was slender and petite, with shiny black hair and sparkling blue eyes. Over the phone she had a soft, sexy, alluring voice, which charmed all the men she talked to. As a result she was bombarded with requests for a date. I doubt that she could have weighed more than 100 pounds dripping wet and therefore I was surprised when she responded to a wannabe lover, "Before this goes any further, you need to know I weigh 300 pounds."

After I stopped laughing, I asked Billie why she did that and she said, "I'm in a happy relationship and I'm not interested in these telephone jokers. It shuts them down every time."

By the time I moved my office to France Place I was developing some great leads. One of them was a bowling alley in one of the northern Twin City Suburbs. The applicants were a brother and sister, Patrick and Kelly O'Reilly. You could tell immediately that they were related; there was something about their eyes that only seemed half open. Kelly, an attractive brunette, her eyes made her look sexy, on Patrick it looked like he was always about to fall asleep. However, he was a very bright guy, sleepy he was not.

His sister, who had a charming personality, was experienced in mortgage banking and thought all of those standards and rules would be the same for commercial and SBA loans. While much of the application was quite adequate, other parts weren't precise enough or believable for our sophisticated and picky underwriters. The most vivid evidence of this was the financial statement of Robert Howard, the bowling alley manager, who the O'Reilly's wished to retain, as neither of them had any specialized experience in the bowling alley business. Patrick's background included ownership of a successful auto parts store and Kelly was versed in mortgage lending; she was also licensed as a real estate broker.

Mr. Howard's interest was to be a minor position. Patrick's thinking was to *give* him enough stock so he would want to stay with the business. Patrick was putting up all of the sizable cash injection and would be the controlling stockholder. The balance sheet Kelly helped Robert prepare showed $100,000 in household furnishings. Kelly explained, "If I don't jack up that figure, he would show a negative net worth."

I said, "Kelly, that household goods figure is wildly unrealistic. Robert tells me he has four rambunctious children. I have five kids myself and when they were growing up, there was no way our home's furniture could be worth even $10,000."

Kelly pouted a bit and said, "Patrick and I really want him to be a part of the ownership of the bowling alley. We don't want to be the day to day managers."

I replied, "I understand your motive. Let's approach it from a different perspective. Why don't we leave Robert off the ownership in the application? Show him being retained as manager; then award him the minority stock after the loan is booked and we don't have to show the underwriters his weak credit report and upside down balance sheet. They will like his management experience. We a have some underwriters that assume bad credit is somehow contagious. After all it doesn't change the $200,000 cash injection, which is entirely being furnished by Patrick."

I ran the idea past Patrick and he was okay with it and I sent in off to Ken Galli in Sacramento for approval. A week or so later the loan was approved as a 504 loan. Another loan, size-wise the opposite end of the scale was under the "SBA Express Program." The program is basically an unsecured line of credit up to $50,000. As a "product" they sold well and were easy to process.

The first Express Loan I sold was to the Mosher brothers who operated a small vending machine business. The sold candy bars, pop, and packaged snack foods. They had been in business for 15 years and had excellent credit. A few months after the Express loan was booked, I received a phone call from Andrew Mosher, "Bert, Charles and I would like to talk to you, would you meet us for lunch at the Perkins Restaurant near your office?"

Andrew said, "Charles and I have decided to sell a part of the vending machine route. We have a new soft drink vending business we are putting in a different group of locations. The equipment will mix a variety of healthful fruit and vegetable drinks, ideal for health clubs. The business has really caught fire and we can't keep up with it and don't want to hire help, so we've decided to sell the canned pop and candy route."

I said, "How can I help guys?"

Charles said, "We have a buyer, his name is Orville Germain. We think he'll do well. The specialized part of the business is the repair and maintenance of the vending machines. Currently, Orville is a maintenance man at a machine tool manufacture in Minneapolis. We can provide him training and guidance on the equipment maintenance. Orville says he has no banking connections, so we thought you would be willing to help him and us."

I said, "Sure I'll help him put together an application. If you'll give me a phone number, I'll get the ball rolling."

I gave Orville a phone call and set up a meeting. His application looked pretty good. Although I had seen a credit report Orville assured me it would be clean and he and his wife had never had credit problems. The one thing on the application that bothered me was he had no, specific experience in managing a vending machine business. I pointed out that the Mosher brothers had stated the tough part of the business was the repair and maintenance of the equipment. Charles Mosher made the point, "Any fool can drive around the round, pick up the money, and reload the machines with product. The difficult part is keeping the equipment operating smoothly."

I sent that the application into Las Vegas, and two weeks later, Brian Astle called me to tell me it had been rejected. "Brian," I asked, "was the credit report bad?"

Brian replied, "No it was very good, 780 to be exact. The problem is he has no management experience in the vending machine business."

I said, "Brian, I'd like you to reconsider this application. The vending machine business, with packaged goods like pop and candy bars is not rocket science. I beg you to reconsider this. This fellow is a good man. The tax returns show more than sufficient cash flow. In addition, to the equipment, Orville and his wife will give us a second mortgage on their home; they have an equity of more than the loan request."

Brain said, "Bert, you make a good argument, let me run it by Dave and I'll get right back to you."

The next morning, Brian called and said, "Dave went along with your argument. We'll do it."

I called Orville and let him know we had approval. A week later the documents arrived at my office and I set up a closing at Orville's suburban home. His wife, Marie, greeted me and offered me coffee and fresh oatmeal cookies and we started some friendly chatter. In the course of the conversation, Marie said. "Before we had children, I worked for Sandwich Express. We sold sandwiches and pop through vending machines. I was the manager for my location, they have several around the country."

"Damn!" I thought to myself, "If I had known this and included in the original application this deal would have been done much easier and sooner. Note to self, 'Have applicants include the management experience of spouses and others in applications."

A part of my territory was also North Dakota and South Dakota and I visited the SBA District Offices in those states and they were glad we were interested in doing deals in the Dakotas; I gathered that many banks in those states had only lukewarm interest in SBA lending. One of the leads from SBA was from the Olson family near Huron, South Dakota.

The Olsons operated a "PMU" farm; that stands for "Pregnant Mare Urine." While a PMU Farm sounds like it was more of an agricultural deal, it fit into a business category acceptable to the SBA since the harvested urine is used in the manufacturing of the menstrual drug Premarin. The application was to be for a facility to house the horses. The Olson's had small barn, which was not unlike a dairy barn. The mares were in stalls and fitted with a harness like apparatus to collect the urine, with a set of rubber tubes to a central collecting receptacle. Mr. Olson explained, "We prefer board large draft breeds like Clydesdales, Percherons, and Belgians, all are substantially bigger than the typical saddle horse breeds and naturally generate more pee."

Mr. Olson gave me a tour. They had 20 horses "on line," since it was time to let the animals out for a little exercise, Olson and his son released them from their harnesses. For an unexplainable reason, a giant, yet beautiful Clydesdale mare with her chestnut colored coat with big white legs and mane, took a liking to me and insisted on following me about the exercise corral, kind of like a puppy. Gently, affectionately, she nuzzled me. Yet in spite of her extraordinary size, I never felt threatened. Mr. Olson told me, she weighed about 2000 pounds. She followed me about the yard for 15 minutes until it was time to return to the barn.

Mrs. Olson invited me to join them for lunch and I gratefully accepted, as I was miles from a restaurant. Immediately, I noticed a *Scott's Stamp Catalogue* sitting on a coffee table. I said, "Someone must be a stamp collector?"

"That would be me," said Mr. Olson.

We talked stamps and we decided to do some stamp trading on my next visit. When I came back, we put the finishing touches on their application and did some mutually beneficial stamp trading. Over supper Mrs. Olson said, "I want to tell you a funny story about our business. We were over at the Grange Hall and this newcomer came up to me and introduced herself. 'Hi I'm Evelyn Reifschneider; we just bought the old Jensen farm and are just here getting acquainted. What do you folks do?'"

Mrs. Olson continued, "We have 20 horses on line. Evelyn said, I'm sorry. I'm not familiar with that expression, what do you mean?' I said we have 20 pregnant mares and collect their urine. Evelyn said, 'Why in the world would you do that?' I explained the urine of pregnant horses is used in the manufacture of the menstrual drug Premarin. Then she said, 'Do you mean I've been eating horse piss?' I told her, 'I'm afraid so.'"

We all started laughing and then Mrs. Olson pressed on. "Then Evelyn says, well I never felt better, so I guess I'll continue!"

Another interesting project was a hotel project on the banks of the Red River to be in Moorhead, Minnesota just across the river from Fargo, North Dakota. Although Moorhead had very few hotels or motels, it did have three colleges, which were desirous of hosting conventions and other events. Since the colleges were all within the per view of the University of Minnesota System in order to sponsor gatherings, the lodging facilities needed to be within the boundaries of the State of Minnesota. Never mind there were many very satisfactory facilities across the river in Fargo, a city more than twice the size of Moorhead.

The architect for the project was based in Fargo and I spent as much time working on the project in his office as the time on site in Moorhead. This loan would be a multi-million dollar 504 type and therefore I would again be working with Ken Galli, which I always liked, because Ken, unlike Iron Jane, was always looking for a way to do the loan, rather than turn it down. I called Ken and he said, "Well you know the way Bill, my boss, feels about hotel-motel loans. He got burned on something like 28 different projects, and I don't see him approving it, even if I do recommend it."

I asked, "Why did so many go wrong?"

Ken replied, "What happens is they start out doing well, consistent with the projections. Then a couple years later, a competing facility is built. It is bigger, newer, and fancier. Then the hotel we're financing starts having serious vacancy problems and we are forced to foreclose and always take a hit. The question gets down to why this project is disaster proof?"

I said, "Ken, I completely understand Bill's concerns, but there are several situations that makes this different. First it will be on City of Moorhead land with a 100-year lease. It will be on a prime location overlooking the scenic Red River that cannot be matched by a competitor. But best of all the City of Moorhead is willing to provide a partial financial guaranty. I believe their Moody's Bond Rating is Aa, better than the bank's A rating. It looks goof proof to me, since the City of Moorhead will have a vested interest and exercise some control to make sure it is paying Okay. And they will guarantee it to boot."

Ken said, "That does sound like a doable deal. Send it in and I'll run it by Bill and try to get this approved."

I sent the application in and a few weeks later Ken called me to say, "Bill is adamant, we are not doing any hostelry loans period. Nice try, Bert."

Not too long after that defeat, Bruce called me to tell me he was going to be in town and to plan on having lunch with him. I enjoyed visiting with Bruce and consequently was looking forward to a pleasant lunch. Bruce had apparently researched the restaurants close to my office and picked out an especially nice one. We sat down and Bruce ordered a bottle of red wine. I thought, "This is out of character for Bruce, who I had never seen imbibe during working hours." "What the hell is going on?" I said.

Bruce frowned and said, "This in an unpleasant task for me, but I have orders to close your loan production office. This is a part of the restructuring we are undergoing as a result of the merger with Nations Bank. As I told you earlier, they are buying us, and *they* are calling the shots. They don't want to do SBA loans in areas where they don't have depository branches. Have a glass of wine."

He filled my glass and I said, "I guess this means, I'm out of job again?"

Bruce replied, "Not necessarily, if you are willing to take a position elsewhere. I'd really like to keep you on my team. Incidentally, they are moving me from Chicago to Dallas. I guess the good news is the powers that be at Nations Bank like our SBA lending system and they'll merge their SBA group into our system rather than the other way around."

I asked, "Where does that leave me?"

Bruce replied, "We'll keep this office operational for a couple more months, so if you want to look for something locally, you'll have time to look around. But like I said, if you're open to a transfer, I can offer you some options."

As an afterthought, I asked, "What will happen to our illustrious chairman, Dave Coulter? I must confess, I rather like his humorous and insightful memos."

Bruce said, "As I understand it he will be out of a job. But don't feel too sorry for him, he gets a $30 Million buy for leaving."

We polished off the bottle of wine and the following morning I began another laborious job search. The year was 1999 and I had just turned 61 years old. With daughter Juli still in college and having no fortune on which to retire, I needed to work for a couple more years for sure.

Employers are forbidden to let an applicant's age color their decision about hiring a person. For example Wells Fargo, which had recently absorbed Norwest, which a couple of months earlier had taken over Eastern Heights Bank, which was owned by 3M and where I did my personal business ran an ad for an SBA salesperson. My credentials fit exactly what they were looking for if the ad was to be believed. Bank of America had trained me on the identical computer programs used by Wells Fargo.

I was not granted an interview and happened to meet the guy they hired, a young comparatively inexperienced guy with a dull personality and a weak handshake. My other forays into finding another job based in the Twin Cities were equally fruitless. I called Bruce after about six weeks and said, "Bruce, I really think I would like to stay with Bank of America. I have to say you folks have treated me well. What have you in mind?"

Bruce said, "Bert, I have three options for you, but all of course would involve a transfer. I could put you to work in sales in either Kansas City or in St. Louis. Or a third choice would be you moving to Las Vegas as they are looking for experienced underwriters; they'd love to have you."

I replied, "My wife is not interested in moving, but I wouldn't mind commuting to Kansas City. It is a six and a half hour drive, all on I-35. As you know I worked there for RTC and have a network of good friends there. Kansas City would work out well for me."

Bruce said, "Good, I'd like you to report to our offices in the Community Banking Division at 1200 Main Street in Kansas City at 8:00 on October first. They are on the fourth floor. I believe you met Diane Weir at our conference in Phoenix earlier this year. She also is a GLIP. The two of you will be covering western Missouri, Kansas, Oklahoma, and northwest Arkansas. Diane has been banking in K.C. for many years, so you'll be doing most of the out of the office work."

I said, "Bruce, I do remember Diane, but at this point can't tell you we are well-acquainted. I will report to Kansas City on the first. Thank you for this opportunity."

Thirty One

Last Stand in Kansas City

Upon arriving in Kansas City, I looked up my old examiner friend. Jerry Swords made an introduction for me to stay at the Kansas City Club. The club is an old-fashioned English style men's club as depicted in Sherlock Holmes Tales. In some ways I was reminded of the Gitchy Gummi Club in Duluth, but instead of being housed in an overgrown house, it was situated in a downtown 12- story building. They offered classy meals, nice rooms, indoor parking. My first weekend over in Kansas City, the Kansas City Club had a scotch tasting event with gentlemen in kilts serving great tasting whiskeys, including a more recent bottle of Queen Victoria's favorite; it was truly excellent.

Best of all the Kansas City Club was located just a couple of blocks from 1200 Main Street where Bank of America occupied several floors. This is where I would be working. The disadvantages were it was somewhat beyond my budget and I wouldn't be able to do my own meal preparation. However, it would do nicely until I could find a suitable apartment.

At the office I renewed my acquaintance with Diane Weir and was furnished a desk opposite hers. The Community Banking Unit consisted of Mike Grube and Scott Berghouse and Janell Thome, a secretary and administrative assistant, whose duties was primarily focused on Mike and Scott's community development projects. My duties were to assist the business bankers in various locations. One of my first projects was to work with

Gary Bradley, a business (sales) banker in Tulsa to obtain financing for a convenience store in a north Tulsa neighborhood. As it happened, Mike was working on a project in the same general neighborhood.

Since I was going to Tulsa anyway, Mike asked if I would take a few pictures for him of the shopping center located across the street from the housing project he was working on. Although it has been many years since I lived in Tulsa, I still had a decent feel for the local geography and realized it was only a couple of blocks from Bradley's customer's proposed convenience store. I called Gary Bradley on the phone. He spoke was a slow drawl and reminded me of my assistant examiner and friend in New Mexico, George Lowry. George's family owned the Clinton, Oklahoma Bank and Trust Company situated in 100 miles west of Oklahoma City. George's accent typified people who lived in what is often called the "Red Dirt Country."

I arrived at the Bank of America building in Tulsa, where Gary Bradley had asked me to meet him in the executive offices on the fifth floor. I sat down in the waiting room in anticipation of Gary's appearance. From his voice on the phone I had it in my mind that he would be a white person somewhat resembling my friend George Lowry. A tall, solidly built, well-dressed black gentleman arrived; I made no move towards him. Finally, the black gentleman spoke, "Would you perhaps be Bert Harris from Kansas City? I'm Gary Bradley."

Surprised and stunned, I said, "You are?"

He smiled and replied, "Yes, I am Gary Bradley."

We sat down on the brown leather couch and Gary outlined the project he wanted my help on. Then he said, "Mrs. Fernandez is expected at about 11:00 O'clock. Gary had already given Mrs. Fernandez the application and I looked it over in some detail. What struck me was in the management section she had written a lengthy elaboration of her career as a mortgage banker at Chase Manhattan Bank. Eloise Fernandez was a Senior Vice President and from her description it was evident she was very proud of her accomplishments at Chase.

I said to Ms. Fernandez, "I see you have had a successful career at Chase, but you haven't touch on your experience in running a convenience store. Our underwriters are very interested in your qualifications and abilities as it relates to the management of this store you wish to build and us to finance. My question to you is, what do you know about operating a convenience store?"

To my surprise and relief she said, "My family owns a string of eight "C" stores south of here. I worked there for eight years. You might say I grew up in the business."

"Eloise," I said. "Why didn't you put that in the management section of the application?"

She replied, "Well, you folks being bankers, I thought you would be more impressed with my financial industry background, like I was one of the guys. You know?"

"Eloise, I can see you are rightly proud of your accomplishments at Chase, but it has nothing to do with your ability to succeed and pay back a loan we are considering to make you for the construction and establishment of a convenience store. Let's rewrite the management piece and I think we might be able to qualify you for the requested financing." I said.

Gary was silently grinning through the whole conversation, but finally said, "Eloise, why don't you come down to my office and we'll make the necessary changes and get this off to the underwriter."

That afternoon I was off to Oklahoma City to meet with Terri Gentry, our local business banker. Bank of America's offices downtown were located across the street from the old First National Bank and Trust Company building, where nearly 40 years earlier my job as an Assistant National Bank Examiner had begun. It still looked pretty much the same. Terri met me and we started to visit and I told her about my recent encounter with Gary Bradley. Terri, who is also black, laughed, "Bert, you know he struck me the same way. I was sure after talking to him on the phone, he would be a white dude from out in the Red Dirt Country."

Terri had a deal that had just been turned down and I was there to try to figure out why. Terri said, "Mrs. MacDonald lives out near Shawnee, just on the outskirts of town. For eight years she has worked in a flower shop downtown but now wants to start her own shop. She and her hubby have a building that was originally used to sell farm products: milk, eggs, cream and all, back when their place was an operating dairy. With a little remodeling it will make a real cute little flower and gift shop. They have lived on the place for ten years, but they aren't farmers. Her husband has been manager of a chain drug store, been there since they moved to Shawnee fifteen years ago."

"What seems to be the problem?" I said.

"Well it's kind of funny. We ran credit reports on both Arthur and Margaret MacDonald. His report is clean; nothing on it, not even a late notice. But hers! Wow! Half of it is positive, a dozen reporting prompt payments and modest balances. But then, here's the weird part, foreclosure on house in Louisiana. Serious delinquencies on credit cards, like Master Card, Visa. They were the same kinds of cards that got good reports for her and Arthur. I don't get it."

"And of course the underwriter turned it down, due to her lousy credit score?" I said.

"Right, but the credit report doesn't make sense?" Terri said.

"Well Terri, here we have a problem where the underwriter will believe anything he or she reads on a credit report. I'll bet that the problem is someone at the credit reporting agency keyed in Mrs. MacDonald's social security number, instead of the correct person. They don't pay those folks much and their employees are more interested in going home at five o'clock, than accuracy. Mrs. MacDonald needs to get that straightened out. That's will be a blockade until the erroneous data is purged from her file."

Terri said, "I'll be damned. Mrs. MacDonald was also puzzled, says she never been to, much less owned a home in Louisiana or knew about the delinquent credit cards. She said her's are always current and paid to zero monthly. Those underwriter jokers will believe anything on a credit report. Even it is completely illogical."

"Terri, that pretty well sums it up. We have underwriters; unfortunately, they are looking at a pile of files that they need to get through so they can go home at five o'clock too. Just like some of the credit report people." I replied.

The credit report is the first thing underwriters look at. If it doesn't pass muster, the application stops dead in its tracks and is automatically rejected. Kris Bell, a business banker, from our branch in Little Rock, Arkansas had a couple of interesting stories. I was coaching her on assisting a client put together an SBA loan application and naturally emphasized the importance of at least what I like to call "an honorable credit report." By this I meant it didn't need to be perfect, but overall needed to have a decent score of say

650 or better. I said, "Kris remember underwriters will believe anything on a credit report."

Kris said, "I had an interesting case involving a customer and his father with the same name."

I said, "Yeah, I know the problem, being the third in my family to have the same name. Luckily, they all had good credit, and also died many years ago."

"Well," said Kris, "In this case the father died in 1986 and the credit agency still had a file. The data was tangled up with the son's report, who was the applicant. I thought him to be an okay credit risk. But the father, the dead guy had some ongoing collection actions, which screwed up the son's credit report since they had the same name."

"How did it turn out?" I asked.

"Well, we finally got the son approved, but it took him a year of pleading and providing a copy of his dad's death certificate." Replied Kris.

Kris wasn't done with her credit report stories. She said, "Here's a funny one. This guy had an odd report for several years this fellow had a satisfactory report. Then for three years there were all kinds of collections, suits and what have you. It looked like for three years he never paid a bill. Then he had a couple of decent items in his report in the last year. Of course his credit score was awful, about as bad as it could get, so I had to tell him he was declined."

The guy said, "I don't understand, I pay my bills when I can, but I was in prison for three years. You mean that counts?"

Kris continued, "You know what, he was even more amazed the interest on the defaulted loan continued to accumulate while he was in jail. Amazing!"

I had to agree and said, "The banking business is about people, all kinds."

One of the most enjoyable things about working in the Kansas City Office was the people I worked with. I generally, went home every other weekend and I drove. But on weekends I had things to do in Kansas City too. Our Community Banking Group had small parties on the weekend. One such party was at Scott Berghouse's home. Mike and I were in charge of purchasing the beverages. We went to a liquor store in Scott's neighborhood. Our instructions were to get beer and wine. Not too difficult an assignment.

The clerk at the liquor store proceeded to give us the history of each of the wine we considered, where the grapes came from, the specific locale in France or Italy, the vintage, and on and on. Finally, Mike says to the gentleman, "Look all I really need to know is does it have alcohol in it?"

The stunned clerk looked at him and said, "Well, most wines we carry have between 10 and 12 percent."

We made our purchases, left and joined the rest of our crew. One of my favorite people at Bank of America was Ken Galli, the underwriter for the larger deals in Sacramento. It seemed like Ken and I always had something in the works. Ken knew when I would be driving back to Minnesota and would call me on my bank provided cell phone as I traveled north on a Friday afternoons, combining a little business and just to keep me company on my journey.

The trips were made more interesting by books on tape, which I borrowed from the public library in Woodbury. At first I would limit my borrowing to only three or four, but when I contemplated a trip away from Kansas City down through Kansas and Oklahoma, I knew that it would be good to have more books to take along. I went to the information desk at the Woodbury Library and said, "How many books on tape do you allow people to take?"

The plump, middle aged, librarian peered over her thick horn rim glasses and said, "We'd really prefer you not take more than 100 tapes during a three week period."

And here I was thinking that they might be upset if I took ten!

By the spring of 2001, I had learned that my Mom was going to be confined to a nursing home after a second bone-breaking fall. She had turn 89 in January and was failing mentally as well as physically. My brother Frank who lived about a mile from Mom in Boulder, Colorado was now shouldering the burden of looking after Mom. On a visit to Boulder that spring Jo and I thought we might look at moving to Boulder to help out with Mom. We discussed to idea with her and Mom offered to let us live in her house once we were able to sell our house. So we put our house on the market and figured once it sold I would retire. I was now eligible to draw Social Security now and Juli was schedule to graduate from the University of Minnesota in June 2001.

In conversation with my boss, Bruce Stewart, I mentioned the possibility of me retiring to Colorado. Bruce being an avid skier said, "I understand why this makes sense as a family matter and knowing your love of skiing it sounds like a sensible decision. Do keep me informed."

Bruce was among the numerous good people I worked with at the Bank of America. There were a number of excellent underwriters. While I was impressed with the skill, wisdom Bank of America would evaluate and approved restaurant loans, which are among the riskiest loans to make, I was disappointed, where policy would override common sense on some classes of loans. Take contractors for example, one of the policy makers decided to discontinue working with general contractors, even those who had been customers for as long as 30 years, that had excellent track records. Taking on new contractors was forbidden. Yet when I saw a better than average application, I had hopes that somehow the policy Gods would look favorably on that kind of submission. Such was the case of Jacob Miller.

Jake was a highly qualified civil engineer with 15 years construction experience. He wanted to go off on his own and start his own construction company building roads, bridges, and other structures. He had a super high credit score, a very large equity in a farm in eastern Oklahoma, which was worth far more than the loan he was applying for to purchase equipment and provide some working capital. What intrigued me most about the application was he had documentation from the Oklahoma state highway department, along with similar information from various counties in eastern Oklahoma and western Arkansas indicating their interest and eagerness to grant Mr. Miller contracts.

Apparently in this part of the world the state of Oklahoma, as well as several counties had let contracts for road and bridge construction and repair projects, for which they were unable to find a contractor to bid on the work. Moreover, these jobs were small, ideal projects for Mr. Miller's proposed company. He would have a virtual monopoly. It would be a great niche and in fact a service to this part of the country, which desperately needed updated roads and bridges. Sadly, the bank's bureaucrats prevailed and the application was denied. Fortunately, I learned a local independent bank snapped up the opportunity to work with Jake.

Another instance of the bank's ironclad "No Policies," was not unlike the situation in Moorhead, Minnesota a couple of years earlier in that it was a loan perceived as a hotel-motel loan. I met Sandra Walsh, a lawyer who had been working for a law firm in Topeka, Kansas. Recently divorced, the cheerful, blond, 50ish, lady had a vision to establish a Bed and Breakfast inn in her hometown, Eldorado, Kansas. Sandra's idea was to purchase a historic home built in 1874, built by one of the town's founders. The house was a classic looking Victorian style home, painted white with a large wraparound front porch, trimmed with liberally placed "Gingerbread" wood decorations. In addition, the house had third story cupola where one could lookout on the town.

The house sat at what was now a city block and was attractively priced at $175.000. The home had spacious rooms and was in good condition. On the ground floor, the house had a large extra room, which was built as an office and perfect for her law office. Ms. Walsh planned on continuing practicing law and expected to continue with clients she had been working with in Topeka as she had a statewide following in her legal specialty. Her most recent tax returns indicated a six-figure income. Her credit score was over 800 and her cash injection far exceeded all of the bank and SBA minimum criteria. At the B & B, even with a downtick in her legal practice revenues, but counting a modest income from the bed and breakfast revenues the debt service projected cash flow was three to one; the bank's minimum standard was 1.25 to one. In addition, her mother and two sisters were enthusiastic about the project and were eager be there to help Sandra with the Bed and Breakfast business. It was a super strong application.

At every bank I had previously been associated with, it was a slam-dunk application and in all likelihood it wouldn't have required an SBA guaranty. Unfortunately, our underwriters saw it only as a hotel loan, and declined it.

I called the underwriter and I will leave out his name to save a decent guy the embarrassment of turning down this excellent request. I was frustrated and furious and said, "What are you thinking, this is an excellent application. A B & B is not a hotel loan. For collateral you have a great historical home in excellent condition, a well-established lawyer with a statewide reputation, as an alternative income source even if the B & B enterprise fails. After all, this a house which would be a desirable home if that was the purchasers intent."

The underwriter replied, "Sorry Bert, but Bill, our illustrious leader has said 'absolutely, no hotel loans!'"

So my next call was to Sandra Walsh, "Sandra, I am very sorry to report that the underwriters see this as a hotel loan and have turned down the application. Let me suggest you try the local bank, I'll wager they'll do it in a heartbeat."

Sandra replied, "The folks at the First National there know me and my family, I'm confident they will make the loan. The house is easily worth the request and my law practice will easily support the payments."

Sandra applied to her local bank and as expected they approved the loan as a conventional home loan, which I image Bank of America's home mortgage department would have too, if we left out the B & B part. As stated earlier, while the bank had unyielding inflexibility when it came to construction companies and anything that remotely looked like a hotel or motel loan, they were at times willing to be quite open minded and creative when it came to other applications. Such was the Jasper Nursery. I received a call from our business banker in Joplin asking me to meet with a customer about financing a plant nursery not to be confused with one for children.

Financing the nursery itself was not beyond the purview of the bank's policy, but the person requesting the loan was different to say the least. Sharon Rogers our business banker said, "Before you go out to the nursery to see the place I have arranged for Mrs. Kemper to visit with you. She is a friend of Allison and you might say her, or maybe I should say HIS fairy godmother and an angel investor."

Before I could question Sharon for details about the gender disagreement, Mrs. Kemper entered Sharon's office and said, "Good morning Mr. Harris, Sharon has told me you are here to help put together an SBA loan application for Allison to buy the Jasper Nursery, I'm Katherine Kemper."

Mrs. Kemper was a fit looking gray haired lady, I would guess to be in her mid-seventies. From her appearance in a well-fitting royal blue pantsuit, with a neatly tied white scarf, she gave off the aura of affluence and that of a cultured person. I greeted her with, "Mrs. Kemper it is nice to meet you. Sharon tells me you are prepared to make a substantial cash investment in the nursery so the Allison Alexander might purchase it."

She smiled in her genteel sort of way and said, "Yes, that is correct I would like to help Allison do this, I have known him, or should I say her for years. A young neighbor of mine for many years, you understand."

Again I noticed the gender confusion. I said, "You both are confusing me, is Allison Alexander a man or a woman?"

Both Sharon and Mrs. Kemper smiled for a moment. Finally Mrs. Kemper spoke, "When you meet Allison, you'll see what we mean. The thing I want you to understand, is while Allison is certainly a very odd sort of being, she has a magically touch with plants, works very hard and has good business sense about the nursery, which is why I'm happy to back the project."

I looked over the application, which was only partially completed; however, the financial pieces that were presented looked decent enough. Following Sharon's instructions I drove out to the nursery. The headquarters for the enterprise was an older farmhouse, which I would judge was built sometime in the early part of the 20th century. Beyond it were several very large, well-kept greenhouses on the left. To the right there were rows and rows of a wide variety of plants and trees neatly arranged. There was no one in the office, so I proceeded to enter the first greenhouse. There was Allison tending a bed of red, white and pink carnations.

She turned to face me and smiled. She was nearly my height, six feet, solidly built and reminded me more of Charles Atlas, the famous body builder, than anyone named Allison I had ever encountered. She wore a frilly white blouse which was somewhat dirty, which given her profession was not unreasonable. Through the thin blouse one could see she was wearing a bra, but with nothing to put into it, I couldn't help but wonder why she had bothered. In spite of wearing lipstick, a touch of rouge, and dangling earrings, her square jaw gave her the aura of a masculine kind of strength. I resisted showing any sign of amusement, as best I could, and said, "Allison Alexander, I presume?"

We shook hands; her grip was strong like some of my old Wyoming rancher customers. She said in a throaty voice, "Yes, and you are the gentleman from the bank?"

I said, "Right, I am Bert Harris, government loan products specialist out of Kansas City. How can I be of assistance?"

Ms. Alexander explained the details of how much money and why it was needed. In addition, she provided some historical financials. It was evident that the nursery had prospered under her/his management since the owner was forced to retire due to health and aging issues a few years earlier. Allison said, "Walmart got wind of our operation and they sent a couple of folks up from Bentonville, Arkansas. That's a short drive from here. Anyway, they looked at our quality roses, carnations, and other flowers and want me to supply them. The order was huge."

I said, "Did you accept the order?"

She said, "Heck no, it would take my entire capacity to supply them and I'd have to run off all my other customers. Walmart is famous for squeezing the last dime out of their suppliers. If I signed on with them and then for whatever reason they decided to drop me, I would have lost all of my old loyal customers. I said, 'thanks, but no thanks.'"

I proceeded to process the application. After driving to Minnesota on Friday night, I received a telephone call from my brother, Frank, just as I had arrived home in Minnesota for the weekend. He said, "Mom (Who was in a nursing home following a nasty fall.) Has taken a turn for the worse and her doctors don't expect her to live much longer. If you want to see her once more before she passes you will need to get out to Boulder quickly."

This would have been about 9 PM and I had just driven from Kansas City, arriving an hour earlier. I said, "Okay, I'll start driving in the morning."

I had just seen Mom a couple of weeks earlier as I had been in Boulder attending my 45th Boulder High School class reunion. Although it was obvious her mind had slipped noticeably, I had understood all her vital signs were good and I full expected she would easily make her 90th birthday five months away. About midnight after Jo and I had gone to bed, Frank called again to report, "Bert, Boulder Manor just called to say Mom passed away in her sleep about an hour ago."

I replied, "I'll be on my way to Boulder in the morning."

Our house hadn't sold and in fact we hadn't even received a single offer. We immediately took it off the market, as we had both daughters, plus Jo's Mom residing in the greater Twin Cities area. Jo's mother was 92, but well, with excellent mental capacity and living at Wintergreen, an independent living facility in nearby Hudson, Wisconsin.

The moving to Colorado was out, but for me retiring seemed like a good idea. The commute back and forth from Kansas City to Minnesota was exhausting, a 900 miles round trip. My four year old Ford Explorer now had over 180,000 miles on it and continuing working in Kansas City, would mean I'd need to purchase a new vehicle, although remarkably it was still very reliable and giving me no trouble. Even the much vilified Firestone tires had served me well; 133,000 miles on the original set. It was now time to spend time at home with my family and think about things besides banking.

I called Bruce Stewart to announce my decision to retire. Since I had previously discussed the concept with him earlier I was surprised as his reaction. Bruce said, "Retiring to Colorado and skiing is one thing, but retiring to Minnesota, where they get tons of snow, but not very interesting skiing. I don't get it."

I replied, "Bruce, this 900 mile weekend commute is wearing me out, and my car too. Besides I have two daughters, Jo and her family there."

To my surprise, Bruce replied, "Bert is there any way I can convince you to stay? You know I just can't replace you with your experience, knowledge and ability to teach our young business bankers your insight into SBA lending is invaluable."

I said, "Bruce, I appreciate your kind words but I feel it is time. Thank you. I have enjoyed working for you and your support."

On October 31st I concluded my 41-year career in the banking business.

After Thoughts

However, after 41 years in the profession I cannot lure myself away for articles about the industry and thinking about the banking business. Since retiring from active participation in the banking business, and especially after the 2008 melt down of the American financial system, I find it impossible not to offer a few comments for what ever the reader may think they are worth. The most glaring thought is how little our society and specifically those in Washington who write the laws which govern and guide the financial industry really understand.

If one turns back to the pages of history to the financial collapse of 1929 and the great depression that follows, It is apparent that a root cause was the fact that commercial banks that take in the public's deposits and loan it out to individuals and businesses are vastly different from so called investment banks that issue securities and sell them to investors, and often to speculators. The Glass Steagall Act of 1933 separated these two diametrically different enterprises. Truly, it was one of the great accomplishments of the Franklin Roosevelt Administration.

On the one hand a commercial banking makes a loan and evaluates on the basis of the borrower, whether corporate or an individual buying an automobile or a home can make the payments to retire the entire debt. Investment securities firms, notice I refrain from calling them banks, put together a security be it a stock or bond or other financing instrument, write a pretty prospectus and sell it to whoever is willing to pay the price. The ultimate value of the security is of no long-term concern because it is off the investment securities dealer's shelves and they are on to the next deal.

So was the case with the underwriting, or lack thereof of the Fannie Mae and Freddie Mac bonds. We were liberalized along with the eliminating of the Glass Steagall Act's restrictions, reverting our financial system back to reinstate the causes of the Great Depression. Various and sundry mortgage banking hucksters proceeded to collect various home mortgages, bundle them up and sell them to Fannie and Freddie. As tough as it was to get perfectly decent SBA guaranteed SBA loans approved at Bank of America, it would seem reasonable that underwriting standards with a long view of the borrower's ultimate ability to repay the loan would prevail. And so it was with the home loans directly produced by the Bank of America; their total in-house subprime portfolio amount to a minuscule 2% of capital.

However, for reasons I am not privy to Ken Lewis, then the chairman and CEO of the bank was seduced either by greed, or as has been rumored pressure from the Fed and other financial regulators to acquire Merrill Lynch and Countrywide. These organizations were loaded with lousy mortgage loans, where the fundamental questions such as the mortgagor's income, were either not asked or in too many cases were falsified by greedy, fast-buck, and unscrupulous mortgage originators. None of these companies gave a thought to the ultimate ability of the borrower to repay the loan. What the hell, they were going to ship them off to Fannie or Freddie and reap the front-end fees and profits.

Executives running the large mega financial institutions saw these transactions as a means of lining their pockets. The mentality of a commercial banker is vastly different from the investment firms, which got caught up in the melee frenzy of taking quick profits. Then it was discovered the portfolios of Fannie and Freddie along with any organization holding these subprime, risky mortgages were holding nothing but junk paper. This caused a rash of defaults, then foreclosures, which lead to huge number of empty homes of the housing market; housing prices plummeted. Which led to the financial debacle of 2008.

Most of these defaulted mortgages were serviced by large organizations, which were totally disconnected from the borrowers. Little attempt was made to work out the problems with the customers. Better flush the episode down the toilet by foreclosing on the property. After all the folks in charge of all this didn't have any personal connection with the borrower.

The possibility that just because a borrower couldn't handle a $1000 payment, but might be able to make a $700 payment was ignored. Better get the damned defaulted mortgage off the books as expediently as possible.

Here in lies one of the many problems I have with large banking organizations such as my former employer. While it is one thing to kick someone out of their home when the person resides in a distant community from yours, it is quite another to foreclose on the family, whose kids play baseball and go to school with your children. The disconnection between the banks and the people and community they serve is disturbing to me. It is at least a piece of the problems in banking today. Monster banks have very simplistic policies that take turn down decent loans and fail to make a sincere effort to work out problems with their customers to mutually beneficial solutions.

Let me say that as employee, I was treated very well by the Bank of America. They hired me when I was 58 years old, clearly at the end of my career. Other large banks would not even grant me interviews for positions I was clearly superbly well qualified for, which annoyed me, especially after I got to meet some of the people that applied for the jobs I had applied for. It was trying to adequately serve the bank's customers within the bank's underwriting guidelines and systems that were the cornerstone of my frustrations as an employee.

The financial debacle of 2008 leads me to ask the question are these super large, multifaceted organizations, "To Big to Succeed," if adequate serving the customers financial needs is any criteria.

The *Troubled Asset Relief Program,* (TARP) illustrates this problem as clearly as any political action could. The bill as proposed by congress was intended to remove troubled assets from the various financial institutions. This included banks, Insurance companies and investment firms like Mr. Paulson's former firm, Goldman Sachs. Mr. Paulson's mentality was without the long-term view. He believed in put together a securities offering and sell it to whomever will ever pay the price. He could care less if the debtors ultimately paid off the loan.

So he chose to revise TARP, with the simplistic answer. Instead of actually removing the "troubled assets," He doled out large gobs of cash to various large institutions regardless of whether they needed the money or not. The troubled assets remained. This was like your doctor telling you, "You have cancer." But instead of removing the tumor he gives you a million dollars.

You're thinking a million bucks is nice, but I'm going to die if the malignant tumor is not removed. Secretary of the Treasury, Henry Paulson temporarily boosted the capital of the financial firms, but the bad assets remained. This of course resulted in banks severely curtailing their lending activities. I can assure you firsthand from years of experience working out problem loans, if your bank has a portfolio overloaded with bad loans, there will be no enthusiasm for making new ones. Major banks have in some cases as much as twice their capital threatened by substandard assets. Small wonder they are not interested in taking on new business and other inherently riskier loans. While from a conservative banking view this makes perfect sense, it does tend to limit the growth of new ventures. It is a well-known economic fact that small businesses generate as much as 90% of economic growth and hence job creation stagnates in the nine percent range as this final chapter.

It seems to me that the smaller community banks are more beneficial to the creation of economic growth and it is interesting to note the 2008 financial crisis was to some extent a testament to the weakness of the complex institutions created by the liberalization of financial regulations in during the Clinton years when we had a collaboration of greedy financial interests joining forces with social liberals who wished to make ownership more available to the masses. The smaller banks that have gotten in difficulty and failed were almost without exception institutions that made speculative loans for real estate development projects. This was not unlike the root causes of the S&L crisis of the 1980s.

The morning that I wrote this I noticed I was growing a great festering carbuncle on my nose, a smaller version to be sure, but nonetheless reminiscent of J. P. Morgan's famous proboscis; which tells me it is time to conclude this memoir.

26709082R00264

Made in the USA
Charleston, SC
16 February 2014